# A·N·N·U·A·L E·D·I·T·I·O·N·S

# American Government

## 99/00

*Twenty-Ninth Edition*

## EDITOR

**Bruce Stinebrickner**
*DePauw University*

Professor Bruce Stinebrickner teaches American politics in the Department of Political Science at DePauw University in Greencastle, Indiana. He has also taught American politics at Lehman College of the City University of New York, at the University of Queensland in Brisbane, Australia, and in a DePauw program for Argentine students in Buenos Aires. He received his Ph.D. from Yale University in 1974. In his courses and publications on American politics, Professor Stinebrickner brings to bear valuable insights gained from living, teaching, and lecturing abroad.

*Dushkin/McGraw-Hill*
Sluice Dock, Guilford, Connecticut 06437

**Visit us on the Internet**
*http://www.dushkin.com/annualeditions/*

**Credits**

**1. Foundations of American Politics**
Facing overview—Constitutional Convention illustration courtesy of the Library of Congress.
**2. Structures of American Politics**
Facing overview—Photo © 1919 by McPheeters and Krouier.
**3. Process of American Politics**
Facing overview—AP/Wide World photo by Wilfredo Lee.
**4. "Products" of American Politics**
Facing overview—Photo of B-1-B bomber courtesy of United States Air Force.

**Copyright**

Cataloging in Publication Data
Main entry under title: Annual Editions: American government. 1999/2000.
    1. U.S.—Politics and government—1945—Periodicals. I. Stinebrickner, Bruce, *comp*. II. Title: American Government.
ISBN 0–07–030303–7        320.9'73'0924'05        76-180265        ISSN 0891-3390
JK1.A7A

Twenty-Ninth Edition

Cover image © 1999 PhotoDisc, Inc.

Printed in the United States of America        1234567890BAHBAH5432109        Printed on Recycled Paper

Members of the Advisory Board are instrumental in the final selection of articles for each edition of ANNUAL EDITIONS. Their review of articles for content, level, currentness, and appropriateness provides critical direction to the editor and staff. We think that you will find their careful consideration well reflected in this volume.

## Editors/Advisory Board

## EDITOR

**Bruce Stinebrickner**
*DePauw University*

## ADVISORY BOARD

**Agar Adamson**
*Acadia University*

**Ryan J. Barilleaux**
*Miami University*

**Joseph M. Bristow**
*County College of Morris*

**Leonard Cardenas**
*Southwest Texas State University*

**Andrew W. Dobelstein**
*University of North Carolina
Chapel Hill*

**Michael Fischetti**
*Montgomery College*

**Robert Friedman**
*California State University
Sacramento*

**Lawrence R. Godtfredsen**
*Babson College*

**John C. Green**
*University of Akron*

**Robert W. Lane**
*Saginaw Valley State University*

**Eloise F. Malone**
*U.S. Naval Academy*

**Robert J. Marbach**
*West Chester University*

**George McKenna**
*CUNY, City College*

**Kenneth Palmer**
*University of Maine
Orono*

**Theodore B. Pedeliski**
*University of North Dakota*

**Robert S. Ross**
*California State University
Chico*

**Steven J. Showalter**
*Lee College*

**Michael E. Siegel**
*American University*

**Valerie J. Simms**
*Northeastern Illinois University*

**Lois T. Vietri**
*University of Maryland
College Park*

**Lois Duke Whitaker**
*Georgia Southern University*

**Cecil Harvey Williams**
*Christopher Newport University*

**Edward N. Wright**
*University of Southern Colorado*

## Staff

## EDITORIAL STAFF

**Ian A. Nielsen,** Publisher
**Roberta Monaco,** Senior Developmental Editor
**Dorothy Fink,** Associate Developmental Editor
**Addie Raucci,** Senior Administrative Editor
**Cheryl Greenleaf,** Permissions Editor
**Joseph Offredi,** Permissions/Editorial Assistant
**Diane Barker,** Proofreader
**Lisa Holmes-Doebrick,** Program Coordinator

## PRODUCTION STAFF

**Brenda S. Filley,** Production Manager
**Charles Vitelli,** Designer
**Lara M. Johnson,** Design/
Advertising Coordinator
**Laura Levine,** Graphics
**Mike Campbell,** Graphics
**Tom Goddard,** Graphics
**Juliana Arbo,** Typesetting Supervisor
**Jane Jaegersen,** Typesetter
**Marie Lazauskas,** Word Processor
**Kathleen D'Amico,** Word Processor
**Larry Killian,** Copier Coordinator

iii

# To the Reader

In publishing ANNUAL EDITIONS we recognize the enormous role played by the magazines, newspapers, and journals of the public press in providing current, first-rate educational information in a broad spectrum of interest areas. Many of these articles are appropriate for students, researchers, and professionals seeking accurate, current material to help bridge the gap between principles and theories and the real world. These articles, however, become more useful for study when those of lasting value are carefully collected, organized, indexed, and reproduced in a low-cost format, which provides easy and permanent access when the material is needed. That is the role played by ANNUAL EDITIONS.

New to ANNUAL EDITIONS is the inclusion of related World Wide Web sites. These sites have been selected by our editorial staff to represent some of the best resources found on the World Wide Web today. Through our carefully developed topic guide, we have linked these Web resources to the articles covered in this ANNUAL EDITIONS reader. We think that you will find this volume useful, and we hope that you will take a moment to visit us on the Web at *http://www.dushkin.com* to tell us what you think.

Annual Editions: American Government 99/00 is the twenty-ninth edition of a book that has become a mainstay in many introductory courses on American politics. The educational goal is to provide a readable collection of up-to-date articles that are informative, interesting, and stimulating to students beginning their study of the American political system.

The past year has been quite a year in American politics. In January 1998, a sex scandal involving President Bill Clinton and a White House intern named Monica Lewinsky first came to the public's attention. For 8 months, the president publicly denied any sexual wrongdoing with her, even as evidence to the contrary leaked into the public domain. In August testimony before a grand jury, Clinton changed his story and admitted sexual wrongdoing and a subsequent cover-up. Then, independent counsel Kenneth Starr made a lengthy referral to the House of Representatives recommending that the president be impeached.

The Clinton scandal and the Starr referral were expected to harm the candidacies of Democrats in the November congressional elections. To the contrary, Democrats narrowed the Republican margin in the House by five seats and lost no seats in the Republican-controlled Senate. A few days after these surprising election results, Republican Speaker Newt Gingrich announced that he was going to step down from the Speakership and resign from the House of Representatives.

The 1998 November election results seemed to spell the end of any serious impeachment effort, but that perception turned out to be wrong. In December, the House of Representatives passed two articles of impeachment against the president by a nearly straight party-line vote, one for perjury and one for obstruction of justice. For only the second time in U.S. history, a president had been impeached in the House. In a dramatic development during the House floor debate on the articles of impeachment, Congressman Bob Livingston of Louisiana, whom House Republicans had chosen to succeed Gingrich as speaker, announced his withdrawal because of recent revelations about past marital infidelity.

In January 1999, the president's impeachment trial began in the Senate amidst clear indications that fewer than the constitutionally required two-thirds of the Senate would vote to convict. This time expectations have been fulfilled. As I already suggested, it has been quite a year in American politics since the previous edition of this book went to press in early 1998!

The systems approach provides a rough organizational framework for this book. The first unit focuses on ideological and constitutional underpinnings of American politics, from both historical and contemporary perspectives. The second unit treats the major institutions of the national government. The third covers the "input" or "linkage" mechanisms of the system: political parties, elections, interest groups, and media. The fourth and concluding unit shifts the focus to policy choices that confront the government in Washington and resulting "outputs" of the political system. Also included in this book are *World Wide Web* sites that can be used to explore topics in American politics. These sites are cross-referenced by number in the *topic guide*.

Each year thousands of articles about American politics are published, and deciding which to reprint in a collection of readings such as this is not always easy. Since no position on the political spectrum has a monopoly on truth, articles are chosen with an eye toward providing viewpoints from left, right, and center. About half of the selections in this book are new to this year's edition.

Next year will bring another opportunity for change, and you, the reader, are invited to participate in the process. Please complete and return the postpaid *article rating form* on the last page of the book and let us know your reactions and your suggestions for improvement.

Bruce Stinebrickner
*Editor*

# Contents

## A. BASIC DOCUMENTS

## B. CONTEMPORARY VIEWS AND VALUES

**UNIT 1**

## Foundations of American Politics

The fifteen selections in this unit outline the foundations of American politics. In addition to primary documents, there are discussions of contemporary political ideals and viewpoints as well as recent commentaries on constitutional issues.

---

The concepts in bold italics are developed in the article. For further expansion please refer to the Topic Guide and the Index.

The concepts in bold italics are developed in the article. For further expansion please refer to the Topic Guide and the Index.

**Overview** **74**

## UNIT 2

## Structures of American Politics

The fifteen articles in this unit examine the structure and present status of the American presidency, Congress, judiciary, and bureaucracy.

The concepts in bold italics are developed in the article. For further expansion please refer to the Topic Guide and the Index.

UNIT 4

# "Products" of American Politics

The six selections in this unit examine the domestic, economic, foreign, and defense policies that American government produces.

The concepts in bold italics are developed in the article. For further expansion please refer to the Topic Guide and the Index.

The concepts in bold italics are developed in the article. For further expansion please refer to the Topic Guide and the Index.

# Topic Guide

This topic guide suggests how the selections and World Wide Web sites found in the next section of this book relate to topics of traditional concern to students and professionals involved with the study of American politics. It is useful for locating interrelated articles and Web sites for reading and research. The guide is arranged alphabetically according to topic.

The relevant Web sites, which are numbered and annotated on pages 4 and 5, are easily identified by the Web icon (◎) under the topic articles. By linking the articles and the Web sites by topic, this ANNUAL EDITIONS reader becomes a powerful learning and research tool.

# ● AE: American Government

The following World Wide Web sites have been carefully researched and selected to support the articles found in this reader. If you are interested in learning more about specific topics found in this book, these Web sites are a good place to start. The sites are cross-referenced by number and appear in the topic guide on the previous two pages. Also, you can link to these Web sites through our DUSHKIN ONLINE support site at *http://www.dushkin.com/online/*.

**The following sites were available at the time of publication. Visit our Web site—we update DUSHKIN ONLINE regularly to reflect any changes.**

## General Sources

### 1. The Federal Web Locator
*http://www.law.vill.edu/Fed-Agency/fedwebloc.html*
Use this handy site as a launching pad for the Web sites of U.S. federal agencies, departments, and organizations. It is well organized and easy to use for informational and research purposes.

### 2. John F. Kennedy School of Government
*http://www.ksg.harvard.edu*
Starting from Harvard University's KSG page, you will be able to click on a huge variety of links to information about American politics and government, ranging from political party and campaign data to debates of enduring issues.

### 3. Library of Congress
*http://www.loc.gov*
Examine this Web site to learn about the extensive resource tools, library services/resources, exhibitions, and databases available through the Library of Congress in many different subfields of government studies.

## Foundations of American Politics

### 4. American Studies Web
*http://www.georgetown.edu/crossroads/asw/*
This eclectic site provides links to a wealth of Internet resources for research in American studies, including agriculture and rural development, government, and race and ethnicity.

### 5. Federalism: Relationship between Local and National Governments
*http://www.infidels.org/~nap/index.federalism.html*
Federalism versus states' rights has always been a spirited debate in American government. Visit this George Mason University site for links to many articles and reports on the subject.

### 6. Opinion, Inc.: The Site for Conservative Opinion on the Web
*http://www.opinioninc.com*
Open this site for access to political, cultural, and Web commentary on a number of issues from a conservative political viewpoint. The site is updated frequently.

### 7. Scanned Originals of Early American Documents
*http://www.law.emory.edu/FEDERAL/*
Through this Emory University site you can view scanned originals of the Declaration of Independence, the Constitution, and the Bill of Rights. The transcribed texts are also available, as are *The Federalist* papers.

### 8. Smithsonian Institution
*http://www.si.edu*
This site provides access to the enormous resources of the Smithsonian, which holds some 140 million artifacts and specimens in its trust for "the increase and diffusion of knowledge." Here you can learn about American social, cultural, economic, and political history, from a variety of viewpoints.

### 9. The Written Word
*http://www.mdle.com/WrittenWord/*
This is an online journal of economic, political, and social commentary, primarily from a center or left-of-center viewpoint. The site provides links to governmental and political Web resources.

## Structures of American Politics

### 10. Department of State
*http://www.state.gov*
View this site for understanding into the workings of a major U.S. executive branch department. Links explain exactly what the Department does, what services it provides, and what it says about U.S. interests around the world, and they also provide much more information.

### 11. Federal Reserve System
*http://woodrow.mpls.frb.fed.us/info/sys/index.html*
Consult this page to learn the answers to FAQs about the Fed, the structure of the Federal Reserve system, monetary policy, and more. It provides links to speeches and interviews as well as essays and articles presenting different views on the Fed.

### 12. Policy Digest Archives
*http://www.public-policy.org/~ncpa/pd/pdindex.html*
Through this site of the National Center for Policy Analysis, access discussions on an array of topics that are of major interest in the study of American government, from regulatory policy and privatization to economy and income.

### 13. Supreme Court/Legal Information Institute
*http://supct.law.cornell.edu/supct/index.html*
Open this site for current and historical information about the Supreme Court. The LII archive contains many opinions issued since May 1990 as well as a collection of nearly 600 of the most historical decisions of the Court.

### 14. United States House of Representatives
*http://www.house.gov*
This Web page of the House of Representatives will lead you to information about current and past House members and agendas, the legislative process, and so on. You can learn about events on the House floor as they happen.

### 15. United States Senate
*http://www.senate.gov*
This Web page of the U.S. Senate will lead you to information about current and past Senate members and agendas, legislative activities, committees, and so on.

### 16. The White House
*http://www.whitehouse.gov/WH/Welcome.html*
Visit the White House home page for direct access to information about commonly requested federal services, the

White House Briefing Room, and the presidents and vice presidents. The Virtual Library allows you to search White House documents, listen to speeches, and view photos.

## Process of American Politics

### 17. The Henry L. Stimson Center
*http://www.stimson.org*
Stimson, a nonprofit and (self-described) nonpartisan organization, focuses on issues where policy, technology, and politics intersect. Use this site to find assessments of U.S. foreign and domestic policy and other topics.

### 18. Marketplace of Political Ideas/University of Houston Library
*http://info.lib.uh.edu/politics/markind.htm*
Here is a collection of links to campaign, conservative/liberal perspectives, and political party sites. There are General Political Sites, Democratic Sites, Republican Sites, Third Party Sites, and much more.

### 19. National Journal's Cloakroom
*http://www.Cloakroom.com*
This is a major site for information on American government and politics. There are reportage and discussion of campaigns, congressional calendar, a news archive, and more for politicos and policy makers. Membership is required, however, to access much of the information.

### 20. Political Pages
*http://montego.ais.org/~paxton/other.html*
Dean Paxton's site will point you to a number of resources for domestic and international political and governmental news, including the LSU Political Science WWW Server, which is maintained by a dedicated group of professionals.

### 21. Poynter Online
*http://www.poynter.org/research/research.htm*
This research site of the Poynter Institute for Media Studies provides extensive links to information and resources about the media, including media ethics and reportage techniques. Many bibliographies and Web sites are included.

### 22. RAND
*http://www.rand.org*
RAND is a nonprofit institution that works to improve public policy through research and analysis. Links offered on this home page provide for keyword searches of certain topics and descriptions of RAND activities and major research areas.

### 23. Social Influence
*http://www.public.asu.edu/~kelton*
This site focuses on the nature of persuasion, compliance, and propaganda, with many practical examples and applications. Students of such topics as the roles of public opinion and media influence in policy making may find these discussions of interest.

## "Products" of American Politics

### 24. American Diplomacy
*http://www.unc.edu/depts/diplomat/*
*American Diplomacy* is an intriguing online journal of commentary, analysis, and research on U.S. foreign policy and its results around the world.

### 25. Cato Institute
*http://www.cato.org/research/ss_prjct.html*
The Cato Institute presents this page to discuss its Project on Social Security Privatization. The site and its links begin from the belief that privatization of the U.S. Social Security system is a positive goal that will empower workers.

### 26. Clinton Foreign Policy Page
*http://www.geocities.com/CapitolHill/8514/*
For a change of pace from the sites of journals, think tanks, and government organizations, check out Eddie Robert's personal home page. Roberts, an individual who is very critical of President Bill Clinton's foreign policy, provides space for you to respond to his opinions.

### 27. Foreign Affairs
*http://www.foreignaffairs.org*
This home page of the well-respected foreign policy journal is a valuable research tool. It allows users to search the journal's archives and provides indexed access to the field's leading publications, documents, online resources, and so on. Links to dozens of other related Web sites are possible from here.

### 28. The Gallup Organization
*http://www.gallup.com*
Open this Gallup Organization home page for links to an extensive archive of public opinion poll results and special reports on a variety of topics related to American society, politics, and government.

### 29. Tax Foundation
*http://www.taxfoundation.org/index.html*
Ever wonder where your taxes go? Consult the site of this self-described "nonprofit, nonpartisan policy research organization" to learn the history of "Tax Freedom Day," tax burdens around the United States, and other information about your tax bill or taxes in general.

### 30. STAT-USA
*http://www.stat-usa.gov/stat-usa.html*
This essential site, a service of the Department of Commerce, contains daily economic news, frequently requested statistical releases, information on export and international trade, domestic economic news and statistical series, and databases.

### 31. U.S. Information Agency
*http://www.usia.gov/usis.html*
This wide-ranging page of the USIA provides definitions, related documentation, and a discussion of topics of concern to students of American government. It addresses today's Hot Topics as well as ongoing issues that form the foundation of the field. Many Web links are provided.

**We highly recommend that you review our Web site for expanded information and our other product lines. We are continually updating and adding links to our Web site in order to offer you the most usable and useful information that will support and expand the value of your Annual Editions. You can reach us at:** *http://www.dushkin.com/annualeditions/.*

www.dushkin.com/online/

# Unit 1

## Unit Selections

*Basic Documents*

1. **The Declaration of Independence, 1776**
2. **The Constitution of the United States, 1787**
3. **The Size and Variety of the Union as a Check on Faction,** James Madison
4. **Checks and Balances,** James Madison
5. **The Judiciary,** Alexander Hamilton

*Contemporary Views and Values*

6. **What Good Is Government?** William J. Bennett and John J. Dilulio Jr.
7. **Chomp!** Jim Hightower
8. **What's Wrong with America: Open Season on Uncle Sam,** John Carlin
9. **When Naptime Is Over,** Robert B. Reich

*Constitutional and Legal Matters*

10. **Race and the Constitution,** Thurgood Marshall
11. **Vigilante Justices,** Antonin Scalia
12. **Breaking Thurgood Marshall's Promise,** A. Leon Higginbotham Jr.
13. **More than Sex: Why the Courts Are Missing the Point,** Ellen Yaroshefsky
14. **The Case for Impeachment,** Stuart Taylor Jr.
15. **The Case against Impeachment,** Kirk Victor

## Key Points to Consider

❖ What do you think would surprise the Founders most about the values and ideals held by Americans today?

❖ Which ideals, ideas, and values seem likely to remain central to American politics, and which seem likely to erode and gradually disappear?

❖ To what rights do you think all Americans are entitled? Do all Americans have these rights now? If not, why not?

❖ What provisions of the U.S. Constitution do you think are particularly wise and desirable? Which provisions, including ones that have been superseded by amendments, seem unwise and undesirable?

❖ What makes constitutional interpretation and reinterpretation necessary in the American political system? Why, at the same time, do the very words of the Constitution remain a respected foundation of the entire system of government? What groups seem most likely to become visible, active forces on the American political scene in the way that African Americans and women have in the recent past? Why?

❖ Do you consider yourself a conservative, a liberal, a socialist, a reactionary, or what? Why?

 **Links**

## www.dushkin.com/online/

4. **American Studies Web**
   http://www.georgetown.edu/crossroads/asw/
5. **Federalism: Relationship between Local and National Governments**
   http://www.infidels.org/~nap/index.federalism.html
6. **Opinion, Inc.: The Site for Conservative Opinion on the Web**
   http://www.opinioninc.com
7. **Scanned Originals of Early American Documents**
   http://www.law.emory.edu/FEDERAL/
8. **Smithsonian Institution**
   http://www.si.edu
9. **The Written Word**
   http://www.mdle.com/WrittenWord/

These sites are annotated on pages 4 and 5.

This unit treats some of the less concrete aspects of the American political system—historic ideals, contemporary ideas and values, and constitutional and legal issues. These dimensions of the system are not immune to change. Instead, they interact with the wider political environment in which they exist and are modified accordingly. Usually this interaction is a gradual process, but sometimes events foster more rapid change. Human beings can be distinguished from other species by their ability to think and reason at relatively high levels of abstraction. In turn, ideas, ideals, values, and principles can and do play important roles in politics. Most Americans value ideals such as democracy, freedom, equal opportunity, and justice. Yet the precise meanings of these terms and the best ways of implementing them are the subject of much dispute in the political arena. Such ideas and ideals, as well as disputes about their "real" meanings, are important elements in the practice of American politics.

Although the selections in this unit span more than 200 years, they are clearly related to one another. Understanding contemporary political viewpoints is easier if the ideals and principles of the past are also taken into account. In addition, we can better appreciate the significance of historic documents such as the Declaration of Independence and the Constitution if we are familiar with contemporary ideas and perspectives. The interaction of different ideas and values plays an important part in the continuing development of the "foundations" of the American political system.

The first subsection includes several historic documents from the eighteenth century. The first is the Declaration of Independence. Written in 1776, it proclaims the Founders' views of why independence from England was justified and, in so doing, identifies certain "unalienable" rights that "all men" are said to possess. The second document, the Constitution of 1787, remains in effect to this day. It provides an organizational blueprint for the structure of American national government, outlines the federal relationship between the national government and the states, and expresses limitations on what government can do. Twenty-seven amendments have been added to the original Constitution in two centuries. In addition to the Declaration of Independence and the Constitution, the first section includes three selections from *The Federalist* papers, a series of newspaper articles written in support of the proposed new Constitution. Appearing in 1787 and 1788, *The Federalist* papers treated various provisions of the new Constitution and argued that putting the Constitution into effect would bring about good government. The second subsection treats contemporary political ideas and viewpoints. As selections in this section illustrate, efforts to apply or act on political beliefs in the context of concrete circumstances often lead to interesting commentary and debate. "Liberal" and "conservative" are two labels often used in American political discussions, but political views and values have far more complexity than can be captured by these two terms.

Selections in the third subsection show that constitutional and legal issues and interpretations are tied to historic principles as well as to contemporary ideas and values. It has been suggested that, throughout American history, almost every important political question has at one time or another appeared as a constitutional or legal issue.

The historic documents and some other selections in this unit can be more difficult to understand than most articles in other units. Some of them may have to be read and reread carefully to be fully appreciated. But to grapple with the important material treated here is to come to grips with a variety of conceptual blueprints for the American political system. To ignore the theoretical issues raised would be to bypass an important element of American politics today.

# Foundations of American Politics

# The Declaration of Independence

WHEN in the Course of human events, it becomes necessary for one people to dissolve the political bands which have connected them with another, and to assume among the powers of the earth, the separate and equal station to which the Laws of Nature and of Nature's God entitle them, a decent respect to the opinions of mankind requires that they should declare the causes which impel them to the separation.—We hold these truths to be self-evident, that all men are created equal, that they are endowed by their Creator with certain unalienable Rights, that among these are Life, Liberty and the pursuit of Happiness.—That to secure these rights, Governments are instituted among Men, deriving their just powers from the consent of the governed.—That whenever any Form of Government becomes destructive of these ends, it is the Right of the People to alter or to abolish it, and to institute new Government, laying its foundation on such principles and organizing its powers in such form, as to them shall seem most likely to effect their Safety and Happiness. Prudence, indeed, will dictate that Governments long established should not be changed for light and transient causes; and accordingly all experience hath shewn, that mankind are more disposed to suffer, while evils are sufferable, than to right themselves by abolishing the forms to which they are accustomed. But when a long train of abuses and usurpations, pursuing invariably the same Object evinces a design to reduce them under absolute Despotism, it is their right, it is their duty, to throw off such Government, and to provide new Guards for their future security.—Such has been the patient sufferance of these Colonies; and such is now the necessity which constrains them to alter their former Systems of Government. The history of the present King of Great Britain is a history of repeated injuries and usurpations, all having in direct object the establishment of an absolute Tyranny over these States. To prove this, let Facts be submitted to a candid world.—He has refused his Assent to Laws, the most wholesome and necessary for the public good.—He has forbidden his Governors to pass Laws of immediate and pressing importance, unless suspended in their operation till his Assent should be obtained; and when so suspended, he has utterly neglected to attend to them.—He

has refused to pass other Laws for the accommodation of large districts of people, unless those people would relinquish the right of Representation in the Legislature, a right inestimable to them and formidable to tyrants only.—He has called together legislative bodies at places unusual, uncomfortable, and distant from the depository of their public Records, for the sole purpose of fatiguing them into compliance with his measures.—He has dissolved Representative Houses repeatedly, for opposing with manly firmness his invasions on the rights of the people.—He has refused for a long time, after such dissolutions, to cause others to be elected; whereby the Legislative powers, incapable of Annihilation, have returned to the People at large for their exercise; the State remaining in the meantime exposed to all the dangers of invasion from without, and convulsions within.—He has endeavoured to prevent the population of these States; for that purpose obstructing the Laws for Naturalization of Foreigners; refusing to pass others to encourage their migrations hither, and raising the conditions of new Appropriations of Lands.—He has obstructed the Administration of Justice, by refusing his Assent to Laws for establishing Judiciary powers.—He has made Judges dependent on his Will alone, for the tenure of their offices, and the amount and payment of their salaries.—He has erected a multitude of New Offices, and sent hither swarms of Officers to harass our people, and eat out their substance. He has kept among us, in times of peace, Standing Armies without the Consent of our legislatures.—He has affected to render the Military independent of and superior to the Civil power.—He has combined with others to subject us to a jurisdiction foreign to our constitution, and unacknowledged by our laws; giving his Assent to their Acts of pretended Legislation:—For quartering large bodies of armed troops among us:—For protecting them, by a mock Trial, from punishment for any Murders which they should commit on the Inhabitants of these States:—For cutting off our Trade with all parts of the world:—For imposing Taxes on us without our Consent:—For depriving us in many cases, of the benefits of Trial by Jury:—For transporting us beyond Seas to be tried for pretended offences:—For abolishing the free System of English Laws in a neighboring Province, establishing therein an Arbitrary government, and enlarging its Boundaries so as to render it at once an example and fit instrument for introducing the same absolute rule into these Colonies:—For taking away our Charters, abolishing our most valuable Laws and altering fundamentally the Forms of our Governments:—For suspending our own Legislatures, and declaring themselves invested with power to legislate for us in all cases whatsoever.—He has abdicated Government here, by declaring us out of his Protection and waging War against us.—He has plundered our seas, ravaged our Coasts, burnt our towns, and destroyed the lives of our people.—He is at this time transporting large Armies of foreign Mercenaries to compleat the works of death, desolation and tyranny, already begun with circumstances of Cruelty & perfidy scarcely paralled in the most barbarous ages, and totally unworthy the Head of a civilized nation.—He has constrained our fellow Citizens taken Captive on the high Seas to bear Arms gainst their Country, to become the executioners of their friends and Brethren, or to fall themselves by their Hands.—He has excited domestic insurrections amongst us, and has endeavoured to bring on the inhabitants of our frontiers, the merciless Indian Savages, whose known rule of warfare, is an undistinguished destruction of all ages, sexes and conditions. In every stage of these Oppressions We have Petitioned for Redress in the most humble terms: Our repeated Petitions have been answered only by repeated injury. A Prince, whose character is thus marked by every act which may define a Tyrant, is unfit to be the ruler of a free people. Nor have We been wanting in attentions to our British brethren. We have warned them from time to time of attempts by their legislature to extend an unwarrantable jurisdiction over us. We have reminded them of the circumstances of our emigration and settlement here. We have appealed to their native justice and magnanimity, and we have conjured them by the ties of our common kindred to disavow these usurpations, which would inevitably interrupt our connections and correspondence. They too have been deaf to the voice of justice and of consanguinity. We must, therefore, acquiesce in the necessity, which denounces our Separation, and hold them, as we hold the rest of mankind, Enemies in War, in Peace Friends.—

WE, THEREFORE, the Representatives of the UNITED STATES OF AMERICA, in General Congress, Assembled, appealing to the Supreme Judge of the world for the rectitude of our intentions, do, in the Name, and by Authority of the good People of these Colonies, solemnly publish and declare, That these United Colonies are, and of Right ought to be FREE AND INDEPENDENT STATES; that they are Absolved from all Allegiance to the British Crown, and that all political connection between them and the State of Great Britain, is and ought to be totally dissolved; and that as Free and Independent States, they have full Power to levy War, conclude Peace, contract Alliances, establish Commerce, and to do all other Acts and Things which Independent States may of right do.—And for the support of this Declaration, with a firm reliance on the protection of divine Providence, we mutually pledge to each other our Lives, our Fortunes and our sacred Honor.

# The History of The Constitution of the United States

**CONSTITUTION OF THE UNITED STATES.** The Articles of Confederation did not provide the centralizing force necessary for unity among the new states and were soon found to be so fundamentally weak that a different political structure was vital. Conflicts about money and credit, trade, and suspicions about regional domination were among the concerns when Congress on February 21, 1787, authorized a Constitutional Convention to revise the Articles. The delegates were selected and assembled in Philadelphia about three months after the call. They concluded their work by September.

The delegates agreed and abided to secrecy. Years afterward James Madison supported the secrecy decision writing that "no man felt himself obliged to retain his opinions any longer than he was satisfied of their propriety and truth, and was open to the force of argument." Secrecy was not for all time. Madison, a delegate from Virginia, was a self-appointed but recognized recorder and took notes in the clear view of the members. Published long afterward, Madison's *Journal* gives a good record of the convention.

The delegates began to assemble on May 14, 1787, but a majority did not arrive until May 25. George Washington was elected President of the Convention without opposition. The lag of those few days gave some of the early arrivals, especially Madison, time to make preparations on substantive matters, and Gov. Edmund Jennings Randolph presented a plan early in the proceedings that formed the basis for much of the convention deliberations. The essentials were that there should be a government adequate to prevent foreign invasion, prevent dissension among the states, and provide for general national development, and give the national government power enough to make it superior in its realm. The decision was made not merely to revise the articles but to create a new government and a new constitution.

One of the most crucial decisions was the arrangement for representation, a compromise providing that one house would represent the states equally, the other house to be based on popular representation (with some modification due to the slavery question). This arrangement recognized political facts and concessions among men with both theoretical and practical political knowledge.

**Basic Features.** Oliver Wendell Holmes, Jr., once wrote that the provisions of the Constitution were not mathematical formulas, but "organic living institutions *[sic]* and its origins and growth were vital to understanding it." The constitution's basic features provide for a supreme law—notwithstanding any other legal document or practice, the Constitution is supreme, as are the laws made in pursuance of it and treaties made under the authority of the United States.

The organizational plan for government is widely known. Foremost is the separation of powers. If the new government were to be limited in its powers, one way to keep it limited would have been executive, legislative, and judicial power [given] to three distinct and non-overlapping branches. A government could not actually function, however, if the separation meant the independence of one branch from the others. The answer was a design to insure cooperation and the sharing of some functions. Among these are the executive veto and the power of Congress to have its way if it musters a super-majority to override that veto. The direction of foreign affairs and the war power are both dispersed and shared. The appointing power is shared by the Senate and the president; impeaching of officers and financial controls are powers shared by the Senate and the House.

A second major contribution by the convention is the provision for the judiciary, which gave rise to the doctrine of judicial review. There is some doubt that the delegates comprehended this prospect but Alexander Hamilton considered it in *Federalist* No. 78: "The interpretation of the laws is a proper and peculiar province of the Courts.... Wherever a particular statute contravenes the Constitution, it will be the duty of the judicial tribunals to adhere to the latter and disregard the former."

Another contribution is the federal system, an evolution from colonial practice and the relations between the colonies and the mother country. This division of authority between the new national government and the states recognized the doctrine of delegated and reserved powers. Only certain authority was to go to the new government; the states were not to be done away with and much of the Constitution is devoted to insuring that they were to be maintained even with the stripping of some of their powers.

It is not surprising, therefore, that the convention has been called a great political reform caucus composed of both revolutionaries and men dedicated to democracy. By eighteenth-century standards the Constitution was a democratic document, but standards change and the Constitution has changed since its adoption.

**Change and Adaptation.** The authors of the Constitution knew that provision for change was essential and provided for it in Article V, insuring that a majority could amend, but being restrictive enough that changes were not likely for the "light and transient" causes Jefferson warned about in the Declaration of Independence.

During the period immediately following the presentation of the Constitution for ratification, requiring assent of nine states to be effective, some alarm was expressed that there was a major defect: there was no bill of rights. So, many leaders committed themselves to the presentation of constitutional amendments for the purpose. Hamilton argued that the absence of a bill of rights was not a defect; indeed, a bill was not necessary. "Why," he wrote, in the last of *The Federalist Pa-*

*pers,* "declare things that shall not be done which there is no power to do?" Nonetheless, the Bill of Rights was presented in the form of amendments and adopted by the states in 1791.

Since 1791 many proposals have been suggested to amend the Constitution. By 1972 sixteen additional amendments had been adopted. Only one, the Twenty-first, which repealed the Eighteenth, was ratified by state conventions. All the others were ratified by state legislatures.

Even a cursory reading of the later amendments shows they do not alter the fundamentals of limited government, the separation of powers, the federal system, or the political process set in motion originally. The Thirteenth, Fourteenth, Fifteenth, and Nineteenth amendments attempt to insure equality to all and are an extension of the Bill of Rights. The others reaffirm some existing constitutional arrangements, alter some procedures, and at least one, the Sixteenth, states national policy.

Substantial change and adaptation of the Constitution beyond the formal amendments have come from national experience, growth, and development. It has been from the Supreme Court that much of the gradual significant shaping of the Constitution has been done.

Government has remained neither static nor tranquil. Some conflict prevails continually. It may be about the activities of some phase of government or the extent of operations, and whether the arrangement for government can be made responsive to current and prospective needs of society. Conflict is inevitable in a democratic society. Sometimes the conflict is spirited and rises to challenge the continuation of the system. Questions arise whether a fair trial may be possible here or there; legislators are alleged to be indifferent to human problems and pursue distorted public priorities. Presidents are charged with secret actions designed for self-aggrandizement or actions based on half-truths. Voices are heard urging revolution again as the only means of righting alleged wrongs.

The responses continue to demonstrate, however, that the constitutional arrangement for government, the allocation of powers, and the restraints on government all provide the needed flexibility. The Constitution endures.

—Adam C. Breckenridge, *University of Nebraska-Lincoln*

# The Constitution of the United States

**We the People of the United States, in Order to form a more perfect Union, establish Justice, insure domestic Tranquility, provide for the common defence, promote the general Welfare, and secure the Blessings of Liberty to ourselves and our Posterity, do ordain and establish this Constitution for the United States of America.**

## ARTICLE. I.

SECTION. 1. All legislative Powers herein granted shall be vested in a Congress of the United States, which shall consist of a Senate and House of Representatives.

SECTION. 2. The House of Representatives shall be composed of Members chosen every second Year by the People of the several States, and the Electors in each State shall have the Qualifications requisite for Electors of the most numerous Branch of the State Legislature.

No Person shall be a Representative who shall not have attained to the age of twenty five Years, and been seven Years a Citizen of the United States, and who shall not, when elected, be an Inhabitant of that State in which he shall be chosen.

Representatives and direct Taxes shall be apportioned among the several States which may be included within this Union, according to their respective Numbers, which shall be determined by adding to the whole Number of free Persons, including those bound to Service for a Term of Years, and excluding Indians not taxed, three fifths of all other Persons. The actual Enumeration shall be made within three Years after the first Meeting of the Congress of the United States, and within every subsequent Term of ten Years, in such Manner as they shall by Law direct. The Number of Representatives shall not exceed one for every thirty Thousand, but each State shall have at Least one Representative; and until such enumeration shall be made, the State of New Hampshire shall be entitled to chuse three, Massachusetts eight, Rhode-Island and Providence Plantations one, Connecticut five, New-York six, New Jersey four, Pennsylvania eight, Delaware one, Maryland six, Virginia ten, North Carolina five, South Carolina five, and Georgia three.

When vacancies happen in the Representation from any State, the Executive Authority thereof shall issue Writs of Election to fill such Vacancies.

The House of Representatives shall chuse their Speaker and other Officers; and shall have the sole Power of Impeachment.

SECTION. 3. The Senate of the United States shall be composed of two Senators from each State, chosen by the Legislature thereof, for six years; and each Senator shall have one Vote.

Immediately after they shall be assembled in Consequence of the first Election, they shall be divided as equally as may be into three Classes. The Seats of the Senators of the first Class shall be vacated at the Expiration of the second Year, of the second Class at the Expiration of the fourth Year, and of the third Class at the Expiration of the sixth Year, so that one third may be chosen every second year; and if Vacancies happen by Resignation, or otherwise, during the Recess of the Legislature of any State, the Executive thereof may make temporary Appointments until the next Meeting of the Legislature, which shall then fill such Vacancies.

No Person shall be a Senator who shall not have attained to the Age of thirty Years, and been nine Years a Citizen of the United States, and who shall not, when elected, be an Inhabitant of that State for which he shall be chosen.

The Vice President of the United States shall be President of the Senate, but shall have no Vote, unless they be equally divided.

The Senate shall chuse their other Officers, and also a President pro tempore, in the Absence of the Vice President, or when he shall exercise the Office of President of the United States.

The Senate shall have the sole Power to try all Impeachments. When sitting for that Purpose, they shall be on Oath or Affirmation. When the President of the United States is tried the Chief Justice shall preside: And no Person shall be convicted without the Concurrence of two thirds of the Members present.

Judgment in Cases of Impeachment shall not extend further than to removal from Office, and disqualification to hold and enjoy any Office of honor, Trust or Profit under the United States: but the Party convicted shall nevertheless be liable and subject to Indictment, Trial, Judgment and Punishment, according to Law.

SECTION. 4. The Times, Places and Manner of holding Elections for Senators and Representatives, shall be prescribed in each State by the Legislature thereof; but the Congress may at any time by Law make or alter such Regulations, except as to the Places of chusing Senators.

The Congress shall assemble at least once in every Year, and such Meeting shall be on the first Monday in December, unless they shall by Law appoint a different Day.

SECTION. 5. Each House shall be the Judge of the Elections, Returns and Qualifications of its own Members, and a Majority of each shall constitute a Quorum to do Business; but a smaller Number may adjourn from day to day, and may be authorized to compel the Attendance of absent Members, in such Manner, and under such Penalties as each House may provide.

Each House may determine the Rules of its Proceedings, punish its Members for disorderly Behaviour, and, with the Concurrence of two thirds, expel a Member.

Each House shall keep a Journal of its Proceedings, and from time to time publish the same, excepting such Parts as may in their Judgment require Secrecy; and the Yeas and Nays of the Members of either House on any question shall, at the Desire of one fifth of those Present, be entered on the Journal.

Neither House, during the Session of Congress, shall, without the Consent of the other, adjourn for more than three days, nor to any other Place than that in which the two Houses shall be sitting.

SECTION. 6. The Senators and Representatives shall receive a Compensation for their Services, to be ascertained by Law, and paid out of the Treasury of the United States. They shall in all Cases, except Treason, Felony and Breach of the Peace, be privileged from Arrest during their Attendance at the Session of their respective Houses, and in going to and returning from the same; and for any Speech or Debate in either House, they shall not be questioned in any other Place.

No Senator or Representative shall, during the Time for which he was elected, be appointed to any civil Office under the Authority of the United States, which shall have been created, or the Emoluments whereof shall have been encreased during such time; and no Person holding any Office under the United States, shall be a Member of either House during his Continuance in Office.

SECTION. 7. All Bills for raising Revenue shall originate in the House of Representatives; but the Senate may propose or concur with amendments as on other Bills.

Every Bill which shall have passed the House of Representatives and the Senate, shall, before it become a Law, be presented to the President of the United States; If he approve he shall sign it, but if not he shall return it, with his Objections to that House in which it shall have originated, who shall enter the Objections at large on their Journal, and proceed to reconsider it. If after such Reconsideration two thirds of that House shall agree to pass the Bill, it shall be sent, together with the Objections, to the other House, by which it shall likewise be reconsidered, and if approved by two thirds of that House, it shall become a Law. But in all such Cases the Votes of both Houses shall be determined by Yeas and Nays, and the Names of the Persons voting for and against the Bill shall be entered on the Journal of each House respectively. If any Bill shall not be returned by the President within ten Days (Sundays excepted) after it shall have been presented to him, the Same shall be a Law, in like Manner as if he had signed it, unless the Congress by their Adjournment prevent its Return, in which Case it shall not be a Law.

Every Order, Resolution, or Vote to which the Concurrence of the Senate and House of Representatives may be necessary (except on a question of Adjournment) shall be presented to the President of the United States; and before the Same shall take Effect, shall be approved by him, or being disapproved by him, shall be repassed by two thirds of the Senate and House of Representatives, according to the Rules and Limitations prescribed in the Case of a Bill.

SECTION. 8. The Congress shall have Power To lay and collect Taxes, Duties, Imposts and Excises, to pay the Debts and provide for the common Defence and general Welfare of the United States; but all Duties, Imposts and Excises shall be uniform throughout the United States;

To borrow Money on the credit of the United States;

To regulate Commerce with foreign Nations, and among the several States, and with the Indian Tribes;

To establish an uniform Rule of Naturalization, and uniform Laws on the subject of Bankruptcies throughout the United States;

To coin Money, regulate the Value thereof, and of foreign Coin, and fix the Standard of Weights and Measures;

To provide for the Punishment of counterfeiting the Securities and current Coin of the United States;

To establish Post Offices and post Roads;

To promote the Progress of Science and useful Arts, by securing for limited Times to Authors and Inventors the exclusive Right to their respective Writings and Discoveries;

To constitute Tribunals inferior to the supreme Court;

To define and punish Piracies and Felonies committed on the high Seas, and Offences against the Law of Nations;

To declare War, grant Letters of Marque and Reprisal, and make Rules concerning Captures on Land and Water;

To raise and support Armies, but no Appropriation of Money to that Use shall be for a longer Term than two Years;

To provide and maintain a Navy;

To make Rules for the Government and Regulation of the land and naval Forces;

To provide for calling forth the Militia to execute the Laws of the Union, suppress Insurrections and repel Invasions;

To provide for organizing, arming, and disciplining, the Militia, and for governing such Part of them as may be employed in the Service of the United States, reserving to the States respectively, the Appointment of the Officers, and the Authority of training the Militia according to the discipline prescribed by Congress;

To exercise exclusive Legislation in all Cases whatsoever, over such District (not exceeding ten Miles square) as may, by Cession of Particular States, and the Acceptance of Congress, become the Seat of the Government of the United States, and to exercise like Authority over all Places purchased by the Consent of the Legislature of the State in which the Same shall be, for the Erection of Forts, Magazines, Arsenals, dock-Yards, and other needful Buildings;—And

To make all Laws which shall be necessary and proper for carrying into Execution the foregoing Powers, and all other Powers vested by this Constitution in the Government of the United States, or in any Department or Officer thereof.

SECTION. 9. The Migration or Importation of such Persons as any of the States now existing shall think proper to admit, shall not be prohibited by the Congress prior to the Year one thousand eight hundred and eight, but a Tax or duty may be imposed on such Importation, not exceeding ten dollars for each Person.

The Privilege of the Writ of Habeas Corpus shall not be suspended, unless when in Cases of Rebellion or Invasion the public Safety may require it.

No Bill of Attainder or ex post facto Law shall be passed.

No Capitation, or other direct, Tax shall be laid, unless in Proportion to the Census or Enumeration herein before directed to be taken.

No Tax or Duty shall be laid on Articles exported from any State.

No Preference shall be given by any Regulation or Commerce or Revenue to the Ports of one State over those of another; nor shall Vessels bound to, or from, one State, be obliged to enter, clear or pay Duties in another.

No Money shall be drawn from the Treasury, but in Consequence of Appropriations made by Law; and a regular Statement and Account of the Receipts and Expenditures of all public Money shall be published from time to time.

No Title of Nobility shall be granted by the United States: And no Person holding any Office of Profit or Trust under them, shall, without the Consent of the Congress, accept of any present Emolument, Office, or Title, of any kind whatever, from any King, Prince, or foreign State.

SECTION. 10. No State shall enter into any Treaty, Alliance, or Confederation; grant Letters of Marque and Reprisal; coin Money; emit Bills of Credit; make any Thing but gold and silver Coin a Tender in Payment of Debts; pass any Bill of Attainder, ex post facto Law, or Law impairing the Obligation of Contracts, or grant any Title of Nobility.

No State shall, without the Consent of the Congress, lay any Imposts or Duties on Imports or Exports, except what may be absolutely necessary for executing its inspection Laws: and the net Produce of all Duties and Imposts, laid by any State on Imports or Exports, shall be for the Use of the Treasury of the United States; and all such Laws shall be subject to the Revision and Controul of the Congress.

No state shall, without the Consent of Congress, lay any Duty of Tonnage, keep Troops, or Ships of War in time of Peace, enter into any Agreement or Compact with another State, or with a foreign Power, or engage in War, unless actually invaded, or in such imminent Danger as will not admit of delay.

## ARTICLE. II.

SECTION. 1. The executive Power shall be vested in a President of the United States of America. He shall hold his Office during the Term of four Years, and, together with the Vice President, chosen for the same Term, be elected as follows

Each State shall appoint, in such Manner as the Legislature thereof may direct, a Number of Electors, equal to the whole Number of Senators and Representatives to which the State may be entitled in the Congress: but no Senator or Representative, or Person holding an Office of Trust or Profit under the United States, shall be appointed an Elector.

The Electors shall meet in their respective States, and vote by Ballot for two Persons, of whom one at least shall not be an Inhabitant of the same State with themselves. And they shall make a List of all the persons voted for, and of the Number of Votes for each; which List they shall sign and certify, and transmit sealed to the Seat of Government of the United States, directed to the President of the Senate. The President of the Senate shall, in the Presence of the Senate and House of Representatives, open all the Certificates, and the Votes shall then be counted. The Person having the greatest Number of Votes shall be the President, if such Number be a Majority of the whole Number of Electors appointed; and if there be more than one who have such Majority, and have an equal Number of Votes, then the House of Representatives shall immediately chuse by Ballot one of them for President; and if no Person have a Majority, then from the five highest on the List the said House shall in like Manner chuse the President. But in chusing the President, the Votes shall be taken by States, the Representation from each State having one Vote; a quorum for this Purpose shall consist of a Member or Members from two thirds of the States, and a Majority of all the States shall be necessary to a Choice. In every Case, after the Choice of the President, the Person having the greatest Number of Votes of the Electors shall be the Vice President. But if there should remain two or more who have equal Votes, the Senate shall chuse from them by Ballot the Vice President.

The Congress may determine the Time of chusing the Electors, and the Day on which they shall give their Votes; which Day shall be the same throughout the United States.

No Person except a natural born Citizen, or a Citizen of the United States, at the time of the Adoption of this Constitution, shall be eligible to the Office of President; neither shall any person be eligible to that Office who shall not have attained to the Age of thirty five Years, and been fourteen Years a Resident within the United States.

In Case of the Removal of the President from Office, or of his Death, Resignation, or Inability to discharge the Powers and Duties of the said Office, the Same shall devolve on the Vice President, and the Congress may by Law provide for the Case of Removal, Death, Resignation or Inability, both of the President and Vice President, declaring what Officer shall then act as President, and such Officer shall act accordingly, until the Disability be removed, or a President shall be elected.

The President shall, at stated Times, receive for his Services, a Compensation, which shall neither be encreased nor diminished during the Period for which he shall have been elected, and he shall not receive within that period any other Emolument from the United States, or any of them.

Before he enter on the Execution of his Office, he shall take the following Oath or Affirmation:—"I do solemnly swear (or affirm) that I will faithfully execute the Office of President of the United States, and will to the best of my Ability, preserve, protect and defend the Constitution of the United States."

SECTION. 2. The President shall be Commander in Chief of the Army and Navy of the United States, and of the Militia of the several States, when called into the actual Service of the United States; he may require the Opinion, in writing, of the principal Officer in each of the executive Departments, upon any Subject relating to the Duties of their respective Offices, and he shall have Power to grant Reprieves and Pardons for Offences against the United States, except in Cases of Impeachment.

He shall have Power, by and with the Advice and Consent of the Senate, to make Treaties, provided two thirds of the Senators present concur; and he shall nominate, and by and with the Advice and Consent of the Senate, shall appoint Ambassadors, other public Ministers and Consuls, Judges of the supreme Court, and all other Officers of the United States, whose Appointments are not herein otherwise provided for, and which shall be established by Law: but the Congress may by Law vest the Appointment of such inferior Officers, as they think proper, in the President alone, in the Courts of Law, or in the Heads of Departments.

The President shall have Power to fill up all Vacancies that may happen during the Recess of the Senate, by granting Commissions which shall expire at the End of their next Session.

SECTION. 3. He shall from time to time give to the Congress Information of the State of the Union, and recommend to their Consideration such Measures as he shall judge necessary and expedient; he may, on extraordinary Occasions, convene both Houses, or either of them, and in Case of Disagreement between them, with Respect to the Time of Adjournment, he may adjourn them to such Time as he shall think proper; he shall receive Ambassadors and other public Ministers; he shall take Care that the Laws be faithfully executed, and shall Commission all the Officers of the United States.

SECTION. 4. The President, Vice President and all civil Officers of the United States, shall be removed from Office on Impeachment for, and Conviction of, Treason, Bribery, or other high Crimes and Misdemeanors.

## ARTICLE. III.

SECTION. 1. The judicial Power of the United States, shall be vested in one supreme Court, and in such inferior Courts as the Congress may from time to time ordain and establish. The Judges, both of the supreme and inferior Courts, shall hold their Offices during good Behaviour, and shall, at stated Times, receive for their Services, a Compensation, which shall not be diminished during their Continuance in Office.

SECTION. 2. The judicial Power shall extend to all Cases, in Law and Equity, arising under this Constitution, the Laws of the United States, and Treaties made, or which shall be made, under their Authority;—to all Cases affecting Ambassadors, other public Ministers and Consuls;—to all Cases of admiralty and maritime Jurisdiction;—to Controversies to which the United States shall be a Party;—to Controversies between two or more States;—between a State and Citizens of another State;—between Citizens of different States;—between Citizens of the same State claiming Lands under Grants of different States, and between a State, or the Citizens thereof, and foreign States, Citizens or Subjects.

In all Cases affecting Ambassadors, other public Ministers and Consuls, and those in which a State shall be Party, the supreme Court shall have original Jurisdiction. In all the other Cases before mentioned, the supreme Court shall have appellate Jurisdiction, both as to Law and Fact, with such Exceptions, and under such Regulations as the Congress shall make.

The Trial of all Crimes, except in Cases of Impeachment, shall be by Jury; and such Trial shall be held in the State where the said Crimes shall have been committed; but when not committed within any State, the Trial shall be at such Place or Places as the Congress may by Law have directed.

SECTION. 3. Treason against the United States, shall consist only in levying War against them, or in adhering to their Enemies, giving them Aid and Comfort. No Person shall be convicted of Treason unless on the Testimony of two Witnesses to the same overt Act, or on Confession in open Court.

The Congress shall have Power to declare the Punishment of Treason, but no Attainder of Treason shall work Corruption of Blood, or Forfeiture except during the Life of the Person attained.

## ARTICLE. IV.

SECTION. 1. Full Faith and Credit shall be given in each State to the public Acts, Records, and judicial Proceedings of every other State. And the Congress may by general Laws prescribe the Manner in which such Acts, Record and Proceedings shall be proved, and the Effect thereof.

SECTION. 2. The Citizens of each State shall be entitled to all Privileges and Immunities of Citizens in the several States.

A Person charged in any State with Treason, Felony, or other Crime, who shall flee from Justice, and be found in another State, shall on Demand of the executive Authority of the State from which he fled, be delivered up, to be removed to the State having Jurisdiction of the Crime.

No Person held to Service or Labour in one State, under the Laws thereof, escaping into another, shall, in Consequence of any Law or Regulation therein, be discharged from such Service or Labour, but shall be delivered up on Claim of the Party to whom such Service or Labour may be due.

SECTION. 3. New States may be admitted by the Congress into this Union; but no new State shall be formed or erected within the Jurisdiction of any other State; nor any State be formed by the Junction of two or more States, or Parts of States, without the Consent of the Legislatures of the States concerned as well as of the Congress.

The Congress shall have Power to dispose of and make all needful Rules and Regulations respecting the Territory or other Property belonging to the United States; and nothing in this Constitution shall be so construed as to Prejudice any Claims of the United States, or of any particular State.

SECTION. 4. The United States shall guarantee to every State in this Union a Republican Form of Government, and shall protect each of them against Invasion; and on Application of the Legislature, or of the Executive (when the Legislature cannot be convened) against domestic Violence.

## ARTICLE. V.

The Congress, whenever two thirds of both Houses shall deem it necessary, shall propose Amendments to this Constitution, or, on the Application of the Legislature of two thirds of the several States, shall call a Convention for proposing Amendments, which, in either Case, shall be valid to all Intents and Purposes, as Part of this Constitution, when ratified by the Legislatures of three fourths of the several States, or by Conventions in three fourths thereof, as the one or the other Mode of Ratification may be proposed by the Congress; Provided that no Amendment which may be made prior to the Year One thousand eight hundred and eight shall in any Manner affect the first and fourth Clauses in the Ninth Section of the first Article; and that no State, without its Consent, shall be deprived of its equal Suffrage in the Senate.

## ARTICLE. VI.

All Debts contracted and Engagements entered into, before the Adoption of this Constitution, shall be as valid against the United States under this Constitution, as under the Confederation.

This Constitution, and the Laws of the United States which shall be made in Pursuance thereof; and all Treaties made, or which shall be made, under the Authority of the United States, shall be the supreme Law of the Land; and the Judges in every State shall be bound thereby, any Thing in the Constitution or Laws of any State to the Contrary notwithstanding.

The Senators and Representatives before mentioned, and the Members of the several State Legislatures, and all executive and judicial Officers, both of the United States and of the several States, shall be bound by Oath or Affirmation, to support this Constitution; but no religious Test shall ever be required as a Qualification to any Office or public Trust under the United States.

## ARTICLE. VII.

The Ratification of the Conventions of nine States, shall be sufficient for the Establishment of this Constitution between the States so ratifying the Same.

Done in Convention by the Unanimous Consent of the States present the Seventeenth Day of September in the Year of our Lord one thousand seven hundred and Eighty seven and of the Independence of the United States of America the Twelfth In witness whereof We have hereunto subscribed our Names,

Go. WASHINGTON—Presidt. and deputy from Virginia

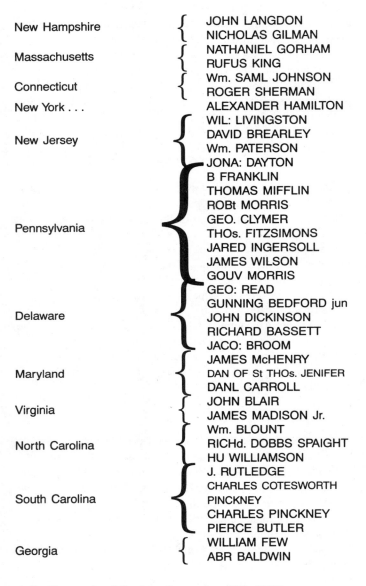

| New Hampshire | JOHN LANGDON<br>NICHOLAS GILMAN |
| Massachusetts | NATHANIEL GORHAM<br>RUFUS KING |
| Connecticut | Wm. SAML JOHNSON<br>ROGER SHERMAN |
| New York . . . | ALEXANDER HAMILTON |
| New Jersey | WIL: LIVINGSTON<br>DAVID BREARLEY<br>Wm. PATERSON<br>JONA: DAYTON |
| Pennsylvania | B FRANKLIN<br>THOMAS MIFFLIN<br>ROBt MORRIS<br>GEO. CLYMER<br>THOs. FITZSIMONS<br>JARED INGERSOLL<br>JAMES WILSON<br>GOUV MORRIS |
| Delaware | GEO: READ<br>GUNNING BEDFORD jun<br>JOHN DICKINSON<br>RICHARD BASSETT<br>JACO: BROOM |
| Maryland | JAMES McHENRY<br>DAN OF St THOs. JENIFER<br>DANL CARROLL |
| Virginia | JOHN BLAIR<br>JAMES MADISON Jr. |
| North Carolina | Wm. BLOUNT<br>RICHd. DOBBS SPAIGHT<br>HU WILLIAMSON |
| South Carolina | J. RUTLEDGE<br>CHARLES COTESWORTH PINCKNEY<br>CHARLES PINCKNEY<br>PIERCE BUTLER |
| Georgia | WILLIAM FEW<br>ABR BALDWIN |

In Convention Monday, September 17th 1787.

Present The States of

New Hampshire, Massachusetts, Connecticut, Mr. Hamilton from New York, New Jersey, Pennsylvania, Delaware, Maryland, Virginia, North Carolina and Georgia.

Resolved,

That the preceeding Constitution be laid before the United States in Congress assembled, and that it is the Opinion of this Convention, that it should afterwards be submitted to a Convention of Delegates, chosen in each State by the People thereof, under the Recommendation of its Legislature, for their Assent and Ratification; and that each Convention assenting to, and ratifying the Same, should give Notice thereof to the United States in Congress assembled. Resolved, That it is the Opinion of this Convention, that as soon as the Conventions of nine States shall have ratified this Constitution, the United States in Congress assembled should fix a Day on which Electors should be appointed by the States which shall have ratified the same, and a Day on which the Electors should assemble to vote for the President, and the Time and Place for commencing Proceedings under this Constitution. That after such Publication the Electors should be appointed, and the Senators and Representatives elected: That the Electors should meet on the Day fixed for the Election of the President, and should transmit their Votes certified, signed, sealed and directed, as the Constitution requires, to the Secretary of the United States in Congress assembled, that the Senators and Representatives should convene at the Time and Place assigned; that the Senators should appoint a President of the Senate, for the sole Purpose of receiving, opening and counting the Votes for President; and, that after he shall be chosen, the Congress, together with the President, should, without Delay, proceed to execute this Constitution.

By the Unanimous Order of the Convention

Go. WASHINGTON—Presidt.

W. JACKSON Secretary.

## RATIFICATION OF THE CONSTITUTION

| State | Date of ratification |
| --- | --- |
| Delaware | Dec 7, 1787 |
| Pennsylvania | Dec 12, 1787 |
| New Jersey | Dec 19, 1787 |
| Georgia | Jan 2, 1788 |
| Connecticut | Jan 9, 1788 |
| Massachusetts | Feb 6, 1788 |
| Maryland | Apr 28, 1788 |
| South Carolina | May 23, 1788 |
| New Hampshire | June 21, 1788 |
| Virginia | Jun 25, 1788 |
| New York | Jun 26, 1788 |
| Rhode Island | May 29, 1790 |
| North Carolina | Nov 21, 1789 |

**ARTICLES IN ADDITION TO, AND AMENDMENT OF, THE CONSTITUTION OF THE UNITED STATES OF AMERICA, PROPOSED BY CONGRESS, AND RATIFIED BY THE SEVERAL STATES, PURSUANT TO THE FIFTH ARTICLE OF THE ORIGINAL CONSTITUTION.**

### AMENDMENT I.

Congress shall make no law respecting an establishment of religion, or prohibiting the free exercise thereof; or abridging the freedom of speech, or of the press; or the right of the people peaceably to assemble, and to petition the Government for a redress of grievances.

## AMENDMENT II.

A well regulated Militia, being necessary to the security of a free State, the right of the people to keep and bear Arms, shall not be infringed.

## AMENDMENT III.

No Soldier shall, in time of peace be quartered in any house, without the consent of the Owner, nor in time of war, but in a manner to be prescribed by law.

## AMENDMENT IV.

The right of the people to be secure in their persons, houses, papers, and effects, against unreasonable searches and seizures, shall not be violated, and no Warrants shall issue, but upon probable cause, supported by Oath or affirmation, and particularly describing the place to be searched, and the persons or things to be seized.

## AMENDMENT V.

No person shall be held to answer for a capital, or otherwise infamous crime, unless on a presentment or indictment of a Grand Jury, except in cases arising in the land or naval forces, or in the Militia, when in actual service in time of War or public danger; nor shall any person be subject for the same offence to be twice put in jeopardy of life or limb; nor shall be compelled in any criminal case to be a witness against himself, nor be deprived of life, liberty, or property, without due process of law; nor shall private property be taken for public use, without just compensation.

## AMENDMENT VI.

In all criminal prosecutions, the accused shall enjoy the right to a speedy and public trial, by an impartial jury of the State and district wherein the crime shall have been committed, which district shall have been previously ascertained by law, and to be informed of the nature and cause of the accusation; to be confronted with the witnesses against him; to have compulsory process for obtaining witnesses in his favor, and to have the Assistance of Counsel for his defence.

## AMENDMENT VII.

In Suits at common law, where the value in controversy shall exceed twenty dollars, the right of trial by jury shall be preserved, and no fact tried by a jury, shall be otherwise re-examined in any Court of the United States, than according to the rules of the common law.

## AMENDMENT VIII.

Excessive bail shall not be required, nor excessive fines imposed, nor cruel and unusual punishments inflicted.

## AMENDMENT IX.

The enumeration in the Constitution, of certain rights, shall not be construed to deny or disparage others retained by the people.

## AMENDMENT X.

The powers not delegated to the United States by the Constitution, nor prohibited by it to the States, are reserved to the States respectively, or to the people.

## AMENDMENT XI.

**(Adopted Jan. 8, 1798)**

The Judicial power of the United States shall not be construed to extend to any suit in law or equity, commenced or prosecuted against one of the United States by Citizens of another State, or by Citizens or Subjects of any Foreign State.

## AMENDMENT XII.

**(Adopted Sept. 25, 1804)**

The Electors shall meet in their respective states and vote by ballot for President and Vice-President, one of whom, at least, shall not be an inhabitant of the same state with themselves; they shall name in their ballots the person voted for as President, and in distinct ballots the person voted for as Vice-President, and they shall make distinct lists of all persons voted for as President, and of all persons voted for as Vice-President, and of the number of votes for each, which lists they shall sign and certify, and transmit sealed to the seat of the government of the United States, directed to the President of the Senate;—The President of the Senate shall, in the presence of the Senate and House of Representatives, open all the certificates and the votes shall then be counted;—The person having the greatest number of votes for President, shall be the President, if such number be a majority of the whole number of Electors appointed; and if no person have such majority, then from the persons having the highest numbers not exceeding three on the list of those voted for as President, the House of Representatives shall choose immediately, by ballot, the President. But in choosing the President, the votes shall be taken by states, the representation from each state having one vote; a quorum for this purpose shall consist of a member or members from two-thirds of the states, and a majority of all the states shall be necessary to a choice. And if the House of Representatives shall not choose a President whenever the right of choice shall devolve upon them, before the fourth day of March next following, then the Vice-President shall act as President, as in the case of the death or other constitutional disability of the President.—The person having the greatest number of votes as Vice-President, shall be the Vice-President, if such number be a majority of the whole number of Electors appointed, and if no person have a majority, then from the two highest numbers on the list, the Senate shall choose the Vice-President; a quorum for the purpose shall consist of two-thirds of the whole number of Senators, and a majority of the whole number shall be necessary to a choice. But no person constitutionally ineligible to the office of President shall be eligible to that of Vice-President of the United States.

## AMENDMENT XIII.

### (Adopted Dec. 18, 1865)

SECTION 1. Neither slavery nor involuntary servitude, except as a punishment for crime whereof the party shall have been duly convicted, shall exist within the United States, or any place subject to their jurisdiction.

SECTION 2. Congress shall have power to enforce this article by appropriate legislation.

## AMENDMENT XIV.

### (Adopted July 28, 1868)

SECTION 1. All persons born or naturalized in the United States and subject to the jurisdiction thereof, are citizens of the United States and of the State wherein they reside. No State shall make or enforce any law which shall abridge the privileges or immunities of citizens of the United States; nor shall any State deprive any person of life, liberty, or property, without due process of law; nor deny to any person within its jurisdiction the equal protection of the laws.

SECTION 2. Representatives shall be apportioned among the several States according to their respective numbers, counting the whole number of persons in each State, excluding Indians not taxed. But when the right to vote at any election for the choice of electors for President and Vice President of the United States, Representatives in Congress, the Executive and Judicial officers of a State, or the members of the Legislature thereof, is denied to any of the male inhabitants of such State, being twenty-one years of age, and citizens of the United States, or in any way abridged, except for participation in rebellion, or other crime, the basis of representation therein shall be reduced in the proportion which the number of such male citizens shall bear to the whole number of male citizens twenty-one years of age in such State.

SECTION 3. No person shall be a Senator or Representative in Congress, or elector of President and Vice President, or hold any office, civil or military, under the United States, or under any State, who, having previously taken an oath, as a member of Congress, or as an officer of the United States, or as a member of any State legislature, or as an executive or judicial officer of any State, to support the Constitution of the United States, shall have engaged in insurrection or rebellion against the same, or given aid or comfort to the enemies thereof. But Congress may by a vote of two-thirds of each House, remove such disability.

SECTION 4. The validity of the public debt of the United States, authorized by law, including debts incurred for payment of pensions and bounties for services in suppressing insurrection or rebellion, shall not be questioned. But neither the United States nor any State shall assume or pay any debt or obligation incurred in aid of insurrection or rebellion against the United States, or any claim for the loss or emancipation of any slave; but all such debts, obligations and claims shall be held illegal and void.

SECTION 5. The Congress shall have power to enforce, by appropriate legislation, the provisions of this article.

## AMENDMENT XV.

### (Adopted March 30, 1870)

SECTION 1. The right of citizens of the United States to vote shall not be denied or abridged by the United States or by any State on account of race, color, or previous condition of servitude.

SECTION 2. The Congress shall have power to enforce this article by appropriate legislation.

## AMENDMENT XVI.

### (Adopted Feb. 25, 1913)

The Congress shall have power to lay and collect taxes on incomes, from whatever source derived, without apportionment among the several States, and without regard to any census or enumeration.

## AMENDMENT XVII.

### (Adopted May 31, 1913)

The Senate of the United States shall be composed of two Senators from each State, elected by the people thereof, for six years; and each Senator shall have one vote. The electors in each State shall have the qualifications requisite for electors of the most numerous branch of the State legislatures.

When vacancies happen in the representation of any State in the Senate, the executive authority of such State shall issue writs of election to fill such vacancies: *Provided,* That the legislature of any State may empower the executive thereof to make temporary appointments until the people fill the vacancies by election as the legislature may direct.

This amendment shall not be so construed as to affect the election or term of any Senator chosen before it becomes valid as part of the Constitution.

## AMENDMENT XVIII.

### (Adopted Jan. 29, 1919)

SECTION 1. After one year from the ratification of this article the manufacture, sale or transportation of intoxicating liquors within, the importation thereof into, or the exportation thereof from the United States and all territory subject to the jurisdiction thereof for beverage purposes is hereby prohibited.

SECTION 2. The Congress and the several States shall have concurrent power to enforce this article by appropriate legislation.

SECTION 3. This article shall be inoperative unless it shall have been ratified as an amendment to the Constitution by the legislatures of the several States, as provided in the Constitution, within seven years from the date of the submission hereof to the States by the Congress.

# AMENDMENT XIX.

**(Adopted Aug. 26, 1920)**

The right of citizens of the United States to vote shall not be denied or abridged by the United States or by any State on account of sex.

Congress shall have power to enforce this article by appropriate legislation.

# AMENDMENT XX.

**(Adopted Feb. 6, 1933)**

SECTION 1. The terms of the President and Vice President shall end at noon on the 20th day of January, and the terms of Senators and Representatives at noon on the 3d day of January, of the years in which such terms would have ended if this article had not been ratified; and the terms of their successors shall then begin.

SECTION 2. The Congress shall assemble at least once in every year, and such meeting shall begin at noon on the 3d day of January, unless they shall by law appoint a different day.

SECTION 3. If, at the time fixed for the beginning of the term of the President, the President elect shall have died, the Vice President elect shall become President. If a President shall not have been chosen before the time fixed for the beginning of his term, or if the President elect shall have failed to qualify, then the Vice President elect shall act as President until a President shall have qualified; and the Congress may by law provide for the case wherein neither a President elect nor a Vice President elect shall have qualified, declaring who shall then act as President, or the manner in which one who is to act shall be selected, and such person shall act accordingly until a President or Vice President shall have qualified.

SECTION 4. The Congress may by law provide for the case of the death of any of the persons from whom the House of Representatives may choose a President whenever the right of choice shall have devolved upon them, and for the case of the death of any of the persons from whom the Senate may choose a Vice President whenever the right of choice shall have devolved upon them.

SECTION 5. Sections 1 and 2 shall take effect on the 15th day of October following the ratification of this article.

SECTION 6. This article shall be inoperative unless it shall have been ratified as an amendment to the Constitution by the legislatures of three-fourths of the several States within seven years from the date of its submission.

# AMENDMENT XXI.

**(Adopted Dec. 5, 1933)**

SECTION 1. The eighteenth article of amendment to the Constitution of the United States is hereby repealed.

SECTION 2. The transportation or importation into any State, Territory, or possession of the United States for delivery or use therein of intoxicating liquors, in violation of the laws thereof, is hereby prohibited.

SECTION 3. This article shall be inoperative unless it shall have been ratified as an amendment to the Constitution by conventions in the several States, as provided in the Constitution, within seven years from the date of the submission hereof to the States by the Congress.

# AMENDMENT XXII.

**(Adopted Feb. 27, 1951)**

SECTION 1. No person shall be elected to the office of the President more than twice, and no person who has held the office of President, or acted as President, for more than two years of a term to which some other person was elected President shall be elected to the office of the President more than once. But this Article shall not apply to any person holding the office of President when this Article was proposed by the Congress, and shall not prevent any person who may be holding the office of President, or acting as President, during the term within which this Article becomes operative from holding the office of President or acting as President during the remainder of such term.

SECTION 2. This Article shall be inoperative unless it shall have been ratified as an amendment to the Constitution by the legislatures of three-fourths of the several States within seven years from the date of its submission to the States by the Congress.

# AMENDMENT XXIII.

**(Adopted Mar. 29, 1961)**

SECTION 1. The District constituting the seat of Government of the United States shall appoint in such manner as the Congress may direct:

A number of electors of President and Vice President equal to the whole number of Senators and Representatives in Congress to which the District would be entitled if it were a State, but in no event more than the least populous State; they shall be in addition to those appointed by the States, but they shall be considered, for the purposes of the election of President and Vice President, to be electors appointed by a State; and they shall meet in the District and perform such duties as provided by the twelfth article of amendment.

SECTION 2. The Congress shall have power to enforce this article by appropriate legislation.

# AMENDMENT XXIV.

**(Adopted Jan. 23, 1964)**

SECTION 1. The right of citizens of the United States to vote in any primary or other election for President or Vice President, for electors for President or Vice President, or for Senator or Representative in Congress, shall not be denied or abridged by the United States or any State by reason of failure to pay any poll tax or other tax.

SECTION 2. The Congress shall have the power to enforce this article by appropriate legislation.

## AMENDMENT XXV.

**(Adopted Feb. 10, 1967)**

SECTION 1. In case of the removal of the President from office or of his death or resignation, the Vice President shall become President.

SECTION 2. Whenever there is a vacancy in the office of the Vice President, the President shall nominate a Vice President who shall take the office upon confirmation by a majority vote of both houses of Congress.

SECTION 3. Whenever the President transmits to the President pro tempore of the Senate and the Speaker of the House of Representatives his written declaration that he is unable to discharge the powers and duties of his office, and until he transmits to them a written declaration to the contrary, such powers and duties shall be discharged by the Vice President as Acting President.

SECTION 4. Whenever the Vice President and a majority of either the principal officers of the executive departments or of such other body as Congress may by law provide, transmit to the President pro tempore of the Senate and the Speaker of the House of Representatives their written declaration that the President is unable to discharge the powers and duties of his office, the Vice President shall immediately assume the powers and duties of the office as Acting President.

Thereafter, when the President transmits to the President pro tempore of the Senate and the Speaker of the House of Representatives his written declaration that no inability exists, he shall resume the powers and duties of his office unless the Vice President and a majority of either the principal officers of the executive department or of such other body as Congress may by law provide, transmit within four days to the President pro tempore of the Senate and the Speaker of the House of Representatives their written declaration that the President is unable to discharge the powers and duties of his office. Thereupon Congress shall decide the issue, assembling within forty-eight hours for that purpose if not in session. If the Congress within twenty-one days after receipt of the latter written declaration, or, if Congress is not in session, within twenty-one days after Congress is required to assemble, determines by two-thirds vote of both Houses that the President is unable to discharge the powers and duties of his office, the Vice President shall continue to discharge the same as Acting President; otherwise, the President shall resume the powers and duties of his office.

## AMENDMENT XXVI.

**(Adopted June 30, 1971)**

SECTION 1. The right of citizens of the United States, who are 18 years of age or older, to vote shall not be denied or abridged by the United States or by any state on account of age.

SECTION 2. The Congress shall have the power to enforce this article by appropriate legislation.

## AMENDMENT XXVII.

**(Adopted May 7, 1992)**

No law, varying the compensation for the services of the Senators and Representatives, shall take effect, until an election of Representatives shall have intervened.

# THE SIZE AND VARIETY OF THE UNION AS A CHECK ON FACTION

## *FEDERALIST* NO. 10

### (MADISON)

*To the People of the State of New York:*

AMONG the numerous advantages promised by a well-constructed Union, none deserves to be more accurately developed than its tendency to break and control the violence of faction. The friend of popular governments never finds himself so much alarmed for their character and fate, as when he contemplates their propensity to this dangerous vice. He will not fail, therefore, to set a due value on any plan which, without violating the principles to which he is attached, provides a proper cure for it. The instability, injustice, and confusion introduced into the public councils, have, in truth, been the mortal diseases under which popular governments have everywhere perished; as they continue to be the favorite and fruitful topics from which the adversaries to liberty derive their most specious declamations. The valuable improvements made by the American constitutions on the popular models, both ancient and modern, cannot certainly be too much admired; but it would be an unwarrantable partiality, to contend that they have as effectually obviated the danger on this side, as was wished and expected. Complaints are everywhere heard from our most considerate and virtuous citizens, equally the friends of public and private faith, and of public and personal liberty, that our governments are too unstable, that the public good is disregarded in the conflicts of rival parties, and that measures are too often decided, not according to the rules of justice and the rights of the minor party, but by the superior force of an interested and overbearing majority. However anxiously we may wish that these complaints had no foundation, the evidence of known facts will not permit us to deny that they are in some degree true. It will be found, indeed, on a candid review of our situation, that some of the distresses under which we labor have been erroneously charged on the operation of our governments; but it will be found, at the same time, that other causes will not alone account for many of our heaviest misfortunes; and, particularly, for that prevailing and increasing distrust of public engagements, and alarm for private rights, which are echoed from one end of the continent to the other. These must be chiefly, if not wholly, effects of the unsteadiness and injustice with which a factious spirit has tainted our public administrations.

By a faction, I understand a number of citizens, whether amounting to a majority or minority of the whole, who are united and actuated by some common impulse of passion, or of interest, adverse to the rights of other citizens, or to the permanent and aggregate interests of the community.

There are two methods of curing the mischiefs of faction: the one, by removing its causes; the other, by controlling its effects.

There are again two methods of removing the causes of faction: the one, by destroying the liberty which is essential to its existence; the other, by giving to every citizen the same opinions, the same passions, and the same interests.

It could never be more truly said than of the first remedy, that it was worse than the disease. Liberty is to faction what air is to fire, an aliment without which it instantly expires. But it could not be less folly to abolish liberty, which is essential to political life, because it nourishes faction, than it would be to wish the annihilation of air, which is essential to animal life, because it imparts to fire its destructive agency.

The second expedient is as impracticable as the first would be unwise. As long as the reason of man continues fallible, and he is at liberty to exercise it, different opinions will be formed. As long as the connection subsists between his reason and his self-love, his opinions and his passions will have a reciprocal influence on each other; and the former will be objects to which the latter will attach themselves. The diversity in the faculties of men, from which the rights of property originate, is not less an insuperable obstacle to a uniformity of interests. The protection of these faculties is the first object of government. From the protection of different and unequal faculties of acquiring property, the possession of different degrees and kinds of property immediately results; and from the influence of these on the sentiments and views of the respective proprietors, ensues a division of the society into different interests and parties.

The latent causes of faction are thus sown in the nature of man; and we see them everywhere brought into different degrees of activity, according to the different circumstances of civil society. A zeal for different opinions concerning religion, concerning government, and many other points, as well of speculation as of practice; an attachment to different leaders ambitiously contending for pre-eminence and power; or to persons of other descriptions whose fortunes have been interesting to the human passions, have, in turn, divided mankind into parties, inflamed them with mutual animosity, and rendered them much more disposed to vex and oppress each other than to co-operate for their common good. So strong is this propensity of mankind to fall into mutual animosities, that where no substantial occasion presents itself, the most frivolous and fanciful distinctions have been sufficient to kindle their unfriendly passions and excite their most violent conflicts. But the most common and durable source of factions has been the various and unequal distribution of property. Those who hold and those who are without property have ever formed distinct interests in society.

Those who are creditors, and those who are debtors, fall under a like discrimination. A landed interest, a manufacturing interest, a mercantile interest, a moneyed interest, with many lesser interests, grow up of necessity in civilized nations, and divide them into different classes, actuated by different sentiments and views. The regulation of these various and interfering interests forms the principal task of modern legislation, and involves the spirit of party and faction in the necessary and ordinary operations of the government.

No man is allowed to be a judge in his own cause, because his interest would certainly bias his judgment, and, not improbably, corrupt his integrity. With equal, nay with greater reason, a body of men are unfit to be both judges and parties at the same time; yet what are many of the most important acts of legislation, but so many judicial determinations, not indeed concerning the rights of single persons, but concerning the rights of large bodies of citizens? And what are the different classes of legislators but advocates and parties to the causes which they determine? Is a law proposed concerning private debts? It is a question to which the creditors are parties on one side and the debtors on the other. Justice ought to hold the balance between them. Yet the parties are, and must be, themselves the judges; and the most numerous party, or, in other words, the most powerful faction must be expected to prevail. Shall domestic manufactures be encouraged, and in what degree, by restrictions on foreign manufactures? are questions which would be differently decided by the landed and the manufacturing classes, and probably by neither with a sole regard to justice and the public good. The apportionment of taxes on the various descriptions of property is an act which seems to require the most exact impartiality; yet there is, perhaps, no legislative act in which greater opportunity and temptation are given to a predominant party to trample on the rules of justice. Every shilling with which they overburden the inferior number, is a shilling saved to their own pockets.

It is in vain to say that enlightened statesmen will be able to adjust these clashing interests, and render them all subservient to the public good. Enlightened statesmen will not always be at the helm. Nor, in many cases, can such an adjustment be made at all without taking into view indirect and remote considerations, which will rarely prevail over the immediate interest which one party may find in disregarding the rights of another or the good of the whole.

The inference to which we are brought is, that the *causes* of faction cannot be removed, and that relief is only to be sought in the means of controlling its *effects*.

If a faction consists of less than a majority, relief is supplied by the republican principle, which enables the majority to defeat its sinister views by regular vote. It may clog the administration, it may convulse the society; but it will be unable to execute and mask its violence under the forms of the

Constitution. When a majority is included in a faction, the form of popular government, on the other hand, enables it to sacrifice to its ruling passion or interest both the public good and the rights of other citizens. To secure the public good and private rights against the danger of such a faction, and at the same time to preserve the spirit and the form of popular government, is then the great object to which our inquiries are directed. Let me add that it is the great desideratum by which this form of government can be rescued from the opprobrium under which it has so long labored, and be recommended to the esteem and adoption of mankind.

By what means is this object attainable? Evidently by one of two only. Either the existence of the same passion or interest in a majority at the same time must be prevented, or the majority, having such coexistent passion or interest, must be rendered, by their number and local situation, unable to concert and carry into effect schemes of oppression. If the impulse and the opportunity be suffered to coincide, we well know that neither moral nor religious motives can be relied on as an adequate control. They are not found to be such on the injustice and violence of individuals, and lose their efficacy in proportion to the number combined together, that is, in proportion as their efficacy becomes needful.

From this view of the subject it may be concluded that a pure democracy, by which I mean a society consisting of a small number of citizens, who assemble and administer the government in person, can admit of no cure for the mischiefs of faction. A common passion or interest will, in almost every case, be felt by a majority of the whole; a communication and concert result from the form of government itself; and there is nothing to check the inducements to sacrifice the weaker party or an obnoxious individual. Hence it is that such democracies have ever been spectacles of turbulence and contention; have ever been found incompatible with personal security or the rights of property; and have in general been as short in their lives as they have been violent in their deaths. Theoretic politicians, who have patronized this species of government, have erroneously supposed that by reducing mankind to a perfect equality in their political rights, they would, at the same time, be perfectly equalized and assimilated in their possessions, their opinions, and their passions.

A republic, by which I mean a government in which the scheme of representation takes place, opens a different prospect, and promises the cure for which we are seeking. Let us examine the points in which it varies from pure democracy, and we shall comprehend both the nature of the cure and the efficacy which it must derive from the Union.

The two great points of difference between a democracy and a republic are: first, the delegation of the government, in the latter, to a small number of citizens elected by the rest; secondly, the greater number of citizens, and greater sphere of country, over which the latter may be extended.

The effect of the first difference is, on the one hand, to refine and enlarge the public views, by passing them through the medium of a chosen body of citizens, whose wisdom may best discern the true interest of their country, and whose patriotism and love of justice will be least likely to sacrifice it to temporary or partial considerations. Under such a regulation, it may well happen that the public voice, pronounced by the representatives of the people, will be more consonant to the public good than if pronounced by the people themselves, convened for the purpose. On the other hand, the effect may be inverted. Men of factious tempers, of local prejudices, or of sinister designs, may, by intrigue, by corruption, or by other means, first obtain the suffrages, and then betray the interests, of the people. The question resulting is, whether small or extensive republics are more favorable to the election of proper guardians of the public weal; and it is clearly decided in favor of the latter by two obvious considerations:

In the first place, it is to be remarked that, however small the republic may be, the representatives must be raised to a certain number, in order to guard against the cabals of a few; and that, however large it may be, they must be limited to a certain number, in order to guard against the confusion of a multitude. Hence, the number of representatives in the two cases not being in proportion to that of the two constituents, and being proportionally greater in the small republic, it follows that, if the proportion of fit characters be not less in the large than in the small republic, the former will present a greater option, and consequently a greater probability of a fit choice.

In the next place, as each representative will be chosen by a greater number of citizens in the large than in the small republic, it will be more difficult for unworthy candidates to practise with success the vicious arts by which elections are too often carried; and the suffrages of the people being more free, will be more likely to centre in men who possess the most attractive merit and the most diffusive and established characters.

It must be confessed that in this, as in most other cases, there is a mean, on both sides of which inconveniences will be found to lie. By enlarging too much the number of electors, you render the representative too little acquainted with all their local circumstances and lesser interests; as by reducing it too much, you render him unduly attached to these, and too little fit to comprehend and pursue great and national objects. The federal Constitution forms a happy combination in this respect; the great and aggregate interests being referred to the national, the local and particular to the State legislatures.

The other point of difference is, the greater number of citizens and extent of territory which may be brought within the compass of republican than of democratic government; and it is this circumstance principally which renders factious combinations less to be dreaded in the former than in the latter. The smaller the society, the fewer probably will be the distinct parties and interests composing it; the fewer the distinct parties and interests, the more frequently will a majority be found of the same party; and the smaller the number of individuals composing a majority, and the smaller the compass within which they are placed, the more easily will they concert and execute their plans of oppression. Extend the sphere and you take in a greater variety of parties and interests; you will make it less probable that a majority of the whole will have a common motive to invade the rights of other citizens; or if such a common motive exists, it will be more difficult for all who feel it to discover their own strength, and to act in unison with each other. Besides other impediments, it may be remarked that, where there is a consciousness of unjust or dishonorable purposes, communication is always checked by distrust in proportion to the number whose concurrence is necessary.

Hence, it clearly appears, that the same advantage which a republic has over a democracy, in controlling the effects of faction, is enjoyed by a large over a small republic,—is enjoyed by the Union over the States composing it. Does the advantage consist in the substitution of representatives whose enlightened views and virtuous sentiments render them superior to local prejudices and to schemes of injustice? It will not be denied that the representation of the Union will be most likely to possess these requisite endowments. Does it consist in the greater

security afforded by a greater variety of parties, against the event of any one party being able to outnumber and oppress the rest? In an equal degree does the increased variety of parties comprised within the Union, increase this security. Does it, in fine, consist in the greater obstacles opposed to the concert and accomplishment of the secret wishes of an unjust and interested majority? Here, again, the extent of the Union gives it the most palpable advantage.

The influence of factious leaders may kindle a flame within their particular States, but will be unable to spread a general conflagration through the other States. A religious sect may degenerate into a political faction in a part of the Confederacy; but the variety of sects dispersed over the entire face of it must secure the national councils against any danger from that source. A rage for paper money, for an abolition of debts, for an equal division of property, or for any other improper or wicked project, will be less apt to pervade the whole body of the Union than a particular member of it; in the same proportion as such a malady is more likely to taint a particular county or distinct, than an entire State.

In the extent and proper structure of the Union, therefore, we behold a republican remedy for the diseases most incident to republican government. And according to the degree of pleasure and pride we feel in being republicans, ought to be our zeal in cherishing the spirit and supporting the character of Federalists.

PUBLIUS

# CHECKS AND BALANCES

## *FEDERALIST* NO. 51

## (MADISON)

*To the People of the State of New York:*

To what expedient, then, shall we finally resort, for maintaining in practice the necessary partition of power among the several departments, as laid down in the Constitution? The only answer that can be given is, that as all these exterior provisions are found to be inadequate, the defect must be supplied, by so contriving the interior structure of the government as that its several constituent parts may, by their mutual relations, be the means of keeping each other in their proper places. Without presuming to undertake a full development of this important idea, I will hazard a few general observations, which may perhaps place it in a clearer light, and enable us to form a more correct judgment of the principles and structure of the government planned by the convention.

In order to lay a due foundation for that separate and distinct exercise of the different powers of government, which to a certain extent is admitted on all hands to be essential to the preservation of liberty, it is evident that each department should have a will of its own; and consequently should be so constituted that the members of each should have as little agency as possible in the appointment of the members of the others. Were this principle rigorously adhered to, it would require that all the appointments for the supreme executive, legislative, and judiciary magistracies should be drawn from the same fountain of authority, the people, through channels having no communication whatever with one another. Perhaps such a plan of constructing the several departments would be less difficult in practice than it may in contemplation appear. Some difficulties, however, and some additional expense would attend the execution of it. Some deviations, therefore, from the principle must be admitted. In the constitution of the judiciary department in particular, it might be inexpedient to insist rigorously on the principle: first, because peculiar qualifications being essential in the members, the primary consideration ought to be to select that mode of choice which best secures these qualifications; secondly, because the permanent tenure by which the appointments are held in that department, must soon destroy all sense of dependence on the authority conferring them.

It is equally evident, that the members of each department should be as little dependent as possible on those of the others, for the emoluments annexed to their offices. Were the executive magistrate, or the judges, not independent of the legislature in this particular, their independence in every other would be merely nominal.

But the great security against a gradual concentration of the several powers in the same department, consists in giving to those who administer each department the necessary constitutional means and personal motives to resist encroachments of the others. The provision for defence must in this, as in all other cases, be made commensurate to the danger of attack. Ambition must be made to counteract ambition. The interest of the man must be connected with the constitutional rights of the place. It may be a reflection on human nature, that such devices should be necessary to control the abuses of government. But what is government itself, but the greatest of all reflections on human nature? If men were angels, no government would be necessary. If angels were to govern men, neither external nor internal controls on government would be necessary. In framing a government which is to be administered by men over men, the great difficulty lies in this: you must first enable the government to control the governed; and in the next place oblige it to control itself. A dependence on the people is, no doubt, the primary control on the government; but experience has taught mankind the necessity of auxiliary precautions.

This policy of supplying, by opposite and rival interests, the defect of better motives, might be traced through the whole system of human affairs, private as well as public. We see it particularly displayed in all the subordinate distributions of power, where the constant aim is to divide and arrange the several offices in such a manner as that each may be a check on the other—that the private interest of every individual may be a sentinel over the public rights. These inventions of prudence cannot be less requisite in the distribution of the supreme powers of the State.

But it is not possible to give to each department an equal power of self-defence. In republican government, the legislative authority necessarily predominates. The remedy for this inconveniency is to divide the legislature into different branches; and to render them, by different modes of election and different principles of action, as little connected with each other as the nature of their common functions and their common dependence on the society will admit. It may even be necessary to guard against dangerous encroachments by still further precautions. As the weight of the legislative authority requires that it should be thus divided, the weakness of the executive may require, on the other hand, that it should be fortified. An absolute negative on the legislature appears, at first view, to be the natural defence with which the executive magistrate should be armed. But perhaps it would be neither altogether safe nor alone sufficient. On ordinary occasions it might not be exerted with the requisite firmness, and on extraordinary occasions it might be perfidiously abused. May not this defect of an absolute negative be supplied by some qualified connection between this weaker department and the weaker branch of the stronger department, by which the latter may be led to support the constitutional rights of the former, without being too much detached from the rights of its own department?

If the principles on which these observations are founded be just, as I persuade myself they are, and they be applied as a criterion to the several State constitutions, and to the federal Constitution, it will be found that if the latter does not perfectly correspond with them, the former are infinitely less able to bear such a test.

There are, moreover, two considerations particularly applicable to the federal system of America, which place that system in a very interesting point of view.

*First.* In a single republic, all the power surrendered by the people is submitted to the administration of a single government; and the usurpations are guarded against by a division of the government into distinct and separate departments. In the compound republic of America, the power surrendered by the people is first divided between two distinct governments, and then the portion allotted to each subdivided among distinct and separate departments. Hence a double security arises to the rights of the people. The different governments will control each other, at the same time that each will be controlled by itself.

*Second.* It is of great importance in a republic not only to guard the society against the oppression of its rulers, but to guard one part of the society against the injustice of the other part. Different interests necessarily exist in different classes of citizens. If a majority be united by a common interest, the rights of the minority will be insecure. There are but two methods of providing against this evil: the one by creating a will in the community independent of the majority—that is, of the society itself; the other, by comprehending in the society so many separate descriptions of citizens as will render an unjust combination of a majority of the whole very improbable, if not impracticable. The first method prevails in all governments possessing an hereditary or self-appointed authority. This, at best, is but a precarious security; because a power independent of the society may as well espouse the unjust views of the major, as the rightful interests of the minor party, and may possibly be turned against both parties. The second method will be exemplified in the federal republic of the United States. Whilst all authority in it will be derived from and dependent on the society, the society itself will be broken into so many parts, interests and classes of citizens, that the rights of individuals, or of the minority, will be in little danger from interested combinations of the majority. In a free government the security for civil rights must be the same as that for religious rights. It consists in the one case in the multiplicity of interests, and in the other in the multiplicity of sects. The degree of security in both cases will depend on the number of interests and sects; and this may be presumed to depend on the extent of country and number of people comprehended under the same government. This view of the subject must particularly recommend a proper federal system to all the sincere and considerate friends of republican government, since it shows that in exact proportion as the territory of the Union may be formed into more circumscribed Confederacies, or States, oppressive combinations of a majority will be facilitated; the best security,

under the republican forms, for the rights of every class of citizens, will be diminished; and consequently the stability and independence of some member of the government, the only other security, must be proportionally increased. Justice is the end of government. It is the end of civil society. It ever has been and ever will be pursued until it be obtained, or until liberty be lost in the pursuit. In a society under the forms of which the stronger faction can readily unite and oppress the weaker, anarchy may as truly be said to reign as in a state of nature, where the weaker individual is not secured against the violence of the stronger; and as, in the latter state, even the stronger individuals are prompted, by the uncertainty of their condition, to submit to a government which may protect the weak as well as themselves; so, in the former state, will the more powerful factions or parties be gradually induced, by a like motive, to wish for a government which will protect all parties, the weaker as well as the more powerful. It can be little doubted that if the State of Rhode Island was separated from the Confederacy and left to itself, the insecurity of rights under the popular form of government within such narrow limits would be displayed by such reiterated oppressions of factious majorities that some power altogether independent of the people would soon be called for by the voice of the very factions whose misrule had proved the necessity of it. In the extended republic of the United States, and among the great variety of interests, parties, and sects which it embraces, a coalition of a majority of the whole society could seldom take place on any other principles than those of justice and the general good; whilst there being thus less danger to a minor from the will of a major party, there must be less pretext, also, to provide for the security of the former, by introducing into the government a will not dependent on the latter, or, in other words, a will independent of the society itself. It is no less certain than it is important, notwithstanding the contrary opinions which have been entertained, that the larger the society, provided it lie within a particular sphere, the more duly capable it will be of self-government. And happily for the *republican cause,* the practicable sphere may be carried to a very great extent, by a judicious modification and mixture of the *federal principle.*

PUBLIUS

# THE JUDICIARY

## FEDERALIST NO. 78

### (HAMILTON)

*To the People of the State of New York:* We proceed now to an examination of the judiciary department of the proposed government.

In unfolding the defects of the existing Confederation, the utility and necessity of a federal judicature have been clearly pointed out. It is the less necessary to recapitulate the considerations there urged, as the propriety of the institution in the abstract is not disputed; the only questions which have been raised being relative to the manner of constituting it, and to its extent. To these points, therefore, our observations shall be confined.

The manner of constituting it seems to embrace these several objects: 1st. The mode of appointing the judges. 2d. The tenure by which they are to hold their places. 3d. The partition of the judiciary authority between different courts, and their relations to each other.

*First.* As to the mode of appointing the judges; this is the same with that of appointing the officers of the Union in general, and has been so fully discussed in the two last numbers, that nothing can be said here which would not be useless repetition.

*Second.* As to the tenure by which the judges are to hold their places: this chiefly concerns their duration in office; the provisions for their support; the precautions for their responsibility.

According to the plan of the convention, all judges who may be appointed by the United States are to hold their offices *during good behavior;* which is conformable to the most approved of the State constitutions, and among the rest, to that of this State. Its propriety having been drawn into question by the adversaries of that plan, is no light symptom of the rage for objection, which disorders their imaginations and judgments. The standard of good behavior for the continuance in office of the judicial magistracy, is certainly one of the most valuable of the modern improvements in the practice of government. In a monarchy it is an excellent barrier to the despotism of the prince; in a republic it is a no less excellent barrier to the encroachments and oppressions of the representative body. And it is the best expedient which can be devised in any government, to secure a steady, upright, and impartial administration of the laws.

Whoever attentively considers the different departments of power must perceive, that, in a government in which they are separated from each other, the judiciary, from the nature of its functions, will always be the least dangerous to the political rights of the Constitution; because it will be least in a capacity to annoy or injure them. The Executive not only dispenses the honors, but holds the sword of the community. The legislature not only commands the purse, but prescribes the rules by which the duties and rights of every citizen are to be regulated. The judiciary, on the contrary, has no influence over either the sword or the purse; no direction either of the strength or of the wealth of the society; and can take no active resolution whatever. It may truly be said to have neither FORCE NOR WILL, but merely judgment; and must ultimately depend upon the aid of the executive arm even for the efficacy of its judgments.

This simple view of the matter suggests several important consequences. It proves incontestably, that the judiciary is beyond comparison the weakest of the three departments of power*; that it can never attack with success either of the other two; and that all possible care is requisite to enable it to defend itself against their attacks. It equally proves, that though individual oppression may now and then proceed from the courts of justice, the general liberty of the people can never be endangered from that quarter; I mean so long as the judiciary remains truly distinct from both the legislature and the Executive. For I agree, that "there is no liberty, if the power of judging be not separated from the legislative and executive powers."† And it proves, in the last place, that as liberty can have nothing to fear from the judiciary alone, but would have every thing to fear from its union with either of the other departments; that as all the effects of such a union must ensue from a dependence of the former on the latter, notwithstanding a nominal and apparent separation; that as, from the natural feebleness of the judiciary, it is in continual jeopardy of being overpowered, awed, or influenced by its coördinate branches; and that as noth-

*The celebrated Montesquieu, speaking of them, says: "Of the three powers above mentioned, the judiciary is next to nothing."—"Spirit of Laws," vol. i., page 186.—PUBLIUS
†*Idem,* page 181.—PUBLIUS

ing can contribute so much to its firmness and independence as permanency in office, this quality may therefore be justly regarded as an indispensable ingredient in its constitution, and, in a great measure, as the citadel of the public justice and the public security.

The complete independence of the courts of justice is peculiarly essential in a limited Constitution. By a limited Constitution, I understand one which contains certain specified exceptions to the legislative authority; such, for instance, as that it shall pass no bills of attainder, no *ex-post-facto* laws, and the like. Limitations of this kind can be preserved in practice no other way than through the medium of courts of justice, whose duty it must be to declare all acts contrary to the manifest tenor of the Constitution void. Without this, all the reservations of particular rights or privileges would amount to nothing.

Some perplexity respecting the rights of the courts to pronounce legislative acts void, because contrary to the constitution, has arisen from an imagination that the doctrine would imply a superiority of the judiciary to the legislative power. It is urged that the authority which can declare the acts of another void, must necessarily be superior to the one whose acts may be declared void. As this doctrine is of great importance in all the American constitutions, a brief discussion of the ground on which it rests cannot be unacceptable.

There is no position which depends on clearer principles, than that every act of a delegated authority, contrary to the tenor of the commission under which it is exercised, is void. No legislative act, therefore, contrary to the Constitution, can be valid. To deny this, would be to affirm, that the deputy is greater than his principal; that the servant is above his master; that the representatives of the people are superior to the people themselves; that men acting by virtue of powers, may do not only what their powers do not authorize, but what they forbid.

If it be said that the legislative body are themselves the constitutional judges of their own powers, and that the construction they put upon them is conclusive upon the other departments, it may be answered, that this cannot be the natural presumption, where it is not to be collected from any particular provisions in the Constitution. It is not otherwise to be supposed, that the Constitution could intend to enable the representatives of the people to substitute their *will* to that of their constituents. It is far more rational to suppose, that the courts were designed to be an intermediate body between the people and the legislature, in order, among other things, to keep the latter within the limits assigned to their authority. The interpretation of the laws is the proper and peculiar province of the courts. A constitution is, in fact, and must be regarded by the judges, as a fundamental law. It therefore belongs to them to ascertain its meaning, as well as the meaning of any particular act proceeding from the legislative body. If there should happen to be an irreconcilable variance between the two, that which has the superior obligation and validity ought, of course, to be preferred; or, in other words, the Constitution ought to be preferred to the statute, the intention of the people to the intention of their agents.

Nor does this conclusion by any means suppose a superiority of the judicial to the legislative power. It only supposes that the power of the people is superior to both; and that where the will of the legislature, declared in its statutes, stands in opposition to that of the people, declared in the Constitution, the judges ought to be governed by the latter rather than the former. They ought to regulate their decisions by the fundamental laws, rather than by those which are not fundamental.

This exercise of judicial discretion, in determining between two contradictory laws, is exemplified in a familiar instance. It not uncommonly happens, that there are two statutes existing at one time, clashing in whole or in part with each other, and neither of them containing any repealing clause or expression. In such a case, it is the province of the courts to liquidate and fix their meaning and operation. So far as they can, by any fair construction, be reconciled to each other, reason and law conspire to dictate that this should be done; where this is impracticable, it becomes a matter of necessity to give effect to one, in exclusion of the other. The rule which has obtained in the courts for determining their relative validity is, that the last in order of time shall be preferred to the first. But this is a mere rule of construction, not derived from any positive law, but from the nature and reason of the thing. It is a rule not enjoined upon the courts by legislative provision, but adopted by themselves, as consonant to truth and propriety, for the direction of their conduct as interpreters of the law. They thought it reasonable, that between the interfering acts of an *equal* authority, that which was the last indication of its will should have the preference.

But in regard to the interfering acts of a superior and subordinate author-ity, of an original and derivative power, the nature and reason of the thing indicate the converse of that rule as proper to be followed. They teach us that the prior act of a superior ought to be preferred to the subsequent act of an inferior and subordinate authority; and that accordingly, whenever a particular statute contravenes the Constitution, it will be the duty of the judicial tribunals to adhere to the latter and disregard the former.

It can be of no weight to say that the courts, on the pretence of a repugnancy, may substitute their own pleasure to the constitutional intentions of the legislature. This might as well happen in the case of two contradictory statutes; or it might as well happen in every adjudication upon any single statute. The courts must declare the sense of the law; and if they should be disposed to exercise WILL instead of JUDGMENT, the consequence would equally be the substitution of their pleasure to that of the legislative body. The observation, if it prove any thing, would prove that there ought to be no judges distinct from that body.

If, then, the courts of justice are to be considered as the bulwarks of a limited Constitution against legislative encroachments, this consideration will afford a strong argument for the permanent tenure of judicial offices, since nothing will contribute so much as this to that independent spirit in the judges which must be essential to the faithful performance of so arduous a duty.

This independence of the judges is equally requisite to guard the Constitution and the rights of individuals from the effects of those ill humors, which the arts of designing men, or the influence of particular conjunctures, sometimes disseminate among the people themselves, and which, though they speedily give place to better information, and more deliberate reflection, have a tendency, in the meantime, to occasion dangerous innovations in the government, and serious oppressions of the minor party in the community. Though I trust the friends of the proposed Constitution will never concur with its enemies,* in questioning that fundamental principle of republican government, which admits the right of the people to alter or abolish the established Constitution, whenever they find it inconsistent with their happiness, yet it is not to be inferred from

---

*Vide* "Protest of the Minority of the Convention of Pennsylvania," Martin's Speech, etc.—PUBLIUS

this principle, that the representatives of the people, whenever a momentary inclination happens to lay hold of a majority of their constituents, incompatible with the provisions in the existing Constitution, would, on that account, be justifiable in a violation of those provisions; or that the courts would be under a greater obligation to connive at infractions in this shape, than when they had proceeded wholly from the cabals of the representative body. Until the people have, by some solemn and authoritative act, annulled or changed the established form, it is binding upon themselves collectively, as well as individually; and no presumption, or even knowledge, of their sentiments, can warrant their representatives in a departure from it, prior to such an act. But it is easy to see, that it would require an uncommon portion of fortitude in the judges to do their duty as faithful guardians of the Constitution, where legislative invasions of it had been instigated by the major voice of the community.

But it is not with a view to infractions of the Constitution only, that the independence of the judges may be an essential safeguard against the effects of occasional ill humors in the society. These sometimes extend no farther than to the injury of the private rights of particular classes of citizens, by unjust and partial laws. Here also the firmness of the judicial magistracy is of vast importance in mitigating the severity and confining the operation of such laws. It not only serves to moderate the immediate mischiefs of those which may have been passed but it operates as a check upon the legislative body in passing them; who, perceiving that obstacles to the success of iniquitous intention are to be expected from the scruples of the courts, are in a manner compelled, by the very motives of the injustice they meditate, to qualify their attempts. This is a circumstance calculated to have more influence upon the character of our governments, than but few may be aware of. The benefits of the integrity and moderation of the judiciary have

already been felt in more States than one; and though they may have displeased those whose sinister expectations they may have disappointed, they must have commanded the esteem and applause of all the virtuous and disinterested. Considerate men, of every description, ought to prize whatever will tend to beget or fortify that temper in the courts; as no man can be sure that he may not be to-morrow the victim of a spirit of injustice, by which he may be a gainer to-day. And every man must now feel, that the inevitable tendency of such a spirit is to sap the foundations of public and private confidence, and to introduce in its stead universal distrust and distress.

That inflexible and uniform adherence to the rights of the Constitution, and of individuals, which we perceive to be indispensable in the courts of justice, can certainly not be expected from judges who hold their offices by a temporary commission. Periodical appointments, however regulated, or by whomsoever made, would, in some way or other, be fatal to their necessary independence. If the power of making them was committed either to the Executive or legislature, there would be danger of an improper complaisance to the branch which possessed it; if to both, there would be an unwillingness to hazard the displeasure of either; if to the people, or to persons chosen by them for the special purpose, there would be too great a disposition to consult popularity, to justify a reliance that nothing would be consulted but the Constitution and the laws.

There is yet a further and a weightier reason for the permanency of the judicial offices, which is deducible from the nature of the qualifications they require. It has been frequently remarked, with great propriety, that a voluminous code of laws is one of the inconveniences necessarily connected with the advantages of a free government. To avoid an arbitrary discretion in the courts, it is indispensable that they should be bound down by strict rules and precedents, which serve to define and point out their duty in

every particular case that comes before them; and it will readily be conceived from the variety of controversies which grow out of the folly and wickedness of mankind, that the records of those precedents must unavoidably swell to a very considerable bulk, and must demand long and laborious study to acquire a competent knowledge of them. Hence it is, that there can be but few men in the society who will have sufficient skill in the laws to qualify them for the stations of judges. And making the proper deductions for the ordinary depravity of human nature, the number must be still smaller of those who unite the requisite integrity with the requisite knowledge. These considerations apprise us, that the government can have no great option between fit character; and that a temporary duration in office, which would naturally discourage such characters from quitting a lucrative line of practice to accept a seat on the bench, would have a tendency to throw the administration of justice into hands less able, and less well qualified, to conduct it with utility and dignity. In the present circumstances of this country, and in those in which it is likely to be for a long time to come, the disadvantages on this score would be greater than they may at first sight appear; but it must be confessed, that they are far inferior to those which present themselves under the other aspects of the subject.

Upon the whole, there can be no room to doubt that the convention acted wisely in copying from the models of those constitutions which have established *good behavior* as the tenure of their judicial offices, in point of duration; and that so far from being blamable on this account, their plan would have been inexcusably defective, if it had wanted this important feature of good government. The experience of Great Britain affords an illustrious comment on the excellence of the institution.

PUBLIUS

# What Good Is Government????

### William J. Bennett & John J. DiIulio, Jr.

NOBODY NEEDS to persuade most Americans that their national government is too big, taxes and regulates too much, and fails to accomplish enough of genuine public value. Much of what emanates from Washington is an uneconomical, uncoordinated, unholy mess, and almost everyone knows it. When President Clinton declared, in his 1996 State of the Union address, that "the era of big government is over," he was belatedly responding to the political pressures generated by this deep-seated knowledge, which ever since the days of Ronald Reagan has been the motive force behind conservative and Republican victories at the polls. Indeed, Clinton himself won the presidency in 1992 and then won it again in 1996 largely by exploiting conservative themes about relimiting government and restoring civil society.

For conservatives, there would thus seem to be cause for satisfaction at this new coincidence of views between the leadership of both political parties. But of late, conservatives have been doing more fretting than celebrating. Some complain that today's Republican-led Congress is proving itself incapable of sustaining the "revolution" launched by its immediate predecessor after 1994. Others lament the "loss of political momentum" represented, for example, by the Clinton administration's slow but steady gutting of the work requirements in the 1996 welfare-reform law.

---

WILLIAM J. BENNETT *is co-director of Empower America and John M. Olin fellow in cultural-policy studies at the Heritage Foundation. His most recent book is* Our Sacred Honor. JOHN J. DIIULIO, JR. *is professor of politics and public affairs at Princeton and the co-editor (with Frank Thompson) of* Medicaid and the States, *forthcoming from Brookings.*

Still others carp that the latest bipartisan budget bill increases social spending by $70 billion in just its first year. The worry, in short, is that the fight against big government has no sooner begun than it is being toned down, qualified, or even abandoned, by Republicans and conservatives themselves no less than by Democrats and liberals.

There is something to this worry. But it also reflects the current state of confusion on both sides of the political aisle over exactly what our national government does, exactly what it can or should do, and what the American people want it to do. We are caught in one of those historic moments of transition, between one model of government, now 60 years old, with whose virtues and (especially) with whose defects we have become intimately familiar, and another model still very much in the making and yet to be adequately defined. In what follows we mean to contribute, however, tentatively, to such a definition, in the first place by dispelling some false ideas.

II

TO BEGIN at the beginning: *is the era of big government over, and if not, is it likely to be over any time soon? The realistic answer to both questions is no.

Virtually every aspect of our lives is now touched by government. Washington underwrites support for the elderly and the disabled, for medical research, space missions, art museums, farmers, and mass transit. It subsidizes public television and mandates the number of hours that commercial networks must devote to "children's programs." It pays people to "volunteer" for national service. It builds prisons and supports public-housing projects and even midnight basketball. It provides food stamps, health care, college scholarships, loans, and grants. It involves itself in university admissions, hiring practices, family-leave policies, civil-rights laws, banking insurance and regulation, professional accrediting, air-traffic control, and parks administration. Among its obligations are protecting our air, water, and food; regulating tobacco and automobiles; constructing interstate highways; keeping out illegal immigrants and drugs; and providing pensions to our veterans.

This is only a partial list—and, needless to say, it all costs a lot. On the basis of the budget that has now become law, Americans will have at least $1.7 trillion-a-year's worth of national government as far as the fiscal eye can see. By every estimate, annual federal spending will top $2 trillion before the year 2003.

In order to get some earthly perspective on such astronomical figures, consider the humble fiscal facts behind the welfare-reform law, universally and deservedly acknowledged to be the single most far-reaching legislative action of the historic 104th Congress. This act abolished a means-tested federal-state program for low-income households, Aid to Families with Dependent Children (AFDC). But AFDC accounted for only about $22 billion a year in federal spending—much less than two cents of every federal dollar. And the act *continued* federal cash assistance via block grants to states, at funding levels largely comparable to AFDC.

Again: last June, members of the House commerce committee voted to cut $15 billion over five years from Medicaid, the joint federal-state program that provides health-care insurance to some 35 million low-income, elderly, and disabled Americans. But between 1988 and 1994, Medicaid spending *grew* by about $100 billion, roughly $77 billion of which were federal dollars, and will likely grow by another $40 billion or more by 2002. And incidentally, the same House panel that voted for the much-publicized $15 billion in cuts also approved a new $16-billion grant to the states to expand health-care coverage for uninsured children.

Where do the other hundreds of billions in federal money go every year? Roughly half goes to the "3 15's and a nickel"—15 percent each to national defense, grants to states and localities, and net interest payments, and 5 percent to other federal operations. The other half goes to payments to individuals. Of the latter, half again are made via entitlement programs that directly benefit the majority of all Americans, including many with annual incomes of $50,000 or more.

And what can be cut from all this? By the time the 104th Congress arrived in Washington in January 1995, the proportion of "big government" that consisted of nondefense discretionary spending, including such items as Head Start, public housing, and interstate highways, had already been squeezed by almost half in the 1990 Omnibus Budget Reconciliation Act and still further in its 1993 successor. In 1995 and 1996, as we have seen, programs for low-income families and individuals followed suit, absorbing over 90 percent of all cuts to entitlement programs.

The reason the only sizable cuts in the "nanny state" have fallen on programs for the poor rather than on those benefiting the middle class and the affluent is simple. In survey after survey, clear majorities of Americans have said that they would rather *prevent* cuts to most federal programs than balance the budget or shrink the deficit. As many as 80 percent or more favor maintaining or expanding Social Security and Medicare. For Medicaid the parallel figure is over 70 percent, and over 60 percent favor student loans, veterans' hospitals, environmental protection, unemployment insurance, and other programs. In a period like the present one, when economic growth has boosted tax revenues and shrunk the deficit, there is likely to be even less pressure for significant cuts to big-ticket entitlements and discretionary spending programs for the nonpoor.

III

THE LARGE majorities in favor of retaining government entitlement programs raise a question about what was in the mind of the American people when in 1994 they gave control of both the House and the Senate to the Republicans. Certainly many of those newly elected Senators and Congressmen read the results as a mandate to downsize government.

But the election results can also be read in other ways. For one thing, the Republican victory, which was in any case not the landslide it is sometimes depicted as being, may have had less to do with ideas than with long-term electoral trends. Thus, in every election from 1968 to 1992, the percentage of the vote going to Republicans in congressional battles had been higher than the percentage of seats actually won by Republicans. What happened in 1994 is that the party finally succeeded in closing the gap. In the words of the political scientist Gary C. Jacobson, "Most of the seats the [GOP] added in 1994 were seats a Republican should have held in the first place."

For Republicans, the good news is that the factors behind this trend are likely to continue. One such factor is the increasing suburbanization of the electorate. Another is the increasing consolidation of the Republican hold on the South. (In 1996, Republicans added Southern House seats even as they lost seats elsewhere, and the South was also the only region where Bob Dole's popular vote nosed out Bill Clinton's.) Finally, gathering Republican strength at the state level is a bellwether of greater strength at the national level.

We hardly mean to suggest that issues and ideas have played no role in all this: nobody who followed the course of Hillary Clinton's health-care fiasco could contend such a thing. More broadly, as the political analyst Everett Carll Ladd has written, Republicans have indeed benefited from an ongoing "philosophical realignment": ever larger majorities of voters have become more conservative, "especially in the sense of being far less inclined to accept claims that more government represents progress." As we noted above, when Bill Clinton won the presidency, he did so in large measure by playing to this growing conservative mood.

Nevertheless, Ladd argues, the continuities in voting behavior "are in many ways more striking than the . . . departures." So far, the philosophical realignment has produced no decisive party realignment and consolidated no conservative governing majority. In 1996, Ladd concludes,

> Voters again elected a President of one party and gave congressional majorities to the other. . . . They again signaled a desire to curb the growth of national government, though not to cut it greatly.

This seems to us to sum up the situation very well. The public may not have the scale of government it prefers, but there is little evidence that it wants government to withdraw from the *spheres* in which it is now involved, or to downsize simply for the sake of downsizing. This reading of the mood of the electorate was confirmed, moreover, when the

Republican majority in Congress did set out to cut government "greatly." In mid-1995, House Republicans proposed eliminating no less than $1.4 trillion in projected federal spending by the year 2002, while Senate Republicans proposed cuts of $961 billion. In 1996, a House budget-committee resolution called for terminating, turning into block grants, or privatizing 3 cabinet departments, 284 programs, 69 commissions, and 13 agencies.

The effect of these ambitious proposals was that, between December 1994 and June 1996, the 104th Congress's net approval rating fell like a rock. In the meantime, the President's steadily improved. In March 1995, according to an ABC News/*Washington Post* poll, almost twice as many people were worried that Republicans would go too far in cutting needed programs than that Democrats would go too far in defending wasteful ones.

THE SHIFT in public sentiment can be explained in part by willful Democratic exaggerations of the size and scope of the proposed Republican cuts. But that is only one element of the story. Another has to do with the inability of the Republican leadership to offer a persuasive defense of their plans against reasonable criticism and concerns.

Consider Medicare. When this program first became law in 1965, estimated spending for 1990 was projected at $8 billion. By the time 1990 rolled around, *actual* Medicare spending was nearly $160 billion and rising; by 1995, the system was (as it remains) headed for bankruptcy. In the words of the *Wall Street Journal*, "Medicare is growing so fast that by 2001 it will overtake all federal spending on defense; by 2005 it will exceed defense by $100 billion."

What to do? In the 104th Congress, the GOP proposed to cap overall Medicare spending. That proposal is now history. In the 105th Congress, the party has sought to modify the program by giving its beneficiaries financial incentives to economize (mostly by shifting from fee-for-service to so-called medical savings accounts). The elderly, Republicans argue, need more "choice," while future technologies will inevitably yield better care for all at less cost. But conservative lawmakers have so far failed to explain how we are to reduce the rate of growth in Medicare without causing millions of elderly Americans to receive less financial help from Washington, get worse care, or be thrown back on their own savings or the support of their often resistant or resourceless families.

It clearly will not do to assert that the public has already "voted for" cuts in Medicare or, for that matter, any of the other major entitlement programs. What the public has voted for is more complicated than that, and what it will stand for, it seems, is very little. In the absence of compelling alternatives, most Americans prefer the status quo, far from perfect though they know it to be, to radical retrenchment.

Faced with these apparently intractable facts, some conservatives have persuaded themselves that other means exist to solve the problem of big government. One, which goes by the name of devolution, is to kick things back from Washington to the states. Another is to hand them over to "civil society." Both these ideas are estimable in and of themselves; but as solutions to the perceived problem, they are partial at best.

IV

**D**EVOLUTION—VESTING as much decision- and policy-making power as possible in what Edmund Burke called the "little platoons" of society—is an idea for which a strong case can be made: philosophical, political, and practical. Why indeed should anyone assume that a Secretary of Health and Human Services in Washington knows better than the governor of Michigan what is good for the children of that state, or which welfare approach will work best there? Moreover, popular support for devolution is high, mirroring the popular disapproval of big government and bloated bureaucracy.

Best of all, evidence is accumulating that local initiative works. In the areas of welfare and education, what Governors Tommy Thompson of Wisconsin, John Engler of Michigan, and Arne Carlson of Minnesota have been able to accomplish in a few short years puts Washington to shame, and the same goes, in the area of criminal justice, for Mayor Rudolph Giuliani of New York City.

But for all its virtues, the paradoxical fact is that devolution *per se* does nothing to contain the size and scope of federal power. Many federal programs are already highly devolved to state and local governments through block grants. The real "Washington bureaucracy" is composed not of the two million nondefense

federal bureaucrats—about the same number as in 1960, before the fifteenfold growth in expenditures since the Great Society—but of the millions and millions of people who work indirectly for the national government as employees of state and local agencies, private firms, and nonprofit organizations that are largely if not entirely funded by federal dollars. About 90 percent of federal civilian workers live elsewhere than Washington and its environs, a reality brought home with tragic poignancy by the Oklahoma City bombing.

As the political scientist Donald F. Kettl has documented, today's national government is "government by proxy." Only about 4 percent of the federal budget, Kettl estimates, goes to programs or services that the federal government delivers directly. Mainly the tasks are performed by state and local governments, followed by private and nonprofit contractors. Indeed, every national domestic-policy initiative of the past six decades has been a version of government by proxy.

Thus, the interstate highway system was built through grants to state and local governments and contracts with private construction companies. Under the direction of state health and human-services officials, private financial intermediaries manage most of the Medicare and Medicaid programs. Contractors perform the clean-ups at the Superfund sites of the Environmental Protection Agency (EPA). Universities and other nonprofit organizations devise and direct federally-funded projects in areas ranging from biomedical research to juvenile justice. The federal prison system and the Federal Aviation Administration—two of the relatively few federal agencies that do directly administer federal laws—rely heavily on private contractors to perform many different functions. Even financing and payments under the Social Security Act are administered by the states (subject to review by the U.S. Department of Health and Human Services).

As for the now-defunct AFDC program, it was administered as a joint federal-state program on the basis of a legal commitment by Washington to match state spending; in effect, AFDC was an entitlement to state governments, and was accordingly managed under a mind-boggling array of local eligibility requirements, work provisions, and more. For well over a decade now, Medicaid too has been evolving into a highly decentralized program in which states take the lead in defining eligibility criteria, streamlining payment procedures, and deciding which, if any, costly auxiliary services get provided.

Supporters of devolution tend to speak of block grants not only as if they were something new but as if they were a proven device for cutting spending and/or a sure-fire way of improving performance. They are neither.

Between 1966 and 1993, there were 23 block-grant programs for the states, fifteen of which were still in effect when the 104th Congress was elected. Total federal aid to the states was $127 billion in 1980; in 1994, *after* the Reagan years with their ostensible commitment to cutting back, it was an estimated $170 billion.

Nor, as John P. Walters has shown, do block grants necessarily guarantee greater efficiency or even a greater degree of control on the part of citizens. Block grants can simply "transfer wealth and authority to state and local bureaucrats who are . . . often less efficient, less responsive, and more prone to corruption than federal bureaucrats." In addition, "devolving federal power" has often meant reducing the federal government's capacity to monitor and correct. It has helped produce fraud and record overpayments in Medicare; the flawed Hubble space telescope; some of the worst defense-procurement scandals ever; the illegal diversion of tens of millions of dollars in food stamps; spectacular defaults in the guaranteed student-loan program; excessive costs in the Superfund; the failure of the Internal Revenue Service's computer-modernization project; and malfeasance of Teapot Dome proportions in the Department of Housing and Urban Development.

In the proper hands, devolution can be a potent weapon in the arsenal of a society attempting to recover the habits of self-government. But it is only one weapon, and its utility is limited. In the wrong hands, moreover, devolution is just as likely to be a recipe for spending money that the federal government does not have, for purposes that no one has clearly specified, with results that cannot be measured or evaluated until it is too late.

V

THIS BRINGS us to the other great hope of conservatives: civil society. By this is meant the entire network of churches, charities, community groups, and other voluntary associations and institutions upon which our society has always depended for its successful functioning. According to at least one reading of the evidence, this network has been eviscerated by the growth and self-aggrandizement of government; families, churches, and community groups have been forced to surrender their authority to bureaucratic experts, with disastrous consequences not only for civility but for civilization itself. The retreat of government from the field would thus be a hopeful sign of progress, allowing these institutions to revive and resume their normal functions, which they have anyway always performed with far greater effectiveness.

Here, too, the evidence is in fact somewhat mixed. One thing still unclear, for example, is the degree to which government has indeed "crowded out" familial, communal, corporate, and philanthropic activity. In articles published in 1995 and 1996, the political scientist Robert Putnam contended that fewer and fewer Americans were voting, joining the PTA, going to church, or participating in other civic associations and group activities, while more and more were "bowling alone." But Putnam's thesis has come under severe challenge by analysts who assert that, to the contrary, the number of Americans volunteering for groups and causes remains huge and shows no signs of declining. Bowling leagues may be down, but soccer leagues are up.

An even tougher question to answer is whether volunteer programs can operate on a large enough scale to deal effectively with hard-core social problems. A few years ago, Public/Private Ventures, a policy-research organization with which one of us has been affiliated, completed a systematic evaluation of the Big Brothers Big Sisters of America program. The findings were remarkably encouraging: for low-income children, many of them abused or neglected, just a few hours a week with a "Big" yielded a 50-percent average reduction in first-time drug use, a 33-percent reduction in violent behavior, and measurable improvements in school performance. But the number of children who could benefit from this program or one like it remains far in excess of the number of adults who volunteer for it.

Whether such institutions are growing in number is again difficult to say. Most urban black churches, for example, run or participate directly in community-service activities that reach beyond their own membership—staffing day-care facilities, offering drug- and alcohol-abuse prevention programs, administering food banks, building shelters, serving as after-school safe havens, and more. But are such faith-based social programs more or less common today than they were ten, twenty, or thirty years ago?

In any case, the basic issue may be less one of numbers, or even of efficacy, than of sheer capacity. According to Princeton's Julian Wolpert, about 125,000 organizations in America operate as charities with receipts of at least $25,000 a year. Their combined revenues and expenditures are about $350 billion annually—roughly *one-seventh* of what is spent by federal, state, and local government. Moreover, a third of those revenues come from government itself. If all of America's grant-making private foundations gave away all of their income and all of their assets, they could cover only a year's worth of current government expenditures on social welfare. It is unlikely that Americans will donate much more than their present 2 percent of annual household income, or that corporate giving will take up any significant proportion of the slack in the event of further government reductions.

An energetic civil society is a blessing beyond compare, and government is no substitute for its myriad institutions. But getting government out of our lives would not *ipso facto* lead to a rebirth of those institutions, particularly ones that may have atrophied, and particularly if they have atrophied for reasons that are as much cultural (think, for instance, of the influence of television and the movies) as political. Nor, in the end, can civil institutions themselves, no matter how energetic, be a substitute for government.

VI

**B**UT WHAT sort of government do we need? In 1964, former President Eisenhower said:

> We Republicans believe in limited government, but also in effective government. We believe in keeping government as close to the people as possible. . . . But we do not shrink from a recognition that there are national problems that require national solutions.

Thirty-three years later, Eisenhower's words seem more relevant than ever, encapsulating a truly national view of our situation and suggesting not just a Republican but a republican way forward.

Perhaps the first lesson these words suggest is the need for all Americans, including those most offended by the depredations of big government, to make their peace with the persistent popular majorities whose duly-elected representatives have supported and sustained the national government's post-New Deal role. That role in itself is not the problem; however they may grumble, Americans want government to perform it, or something like it. Nor is the problem *simply* one of the size of government. Rather, partly on account of sheer size, but more on account of bad ideas in the hands of executors with arbitrary and unaccountable authority, our national government has fatally lost sight of what James Madison called the "permanent and aggregate interests of the community"— that is, of the public interest.

Only now, thanks to widespread disgust with what those ideas and that arbitrary authority have created, are we beginning to take stock of how badly the public interest has been served across the board: from law enforcement, to education, to family policy, to race relations, to tax law. Most saliently, unelected federal officials—whether bureaucrats or judges—have been permitted to define the public interest as they see fit and, through the reach of national power, to impose their understanding over and against the clearly expressed wishes both of representative institutions and of state and local governments, businesses, civic organizations, neighborhoods, and individuals. If our standard is to keep government "as close to the people as possible," then one of the most hopeful pieces of legislation passed by the 104th Congress was a little-noticed provision, authored by Senator Spencer Abraham, restricting the ability of federal judges to continue defying persistent public demands for laws prohibiting the arbitrary release of violent criminals. Similar sorts of restorative lawmaking are a prime desideratum.

Here is where the true value of devolution and civil society makes itself felt. For the foreseeable future, it seems, the social-policy "action" in America will be emanating less from Washington than from the states and localities, as well as from the sphere of private enterprise. That is all to the good. The seeds of a new reconstruction are being sown: from welfare reform to the revolution in health care, a whole array of promising initiatives, none of them conceived or directed by Washington (though some are at least partly subsidized by Washington), is beginning to undo the accumulated damage of a quarter-century and thereby to change the underlying relation of government and society. The eventual effect of these initiatives, if they are not impeded by the dead hand of the federal behemoth, will be to alter the definition not only of American politics, but of government itself.

In this period of experimentation, the role of responsible elected representatives in Washington is to monitor, to assess, to criticize, and even to propose—but first and foremost to foster and encourage. And in the meantime, there is plenty of other work to be done at the national level by a political class—in the nature of things, a conservative political class—bent not on dismantling but (to revert to Eisenhower's language) on limiting government and making it more effective. There may well be some federal agencies we would be better off without—the National Endowment for the Arts is one. On the other hand, calls to eliminate the EPA, for example, are unrealistic and out of touch with the wishes of the electorate; Americans want federal controls on the air they breathe as much as on the meat they consume. Still, *someone* has to start the decade-long task of bringing the morass of federal environmental regulations and the litigation they have spawned into line with the public interest properly understood. And the EPA is only one instance, if among the most egregious, of a much more pervasive problem.

Improving the performance of government hardly exhausts the matter, however. Perhaps the most pernicious legacy of the era of expanded government has been to engender widespread public mistrust of, precisely, government itself. This mistrust is founded on larger considerations than federal waste and inefficiency.

It has often been remarked how liberalism, by creating ever new categories of rights, and by relentlessly expanding the sphere of "entitlement," has devalued the habits of self-reliance and individual responsibility that are critical to economic and social advancement. What is less often remarked is the extent to which these same sturdy habits, the defining marks of a free citizenry, are and must be constitutive of the entire American political order. Should we really be surprised when people inculcated with the thoroughly infantilizing idea that government exists to take care of their "needs" begin to regard that government with increasing petulance and disrespect?

During the 1992 presidential debate in Richmond, Virginia, a middle-aged man stood up in the audience and asked the three candidates: "We're not under oath at this point, but could you make a commitment to the citizens of the United States to meet our *needs?*—and we have many." Neither George Bush, nor Ross Perot, nor, assuredly, Bill Clinton dared challenge the premise of the question. Every parent knows the symptoms of this insatiable disease; a wise one takes steps to prevent them from developing.

To this injury has been added still another: the breaking-down—the deconstruction—of our common American culture, of the American idea. Liberalism brought us not only the era of big government, now officially declared to be over, but the era of official, government-sponsored polarization. It was a bureau of the federal government that in the late 1960's began systematically to infiltrate our way of doing business and educating our young with the insidious practice of counting by race; and it is our national government that through its dogged adherence to these policies and a galaxy of related ones continues daily to go about dividing us by race, gender, and ethnicity, setting us each against the other and then wondering aloud why we cannot "talk."

No amount of devolution, no revival of civil society, can by themselves recreate this bedrock condition of our political existence: the knowledge that we are one nation, indivisible. To the contrary, the very act of draining authority away from Washington, and of encouraging the spirit of individual and civic initiative, may, in the absence of countervailing forces, tend rather to hasten than to impede the further atomizing of society. But neither is it imaginable that we can simply demand of citizens respect for a national government that has shown itself unworthy of their respect.

There is a trap here to which conservatives in particular may be susceptible. As Gertrude Himmelfarb has written in these pages,* in their impassioned and wholly understandable rush to decry big government and extol the virtues of civil society, many otherwise sensible conservatives have come perilously close to delegitimating the idea of government itself. Others, of a frankly libertarian stripe, have gone even farther; characterizing 60 years of expanded government programs as

*"For the Love of Country," [*Commentary,*] May 1997.

a kind of scam perpetrated on a society of native individualists yearning to breathe free, they not only seek to limit government but practically to do away with it.

THE TASK as we see it is instead to limit government; to make it more effective; and to keep it as close to the people as possible. But it is also to conserve, to rebuild, and to restore. The restoration of the American government as a true expression of the American idea cannot be achieved by an act of Congress, or triggered by a provision in a spending bill, or, alas, materialized in an act of will by the American people. It is a task for national leadership, and only national leadership can accomplish it. Ronald Reagan, who paradoxically came to office on a platform for re-limiting government, may have come closer than any statesman in living memory both to grasping what is required for the task and, in his person and spirit, to suggesting the elementary grounds for its realization.

It has been a long time since an American President could say with perfect assurance, as our first President did in his Farewell Address:

> This government, the offspring of our own choice uninfluenced and unawed, ... has a just claim to your confidence and your support. Respect for its authority, compliance with its laws, acquiescence in its measures are duties enjoined by the fundamental maxims of true liberty.

Thanks to decades of often mindless expansion, and even more so to policies that have undermined the habits of freedom, respect for the authority of government is at a low point in our country. But in a fundamental sense, that government remains what it was 200 years ago: the "offspring of our own choice." Without destroying the institution itself, we should study to fashion a better one, of which we can more honestly say that it exercises "a just claim on [our] confidence and [our] support."

# CHOMP!

## How a 17th-century British scam morphed into a global monster—and what we can do about it

### By Jim Hightower

**They tell me advice sells, so here goes:**
- Don't ever buy a pit bull from a one-armed man.
- Never sign nothin' by neon light.
- Always drink upstream from the herd.

Oh, and one more: Never, ever believe the "conventional wisdom," which is to wisdom what "near beer" is to beer. Only not as close.

This is especially true when it comes to our political system. The powers-that-be, for example, tell us over and over that we are not willing to undertake any significant political change. Americans are overwhelmingly middle-of-the-road, they say, and not interested in any kind of "ism."

This is a trick play designed to keep America's political debate from focusing on an insidious new "ism" that has crept into our lives: *corporatism.* Few politicians, pundits, economists, or other officially sanctioned mouthpieces for what passes as public debate in this country want to touch the topic, but—as most ordinary folks have learned—the corporation has gotten way too big for its britches, intruding into every aspect of our lives and forcing changes in how we live.

Less than a decade ago, for example, your medical needs rested in the hands of a doctor whom *you* got to choose. But quicker than a hog eats supper, America's health care system—including your personal doc—got swallowed damn-near whole by a handful of corporate mutants called HMOs, most of which are tentacles of Prudential, Travelers, and other insurance giants.

When did we vote on this? Did I miss the national referendum in which we decided that remote corporate executives with an army of bean counters would displace my handpicked doctor, and would decide which (if any) hospital I can enter, how long I can stay, what specialists I can consult? I know Congress did not authorize this fundamental shift. To the contrary, in 1994 Congress rightly trashed the Clinton health care plan on the grounds that it would do exactly what's being done to us now: put the bean counters in charge. Only back then we were warned by the infamous "Harry and Louise" televi-

sion spots that it would be government bean counters managing our health.

What irony. For years the very companies that financed the "Harry and Louise" ads have flapped their arms wildly to scare us about that old bugaboo, "socialized" medicine, while they blindsided us with something even harsher: corporatized medicine, a new form of "care" in which the Hippocratic Oath has been displaced by a bottom-line ethos. Now our health care is in the hands of people like Richard Scott, a mergers and acquisitions lawyer who headed up the Columbia/HCA Healthcare Corporation, a $20-billion-a-year HMO, until last July when he was forced out under a cloud of scandal about Medicare fraud. During Scott's tenure, Columbia/HCA demanded that its local hospital executives return a 20 percent annual profit to headquarters, or else. How did they meet his demand? By cutting back on services, on employees, and ultimately on us patients.

One place Scott did not cut back, however, was on his own paycheck. In 1995, he took a 43 percent salary hike, which meant he drew a million bucks from the till. Every *month.* But Scott is far less generous when it comes to taking responsibility for meeting the needs of America's sick. "Do we have an obligation to provide health care for everybody?" he recently asked rhetorically. "Where do we draw the line? Is any fast-food restaurant obligated to feed everyone who shows up?"

While it is true that corporations have long been a fact of life in America, since the 1970s they have metamorphosed into something different and disquieting. Corporations have become the governing force in our society, reshaping American life to fit nothing more enlightened than the short-term profile sheets of greedy CEOs. Everything from our amusements to our government, from our public schools to our popular culture—has become thoroughly corporatized.

The true symbol of America is no longer Old Glory, but the corporate logo. No public space, no matter how sacrosanct, is free from the threat of having "Mountain Dew," "Citibank," or "Nike" plastered on it. Not even space itself is off-limits:

From *Utne Reader*, March/April 1998, pp. 57-61, 102-103. Excerpted from *There's Nothing in the Middle of the Road But Yellow Stripes and Dead Armadillos* by Jim Hightower. © 1997 by Jim Hightower. Reprinted by permission of HarperCollins Publishers, Inc.

One visionary business enterprise is already working on launching a low-trajectory satellite equipped with what amounts to an extraterrestrial billboard that will be programmed to beam logos back to earth from the night sky. No matter where you live, from Boston to Bora Bora, you'll be able to gaze into the vast darkness, as humans have for thousands of years, and absorb the natural wonder of the moon, the Milky Way, and, yes, an orbiting ad for Mylanta. Lovely.

**Every once in a while we come across a news item about a corporation acting contrary to form.** For instance, the story of John Tu and David Sun, founders of Kingston Technologies in California, who sold a majority stake in their computer-chip enterprise for one and a half billion big ones and put $100 million of it into bonuses and special benefit programs for their 523 employees.

"What in the name of Ebenezer Scrooge are you two up to?" screeched their high-tech corporate peers. Nothing, it turns out. An amazed media found that this was not a publicity ploy or a tax dodge—it was, simply, sharing. Tu and Sun quietly explained that the hardworking people at Kingston are what made it possible for them as owners to prosper, so it felt right to reward them for their contribution.

Such acts of responsibility are so antithetical to accepted boardroom practice that when they occur it's big news. Indeed, immediately after the Kingston Technologies story broke, business analysts rushed forward to dump cold water on the fantasy that this is the way things should be done in today's complex corporate economy. Kingston Technologies, the critics scoffed, was a privately held company, so Messrs. Tu and Sun could be whimsical with company funds because they weren't subject to the short-term profit pressures from Wall Street investors. The "corporate system," the analysts explained, has no room for beneficence toward employees, communities, or the environment. None other than economist Milton Friedman himself, the patron saint of Wall Street excess, gave academic credence to such myopic thinking by asking and answering his own rhetorical question: "So the question is, do corporate executives, provided they stay within the law, have responsibilities in their business activities other than to make as much money for their stockholders as possible? And my answer to that is, no they do not."

So *my* question is, if the corporate structure exists only for stockholders, as Dr. Friedman makes clear, and since two-thirds of us are not stockholders, why should the larger public be so permissive toward this particular business structure? You don't have to be the brightest light on the block to figure out that if the "corporate system" makes John Tu and David Sun the anomalies (and, in some executive quarters, the pariahs) of American business, then it's time to fix the system. I know the wisdom of the oft-cited aphorism "If it ain't broke, don't fix it," but the equally sagacious corollary to that is "If it is broke, run get the toolbox."

**What is this thing called the "corporation" and why is it here?** It's time to put this basic question back into political play. The corporation has become a given in our culture, not unlike smog and Wayne Newton. It has been with us so long we assume it is part of the natural order.

Not so. Practically all of our nation's founders were appropriately anti-corporate (although you'll never find that in any standard textbooks of American history), and at the time of the Continental Congress, only about 40 corporations existed in our land, and they were kept on a very short leash.

Like powdered wigs and boiled beef, the corporation is a British invention, essentially created by the Crown as a vehicle to amass the capital needed to loot the wealth of its colonies. Of course, looting was nothing new, but this "joint stock" connivance was a devilishly radical scheme. For the first time, ownership of an enterprise was separated from responsibility for the enterprise. If an individual businessperson loots, pollutes, or otherwise behaves illegally, he or she is individually accountable to the community for those actions—that is, they get their sorry asses hauled into court, and get fined, put out of business, and/or tossed in the slammer. But the corporation is a legal fiction that lets the investors who own the business off the hook whenever the business behaves badly (read: steals, kills, poisons, pillages, corrupts, and so on), avoiding individual responsibility for illegal actions done in their name, even when such actions profit them enormously.

Like letting a cat loose in a fish market, this structure invites mischief, which is why the founders of our republic believed corporate charters should be granted only to serve the greater public interest. Through most of the 19th century, states typically limited each corporation they chartered to one kind of business, prohibited it from owning other businesses, strictly limited the amount of capital it could amass, required the stockholders to be local residents, spelled out specific benefits the corporation had to deliver to the community, and put a 20- to 50-year limit on the life of the charter. And, imagine this, legislatures were not shy about yanking charters when a corporation went astray from its stated mission or acted irresponsibly.

But just as America's founders clearly saw the dangers of the corporate entity, greedy hustlers saw its phenomenal potential to help them make a killing. And the latter began early on to lather up politicians with money to try to loosen up the chartering process. During the Civil War, numerous corporations were chartered to supply the Union Army, and the commander-in-chief, Abraham Lincoln, did not find it a positive experience. In an ominous foreboding of corrupt practices among today's Pentagon contractors, many of these corporations delivered shoddily made shoes, malfunctioning guns, and rotten meat. Honest Abe viewed the rise of corporations as a disaster, and warned in an 1864 letter that "as a result of the war, corporations have been enthroned and an era of corruption in high places will follow . . . until all wealth is aggregated in a few hands, and the Republic is destroyed."

Sure enough, during the next three decades, assorted industrialists and corporate flimflam artists known collectively as the robber barons were enthroned and took hold of both the economy and the government. Corruption did abound, from statehouses to the White House, and the concentration of wealth in the clutching hands of such families as the Astors,

# TAMING THE CORPORATE BEAST

## New strategies for making business work for all of us

For as long as there have been corporations, citizens have fought to limit their power and make them more accountable to the public. Two of the most innovative strategies to emerge in recent years—the corporate charter movement and social auditing—are encouraging, but they also demonstrate just how tough it can be to rein in megacorporations.

*Corporate charters.* This movement, led by environmentalist and labor activist Richard Grossman and his Provincetown, Massachusetts-based Program on Corporations, Law and Democracy, seeks to embolden citizens and lawmakers to toughen—or rather enforce—state corporate charter laws. These laws, which have been on the books for decades, give legislatures the power to limit corporations' activities and revoke their right to do business in their state.

Grossman acknowledges that, in an era of intense interstate competition for jobs and corporate tax revenues, few state governments are likely to pull the plug on any major employer. Still, he says, the question of who really governs the country—citizens or corporations—must be addressed. "By what authority are they participating in elections, by what authority are they lobbying politically, by what authority are they in our schools?" he asks. "We've been engaging people all over the country in these questions." And only when citizens begin looking seriously at reforming corporate charters will companies sit up and take notice.

To show how powerful these tools can be, Grossman points to the way some corporations have persuaded legislatures to write additional protections into state charter regulations to shield them from hostile takeovers. These particular charter changes, known as constituency statues, can now be used in 29 states to protect corporate directors from shareholder lawsuits if they make a decision—from mergers and acquisitions to plant closings—that may be beneficial to workers or the local community, but not necessarily to the pocketbooks of stockholders. In a 1987 Pennsylvania case, for instance, the court ruled that Commonwealth National Financial Corporation could approve a merger with Mellon Bank even though the bid was lower than that of its other suitor, Meridian Bancorp. Citing the state's constituency statute, the court ruled that the board was not shirking its fiduciary duties because its employees would have greater opportunities with Mellon than with Meridian.

This may not represent a radical transfer of power—citizens still don't have the right to sue if their needs are ignored—but, as Marjorie Kelly, editor and publisher of *Business Ethics,* has written, strengthening constituency statutes could usher in "a kind of Copernican revolution . . . [in which] stockholders are no longer the exact center of the corporate solar system."

*Social audits.* Not all corporations, of course, are slaves to the bottom line. In fact, some companies are so concerned about their impact on the world that they voluntarily undergo comprehensive evaluations of their operations by independent auditors. These audits, based primarily on social and environmental factors, were popularized three years ago by Ben & Jerry's and The Body Shop in response to criticism of their reputations as socially responsible companies. Now, a number of mainstream companies—including every major accounting firm—are embracing the concept as well.

The Body Shop's 1995 audit, which was performed by Kirk Hanson, long-time director of the Business Enterprise Trust at Stanford University, demonstrated both the promise and the perils of this trend. Hanson measured the Body Shop's performance using the so-called "social indicator" method pioneered by ethical investment firms. This method, which has been criticized by some for being too self-serving, gives greater weight to a company's policies on popular political issues (such as animal testing, human rights, energy conservation) than it gives to its performance in areas directly affecting its stakeholders (such as employee relations, corporate governance, product quality). Hanson gave the company low marks in the more traditional areas of social responsibility—wages, working conditions, product quality, management accountability—while praising its environmental efforts and publicity campaigns about social issues.

Other social audit models can be used. Among the most popular are the social balance sheet (which integrates financial and social reporting by assigning a dollar value to a company's social impact) and benchmarking by objectives (which compares actual company performance with stated objectives). These methods are the primary tools of the accounting firms that are so aggressively pushing corporate social auditing into the mainstream business world, because they know a potential gold mine when they see one. None of these techniques are perfect, says Curtis Verschoor, an accounting professor at DePaul University, and in the absence of credible, recognized standards of ethical behavior, they will inevitably be inconclusive. Still, it's a positive step. "Even if these audits are only done by a few people on a voluntary basis," says Verschoor, "it will lead the way to more socially responsible behavior on the part of corporations."

— Craig Cox

*Program on Corporations, Law & Democracy, 211.5 Bradford St., Provincetown, MA 02657; phone/fax 508/487-3151.*

*Institute for Social and Ethical Accountability, 1st Floor, Vine Court, 112 116, Whitechapel Rd., London EL 1JE, UK; phone 44 (0) 171/377-5866; fax 44 (0) 171/377-5720; Web site is located at www.accountability.org.uk; e-mail Secretariat@AccountAbility.org.uk.*

the Vanderbilts, the Rockefellers, and the Morgans reached proportions unheard of . . . until today.

The power of the modern corporation dates back to this era, aided by two major legal shifts. First was the emasculation of the state "corporate charter," as power brokers goaded spineless and frequently corrupt politicians to remove, bit by bit and state by state, restrictions imposed to protect the public. Today the corporate chartering process is so perfunctory that it can be handled by a phone call.

The other big change came in 1886, when the U.S. Supreme Court essentially made the corporation bulletproof. In a stunning and totally irrational decision made without bothering to hear any formal arguments (indeed, the learned justices said they did not want to hear any arguments), the Court abruptly decreed in a case brought by a railroad company that a corporation is "a person," with the same constitutional protections that you and I have. Dr. Frankenstein could not have done better than the courts and legislators. In only a century, the corporation was transformed into a superhuman creature of the law, superior to you and me, because it has civil rights without any civil responsibilities. It is legally obligated to be selfish; it cannot be thrown into jail; it can deduct from its tax bill any fines it gets for wrongdoing; and it can live forever.

Corporations are the dominant institutions of our time, exercising the sort of power wielded by the church during the Middle Ages or by the nation-state in more recent times. In fact, some corporations are actually bigger than nations in terms of money. Mitsubishi is the 22nd largest economy on earth, ranked ahead of Indonesia. General Motors is number 26, bigger than Denmark or Thailand. Ford is 31st, ahead of South Africa and Saudi Arabia. Toyota, Shell, Exxon, Wal-Mart, Hitachi, and AT&T are all in the top 50.

If you read the business pages, you will find the captains of industry unabashedly declaring their independence from any social contract or community mores, and from nations themselves, even the most powerful nations. Ralph Nader told me about a telling moment at General Motors' stockholders meeting in 1996. The setting was appropriately ceremonious, with CEO John Smith and the board of directors arrayed like ministers of state across an elevated platform in a grand ballroom. At one point, a lone stockholder gained recognition to speak, and noting that GM had eliminated some 73,000 U.S. jobs in the past decade, asked politely if Smith and the members of the board would rise and join him in pledging allegiance to the American flag on display on the side of the platform. After some embarrassed tittering among the board members and scurrying of legal counsels back and forth behind the podium, Smith announced that the bottom line was no, they would not. Of course, even though there was a small army of reporters present, not a whisper of this revealing exchange made the news.

**No single step, no magic fix-it, is going to deflate the arrogance of these elite investors and managers, but one strong hammer our democracy needs in its toolbox is a corporate charter with teeth.** Just as the larger community specifies what it expects of welfare mothers, so must we set strict terms on the much more generous privileges bestowed on corporations. They must assume some individual responsibility for the malfeasance of their enterprises. And corporate charters, like politicians, should be subject to term limits. Such meaningful changes—along with a straightforward six-word constitutional amendment that says "a corporation is not a person"—would begin to mitigate the destructive, single-minded profit drive of the corporation and bring business back into balance with the greater goals of our society.

Challenging hegemonic corporate power head-on is made all the more difficult by the gutlessness that prevails among our present political leaders. This is a struggle that has to be organized and fought with no expectation of help from those in high positions. On the bright side, people already are focusing on the target, organizing, and fighting back, with newly aggressive groups like the Association of Community Organizations for Reform Now (ACORN), the AFL-CIO, the Alliance for Democracy, the Institute for Local Self-Reliance, the New Party, and the Program on Corporations, Law, and Democracy (see box, "Taming the Corporate Beast" ).

And when we think it is too difficult, even impossible, to win such a battle, it is worth remembering that Americans just like us have done this before—and won. Remember that everything Lincoln foresaw—enthronement, corruption, aggregation, and destruction—came true over the next 40 years, except the last: destruction of the republic. This is because ordinary people rose up against the corporate giants and the corrupt politicians. In historic battles from the early 1880s into the early 1900s, the republic was saved from the robber barons by a coalition of the Populist Movement, the labor movement, African American activists, the muckraking press, and thousands of national and local leaders. Together they forged a new politics that elected populists, socialists, radicals, and other noncorporatists to legislative seats, governorships, and Congress. And while they never elected a president, they did force both the Democratic and the Republican parties to embrace their reform agenda, producing the nation's first trust-busting laws, the first minimum-wage-and-hour laws, laws about food purity, women's suffrage, the first national conservation program, the direct election of U.S. senators, and other populist, working people's reforms.

Yes, corporations today are more powerful than any robber baron could have dreamed, but they remain a creation of government. The Supreme Court also ruled in 1906 that "The corporation is a creature of the state. It is presumed to be incorporated for the benefit of the public." When it ceases to be a benefit—declaring itself above the common good—then we can cease to sanction incorporation.

As powerful as the corporation seems, remember this: No building is too tall for even the smallest dog to lift its leg on.

*Jim Hightower, former Texas commissioner of agriculture, is now a radio talk show host and the editor of a newsletter called* The Hightower Lowdown *(www.jimhightower.com). This article was excerpted from* There's Nothing in the Middle of the Road but Yellow Stripes and Dead Armadillos *by Jim Hightower. Copyright © 1997 by Jim Hightower. Reprinted by arrangement with HarperCollins Publishers, Inc.*

# What's wrong with America

## Open Season on Uncle Sam

*Inevitably, the world's only remaining superpower comes in for a good deal
of criticism. Not only is the U.S. the 800-pound gorilla in the neighborhood;
is it arguably smug, arrogant, self-centered, unpredictable, and occasionally just plain
wrong. Now, several recent incidents have raised the chronic level of sniping in the
global press to near-flood proportions. Our cover package:*

THE INDEPENDENT

We savored a rare bipartisan happy hour in Washington early in May. The occasion was a ceremony on Pennsylvania Avenue, a few steps down from the White House, to mark the naming of a large, blank government building after Ronald Reagan, a former president who has already acquired in life the status of a divinity. The entire Congress seemed to be there, Republicans and Democrats, all friends for a day. Nancy Reagan was there—face stretched drum tight, eyes that once blinked now set in a round, manic stare, ditto for Bob Dole.

President Bill Clinton, with his genius for these schmuckfests, was at his unctuous best. Milking the nostalgia. Biting his lower lip. Acting the patriot's part against the cinema-screen backdrop of a giant American flag. "I think we feel the essence of his presence," said the Groper of the Gipper. "His unflagging optimism, his proud patriotism, his unabashed faith in the American people." The crowd roared, raising a breeze that caused the giant flag to flutter. I wanted to be sick. This was grotesque.

What's my problem? All my problems with America, that's what. The dumb certitude; the blind conformity; the contempt for the poor; the facile amiability; the ostentatious religiosity; the callous laws; the love of guns; the Hollywood sensibility; the all-consuming fetish for material success; the showy insubstantiality of the politics; the celebrity junk; the infantile literal-mindedness; and the faith, withal, in America's planetary moral superiority—in the notion that the American way of life is the best ever devised, that America is, in Lincoln's phrase, "the last best hope" for mankind.

Let us start by examining the thing that impelled me to come to Washington in the first place: the reckless inattention to the suffering that American imperial might has inflicted on the unfortunate of the Earth. Had I not spent the 1980s in Latin America, I might look on the U.S. in a different light. But Uncle Sam's fingerprints were everywhere in those days, and it was there that my appetite to know the northern colossus was first picked.

First I was in Argentina, with its extraordinarily evil generals. Then I spent six years covering the blood-soaked little countries of Central America. It was there that I became fascinated, appalled but also intrigued, by the barbarism Reagan's government was prepared to encourage in the name of democracy.

It was partly because I made so many excellent American friends during those years that I expected something entirely different when I moved to America in January, 1995. I expected that under that nice Mr. Clinton the U.S. might make some atonement. I could not have been further from the truth. The U.S. role in Latin America has been eliminated from the official history.

I myself see Reagan the way the majority of South Africans see their former president, P. W. Botha. The difference being that in the scale of human-rights abuses, Botha falls way short. One statistic will make the point. The South African death squads killed 60, maybe 100 activists during the '80s. In El Salvador, in the first two years of the decade alone, they were killing 1,000 a month. In the immortal words of the chief U.S. military adviser in El Salvador in 1984, "After all, they're only little brown men."

But they were real people, those Salvadorans, Guatemalans, Hondurans, and Nicaraguans. I met them. I saw their disfigured corpses and mutilated limbs. They were as real as Mr. and Mrs. Apple Pie Smith and their charmingly computer-literate children in Toledo, Ohio. But to Washington, and to America in general, their lives had no meaning, the gruesome manner of their deaths no pain. Otherwise they would not be naming airports and buildings after Ronald Reagan. They would be hauling him up before a tribunal to answer for his crimes.

Clinton is a refined Reagan, imbued with the talent not only to pander and charm but to think for himself. Being clever and a man who will subordinate every principle to the task of winning, Clinton pulled off a couple of astute gambits to ensure a crushing victory over Dole and a convincing defeat of George Bush. Six months before the 1996 election, he deprived the hapless Dole of the one policy issue he had left: Clinton signed a welfare reform bill, inspired entirely by Reagan's Republican heirs, that slashed aid to the poor, especially children and single mothers. The move played well with the Middle American rump who cling to the mythical belief that if you cannot make your own way in the land of opportunity, you are a contemptible "loser."

In 1992, when Clinton confronted the more difficult challenge of Bush, once again he invoked the spirit of Reagan, this time by making a display of his enthusiasm for the death penalty. Clinton flew to his home state of Arkansas to be present at the precise moment when a mental retard was put to death by lethal injection. Americans' unthinking devotion to the death penalty emanates from a simplistic habit of mind that is incapable of grasping the shared humanity of strangers. The death penalty will not be an issue in the next election, nor any election in America any time soon. For as rash past candidates have learned to their grief, to oppose legal executions is the political kiss of death.

So would be any notion of reforming the unspeakably brutal American prison system where homosexual rape and sexual slavery are tolerated, almost encouraged—and are the stuff of stand-up jokes on national TV—in much the same way that torture of Guatemalan trade unionists was tolerated and encouraged by the Reagan administration.

America, vast and varied as it is, does have its points. We Europeans correctly like to note that Americans lack irony, which means they lack an adult sense of life's limitations, which means they lack wisdom. Yes, but the other side of that coin is that in their adolescent brio they have a sense of possibility, a random energy and optimism, that drives them to heights of inventiveness and wealth creation to which we world-weary Europeans would not think to aspire. And it would be foolish to suggest that there are not wise, humane Americans aplenty. It is a big country. There are people who care keenly about the plight of strangers, who invest as much zeal on behalf of the little brown men of this world as most of their compatriots do to making money, scarfing hamburgers, and watching TV. But such people are strangers in their own land, their voices drowned by the market-driven American dream machine.

I choose to measure America against its own vast, self-satisfied claims. It is not morally superior to the rest of us. It is not the noblest, finest, most decent society that ever was. It is not the last best hope for mankind. It falls way short. It is too pitiless. America, for all the talk about all people having been created equal, has not learned to temper power with mercy, has not—as a nation—extended the hand of compassion. I will come back and visit my American friends. But—offer me all the money in the world—I won't come back to live.

—*John Carlin, "The Independent" (centrist), London, May 10, 1998.*

# Eight Diagnoses Of the U.S. Case

## 'The Only Civilized Society'?

### It Comes with the Territory

Members of so-called "primitive tribes" always thought it was obvious that their village was located in the center of the universe and that they were the only real people. Such a worldview is thought to be a natural result of their ignorance and isolation. But great civilizations, both ancient and modern, also are deeply convinced that they are (here I quote historians) "the only civilized society in the world," "the chosen people," "always right," and "paving the way for the rest of the human race."

What others find irritating about Americans is their feeling of benign superiority, their claim to being the chosen people. This is not a shortcoming of the Americans. It is a common characteristic of every civilization in a period when history belongs to it.

—*Jerzy Trammer, "Gazeta Wyborcza" (liberal), Warsaw, April 3–4, 1998.*

### The Peril of Being Special

The United States emerged from the cold war as the strongest power on Earth. Yet in the years since the end of that conflict—nearly a decade now—it has failed to shape a coherent foreign policy. Why is that?

While there are many reasons, a crucial one is the prevailing sense of American exceptionalism. This belief—that the U.S. is fundamentally different from other countries in its nature and behavior, and therefore ordinary rules do not apply to it—distorts America's worldview. Americans have always maintained they are more moral and disinterested than others—for example, that power politics is a game played by the rest of the world but not by them.

During the cold war the American exceptionalism was essentially justifiable, as its behavior relative to that of its adversary—the Soviet Union—was almost always morally superior. Thus when some Americans indignantly repudiated the doctrine of "moral equivalence," they had a point: The two superpowers were *not* morally equivalent. But—and this is crucial—the validity of that point depended much less on the exceptional virtue of the United States than it did on the exceptional vileness of the totalitarian adversary.

The U.S. does indeed behave better than the great majority of states most of the time, but it is a matter of degree, not a difference in kind. When the chips are down, all states do what they have to to protect their vital interests.

In the absence of an evil empire, and in dealing with the more-or-less ordinary states of the post-communist era, the U.S. is really not much different from other countries. Yet it continues to insist on applying different standards to itself and others. When China sends its forces to put up its flag in an uninhabited South China Sea atoll, it is denounced by Washington, but when the U.S. deems it necessary to send troops into the Caribbean, that is OK. The U.S. thinks it right to apply its own domestic laws to foreign companies operating outside the U.S.—as with the Helms-Burton Act—but it would consider similar behavior toward U.S. companies by a foreign government to be completely unacceptable.

Such application of double standards is bound to store up trouble in the form of cumulative resentment and declining credibility. It is especially incompatible with the claim that the U.S. should be the principal rule setter. Credible rule setters must themselves respect the rules.

Even friendly countries are likely to react as one English politician did to the high-minded Victorian statesman, William Ewart Gladstone: "We don't mind his having an ace or two up his sleeve, but we do resent his insistence that the Lord Almighty put it there."

Or as the orator Edmund Burke more soberly warned the British people 200 years ago: "I must fairly say, I dread our own power and our own ambition; I dread our being too much dreaded. . . . We may say that we shall not abuse this astonishing and hitherto unheard of power. But every other nation will think we shall abuse it. It is impossible but that, sooner or later, this state of things must produce a combination against us which may end in our ruin."

—Owen Harries, "Australian Financial Review" (centrist), Sydney, April 8, 1998.

**Survival of the Fattest**

When the great Thomas Jefferson committed the infant United States to "life, liberty, and the pursuit of happiness" in the Declaration of Independence, he must have known this hedonistic injunction would set his fellow countrymen on a collision course with their older, puritanical instincts. The collision keeps coming round.

# The Sound of One Hand Clapping

## Aftenposten

In Norway, Nepal, and New Zealand, all of us live in a world that is increasingly shaped by the United States and American successes. A nation of immigrants, the U.S. has enormous dynamism, the self-confidence due to a country on top, economic might, technological inventiveness, and political power without parallel. For a world watching it in mild astonishment, America is a laboratory for the future and the world's leader—and other countries prefer to copy it rather than protest.

The conflict with Iraq demonstrated all of this anew, even if military power is but a small part of the picture. The U.S. has, in fact, taken on the role of world policeman—because there are no other candidates. But in addition, and this is more surprising, the Americans have accepted a major role in working toward a stable political order in Europe since the fall of the iron curtain. It is the U.S. that has assumed the political initiative in Europe. It decided the manner in which German reunification was carried out; it launched NATO's "partnership for peace" directly to the East in 1994; it forced the Bosnia agreement that the European Union (EU) was not able to bring about; it steered the expansion of NATO, adding Poland, the Czech Republic, and Hungary last year; it has given the Baltic lands their strongest support in the West. The U.S. takes the lead in all of Europe and the former Soviet Union. Since this has not led to conflict—except for a little grumbling from Paris now and again—the Europeans have in general seemed pleased with the U.S. role. The goals are the same.

America enjoys great authority, for the American version of the free democratic society has emerged as the winner in the political struggle of the postwar era. Today, politicians and economists from the whole word make pilgrimages to New York and Washington to learn how to run an effective financial market. And when crises erupt, as we are seeing in Asia, it is the International Monetary Fund, headquartered in Washington, that runs the show.

There is little or no coercion behind the United States' leadership role. Practical results make the difference for a pragmatic and problem-solving society. Others observe the U.S. solutions and follow in its footsteps. This is true for research, for the computer revolution, and for popular culture. And it is true for higher education. The world's top brains make their way to the best American universities. Early this year, Bonn announced a reform for Germany's crisis-ridden universities—in the direction of an American exam system and better pay for the best teachers. America is showing the world the way.

—Nils Morten Udgaard, "Aftenposten" (conservative) Oslo, Feb. 21, 1998.

Jefferson was a child of rationality and 18th century Enlightenment. But the republic he helped create was rooted not just in warm Virginia, but in wintry Massachusetts to the north, founded in the pursuit of a 17th century notion of goodness. It has left the U.S. a profoundly Protestant country—individualistic, but bent on salvation, on Earth or later. The tension thus created has punctuated American life ever since. When they are not busy trying to outlaw sex, tobacco, or alcohol, Americans enthusiastically pursue them like no other people on Earth.

The cycle is now in one of its neoprohibitionist phases, with smoking under pressure even when committed in private. The war against booze has never ended. "Sin" being an unfashionable concept, "health" is the puritans' weapon. You cannot pursue life, liberty, etc., if you are dead. But Americans also have a passion for quantification, from the biggest buildings to the fat content of yogurt. So it was big news early in June when a new classification of human obesity, the Body Mass Index (BMI), pronounced 29 million unsuspecting Americans fat and 39 million obese. Better still, it has a do-it-yourself formula to judge ourselves.

Many Americans will rush to do that. But they will be the fanatically healthy ones. It is part of the Jeffersonian legacy that the U.S. contains the world's fittest as well as the fattest. It is no secret why so many Americans are obese: They eat junk food and do not exercise. Faced with bad news from the BMI, they will simply resort to slimming pills and continue to pursue happiness in their own sedentary way.

—*"Guardian Weekly" (liberal), London, June 14, 1998.*

## How Israel Calls the Tune

How things have speeded up in the past half century. In its first war back in 1948, Israel took six months to capture most of Palestine and turn half its people into refugees. Two decades later, it took just six days to overrun all of Sinai, the West Bank, and the Golan Heights. And now, in 1998, Israel is well on its way to defeating the United States of America by means of sound bites, those little TV quotation clips no more than six seconds long.

Of course, making the weapon of words effective has required careful planning and tremendous effort over many years. Without the $2 million that a prominent American Zionist is said to have smuggled into Harry Truman's campaign chest during the 1948 presidential elections, for instance, it is doubtful that America would have recognized the newly declared state of Israel with the alacrity it did.

Similar timely investments in U.S. campaign finance have allowed Israel to reap the $60 billion in American aid that has poured into the country since its birth. An astonishing victory in itself—but beyond this, Israel has secured U.S. backing for, or at least acquiescence in, its project to reestablish its purported biblical boundaries of 2,500 years ago.

Much of the credit for this triumph is owed to a veritable fifth column within the U.S. The Israeli lobby in Washington is reckoned to be the second most powerful after the American Association of Retired Persons. The American Israel Public Affairs Committee, or AIPAC, wields a 55,000-strong membership of lobbyists, angry letter writers, and contributors of political funds. More important, it enjoys direct access to the highest levels of government. Small wonder that when Israeli Prime Minister Benjamin Netanyahu snapped his fingers, 81 out of 100 U.S. senators signed a letter demanding that America should refrain from even thinking about publicly blaming Israel for driving the Oslo peace process onto the rocks of its settlements policy.

But now the battle to conquer the U.S. has taken an even more dramatic turn. Israel has managed to get Congress to declare war on the presidency. In May, a majority of the House of Representatives' 435 members signed a letter to Clinton condemning his administration's formula for salvaging peace. One of the letter's authors accused the president of engaging in "extortion" by asking Israel to cede 2 percent more West Bank land. I'm betting that the Clinton administration will sue for a truce with Israel. Clinton will be made to eat his own sound bites. Didn't he say that no country could dictate the terms of peace?

—*Max Rodenbeck, "Cairo Times" (biweekly), Cairo, May 14–27, 1998.*

## Wasting the World

The average American already consumes so much that the U.S. has a worldwide environmental impact amounting to 4 billion people. The U.S., with only 5 percent of the world's population, consumes 32 percent of the world's petroleum and plastics and produces 25 percent of the world's greenhouse gases. Its 265 million people produce more waste than the 2 billion people in China and India. Indeed, the cause of environmental destruction is conspicuous consumption—a lifestyle that is unfortunately "migrating" from the U.S. to the Third World.

However, consumption growth, like population growth, is exponential. If the Americans are to maintain their current rate of consumption, in 24 years the U.S. will be consuming four times more, in 36 years eight times more, and within a lifetime, Americans will be consuming about 64 times as much as they are consuming today.

This American super-consuming society has exported its toxic wastes to Third World countries, its dirty industries to emerging economies. Environment is sacrificed in favor of American investments. These are the real issues that should be the concern of environmentalists in America, and for that matter, environmentalists everywhere. The only solution is for the Americans—and the world—to do away with our consumption frenzy.

—*"The Nation" (independent), Bangkok, April 16, 1998.*

## A Nation of Seinfelds

For weeks, American culture found itself in a state of mourning after the last segment of the supremely popular sitcom *Seinfeld*. There has been no way to fight off the bombardment of "yadda, yadda, yadda."

"Sitcom" is short for situation comedy, a staple of American television since just after World War II. As time went by and political correctness became entrenched, the creators of sitcoms were faced with an increasingly difficult task. To avoid being accused of racism or sexism, they had to give up the reliable sources of their inspiration—politics, class, and ethnic prejudice, along with the traditional view of men's and women's roles in the family. The scope of safe humor shrank. As a result, for the past 10 years the screen has been dominated by comedies "about nothing."

*Seinfeld* was the ideal sitcom. It told the story of four friends in New York whose lives flow "from day to day." Despite the fact that all the characters were older than 30, none of them had started a family, none had really given thought to the future. The preferred lifestyle was egotism and snobbishness and the chosen philosophy cynicism.

If well-received television is viewed in terms of the audience's identification with the subject, *Seinfeld*'s popularity is a sad reflection of the state of American society.

*—Eliza Sarnacka-Mahoney, "Zycie Warszawy" (independent), Warsaw, June 6–7, 1998.*

## Ignorant and Inward Looking

A first-time visitor to America is confounded by the questions repeatedly asked by the citizens of the most advanced and resourceful nation in the world: Where is Kenya on the world map? Where did you learn to speak English so well? How did you get here?

The level of ignorance about Africa and the rest of the world among Americans can only be matched by the influence that American culture—news, music, movies, dress, and capitalist economy—has had on the rest of the world.

Surveys by U.S. media among readers and television viewers indicate that international news is rated least important compared with talk shows, game shows, movies, and local news. But in much of Africa it is the reverse. "It is not uncommon for [African] television viewers to know more about America than their own country," says Radu Herju, a news anchor from Romania.

A trend in which most cities in the U.S. have a single large newspaper focusing on saturation coverage of local news has spawned a population that is inward looking and cannot imagine life in other parts of the world.

*—James Macharia, "East African" (independent weekly), Nairobi, June 8–14, 1998*

## Land of False Smiles

America is a soap bubble that has to be burst," says Dari Milev Dragan. The eccentric Bulgarian avant-garde artist spent more than six months traveling in the U.S., starting with only $2,000 in his pocket and traveling mainly in the West, including 10 days in the Nevada desert. But he says he found everything artificial. "I prefer the long Bulgarian childhood with real games to a childhood in front of a computer," says Dragan. "I prefer Bulgarian savory to the abundance of tasteless food, stray dogs to castrated cats with severed vocal cords and extracted claws. Let them steal my windshield wipers in Bulgaria—I prefer that to being given false smiles."

In America, says Dragan, "They are all scared of being accused of sexual harassment. Americans are extremely cautious on the girlfriends-boyfriends issue. First to a pastry shop, then to the movies, then to a restaurant and discothèque, and only then home under the covers. . . . How can you call it a normal country where a woman sues McDonald's for $2 million for serving hot coffee, which she spills on her bosom?"

*—Ivailo Kitsov, "24 Tchasa" (independent), Sofia, May 16, 1998.*

# Children and Guns: America's Shame

'THESE CRAZY MACHO FANTASIES'

*stern*

If the two boys had had slingshots, there would have been some broken windows and some bruises. But 13-year-old Mitchell Johnson and his 11-year-old friend Andrew Golden went to school with an entire arsenal of deadly weapons. They included a semiautomatic carbine, an unusually powerful deer rifle, and several large-caliber revolvers.

They had several hundred rounds of ammunition and wore camouflage clothing last March when they opened fire on their classmates in Jonesboro, Arkansas. Four girls and a teacher were killed, and nine other children and one adult were wounded.

Two nice boys, one a gifted trumpet player, the other the apple of his mother's eye and his grandparents' favorite. And America once again asked how such murders could happen. Psychologists and politicians pointed, of course, to films and television shows that teach children that violence is the quickest and best way to resolve conflicts. And there was also talk of declining values, dissolving families, and young people under greater and greater stress in an unfriendly world. Just one explanation was a rare commodity: "If those two boys had not had access to that incredible arsenal, the victims would still be alive," said Patrick Tolan of the Institute for Youth Research in Chicago.

It is as simple as that. And as hard to stop. In no other country in the industrial world are children, from early childhood on, so thoroughly familiar with firearms of every sort. And in no other country are they so likely to fall victim to guns. Every two hours, an American between 10 and 19 is killed, and the murder rate for people between 15 and 24 is almost 10 times as high as that it Italy, which holds second place. All in all, about 40,000 Americans die each year from firearms—murders, suicides, and accidents.

The tie between kids and guns is especially close in rural areas, where you may see bumper stickers reading: GOD, GUNS, AND GUTS MADE AMERICA GREAT. So it is no coincidence that in recent months two other teenage attacks with guns also horrified the country. In December, 1997, a 14-year-old in Paducah, Kentucky, shot three classmates during a prayer meeting, and in October a 16-year-old killed two girls at his school in Pearl, Mississippi. [It was in May, after this article went to press, that Kipland Kinkel, 15, allegedly killed his parents and two classmates in Springfield, Oregon.—WPR]

In the Kentucky and Mississippi cases, the boys had taken the guns from their fathers' gun cases. In Arkansas, the Golden boy had stolen them from his grandfather. None of the killers had any trouble using the weapons. Andrew, 11, had learned to shoot from his father, beginning when he was six. This is not considered too early in the South. "Some kids like baseball, and some like guns," people say in Arkansas. Boys go hunting with their dads, and fall and spring vacations at school in many states are arranged to coincide with the beginning of hunting season. Even after the massacre in Jonesboro, many fathers see no reason to change this custom. And the principal of Westside Middle School, where the killings took place, stated the next day: "This tragedy had nothing to do with bearing arms."

The president of the National Rifle Association (NRA), home to 3 million fanatic gun owners, said the killings showed the need for educating

## "Some kids like baseball, and some like guns."

children, as early as possible, how to use guns. When the NRA hears about something like the tragedy in Jonesboro, it replies with its standard slogan: "Guns don't kill people, people kill people." From the point of view of the gun lobby, this is especially true for wars between youth gangs in big cities. The NRA believes that such killers are misguided, rootless kids who would kill even if they did not have a Colt in their hands.

In the United States, there are now between 200 million and 300 million firearms in private ownership. That means roughly one gun per person, infants and the elderly included. But the gun nuts continue to insist on free access to more guns for American citizens. They appeal to the United States constitution. It does, in fact, state the right of the people to keep and bear arms. But this right dates from 200 years ago, when the young republic still feared attacks from an absolute monarch. For such cases, the Americans needed a militia to defend their freedom. Every citizen, a Rambo, was not what the writers of the constitution had in mind.

To make sure that citizens have as much firepower as possible for their self-defense, the NRA has fought to water down any legislation that would limit dealing and owning guns. It is true that 75 especially dangerous weapons have been banned since 1994, but those who already owned these brands did not have to turn them in. And the firms that made these particular models could merely alter them slightly and sell them under new names. A federal law does require that gun buyers wait five days before getting possession of their weapons. This delay is intended to help dealers check the possible criminal backgrounds on gun buyers. But

in most states, except for machine guns, the law is not enforced for sales by one private owner to another. In more than 30 states, anyone may, at any time, carry a pistol around with him—even into a church or courtroom.

America's gun nuts have purchased so much firepower that the country's gun makers are running out of customers. According to the Bureau of Alcohol, Tobacco and Firearms, between 1989 and 1996, average annual production of guns sank from 4.4 million to 3.8 million. So the gun makers have discovered children as customers. "Children are the future of the sport that we love," says the catalog of New England Firearms. And the National Shooting Sports Foundation claims that "age is no barrier. Many youngsters are ready by age 10." Laws prohibit the sale of guns to minors, but this is not a problem: Dad or grandpa already owns an arsenal and is ready to loan a boy a gun or even buy him one.

"We all have these crazy macho fantasies," says Dr. Greg Stanford, who deals with gunshot victims daily in his clinic in Dallas, "that someone will break into our house, and we will be waiting with a shotgun in our hands." But study after study has shown that having a gun in the house makes life more dangerous, not safer. In less than 10 percent of all private use of firearms is self-defense the case. Much more often, children playing with dad's readily available gun wound or kill each other, or marital disputes end in death.

Sometimes gun nuts have to learn in person that John Wayne existed only on the screen. Last year two young men attacked James Boland, 52, a longtime NRA member, intending to rob him. He pulled his .38 Colt and shot one in the arm and the leg. But the man returned his fire, killing Boland with a shot in the chest. Even so, Frederick Boland, the victim's son, did not doubt the virtue of general gun ownership. As he saw it, "My father died exercising his constitutional right to bear arms."

—*Teja Fiedler, "Stern" (liberal newsmagazine), Hamburg, April 2, 1998.*

# Black and White: As Vexed as Ever

AN OLD HORROR IN EAST TEXAS

### The Economist

At dusk on Friday night, at the end of a difficult week in the east Texas town of Jasper, 80 or so boys were playing basketball in the park. Cars were drawn up close to the court, doors open, pumping out a heavy urban beat into the sultry air. Every player was black, all the attendant girlfriends were black, all the hangers-on were black. Did white kids come down and play sometimes? "Who you kidding? They wouldn't be seen with us." "Hey, fool," said another player, "what you think, that everything's all right 'cos the old folk says so? Ain't all right, man. We apart, we always been apart."

The scene, and the conversation, would not be unusual in inner-city America. In a town of 8,000 people, it gives pause. Jasper is a quiet, pretty place, with forests and lakes that look more like Finland than Texas. Down one country road you pass a creek, a meadow dappled in sunshine, then you go on into dense emerald forest. This spot is where the last sinews on James Byrd's neck tore loose, and his head—the face already shredded on the tarmac—bounced off into a ditch. Byrd's murder by three white men [who allegedly dragged him to death chained to the bumper of a pickup] has reminded Jasper—and the rest of America—that relations between the races are as vexed as ever.

The knee-jerk reaction of the national media, as the story broke, was to present east Texas as a white-trash outpost whose public offices are occupied by closet bigots. In fact, as the journalists soon discovered, Jasper has a black mayor and a black school principal. Even the Black Panthers, who sallied into town for a shameless publicity session, praised the white sheriff, Billy Rowles, for his efficient handling of the case. Byrd's family offered unconditional forgiveness to his white killers. Many times in the week of the killing, militant blacks—in town from distant parts to preach their particular form of racial separatism—were shouted down not by whites but by blacks, who said they abhorred violence and vengeance. On the surface, outrage and sorrow brought Jasper together.

The townsfolk were adamant that this awful crime did not represent them. This was true. What represents the town, and makes it so typical, is something much more subtle: a thousand small prejudices and slights that blacks in east Texas feel, but whites rarely notice.

It bothers blacks in Jasper that the bank tellers are almost all white and that they rarely see a black waitress in the more expensive local restaurants. A group of black maids at a local hotel (speaking anonymously for fear of retribution) are particularly candid. They feel humiliated, they say, when security people follow them around the aisles in the Wal-Mart. They wonder why no blacks are "good enough" to work as hotel receptionists. None of them think blacks have a fair deal in the town. "Those signs may have gone," says one of the maids, visibly surprised at her own outspokenness, "but to me they're still there."

On Saturday, Byrd's funeral showed the unstated segregation. Of the 1,000 or so people who attended, fewer than 50 were white. Byrd was laid out in a black funeral home, eulogized in a black church, and buried in the black part of the town cemetery, where blacks have always been buried out of view. "Did they tell you," one of the maids had said unhappily, "they were going to bury him in the back?"

White supremacy may be marginalized, but it is still menacing. A local Ku Klux Klan leader boasts that his group has a strong presence in Jasper. The murder has shed light on the fact that state prisons across the South have become purveyors of white supremacy, recruiting susceptible inmates into violent gangs such as the Aryan Brotherhood. Two of Byrd's alleged killers had been monitored for involvement in a white supremacist group while in prison.

And what of Jasper? This is a community of mutual respect, but it is still distinctly divided at all the levels that matter in ordinary life. What the boys on the basketball court cared about was not whether white kids came and played ball with them. They cared about good jobs, fair treatment—and about the fact that Dennis Rodman, the bad-boy star of the Chicago Bulls, had elected to pay for Byrd's funeral. It sounded awfully like separate but equal.

—*"The Economist" (conservative newsmagazine), London, June 20, 1998.*

# Whatever Happened to Politics?

# When Naptime Is Over

The placid public mood is an illusion. Real issues rumble
beneath the calm and could soon send a wake-up call.

## By Robert B. Reich

THERE'S NO LONGER ANY POLITICAL NEWS, A REPORTER FRIEND
confided recently, explaining why "human interest" stories were oozing like syrup across his
newspaper's front pages. We're in the Bland
Decade now, a time when citizens march on Washington
not to affect politics but to vow they'll be better people
and when politicians speak out mainly to urge niceness:
volunteer your time, enter into dialogues on race, hire
someone off welfare, please. Apparently we need little
more than charity, moral uplift and perhaps a modest program or two. Politics is dead, or so it seems.

The easiest explanation for their torpor is that the nation
is fat, like an overstuffed bear starting hibernation. It's no
longer the economy, stupid. Six years ago, a prolonged
recession hurt white-collar workers, giving some urgency
to the politics of "change." Prosperity, though, is a powerful sedative. Forget politics for now, we seem to be saying. Let's compare stock portfolios, banter about culture
and identity and tut-tut over problems decades hence, like
an insolvent Social Security trust fund or excessive greenhouse gases.

The great economic contests have been won. Communism vanished before it was even vanquished. The Japanese competitive threat is now a sorry heap of bad debt.
European welfare states heave under double-digit unemployment. And here in the land of plenty we've never had
it so good. Wealth is exploding, unemployment is at a
24-year low, inflation is quiescent (the Federal Reserve
Board chairman, Alan Greenspan, publicly raised con-

cerns about *deflation*), the stock market is riding high.
American capitalism is the envy of the world.

But look more closely and the easy explanation falls
short. Most Americans don't have it so good. They have
jobs, but most wages and benefits are stuck or continue
to drop. Wealth has exploded at the top, but the wages
of people in the bottom half are lower today in terms of
purchasing power than they were in 1989, before the last
recession. This is in sharp contrast to every previous recovery in the postwar period. Corporate downsizing and
mass layoffs are still the order of the day, which partly
explains why so few workers demand raises in this tight
labor market. They'd rather keep their jobs.

The reality is that Wall Street's advance hasn't been
widely shared. The richest 1 percent hold more than 35
percent of the nation's wealth. The typical middle-class
family has no more than $7,000 in stocks and $12,500
in mutual funds, according to a 1995 survey by the Federal Reserve and the Treasury Department. Even the recent
market surge isn't likely to have changed this very much,
given what has happened to wages.

Whatever savings Americans do have are imperiled by
hospital bills. A growing portion of the public lacks health
insurance—in 1989, 33 million Americans under age 65
were without it; by 1996, 41.3 million. (The President's
proposal to extend Medicare coverage to early retirees
and displaced workers as young as 55, which would be
the largest expansion in 25 years, is expected to add only
300,000 to the rolls.)

Despite the boom, inequality has widened. The nation's
poverty rate is slightly higher than it was before the last
recession. In 1989, 12.6 million, or 19.6 percent, of the
nation's children lived in poverty; now it's 14.5 million,

---

*Robert B. Reich, professor of social and economic policy
at Brandeis University, was Secretary of Labor during
President Clinton's first term.*

# Almost a century ago, American politics appeared similarly listless despite growing social problems. Within three years there was an outburst of reform: Muckrakers exposed corruption, small businesses railed at monopolies and the middle class demanded fundamental change.

or 20.5 percent. The Conference of Mayors reports rising demand for food and shelter among the homeless. And the successes of the civil rights movement notwithstanding, today's urban schools are more racially segregated than in the 1980's.

SO WHY, THEN, THE PREVAILING POLITICAL SOMNOLENCE? TRADITIONAL politics has been all about who's gaining and who's losing. Yet it has lately become unfashionable, indeed in poor taste, to notice such things. In the present upbeat climate, downbeat data are slightly subversive. It is necessary to minimize all worry about the economy lest the public lose confidence, a perfect tautology. Bankers and business leaders have become cheerleaders in the nationwide pep rally. Onward! Upward!

Recent polls show, accordingly, high rates of consumer confidence. A record 40 percent of consumers queried in the Conference Board's December survey called jobs "plentiful" although, tellingly, only 28 percent expected their own wages to rise. These are the ones who have heard the distant roar of surging wealth and assume that the rising tide will lift them, too—which may explain the record level of consumer debt. Personal bankruptcies are also at a record high.

Will politics revive when the economic tide ebbs and hardships appear like shipwrecks on the tidal flats? Not necessarily. Even in 1992, with the nation mired in recession, political engagement was grudging. Americans wanted "change" to get the economy moving again. But there was no sense of moral urgency. It was simply time to replace old management with new. Most Americans had long before stopped believing in government as a force for much good in their lives.

Some people will say we don't need a vital politics to be a vital society. We can expand the circle of prosperity through grass-roots moral activism, spearheaded by community groups, socially responsible businesses, not-for-profits, religious organizations and compassionate individuals—perhaps all deftly linked by fax and modem, a "virtual" social movement. Commentators rightly stress the importance of such civic engagement. But they make a serious mistake labeling it as an alternative to politics. Throughout our history, civic activism has been the precursor, and the propellant, of political movements.

ALMOST A CENTURY AGO, AMERICAN POLITICS APPEARED SIMILARLY listless despite growing social problems. As today, the economy was booming, jobs were plentiful and vast fortunes were being accumulated. Yet real wages had

stopped growing, and the gulf between rich and poor was widening into a chasm. New technologies (steam engines, railway locomotives, the telephone, steam turbines, electricity) were transforming the nation, pulling families off the farms and immigrants from abroad and depositing many into fetid slums. Wall Street magnates were consolidating their empires. Government was effectively bought by large corporations, and the broad public was deeply cynical. William McKinley won re-election—legend has it, on a pledge to "stand pat"—and as the century closed, the nation seemed politically comatose.

Within three years, however, there was an outburst of reform: muckrakers like Lincoln Steffens and Ida Tarbell exposed corruption, and the middle class demanded fundamental change; small businessmen railed at monopolies; Wisconsin's crusading Governor, Robert La Follette, enacted legislation regulating health and safety in factories; Oregon limited the hours of work for women (no more than 10 per day); Theodore Roosevelt, McKinley's energetic Vice President who took over after McKinley was assassinated, set out to bust the trusts; suffragists marched; campaigns were organized for pure food and drug laws, workers' compensation and a minimum wage. Politics gained new life and meaning.

What happened? Indignation, which had been rising steadily, suddenly burst out and flooded the country. Citizens were already active at the local level, as they are today. Common morality simply couldn't abide the way things were going. Yet instead of opting for revolution or radical change, Americans preferred to spread the benefits of the emerging industrial economy, thereby saving capitalism from its own excesses.

Another foreshadowing occurred in the placid Eisenhower era. The overall economy was doing nicely then as well, even though its benefits had not reached the rural poor, many of whom were black. Politics had grown inert. Ike golfed. In 1954, the Supreme Court decided that separate schools were not equal. In 1957, Eisenhower dispatched Federal troops to Little Rock's Central High School. But who could have predicted that within a few years the civil rights movement would have remolded American politics with the Civil Rights Act of 1964 and the Voting Rights Act of 1965?

The next revival of American politics can be expected to follow a similar course. The current economic boom has bypassed too many; the gap between winners and losers has grown too wide. Fortunately, there is a common morality at the heart of this capitalist democracy that ultimately keeps us on track and keeps us together. Glimpses of it can be had even in these languid times. For example, a majority of Americans supported last year's increase in the minimum wage to $5.15, although only a tiny fraction stood to benefit. It was a matter of simple fairness. Or consider the broad-scale indignation stirred up by revelations of garment sweatshops.

We got another glimpse this summer, when a sudden groundswell of support forced a skinflint Congress to extend health care to millions of children. And a majority of Americans supported the United Parcel Service strikers, not because the public is particularly fond of organized labor but because it seemed unfair for U.P.S. to pay its part-time work force so little.

Recall also the firestorm when, almost exactly two years ago, AT&T announced it was firing some 40,000 employees and then gave the boss stock options that raised his total compensation to $16 million, from $6.7 million. Recall, by contrast, the celebration of Aaron Feuerstein, the owner of Malden Mills in Lawrence, Mass., who, after his synthetic-fleece business burned to the ground, assured his employees that he'd stick by them until the factory was rebuilt.

The pressure keeps rising. A final glimpse came just before the holidays, when the pubic signaled unease about giving the President "fast track" authority to whisk trade treaties through Congress without amendment and most members of the House of Representatives, including many Republicans, refused to support it. That may be a mistake. Trade is good for America. But the public's negative reaction shouldn't be seen as a repudiation of free trade. It was, at bottom, a matter of fairness: trade hurts some people, and we haven't made adequate provision for the losers.

Trade may, in fact, be the precipitating issue this time around. The economic implosion in East Asia will continue to reverberate here, as bahts, won, rupiahs, ringgit and yen drop in value relative to dollars—one of the biggest price-cutting contests in world history. American consumers will have the benefit of bargain-basement sales, but the cheap imports will put additional downward pressure on the wages of lower-skilled Americans. The tumult also will crimp profits of American companies that export to the region, causing more layoffs here. If the Asian flu turns more deadly, the infection here will be all the worse. However resolved, the Asian crisis portends larger jolts, as the global economy absorbs the surging output of 1.2 billion Chinese—more than a fifth of the world's popula-

tion. When the current recovery ends, the underlying reality will be starkly evident and the political debate surrounding trade will intensify.

To an extent, that debate has already begun. The tension between economic nationalism and globalism is emerging as one of the most significant fissures in American politics, and it runs through both parties—as shown by the current dispute over financing for the International Monetary Fund.

But it would be unfortunate indeed if the revival of American politics were to turn on the question of whether the nation should engage in more or less commerce with the rest of the world. The underlying choice is larger, more important and more subtle: ultimately, we must decide whether we want to slow the pace of globalization or else take bold steps to help today's losers share in the benefits of the new economy. I cannot predict the outcome of that great debate to come, but I can express a clear preference. It is that we expand the circle of prosperity and that we do so on a scale that matches the challenge.

A new nationalism founded on shared prosperity might, for example, support "re-employment insurance" that would enable people who lose their jobs to move to new ones with far less disruption and pain than is the norm today. (If the new job paid less, half the difference should be offset for a year by a wage subsidy.)

In that spirit, we could enlarge and expand the earned-income tax credit—a reverse income tax that makes work pay if you're at or near the bottom. We could bring a larger portion of the next generation into the circle of prosperity by rebuilding decaying schools and helping states equalize spending between rich and poor school districts. And we would make sure that *everyone* has access to adequate health care and child care.

To finance all of this—and move beyond the small, feel-good programs that lack adequate scale to make much of a difference—we could simply reverse the current trend in public finance and adopt a truly progressive tax system (including payroll taxes).

None of this will come easily or without a fight. But in the end, the nation will be stronger and better for bringing everyone, or nearly everyone, along. Future historians looking back on the Bland Decade will conclude that, as before, American politics wasn't really dead. It was only caught napping.

# Race and the Constitution

## Thurgood Marshall

*THURGOOD MARSHALL is Associate Justice of the U. S. Supreme Court.* *This article is adapted from a presentation given at the Annual Seminar of the San Francisco Patent and Trademark Law Association, in Maui, Hawaii, May 6, 1987.*

1987 marks the 200th anniversary of the United States Constitution. A commission has been established to coordinate the celebration. The official meetings, essay contests, and festivities have begun.

The planned commemoration will span three years, and I am told 1987 is "dedicated to the memory of the Founders and the document they drafted in Philadelphia."[1] We are to "recall the achievements of our Founders and the knowledge and experience that inspired them, the nature of the government they established, its origins, its character, and its ends, and the rights and privileges of citizenship, as well as its attendant responsibilities."[2]

Like many anniversary celebrations, the plan for 1987 takes particular events and holds them up as the source of all the very best that has followed. Patriotic feelings will surely swell, prompting proud proclamations of the wisdom, foresight, and sense of justice shared by the Framers and reflected in a written document now yellowed with age. This is unfortunate—not the patriotism itself, but the tendency for the celebration to over-

[* Marshall, the first African American justice ever to have served on the Supreme Court, was appointed by President Lyndon B. Johnson in 1967. He resigned in 1991 because of declining health, and he died in January 1993. Ed.]

simplify and overlook the many other events that have been instrumental to our achievements as a nation. The focus of this celebration invites a complacent belief that the vision of those who debated and compromised in Philadelphia yielded the "more perfect Union" it is said we now enjoy.

I cannot accept this invitation, for I do not believe that the meaning of the Constitution was forever "fixed" at the Philadelphia Convention. Nor do I find the wisdom, foresight, and sense of justice exhibited by the Framers particularly profound. To the contrary, the government they devised was defective from the start, requiring several amendments, a civil war, and momentous social transformation to attain the system of constitutional government, and its respect for the individual freedoms and human rights, we hold as fundamental today. When contemporary Americans cite "The Constitution," they invoke a concept that is vastly different from what the Framers barely began to construct two centuries ago.

For a sense of the evolving nature of the Constitution we need look no further than the first three words of the document's preamble: "We the People." When the Founding Fathers used this phrase in 1787, they did not have in mind the majority of America's citizens. "We the People" included, in the words of the Framers, "the whole Number of free persons" (art. I, sec. 2). On a matter so basic as the right to vote, for example, Negro slaves were excluded, although they were counted for representational purposes—at three-fifths each. Women did not gain the right to vote for over 130 years, until the 19th Amendment was ratified in 1920.

These omissions were intentional. The record of the Framers' debates on the slave question is especially clear: The Southern states acceded to the demands of the New England states for giving Congress broad power to regulate commerce, in exchange for the right to continue the slave trade. The economic interests of the regions coalesced: New Englanders engaged in the "carrying trade" would profit from transporting slaves from Africa as well as goods produced in America by slave labor. The perpetuation of slavery ensured the primary source of wealth in the Southern states.

Despite this clear understanding of the role slavery would play in the new republic, use of the words "slaves" and "slavery" was carefully avoided in the original document. Political representation in the lower House of Congress was to be based on the population of "free Persons" in each state, plus three-fifths of all "other Persons" (art. I, sec. 2). Moral principles against slavery, for those who had them, were compromised, with no explanation of the conflicting principles for which the American Revolution had ostensibly been fought: the self-evident truths "that all men are created equal, that they are endowed by their Creator with certain unalienable Rights, that among these are Life, Liberty and the pursuit of Happiness."

It was not the first such compromise. Even these ringing phrases from the Declaration of Independence are filled with irony, for an early draft of what became the Declaration assailed the King of England for suppressing legislative attempts to end the slave trade and for encouraging slave rebellions. The final draft adopted in 1776 did not contain this criticism. And so again at the Constitutional Conven-

From *Social Policy*, Summer 1987, pp. 29-31. This article is adapted from a presentation at the annual seminar of the San Francisco Patent and Trademark Law Association, May 6, 1987.

tion eloquent objections to the institution of slavery went unheeded, and its opponents eventually consented to a document that laid a foundation for the tragic events that were to follow.

Pennsylvania's Gouverneur Morris provides an example. He opposed slavery and the counting of slaves in determining the basis for representation in Congress. At the Convention he objected that:

> the inhabitant of Georgia [or] South Carolina who goes to the coast of Africa, and in defiance of the most sacred laws of humanity tears away his fellow creatures from their dearest connections and damns them to the most cruel bondages, shall have more votes in a Government instituted for protection of the rights of mankind, than the Citizen of Pennsylvania or New Jersey who views with a laudable horror, so nefarious a practice.[3]

And yet Gouverneur Morris eventually accepted the three-fifths accommodation. In fact, he wrote the final draft of the Constitution, the very document the bicentennial will commemorate.

As a result of compromise, the right of the Southern states to continue importing slaves was extended, officially, at least until 1808. We know that it actually lasted a good deal longer, as the Framers possessed no monopoly on the ability to trade moral principles for self-interest. But they nevertheless set an unfortunate example. Slaves could be imported, if the commercial interests of the North were protected. To make the compromise even more palatable, customs duties would be imposed at up to ten dollars per slave as a means of raising public revenues (art. I, sec. 9).

No doubt it will be said, when the unpleasant truth of the history of slavery in America is mentioned during this bicentennial year, that the Constitution was a product of its times, and embodied a compromise that, under other circumstances, would not have been made. But the effects of the Framers' compromise have remained for generations. They arose from the contradiction between guaranteeing liberty and justice to all, and denying both to Negroes.

The original intent of the phrase, "We the People," was far too clear for any ameliorating construction. Writing for the Supreme Court in 1857, Chief Justice Taney penned the following passage in the *Dred Scott* case,[4] on the issue whether, in the eyes of the Framers, slaves were "constituent members of the sovereignty," and were to be included among "We the People":

> We thing they are not, and that they are not included, and were not intended to be included.... They had for more than a century before been regarded as beings of an inferior order, and altogether unfit to associate with the white race...; and so far inferior, that they had no rights which the white man was bound to respect; and that the negro might justly and lawfully be reduced to slavery for his benefit.... [A]ccordingly, a negro of the African race was regarded... as an article of property, and held and bought and sold as such.... [N]o one seems to have doubted the correctness of the prevailing opinion of the time.

And so, nearly seven decades after the Constitutional Convention, the Supreme Court reaffirmed the prevailing opinion of the Framers regarding the rights of Negroes in America. It took a bloody civil war before the 13th Amendment could be adopted to abolish slavery, though not the consequences slavery would have for future Americans.

While the Union survived the Civil War, the Constitution did not. In its place arose a new, more promising basis for justice and equality, the 14th Amendment, ensuring protection of the life, liberty, and property of *all* persons against deprivations without due process, and guaranteeing equal protection of the laws. And yet almost another century would pass before any significant recognition was obtained of the rights of Black Americans to share equally even in such basic opportunities as education, housing, and employment, and to have their votes counted, and counted equally. In the meantime, Blacks joined America's military to fight its wars and invested untold hours working in its factories and on its farms, contributing to the development of this country's magnificent wealth and waiting to share in its prosperity.

What is striking is the role legal principles have played throughout America's history in determining the condition of Negroes. They were enslaved by law, emancipated by law, disenfranchised and segregated by law; and, finally, they have begun to win equality by law. Along the way, new constitutional principles have emerged to meet the challenges of a changing society. The progress has been dramatic, and it will continue.

The men who gathered in Philadelphia in 1787 could not have envisioned these changes. They could not have

imagined, nor would they have accepted, that the document they were drafting would one day be construed by a Supreme Court to which had been appointed a woman and the descendent of an African slave. "We the People" no longer enslave, but the credit does not belong to the Framers. It belongs to those who refused to acquiesce in outdated notions of "liberty," "justice," and "equality," and who strived to better them.

And so we must be careful, when focusing on the events that took place in Philadelphia two centuries ago, that we do not overlook the momentous events which followed, and thereby lose our proper sense of perspective. Otherwise, the odds are that for many Americans the bicentennial celebration will be little more than a blind pilgrimage to the shrine of the original document now stored in a vault in the National Archives. If we seek, instead, a sensitive understanding of the Constitution's inherent defects, and its promising evolution through 200 years of history, the celebration of the "Miracle at Philadelphia"[5] will, in my view, be a far more meaningful and humbling experience. We will see that the true miracle was not the birth of the Constitution, but its life, a life nurtured through two turbulent centuries of our own making, and a life embodying much good fortune that was not.

Thus, in this bicentennial year, we may not all participate in the festivities with flag-waving fervor. Some may more quietly commemorate the suffering, struggle, and sacrifice that has triumphed over much of what was wrong with the original document, and observe the anniversary with hopes not realized and promises not fulfilled. I plan to celebrate the bicentennial of the Constitution as a living document, including the Bill of Rights and the other amendments protecting individual freedoms and human rights.

## Notes

1. Commission on the Bicentennial of the United States Constitution, *First Full Year's Report* (Sept. 1986), p. 7.
2. Commission on the Bicentennial of the United States Constitution, *First Report* (Sept. 1985), p. 6.
3. Max Farrand (ed.), *The Records of the Federal Convention of 1787*, vol. 2 (New Haven: Yale University press, 1911), p. 222.
4. 19 How. (60 U.S.) 393, 405, 407–408 (1857).
5. Catherine D. Bowen, *Miracle at Philadelphia: The Story of the Constitutional Convention, May to September 1787* (Boston: Little, Brown, 1966).

## THE DYING CONSTITUTION

# Vigilante Justices

### *As the Court ignores the Constitution in favor of its conscience, it tramples on democracy— and the rights of the minority.*

ANTONIN SCALIA

THE argument most frequently made in favor of The Living Constitution is a pragmatic one: Such an evolutionary approach is necessary in order to provide the "flexibility" that a changing society requires; the Constitution would have snapped if it had not been permitted to bend and grow. This might be a persuasive argument if most of the "growing" that the proponents of this approach have brought upon us in the past, and are determined to bring upon us in the future, were the *elimination* of restrictions upon democratic government. But just the opposite is true. Historically, and particu-

*Mr. Scalia is a Justice of the U.S. Supreme Court.*

larly in the past 35 years, the "evolving" Constitution has imposed a vast array of new constraints—new inflexibilities— upon administrative, judicial, and legislative action. To mention only a few things that formerly could be done or not done, as the society desired, but now cannot be done:

— admitting in a state criminal trial evidence of guilt that was obtained by an unlawful search;

— permitting invocation of God at public-school graduations;

— electing one of the two houses of a state legislature the way the United States Senate is elected, i.e., on a basis that does not give all voters numerically equal representation;

— terminating welfare payments as soon as evidence of fraud is received,

subject to restoration after hearing if the evidence is satisfactorily refuted;

— imposing property requirements as a condition of voting;

— prohibiting anonymous campaign literature;

— prohibiting pornography.

And the future agenda of constitutional evolutionists is mostly more of the same—the creation of new restrictions upon democratic government, rather than the elimination of old ones. *Less* flexibility in government, not *more*. As things now stand, the federal and state governments may either apply capital punishment or abolish it, permit suicide or forbid it—all as the changing times and the changing sentiments of society may demand. But when capital punishment is held to violate the Eighth

From *National Review*, February 10, 1997, pp. 32-35. Excerpted from *A Matter of Interpretation: Federal Courts and the Law* by Antonin Scalia. © 1997 by Princeton University Press. Reprinted by permission.

Amendment, and suicide is held to be protected by the Fourteenth Amendment, all flexibility with regard to those matters will be gone. No, the reality of the matter is that, generally speaking, devotees of The Living Constitution seek not to facilitate social change but to *prevent* it.

There are, I must admit, a few exceptions to that rule—a few instances in which, historically, greater flexibility *has* been the result of the process. But those exceptions serve only to refute another argument of the proponents of an evolving Constitution: that evolution will always be in the direction of greater personal liberty. They consider that a great advantage, for reasons that I do not entirely understand. All government represents a balance between individual freedom and social order, and it is not true that every alteration of that balance in the direction of greater individual freedom is necessarily good. But in any case, the record of history refutes the proposition that the evolving Constitution will invariably enlarge individual rights. The most obvious refutation is the modern Court's limitation of the constitutional protections afforded to property. The provision prohibiting impairment of the obligation of contracts, for example, has been gutted. I am sure that We the People agree with that development; we value property rights less than did the Founders. So also, we value the right to bear arms less than did the Founders (who thought the right of self-defense to be absolutely fundamental), and there will be few tears shed if and when the Second Amendment is held to guarantee nothing more than the state National Guard. But this just shows that the Founders were right when they feared that some (in their view misguided) future generation might wish to abandon liberties that they considered essential, and so sought to protect those liberties in a Bill of Rights. We may *like* the abridgment of property rights and *like* the elimination of the right to bear arms; but let us not pretend that these are not *reductions* of rights.

My pointing out that the American people may be satisfied with a reduction of their liberties should not be taken as a suggestion that the proponents of The Living Constitution *follow* the desires of the American people in determining how the Constitution should evolve. They follow nothing so precise; indeed, as a group they follow nothing at all.

Perhaps the most glaring defect of Living Constitutionalism, next to its incompatibility with the whole anti-evolutionary purpose of a constitution, is that there is no agreement, and no chance of agreement, upon what is to be the guiding principle of the evolution. *Panta rhei* is not a sufficiently informative principle of constitutional interpretation. What is it that the judge must consult to determine when, and in what direction, evolution has occurred? Is it the will of the majority, discerned from newspapers, radio talk shows, public-opinion polls, and chats at the country club? Is it the philosophy of Hume, or of John Rawls, or of John Stuart Mill, or of Aristotle? As soon as the discussion goes beyond whether the Constitution is static, the evolutionists divide into as many camps as there are individual views of the good, the true, and the beautiful. I think that is inevitably so, which means that evolutionism is simply not a practicable constitutional philosophy.

I DO not suggest, mind you, that originalists always agree upon their answer. There is plenty of room for disagreement as to what the original meaning was, and even more as to how that original meaning applies to the situation before the Court. But the originalist at least knows what he is looking for: the original meaning of the text. Often—indeed, I dare say usually—that is easy to discern and simple to apply. Sometimes (though not very often) there will be disagreement
regarding the original meaning; and sometimes there will be disagreement as to how that original meaning applies to new and unforeseen phenomena. How, for example, does the First Amendment guarantee of "the freedom of speech" apply to new technologies that did not exist when the guarantee was created— to sound trucks, or to government-licensed over-the-air television? In such new fields the Court must follow the trajectory of the First Amendment, so to speak, to determine what it requires— and assuredly that enterprise is not entirely cut-and-dried but requires the exercise of judgment.

But the difficulties and uncertainties of determining original meaning and applying it to modern circumstances are negligible compared with the difficulties and uncertainties of the philosophy which says that the Constitution *changes;*

that the very act which it once prohibited it now permits, and which it once permitted it now prohibits; and that the key to that change is unknown and unknowable. The originalist, if he does not have all the answers, has many of them. For the evolutionist, on the other hand, every question is an open question, every day a new day. No fewer than three of the Justices with whom I have served (Justices Brennan, Marshall, and Blackmun) have maintained that the death penalty is unconstitutional, *even though its use is explicitly contemplated in the Constitution.* The Due Process Clause of the Fifth and Fourteenth Amendments says that no person shall be deprived of life without due process of law; and the Grand Jury Clause of the Fifth Amendment says that no person shall be held to answer for a capital crime without grand-jury indictment. No matter. Under The Living Constitution the death penalty may have *become* unconstitutional. And it is up to each Justice to decide for himself (under no standard I can discern) when that occurs.

In the last analysis, however, it probably does not matter what principle, among the innumerable possibilities, the evolutionist proposes to use in order to determine in what direction The Living Constitution will grow. Whatever he might propose, at the end of the day an evolving constitution will evolve the way the majority wishes. The people will be willing to leave interpretation of the Constitution to lawyers so long as the people believe that it is (like the interpretation of a statute) essentially lawyers' work—requiring a close examination of text, history of the text, traditional understanding of the text, judicial precedent, and so forth. But if the people come to believe that the Constitution is not a text like other texts; that it means, not what it says or what it was understood to mean, but what it should mean, in the light of the "evolving standards of decency that mark the progress of a maturing society"—well, then, they will look for qualifications other than impartiality, judgment, and lawyerly acumen in those whom they select to interpret it. More specifically, they will look for judges who agree with them as to what the evolving standards have evolved to; who agree with them as to what the Constitution ought to be.

It seems to me that that is where we are heading, or perhaps even where we have arrived. Seventy-five years ago, we

# Court Jesters

THE men who wrote the U.S. Constitution dreaded an imperial President, and they feared an unrestrained Congress. Either could destroy the new democratic Republic. So they established an ingenious system of checks and balances to prevent either branch from encroaching too far on the prerogatives of the other. But the Founders considered the judiciary to be inherently the weakest branch of government. They never contemplated what has happened—a willful judiciary that is fencing voters and their elected representatives out of the decision-making process.

Abuse of power by the Supreme Court has long been a serious concern. But the stakes are magnified by the re-election of President Bill Clinton. Mr. Clinton is likely to have the opportunity to nominate one or more members of the High Court. Presumably, he will be inclined to appoint activist Justices whose presence on the Court would aggravate an already untenable situation.

Fortunately, however, members of the U.S. Senate still can prevent our worst fears from being realized. Senators have the right to deny confirmation of activist nominees to the Supreme Court and, for that matter, other courts. Senators should decide that, henceforth, judicial nominees will be required to pledge publicly that they will interpret the Constitution and statutes in accordance with the original intent of the documents and their authors. As the High Court veers further and further from the text and intention of the Constitution, it seems clear that such a promise should be a precondition to confirmation of judicial appointees.

Most Americans paid little attention when Supreme Court Justices first began to substitute their own values for the express provisions of the Constitution. After all, Justices continued to support their decisions by references to the written law even while subverting it. Lately, however, even the pretense that the Court is abiding by the words of the Constitution has worn thin.

"The most important moral, political, and cultural decisions are steadily being removed from democratic control," Judge Robert Bork points out. "A majority of the court routinely enacts its own preference as the command" of the Constitution.

Professor Russell Hittinger terms the situation a "crisis of legitimacy," while Charles W. Colson regards recent trends as the "systematic usurpation of ultimate political power by the American judiciary." Justice Scalia, never one to mince

*Mr. Armstrong, a Colorado businessman, was a U.S. senator from 1979 to 1991.*

words, is even more direct: "day by day, case by case, [the Court] is busy designing a Constitution for a country I do not recognize."

Some will be dismayed by such characterizations. But what else can be said when the Court changes laws from what was intended and written by the authors? Citizens can appeal directly to their elected representatives in state legislatures and Congress; they can request changes in existing laws; if frustrated by elected officials they can seek to replace them next election day. In a democratic society, this is the way the people govern, the way old laws are updated or repealed and new laws enacted.

But when Justices—an unelected elite—arbitrarily substitute their own preferences for the preferences of those who are elected to make laws, they are, in effect, repealing or modifying existing laws or inventing new ones. They become, in George Will's memorable phrase, "our robed masters."

Instinctively most of us shrink from thinking this could be true. But innumerable Supreme Court decisions support Professor Hittinger's contention that "we live today under an altered constitutional regime, where the rules are no longer supplied by a written document but by federal courts defining the powers of government ad hoc."

The Founding Fathers considered it dangerous to leave each state with complete power to regulate commerce. The nation could not long endure if states could discriminate against one another by erecting tariff barriers. Therefore Article I of the Constitution gives to Congress "the power to regulate commerce . . . among the several states." The Constitution could have been written to grant Congress complete power to control all commerce including that which affects only one state or the people within a single state. The Founders decided not to write it that way.

However, the Supreme Court consistently ignores the intent of the Constitution in this area. In the strange case of *Wickard* v. *Filburn,* the Court upheld federal limits on production of wheat even though the crop was never sold in interstate commerce. In fact, the wheat in question was never sold at all. It was consumed at home by the grower. The Court upheld the conviction of Mr. Filburn for violating the limits. In doing so, a majority of the Justices established the bizarre principle that by planting and harvesting wheat on his own property for home consumption, a farmer could substantially affect interstate commerce. With such a precedent that is hard to imagine any form of commerce—for that matter, any

believed firmly enough in a rock-solid, unchanging Constitution that we felt it necessary to adopt the Nineteenth Amendment to give women the vote. The battle was not fought in the courts, and few thought that it could be, despite the constitutional guarantee of Equal Protection of the Laws; that provision

did not, when it was adopted, and hence did not in 1920, guarantee equal access to the ballot but permitted distinctions on the basis not only of age but also of property and of sex. Who can doubt that if the issue had been deferred until today, the Constitution would be (formally) unamended, and the courts

would be the chosen instrumentality of change? The American people have been converted to belief in The Living Constitution, a "morphing" document that means, from age to age, what it ought to mean. And with that conversion has inevitably come the new phenomenon of selecting and confirming federal

human activity—which might not be deemed to "affect" interstate commerce and therefore be subject to federal regulation. Constitutional limitations on the scope of the national government have been effectively repealed by the Court.

When Congress passed the Civil Rights Act of 1964, it was plainly never intended that that Act would require racial quotas in business, education, etc. The law does not provide for such quotas. Indeed, Senator Hubert Humphrey and other backers of the legislation vehemently denied that such an outcome was possible. But within a few years the courts had implemented precisely the quota regime sponsors said could never result.

From their own experience, the Framers of the Constitution feared the establishing of an official religion for Americans. So they drafted a very simple and clear prohibition on the power of Congress to do so. But in *Everson* v. *Board of Education, McCollum* v. *Board of Education, Engle* v. *Vitale,* and many other cases, the Court has tortured the First Amendment to produce judicial outcomes which the amendment's authors would have found inconceivable. So prayers and Bibles are banned from public schools; displays of religious symbols are forbidden; postal workers are prohibited from wishing one another "Merry Christmas"; and schoolchildren are taught that the Pilgrims instituted the first Thanksgiving Day because they wished to commemorate their gratitude to . . . the Indians!

In *Romer* v. *Evans,* the Court struck down a provision of the Colorado Constitution which prohibited Colorado cities from adopting civil-rights ordinances predicated on sexual preference. In a ruling one scholar termed "indecipherable," not only did the Court overrule the people of the state, who had adopted the provision in 1992, the Justices also totally ignored their own ruling in the 1986 case of *Bowers* v. *Hardwick. Bowers* affirmed that the state of Georgia had the constitutional right to provide criminal penalties for homosexual conduct. But *Romer* says the state may not deny special rights to those who engage in the very behavior it is permitted to criminalize.

Some applaud these cases. Among our fellow citizens are some who believe the national government should have unlimited power to regulate commerce, that racial quotas are a good idea and school prayers are not. But the main point is not whether one is pleased or distressed by the outcome of specific cases. What is worrisome is the process by which Justices are hijacking our democratic system of government.

We can well recall with apprehension the boast of Chief Justice Charles Evans Hughes that "the Constitution is what judges say it is."

Before the situation gets any worse, senators should put the White House on notice that no judicial nominee—especially for the Supreme Court—will win confirmation unless the nominee will publicly promise to judge cases in accordance with the meaning intended by the authors of the Constitution and of the various statutes. Such notification will, of course, provoke howls of outrage. The Administration, the American Bar Association, and apologists for the welfare state will be apoplectic. Some TV and newspaper pundits—fortunately not all—will decry any effort to strengthen the Senate's traditional "advice and consent" role in this way.

Insistence on an "original intent" pledge could also delay filling vacancies on various courts. The White House will strongly resist such efforts, and the resulting tensions may make it more difficult for Congress and the President to cooperate on balancing the budget, reforming entitlement programs, etc. If senators were forced to filibuster the confirmation of recalcitrant nominees, it could put a crimp in the whole legislative schedule.

Most senators aren't likely to have the stomach for such a fight. But those who do may prevail. The public is exceedingly cynical about our judicial system. If the issue is properly framed—as a showdown between democracy and elitism—it is very possible the nation will enthusiastically support efforts to curb the abuse of power by "our robed masters." If the public gets behind the idea, then, sooner or later, a majority of senators will also. In the meantime, merely raising the issue will have a beneficial effect on the thought life of nominees and sitting judges.

Cynics may wonder if judicial nominees can be counted on to keep their word if they make an original-intent promise. If they do not, then their faithlessness will merely encourage more drastic reforms.

And what if the effort to extract such promises from nominees should initially fail? In that case, the nation nonetheless will owe a debt of gratitude to any senators who raise the issue. By bringing up this fundamental question, senators can give the whole country an opportunity to participate in the decision. Ultimately, the people are supposed to decide such issues. But they can do so only if the question is put squarely before them.

—WILLIAM L. ARMSTRONG

judges, at all levels, on the basis of their views regarding a whole series of proposals for constitutional evolution. If the courts are free to write the Constitution anew, they will write it the way the majority wants; the appointment and confirmation process will see to that. This, of course, is the end of the Bill of Rights, whose meaning will be committed to the very body it was meant to protect against: the majority. By trying to make the Constitution do everything that needs doing from age to age, we shall have caused it to do nothing at all.

# Breaking Thurgood Marshall's Promise

With the court decision striking down affirmative action at the University of Texas Law School, one man's lifelong belief in racial progress has been dealt another blow.

**By A. Leon Higginbotham Jr.**

OUT OF 268 FIRST-YEAR STUDENTS ENROLLED AT THE LAW school of the University of California at Berkeley, only 1 is African-American. Out of 468 at the University of Texas School of Law, only 4 are. Embedded in these cold acts is a personal story, of how 47 years ago I witnessed the birth of racial justice in the Supreme Court and how now, after 45 years as a lawyer, judge and law professor, I sometimes feel as if I am watching justice die.

In 1946, when Heman Marion Sweatt, an African-American, was denied admission to the University of Texas School of Law, the state set up a makeshift, unaccredited "law school for Negroes." In 1950, toward the end of my first year at Yale Law School, I watched Thurgood Marshall argue Heman Sweatt's case before the Supreme Court. With controlled outrage, Marshall eloquently asserted the constitutional promise of equality for Sweatt, for all African-Americans and, it seemed, for me personally.

In a unanimous opinion, the Supreme Court held that Sweatt had to be admitted to the whites-only school, but

*A. Leon Higginbotham Jr. is a retired chief judge emeritus of the United States Court of Appeals, the Public Service Professor of Jurisprudence at the John F. Kennedy School of Government at Harvard and the author of "Shades of Freedom."*

as a Federal judge later noted, he eventually dropped out "after being subjected to racial slurs from students and professors, cross burnings and tire slashings." Indeed, there were some years between 1950 and 1971 when the school's entering classes did not have a single African-American. Throughout the 1960's, Latino students were officially excluded from university organizations. African-Americans were forbidden to live in or even visit white resident halls. As recently as 1980, the U.S. Department of Health, Education and Welfare concluded that Texas's higher-education system remained segregated, in violation of the 1964 Civil Rights Act.

Gradually this situation began to improve. From the 1970's to 1992, the law school adopted various affirmative-action programs for minority students who could compete successfully. Ultimately, about 10 percent of each entering class tended to be Mexican-American and 5 percent African-American. And from the 1970's on, the school produced nearly 2,000 minority lawyers. Many of these alumni assumed leadership positions, among them Ron Kirk, the Mayor of Dallas, and Frederico Peña, the Secretary of Energy.

Now, with only four African-Americans in the first-year class, these painstakingly won gains are at great risk. This startling reversal arises entirely from decisions by some Federal judges—appointed by Presidents Reagan and

From *The New York Times Magazine*, January 18, 1998, pp. 28-29. © 1998 by The New York Times Company. Reprinted by permission.

Bush—who seem utterly indifferent to the dangers of turning back the clock of racial progress.

No case better demonstrates these judges' callousness than that of Hopwood v. Texas. Cheryl Hopwood, a white woman, along with three white men, claimed that the University of Texas School of Law's affirmative-action program violated the equal-protection clause of the 14th Amendment. The plaintiffs, who had been rejected for admission, alleged that they had a higher grade-point average and test scores than 93 African-American and Mexican-American students who had been admitted.

In 1996, a three-judge panel of the U.S. Court of Appeals for the Fifth Circuit reversed a district court judge and held that the law school could "not use race as a factor in deciding which applicants to admit." Two judges concluded that considering race or ethnicity in admissions would always be unconstitutional—even if it was intended "to combat the perceived effects of a hostile environment," to remedy past discrimination or to promote diversity. The third judge disagreed that diversity could never be a compelling government interest but reasoned that "the admissions process here under scrutiny was not narrowly tailored to achieve diversity." These judges' views are in stark contrast to those of many American educators, among them Nannerl Keohane, the president of Duke University, who testified that "my experience as a teacher at three institutions of higher education and as the president of two others is that diversity benefits students, faculty, institutions and the world of knowledge."

In adopting such drastic reasoning, these three judges—all Reagan or Bush appointees—ignored the history and evidence of discrimination against minorities at the law school, and they ignored some facts of the case—most glaringly, that Hopwood's test scores were higher than those of more than 100 *white* students who were admitted. They also ignored settled precedent. Starting in 1978 with Bakke v. Regents of the University of California, the Supreme Court has consistently maintained that student diversity, when properly devised, is a valid justification for race-based affirmative action.

The state of Texas appealed the panel's majority opinion in Hopwood, requesting a rehearing before all of its 16 active judges. The request was denied. All nine of the judges who either voted against the rehearing or declined to vote were appointed by President Reagan or President Bush; six of the seven dissenting judges were appointed by President Carter or President Clinton.

The dissenters wrote that the majority's opinion "goes out of its way to break ground that the Supreme Court itself has been careful to avoid and purports to overrule a Supreme Court decision." They added that "the radical implications of this opinion . . . will literally change the face of public educational institutions throughout Texas, the other states of this circuit and this nation."

THE MAJORITY OPINION IN HOPWOOD STANDS IN SHARP CONTRAST TO the role that the Fifth Circuit has played in the civil rights era. In the 1950's and 60's, many southern officials, white citizens' councils and vigilante groups urged total defiance of the Federal courts' civil rights decrees. Despite the persistent hostility, virtually every Fifth Circuit judge—all appointed by President Eisenhower—repeatedly affirmed the constitutional rights of black citizens, among them Rosa Parks and Martin Luther King Jr.

When Reagan took office, he pledged to bring a "new breed of conservatism" to the judiciary. Under his and President Bush's Administrations, the judiciary became not only far more conservative but also far more white than it had been. Of 83 appointments to the appeals courts, Reagan appointed only one African-American. Bush appointed two, and one of those was Clarence Thomas. (Carter appointed nine African-Americans, and Clinton has appointed five.)

In 1983, during his less conservative days, Clarence Thomas said, "But for affirmative action laws, God only knows where I would be today." Now that he is on the Supreme Court, he repudiates affirmative action and has made it safe for people like Prof. Lino A. Graglia, of the University of Texas School of Law, to assert openly that "blacks and Mexican-Americans are not academically competitive with whites in selective institutions" because "they have a culture that seems not to encourage achievement. Failure is not looked upon with disgrace." Thomas's skewed and hostile views have also paved the way for the ascent of anti-affirmative-action crusaders like Ward Connerly, a driving force behind California's Proposition 209, the philosophy of which seems to be that anything expressly benefiting African-Americas, no matter how benign, useful or good, is inherently suspect and wrong.

Certainly, it is appropriate for a President to consider what he views as the mandate of the voters who elected him and to nominate those who seem to share his judicial philosophy. Still, it's impossible to ignore the tragic impact of the Reagan and Bush appointments.

In a 1989 employment-discrimination case, Justice Harry Blackmun, a Nixon appointee, wondered whether a majority of the Supreme Court "still believes that . . . race discrimination against nonwhites is a problem in our society, or even remembers that it ever was." This question reverberates today in the chilling legacy of the Hopwood decision. Hopwood has already had a pervasive impact on decreasing minority enrollment in many higher-education institutions. The number of medical-school applications from underrepresented minorities has dropped by 11 percent nationally and 17 percent among students who live in Texas, Louisiana and Mississippi, where the Fifth Circuit now has jurisdiction. The group that represented the plaintiffs in the Texas case recently filed suit to have the affirmative-action program for undergraduates at the University of Michigan declared unconstitutional.

IN DECEMBER 1996, A FEW MONTHS AFTER HOPWOOD WAS DECIDED, I underwent the first of three open-heart surgeries. Late each evening, after my family and friends had left, I would slip in and out of consciousness and dream of a sign that I saw long ago on the bumper of a rickety cab in Lagos, Nigeria. The sign said, in big, bold letters: NO MORE TIME FOR FOOLISHNESS. The long winter ended, the spring rains came and I got better. But still that sign haunted my dreams. As I returned to the work to which I had dedicated my career, I began to understand— slowly and then clearly—the meaning that sign held for me.

At times, this country seems intent on returning to the foolishness of the past. Donald M. Stewart, president of the College Board, has said that in the wake of court decisions like Hopwood, "we're looking at a potential wipeout that could take away an entire generation" of black and Hispanic students. When I think about this potential wipeout, I wonder whether I am still in intensive care, drifting on anesthesia. I ponder: is it a hallucination that in public law schools in California and Texas, the two most populous states in the country, minority enrollment is shrinking almost to the vanishing point? Is the lone black first-year student at Berkeley representative of a dying breed, a tragic echo of James Meredith, who desegregated the University of Mississippi in 1962? How will Texas and California, which are more than a third African-American and Latino, survive with the future shortage of trained minority leadership?

There is a curve of time that separates Heman Sweatt and Cheryl Hopwood. It has been a long while since that spring afternoon in 1950 when, as a first-year Yale law student, I heard the promise of freedom in the voice of Thurgood Marshall. Since then, I have observed commendable progress, lately some tragic retrogression, and now I see even more clearly that, in the long, bloody history of race relations in America, there is no more time for foolishness.

# More Than Sex

## WHY THE COURTS ARE MISSING THE POINT
## An Interview with Vicki Schultz

### By Ellen Yaroshefsky

**W**ith each new case, sexual harassment law changes and expands. But new judgments also close off alternative ways of seeing things. Vicki Schultz, a professor at Yale Law School in New Haven, Connecticut, argues that currently courts recognize incidents of harassment where there is clearly a sexual component, while often ignoring harassment that is not sexual, but that prevents women from doing their jobs. *Ms.* asked Ellen Yaroshefsky, a lawyer who has argued several sexual harassment cases, including a highly publicized (and successful) case involving the United Nations, to talk to Schultz about her work.

**Ellen Yaroshefsky:** We're here to talk about reconceptualizing sexual harassment. But first, tell us how you got started in this field.

**Vicki Schultz:** I was a young assistant professor at the University of Wisconsin, and I met another assistant professor, in the electrical engineering department. She was the only woman in the entire college of engineering. She was a star, she had a Ph.D. from MIT, she had loads of offers when she first went on the market. She ended up coming to Wisconsin because someone there expressed an interest in mentoring her. But this man began to feel threatened by her. A lot of subtle things began happening to my friend, which culminated when she brought her team of graduate students to the lab one day and, lo and behold, the locks had been changed. This was a woman who ultimately brought millions of dollars in grants into the university and had teams of graduate students. It was an outrage that someone would treat the laboratory—partly paid for by the state—as their personal plaything and try to prevent her from doing what it takes to satisfy tenure requirements.

So I thought, this has got to be a problem legally. I found myself asking her questions like, "Did anyone ever leer at you?" "Did anyone ever touch you?" "Did anyone ever make a sexual advance?" She kept saying, "No, that's not what it's about." And so this started me thinking that we need to have a broad conception of the hostile work environment that can take into account things we know to be based on gender, but which really don't bear much relationship to sexuality, or the sex act.

**E.Y.:** It's interesting that your first instinct was to think of it in terms of sexualized behavior, rather than "Does this constitute a hostile work environment?" Because it could have been brought under that, right?

**V.S.:** When courts are looking at the evidence for a hostile work environment case, they tend to want to see sexual advances or other offensive, sexually explicit conduct. If you don't have that, it's very difficult to convince them.

**E.Y.:** I take it that you think that there's something the matter with the way sexual harassment is currently conceptualized.

**V.S.:** There are two kinds of harassment that the courts have recognized. The first, quid pro quo, forbids a supervisor from telling a subordinate she must have sex with him or else suffer adverse consequences on the job.

The other is hostile work environment, where supervisors or coworkers do things that make the work atmosphere more difficult for people based on their gender. Hostile work environment harassment really isn't about sexual exploitation. It's about exclusion—one group trying to make the work atmosphere more difficult for another because they'd really rather not have them around. Or they want to be able to categorize them as inferiors. Sometimes it is sex, but sometimes it's other things that are used to make women look less serious, less capable, different, and out of place on the job.

Over time, quid pro quo—"put out or get out"—has come to be the popular image of harassment. It has overshadowed hostile work environment harassment. We've become obsessively concerned with sexual advances and sexual conduct, and this has had negative consequences for the development of sexual harassment law.

**E.Y.:** But the law allowed a person to sue for either unwanted sexual advances or unwelcome conduct that affected their employment. So why did the courts look primarily to the sexual component?

**V.S.:** The Equal Employment Opportunity Commission guidelines, issued in 1980, focused on unwelcome sexual advances or other conduct of a sexual nature. While the EEOC didn't

From *Ms.*, May/June 1998, pp. 56–61. © 1998 by Ms. Magazine. Reprinted by permission.

say that nonsexual kinds of conduct could not be harassment, many courts blindly or unthinkingly said yes, it has to be sexual conduct to count as a hostile work environment. That's one answer.

**E.Y.:** I think many women and men who have litigated these cases consider those EEOC guidelines a detriment; they sometimes prevent us from being able to go beyond the sexual nature question.

**V.S.:** You're right. The second answer as to why the courts focused on sexual behavior is that the reasoning they adopted in quid pro quo cases spread beyond that context and began to permeate hostile work environment law as well. Essentially we were losing the early quid pro quo cases because the courts said, "Wait a minute! She wasn't fired because she was a woman. She was fired because she refused to have sexual relations with her supervisor."

So feminist advocates and sympathetic lawyers adopted an argument that went something like this: O.K., if a heterosexual, male supervisor makes a sexual advance toward his female subordinate, it is because of a sexual attraction for that woman which he, as a heterosexual, would not experience for a male subordinate. That argument grounds the notion of sex discrimination in sexual desire. Even though I think that was not the intent of the litigators, it really has created a way of looking at the problem that means the courts do not believe all the nonsexual problems that women experience fit within the law.

**E.Y.:** Many litigators understand that sexual harassment is not about attraction, it's about power. Are the courts just deluded, that they don't know that?

**V.S.:** I think the problem is implicit in the reasoning of some of the cases. When the reasoning is that a heterosexual male would not make this demand upon a man, the link to sexual attraction *is* there. I think it is a power issue, but we haven't adequately specified what we mean by that. Yes, lots of things are about power. But the courts need a theory of what kind of power and how is it related and why is that within the scope of Title VII? I'm trying to lay out a theory of how it is about preserving the masculine image of the job and the men who do it.

**E.Y.:** Title VII, the sex discrimination law, was on the books in the sixties. Didn't it cover these nonsexual kinds of cases?

**V.S.:** I don't think there was anything the matter with the law. But, at the time, there had been virtually no integration of the workforce. Women were almost completely stuck in women's jobs. Men were on top and women on bottom, in a job sense. Today women are spread throughout the workforce, but, in many jobs and work settings that used to be claimed exclusively by men, they're in tiny numbers. So we need new ways to think about the actions that are likely to be experienced by women as we invade this new turf. I call a lot of this "competence-undermining harassment."

I have been amazed, in reading the case law, at how often work sabotage is used against women. In *Lipsett* v. *University of Puerto Rico,* a female surgical resident was subjected to a horrible campaign of harassment. Her male colleagues actually falsified a medical report to make it look like she had made a mistake, to make her look stupid. From a public health per-

spective, this is frightening. You would not want to be the patient who had your report falsified in order to serve these men's egos. Most of the time the sabotage or physical attacks are intended to make the woman look like she's done a terrible job so that she'll be fired.

**E.Y.:** Are you saying that the current law isn't adequate to give women remedies for these kinds of actions?

**V.S.:** Absolutely. I've read hundreds of cases. Look at *Reynolds* v. *Atlantic City Convention Center.* Margaret Reynolds was an electrician who was made a subforeman on a project at the convention center, and the men under her rebelled. They did a lot of things that were very humiliating for her. None of it consisted of sexual advances, but there were a few gestures that the court was willing to call sexual: one of them gave her the finger, and another shook his crotch at her. What happened in the court was very typical. The court said, "First of all, let's look at her hostile work environment claim. The conduct has to be sexual; gee, there are only two incidents."

Margaret Reynolds was fired, but a year before, when the foreman had first proposed making her subforeman, the union business agent had said, "Now is not the time, nor will there ever be a time for a woman subforeman." But the court said, no, that wasn't based on gender, and all the nonsexual forms of harassment completely escaped legal scrutiny. All of the most disturbing things that happened to Margaret Reynolds from her point of view completely fell between the cracks, and this happens in case after case after case.

**E.Y.:** But weren't the courts wrong?

**V.S.:** Well, if they were wrong, I can tell you that hundreds of others have been wrong in this way. The law is not what's written down; it's what the courts are actually doing.

**E.Y.:** When Title VII was created, there was nothing in there that suggested that behavior had to be sexual. Are you saying that a law was passed that seemed like it was going to cover these competence-undermining situations, but then the EEOC created guidelines that limited actions to sexual conduct and that's what the courts proceeded to define as a hostile work environment?

**V.S.:** We also have to look outside the legal system to understand how the law became sexualized. The media coverage of cases like Hill-Thomas have solidified for judges the notion that what this is really all about is sexual abuse. Not that that's not a serious problem, but there are equally serious problems that aren't very sexy and that get no coverage.

Think about Shannon Faulkner [the first woman to enroll at The Citadel Military College of South Carolina]: if you only watched television you would come away thinking, "Oh, how terrible for the women's movement, Shannon just couldn't hack it. They should have put up somebody better than that." I didn't hear a lot of talk on TV of how it was a setup, that you could predict it was going to be a hostile education environment or competence-undermining harassment, yet it would have been a great story.

**E.Y.:** The media are always going to cover the "sexiest" piece of any case, but we should expect judges and lawyers to look beyond what the media are covering. Didn't some judges look at the cases and say, "this isn't just about sexual behavior. It is about work sabotage or physical assault"?

**V.S.:** Yes, and I think we should give them credit. But I also think the statement you just made expresses a litigator's optimistic notion that the law is an autonomous realm. You're saying we should expect judges not to be influenced by what happens in the media.

**E.Y.:** I mean the media should not define the law for judges. You're suggesting that because the media have portrayed all these cases as sexual that judges don't see the cases before them in other ways.

**V.S.:** Judges exist in cultural context like anyone else. We need to do a lot more education to create a cultural context in which courts and other policymakers understand that sexuality is not the only arena in which harassment occurs. I think that many of the judges whose decisions I criticize were probably acting in good faith, trying as hard as they could to apply the law.

**E.Y.:** Is it also fair to say that lawyers were too focused on what seemed the most obvious, sexualized behavior, and didn't go beyond that?

**V.S:** I don't know the answer to that because I was never a lawyer in private practice. I can tell you that I'm sometimes stunned when I give talks to groups of lawyers who say, "I'm going to win if I can show sexual advances." Indeed, that was me speaking to my friend saying, "Did he ever leer at you?" trying to create a winning case.

**E.Y.:** So let me understand this: the current state of the law says there is a remedy for competence-undermining behavior, but you're saying it's spotty because some circuits are only looking for sexualized conduct?

**V.S.:** Some circuits have a flat-out ban on looking at nonsexual conduct. Others say that nonsexual forms of harassment will be scrutinized, but when you look at how district courts within that circuit actually apply this, they single out sexual advances as being the most significant forms of harassment, so that it's very hard to win if you don't have them.

**E.Y.:** Is your proposal that we have a new law or just a new interpretation?

**V.S.:** I think there are a lot of things we need to do. They could be done without amending Title VII. I propose a few modest changes in the law.

First of all, judges should not separate sexual from nonsexual forms of conduct. They should look at everything all together. There is support for doing that within the law. There are cases to draw on to give judges some tools so they can have a full and complete picture of the workplace.

Second, where the alleged harassment occurs in a traditionally segregated job setting, judges should presume that the conduct was based on gender.

Say you are the first female electrician or architect, and the men begin to do things like put rats in your lunch box, or put lime in your uniform so when you put it on your skin is burned, or hang a dead animal with a noose over your work station. These kinds of things—including some that are not this blatant—are absolutely predictable when women go into traditionally segregated work settings. The law should presume that, in the absence of the company being able to show proof

to the contrary, the acts are occurring because the person is a woman. This is a very simple little proposal, but I think it would have an enormous effect on lawyers' ability to win some of the cases.

Third, once we move away from a sexual-desire paradigm, we can see how harassment is not just a male/female thing, but also something that occurs between men. Men can be threatened by men who are perceived to be gay, and men who aren't married, and men who align themselves with the interests of women, and men who just are perceived to be "wimps."

Title VII already covers gender stereotyping of this sort, or should do so, based on the Supreme Court's decision in *Price Waterhouse* v. *Hopkins.* In that case, Ann Hopkins was extremely successful in the Washington, D.C., office of the national accounting firm. When she was up for partner, some of the partners told her that in order to be considered more favorably she needed to walk more femininely, talk more femininely, wear makeup, present herself with a more feminine demeanor. She was considered too abrasive. The court held that a firm cannot require someone to meet its image of appropriate gender-based behavior in order to be considered for a job. It's a very simple holding when you reduce it to that core element. And Title VII has been held to apply to men as well as women, so there is no reason why that case should not stand in cases where an employer allows supervisors and coworkers to harass someone because they want him to conform to their notion of manhood. That is also gender stereotyping and gender-based harassment.

Of course, very few courts have recognized it to be so, but I predict that the Supreme Court will in the *Oncale* case, which is pending before it. They will reverse the Fifth Circuit, which held that male-on-male harassment can never be actionable. [Editors' note: Schultz was right. Soon after this interview, in *Oncale* v. *Sundowner Offshore Services, Inc.,* the Supreme Court ruled that same-sex harassment is illegal.] The court will probably want to say as little as possible about the circumstances in which it might be actionable. [Schultz was right again.]

## Courts single out sexual advances as the most significant forms of harassment, so it's hard to win if you don't have them.

**E.Y.:** So you think the law will be that gender stereotyping of lesbians and gays is prohibited under Title VII?

**V.S.:** I would say the law will refer to stereotyping so-called gender-deviant men and women, who may or may not be gay or lesbian. Title VII does not prohibit discrimination based on sexual orientation, so we need an amendment to Title VII to cover sexual orientation as an express category. It is treating lesbians and gays as second-class citizens not to give them the protection against discrimination that we give everyone else in our society.

**E.Y.:** Do you anticipate other changes in the law?

**V.S.:** I think that lawyers could try to think more broadly about the way they bring cases. That would be as transformative, if not more so, than actually changing the law. We need to have large-scale challenges to sex discrimination that occurs throughout a company, from hiring, to assignment, to the way evaluations are done, to the way promotions are granted, to

the way training is given. And we also need to talk about how those kinds of structures create environments in which we can predict that hostility will occur.

It's very expensive and very difficult to bring these cases. I'm hopeful that there will be more cases because of the 1991 Civil Rights Act, which provides jury trials and the right to punitive damages in Title VII cases for the first time. I hope there will be some financial incentive for lawyers to bring the big class action suits. And to go after companies that are thoroughly segregated from top to bottom.

One way to handle this is to say it's not enough to have 5 percent women in a job, it's not enough to have 10 percent. You need to have 50 percent women in this job. You have to go after the structural pattern of segregation as a cause of the hostile work environment.

I don't think any of this requires a change in Title VII, but I'd love to see the EEOC guidelines amended. There could be one sentence to make clear that conduct need not be sexual in nature, and that it can take other forms, including, for example, conduct having the purpose or effect of undermining competence based on gender. Simple addition.

**E.Y.:** When we thought about these things years ago, they seemed relatively simple. But women always face a backlash. Women get blamed, no matter what. Are you concerned that we might hit the next level of blaming the victim if we now start talking about a competence-based evaluation?

**V.S.:** Well, I think you're right, but it's not just that women always get blamed, although we do. It's that somehow ideas that were radically transformative at the time become frozen in the law. We cannot cling stubbornly to ideas that worked well at the time. We always have to try to stay a step ahead and come up with new thoughts.

**E.Y.:** Well said. My fear, though, is that once we start talking about competence-based issues, I can see the other side spending an incredible amount of time in a trial undermining a woman's competence.

**V.S.:** That's already happening. But there are district courts that have held that where harassment has occurred and a person is fired, an employer cannot win just by showing that the person was incompetent. The question is whether the harassment or discrimination itself undermined the person's competence. I also think we need to curb the amount of authority and discretion that supervisors have over their subordinates.

**E.Y.:** But that's a much larger problem of the workforce.

**V.S.:** Yes! But that's the problem to focus on. If we focus on the narrow approach of getting rid of the supervisor, it's too easy for companies. Let's force them to do the harder thing, which is to think about how authority and power and money, and all those things, are distributed. It's not impossible to do. It was a major thrust of the civil rights movement. People went after the fact that foremen had unlimited discretion to hire, fire, control, punish. And that was challenged as a form of subjective decision-making that allowed room for racial bias. So let's think about the structural context in which abuses occur, rather than, or in addition to, focusing on trying to root out the abuses.

**It's not enough to have 10 percent women in a job. You need to have 50 percent. You have to go after the pattern of segregation.**

**E.Y.:** Given the way this culture works, I think people may fear that now we're going to look at competence-based abuses and we'll forget about sexualized conduct, that courts will just jump from one to the other.

**V.S.:** In some contexts, sexualized conduct is one of the most effective ways of undermining competence. I'm saying we might be able to look at sexuality through new eyes and see how it does some things that we haven't really talked about as much. If you read the *Harris* v. *Forklift Systems, Inc.* case, it seems pretty clear that the owner of the company was trying to use sexually explicit conduct as a way of making Teresa Harris, who was a manager, feel that she wasn't as good as he was or the men who were managers. Sexual conduct can serve this function. It's probably not the only function it serves, but it's kind of interesting to look at it that way.

The great thrust of all of the reforms that have occurred under Title VII has been toward making companies more rational and more accountable and more democratic. Early feminists were coming from a perspective that heterosexual sexual relations are a primary shaper and producer of gender inequality for women. What we need to do now is recognize that what happens in the sphere of paid employment is equally important in shaping women's disadvantage. We have to take very seriously the notion that if we're going to be truly free, truly equal, we need to be able to have access to challenging, rewarding, meaningful work that we can do freely and creatively and equally—alongside men, alongside other women, alongside people of all ages and races.

---

# VO!CES

## *"It was all under the pretext of a joke."*

**ANONYMOUS, 29 • JOB WHEN HARASSED: JUNIOR ACCOUNT EXECUTIVE IN PUBLIC RELATIONS; CURRENT JOB: PUBLICIST**

When I was 24, I had a mid-level management position at a large public relations and advertising firm. There was an informal, "jokey" atmosphere around the office. People used to play softball and volleyball together and go out drinking. At first, it seemed fun. But eventually, I realized that the environment was less "jokey" than it was offensive. For example: during a staff lunch once, the president told us that he'd had a sexual dream about a particular female at the office—he was looking straight at me. On another occasion, he asked, "What do all the women at this company have in common?" His answer: "They are all well endowed." And a stripper showed up at the office once as a gift from the general manager to the president.

On one of the first business trips of my career, I went for a drink with the president and the general manager. I thought they were there to mentor me, so I asked them questions about how they had reached where they were. In response, I was told I could get ahead in exchange for sexual favors. It was all under the pretext of a joke, but it make me uncomfortable. I went along with it as if it were a joke because I wanted to be a fun person that they liked. But the whole time I was thinking, "Is this really happening?" I didn't yet know this was sexual harassment, but a part of me knew I should have proof that they were saying these things to me. So I asked them to write their recommendations down, and they did—as a contract on a bar napkin.

Soon afterward there was an investigation of the office climate because a woman had filed a complaint about the president's sexual comments. Since I had the bar napkin, the president and general manager were afraid that I would rat on them to the investigators. That's when they started trying to get rid of me. Ironically, the investigators picked people to question at random and they never spoke to me.

Right before the investigation started I had received high marks on my evaluation and my immediate supervisor had recommended me for a promotion and a raise. But instead, the general manager and president put me on 30-day probation, saying I needed to be more "independent" and "strategic"—very vague charges that were difficult to combat. During the probation period, I was overloaded with work—much of it way above my level of experience. I approached the general manager and asked how I could do my job better. He told me I should have a few drinks with them, hang out more. He also said that I should not have refused an offer to have a beer with him on a particular occasion—one I had avoided because I would have been alone with him. He also asked me to stay over at his house to help him with a party while his wife was out of town. I said no, of course, but by that point I was a complete wreck. I didn't know what to do, what to say.

My immediate supervisor told me that they had asked him to fire me, but he refused because I was doing a wonderful job. I ended up proving myself during the probation period, but my supervisor was ultimately transferred, and after that I was laid off—supposedly for financial reasons.

I filed a complaint with the state department of human rights, claiming that I had lost my job because I had been working in a hostile environment that was sexual in nature. The state came back with a "probable cause" determination, which meant that their investigation found enough evidence to suggest something illegal had occurred. With that, I filed a lawsuit and eventually settled out of court. The harassment and the suit took two and a half years out of my life and made me an emotional wreck. But I felt that I produced important results because by the time the suit was settled, the president and the general manager had been asked to leave and sexual harassment training had been instituted at the company.

# The Case for Impeachment*

BY STUART TAYLOR JR.

**L**et me begin with some concessions and qualifications: It's true that there is something grotesque about wheeling out the awesome machinery of impeachment to determine whether the stuff of a bad porn flick can give rise to "high crimes and misdemeanors." There is something seriously disturbing about the Congress weighing the question of whether the president or the

> **THIS SCANDAL IS FUNDAMENTALLY ABOUT LYING, NOT SEX. THE EVIDENCE THAT THE PRESIDENT OBSTRUCTED JUSTICE IS SUBSTANTIAL. IT IS TIME FOR CLINTON TO GO.**

intern is lying about whether he touched her breasts and genitals "with an intent to arouse or gratify." It's also true that Kenneth Starr's report may wallow in such stuff more than necessary to prove the perjuries. Yuck, to borrow a Monica word.

It's further true that what Clinton has done to the institutions of democracy is not as bad as what President Nixon did in Watergate. Although the evidence that Clinton has committed crimes is at least as strong as the evidence that Nixon did, a criminal cover-up of a sexual affair is not as bad as a criminal cover-up of a burglary aimed at bugging political rivals. And Clinton's perjuries and obstructions are not as bad as the payment of hush money to burglars.

It's finally true that if a majority of the American people demand Clinton's continuance in office—even in the face of Starr's evidence, and even after any congressional hearings or Senate trial—then Clinton should not be removed (and won't be).

But for the time being, as the people and their representatives absorb the detailed evidence and ponder its simultaneously grave and bizarre meaning, there are five key questions to answer:

If there strong evidence that Clinton repeatedly violated criminal laws? Do his actions amount to "high crimes and misdemeanors" within the meaning of the Constitution? Should he be excused as a victim of political persecution, prosecutorial abuse, and invasion of privacy? Has he earned forgiveness and thus continuance in office? And what outcome would be best for the nation?

### THE EVIDENCE OF CLINTON'S CRIMES

This scandal really *is* fundamentally about lying—especially criminal lying—not sex. The proof is this: If Clinton

had testified truthfully when asked on Jan. 17 whether he had had sexual relations with Lewinsky—or even if he had refused on privacy grounds to answer the question—nobody could plausibly have called for impeachment. And there would have been nothing for prosecutors to investigate.

Even if Clinton had lied in that deposition—but then had not sought to influence other witnesses and had come clean after a few days' reflection—I (for one) would have argued against impeachment.

But that's not what happened. What happened is that, advised by his soulmate Dick Morris to stonewall, the president then proceeded to lie to his Cabinet; encouraged Secretary of State Madeleine Albright and others to vouch for his lie; set in motion his scorched-earth, smear-Starr, trash-Tripp, hide-the-evidence defense; and (on Jan. 26) uttered his famous, definitive and inexcusable lie to the American people: "I want you to listen to me. I'm going to say this again. I did not have sexual relations with that woman, Miss Lewinsky. I never told anybody to lie, not a single time. Never. These allegations are false."

But it turns out they were true, except in the exceedingly limited sense that Clinton may have stopped short of explicitly having "told" anybody to lie. Clinton lied under oath in the Jan. 17 deposition in the Paula Jones case, he lied in his Aug. 17 grand jury testimony, and he is lying still. This is what Starr's report shows, through a mass of detailed evidence, which Clinton's lawyers have barely attempted to refute on factual grounds, and which they cannot refute.

On Sunday, three of the president's lawyers—David Kendall, Charles F. C. Ruff and Lanny Breuer—hit the talk shows. They all sang from the same page: The president never perjured himself; this is just about sex. The result was not promising for Clinton. His lawyers were hammered, over and over, with specific, detailed and ex-

**Editor's note on the outcome of the impeachment trial is on page 73.

tremely aggressive questions challenging the veracity of Clinton's sworn testimony in many instances. They could do nothing but duck and weave and hide behind legalisms.

On ABC News' *This Week*, Kendall was sent reeling by questions from George Will like this one: "Is it your position that the president can remember being alone with Miss Lewinsky when she was delivering pizza, but not when she was delivering oral sex?"

At the outset of his deposition in the Jones case, the president took an oath administered by Judge Susan Webber Wright: "Do you swear or affirm . . . that the testimony you are about to give in the matter before the court is the truth, the whole truth, and nothing but the truth, so help you God?" The president answered: "I do."

Instead he lied, over a dozen times. And he lied explicitly enough to fit even a narrow reading of the Supreme Court's definition of perjury as an unambiguously false statement made with intent to deceive.

Let us count some of the ways. Following are excerpts from the deposition transcript, with analysis interspersed:

*Q: At any time were you and Monica Lewinsky together alone in the Oval Office?*

*A: I don't recall, but as I said, when she worked at the legislative affairs office, . . . it seems to me she brought things to me once or twice on the weekends. In that case, whatever time she would be in there, drop it off, exchange a few words and go, she was there. . . .*

*Q: . . . [I]t was possible, then, that you were alone with her, but you have no specific recollection of that ever happening?*

*A: Yes, that's correct. . . .*

*Q: At any time were you and Monica Lewinsky alone in the hallway between the Oval Office and this kitchen area?*

*A: I don't believe so. . . .*

*Q: At any time have you and Monica Lewinsky ever been alone together in any room in the White House?*

*A: . . . I have no specific recollection, . . .*

These are clear, calculated lies—unless you believe that Clinton could have forgotten more than 10 sexual encounters, mostly in that hallway, and many other solo meetings described by Lewinsky, in the Oval Office, the president's private study, the private bathroom across from the study, and elsewhere, the last one just 20 days before the deposition.

*Q: Did she tell you she had been served with a subpoena in this case?*

*A: No. I don't know if she had been. . . .*

Vernon Jordan testified that he had told Clinton about her subpoena on Dec. 19.

*Q: Have you ever talked to Monica Lewinsky about the possibility that she might be asked to testify in this lawsuit?*

*A: I'm not sure, and let me tell you why I'm not sure. [Then he mentioned one time when he might have joked to her in passing that she might be called.]*

Lewinsky testified that she spoke three times with Clinton about the prospect of testifying: in a 2 a.m. phone call on Dec. 17, when he told her that she was on the Jones lawyers' witness list, that she might be able to sign an affidavit to avoid testifying, and that "you can always say you were coming to see Betty or you were bringing me letters"; in a Dec. 28 meeting, in which they discussed what she might do with subpoenaed gifts; and in a Jan. 5 phone call, in which Clinton suggested a misleading explanation that she could give for her involuntary transfer from the White House to the Pentagon.

*Q: Well, have you ever given any gifts to Monica Lewinsky?*

*A: I don't recall. Do you know what they were? . . .*

They had exchanged many gifts of various kinds over many months, as recently as the Dec. 28 meeting, when Clinton gave her at least seven gifts.

*Q: Did you have an extramarital sexual affair with Monica Lewinsky?*

*A: No.*

*Q: If she told someone that she had a sexual affair with you beginning in November of 1995, would that be a lie?*

*A: It's certainly not the truth. It would not be the truth.*

*Q: I think I used the term "sexual affair." And so the record is completely clear, have you ever had sexual relations with Monica Lewinsky as that term is defined in Deposition Exhibit 1, as modified by the court? . . .*

[The modified definition states: "For the purposes of this deposition, a person engages in 'sexual relations' when the person knowingly engages in or causes . . . contact with the genitalia, anus, groin, breast, inner thigh, or buttocks of any person with an intent to arouse or gratify the sexual desire of any person."]

*A: I have never had sexual relations with Monica Lewinsky. I've never had an affair with her.*

In addition, Clinton sat silent while his lawyer Robert Bennett tried to block questions about Lewinsky by misleading (perhaps unwittingly) Judge Wright. Bennett said that Lewinsky "has filed an affidavit, which [the Jones lawyers] are in possession of, saying that there is absolutely no sex of any kind in any manner, shape or form, with President Clinton." He noted that Clinton was "fully aware" of the affidavit, in which Lewinsky denied ever having "sexual relations" with him.

Later in the deposition, Clinton was questioned by Bennett:

*Q: In [Lewinsky's] affidavit, she says this: "I have never had a sexual relationship with the President. . . . ." Is that a true and accurate statement as far as you know it?*

*A: That is absolutely true.*

Clinton has claimed—in his Aug. 17 grand jury testimony, his speech to the nation that night and his current legal defense—that this testimony was "legally accurate." His rationale, spelled out in his grand jury testimony, is that his

> # THE FAMOUS LIE:
>
> "I'm going to say this again, I did not have sexual relations with that woman, Miss Lewinsky."

repeated receipt of oral sex from Lewinsky amounted neither to a "sexual affair," nor to a "sexual relationship"—both of which Clinton said necessarily include sexual intercourse—nor to "sexual relations" as defined in the Jan. 17 deposition.

This rationale is both preposterous and dishonest. It is preposterous because it boils down to saying that while Lewinsky had "sexual relations" with Clinton (by giving him oral sex), *he* had no "sexual relations" with *her*. This tortured notion is based on an unreasonable reading of the definition of "sexual relations" approved by Judge Wright, in the context of a lawsuit accusing Clinton of (let us remember) soliciting oral sex from Paula Jones. No wonder the judge has raised the possibility of holding Clinton in contempt of court.

More important, Clinton's claim is dishonest because it depends on a factual premise that is explicitly and credibly contradicted by Lewinsky: that while passively receiving oral sex over many months from her, Clinton never once touched her breasts or genitals.

During the president's Aug. 17 grand jury testimony, prosecutors pinned him down on this point:

*Q: The question is, if Monica Lewinsky says that while you were in the Oval Office you touched her breasts would she be lying?*

*A: That is not my recollection. My recollection is that I did not have sexual relations with Ms. Lewinsky, . . . as I understood this term to be defined.*

*Q: Including touching her breast, kissing her breast, touching her genitalia?*

*A: That's correct.*

And that, folks, is perjury before a criminal grand jury, unless you believe that Lewinsky lied to the grand jury when she said that Clinton did those things on 10 different occasions, with identified dates, times, and locations.

True, Lewinsky is a (self-described) lifelong liar. But no more so than Clinton. And she is far more believable than he is in this context. Starr's report explains why:

Lewinsky's testimony about her sexual encounters with Clinton is very detailed and specific; she is corroborated by a draft letter she once wrote to Clinton, and by the testimony of seven friends, family members and counselors that she told them explicitly in 1996 and 1997 of how Clinton had fondled her on various occasions; she was an extremely reluctant witness.

Clinton, on the other hand, has a clear motive to contradict Lewinsky's accounts of him fondling her: to preserve some shred of a rationale for insisting that his perjurious denials of "sexual relations" with Lewinsky were truthful.

Clinton can still raise a technical legal defense against charges of perjury in the Jan. 17 deposition—although *not* in his grand jury testimony—by arguing that his lies were not "material" (or important) enough in the context of the Paula Jones lawsuit to be prosecutable. The argument rests on the subsequent decisions by Judge Wright to exclude

the Lewinsky evidence and to dismiss the Jones lawsuit. But the threshold for materiality is "extremely low," in the words of Attorney General Janet Reno.

The evidence that Clinton obstructed justice—mainly through witness-tampering and concealment of subpoenaed gifts—is more subtle but nonetheless substantial. It involves both Lewinsky and Betty Currie, who, Starr's evidence shows, acted as a kind of see-no-evil facilitator of the Clinton-Lewinsky relationship.

It is undisputed that Clinton and Lewinsky had an agreement that they would do what they could to conceal their affair. Starr alleges persuasively that this evolved during the Paula Jones lawsuit into "an understanding [that they would] jointly conceal the truth of their relationship from the judicial process by a scheme" that included lying under oath and the filing of a false affidavit by Lewinsky, at Clinton's suggestion, which the president then used at his deposition in an attempt to head off questions about her; when that failed, he lied under oath about their relationship.

Starr's evidence that Clinton also sought to encourage Betty Currie to lie at a time when she was a possible witness in the Jones case is also substantial.

According to the testimony of reluctant witness Currie, Clinton called his secretary at home on the night of Jan. 17, just after his deposition, and made an unusual request that she come to the office the next day, a Sunday. He wanted to discuss Monica Lewinsky.

After Currie had arrived at her desk on Jan. 18, she later testified, a "concerned" Clinton said a series of things in quick succession—"more like statements than questions"—while indicating by his demeanor that he wanted her to agree with him:

> **STARR'S TENET:**
> "The President has a manifest duty to ensure that his conduct at all times complies with the law of the land."

"You were always there when she was there, right? We were never really alone."

"You could see and hear everything."

"Monica came on to me, and I never touched her, right?"

When asked about this Jan. 18 meeting in his grand jury testimony, Clinton said he had been trying not to influence Currie to lie but "to quickly refresh my memory."

Kendall argues that this could not have been witness-tampering, because Currie has never been called as a witness in the Jones case. That's a plausible, if debatable, legal point, but in the context of Clinton's cover-up campaign, it's less than compelling.

Similarly, Clinton's lawyer can argue that his conversations with Lewinsky and Currie were too elliptical to amount to obstruction of justice. But a president may be held to a high standard of accountability for seeking even subtly to shape the potential testimony of subordinates. That, at least, is suggested by the articles of impeachment against President Nixon, who was charged not with anything as hard to prove as instructing subordinates to lie, but with "approving, condoning, acquiescing in, and counseling witnesses with respect to the giving of false or misleading statements."

## GROUNDS FOR IMPEACHMENT

Are Clinton's alleged perjuries and obstructions "high crimes"? Do they qualify as grounds for impeachment? Or is this all "personal and not impeachable," in the words of Clinton counsel Kendall?

The answer to that question will be informed by politics and the public's will, but also by the Constitution and the precedents. These suggest that a President should not be impeached in the absence of grave misconduct, but leave unclear how grave it must be. Criminality in the strict legal sense appears to be neither necessary nor sufficient. The seven officials (all judges) who have been removed from office by the Senate since 1803 faced charges as diverse as drunkenness on the bench and "loose morals" (John Pickering in 1803), income tax evasion (Harry E. Claiborne in 1986), and perjury (Alcee L. Hastings, also charged with bribery, and Walter L. Nixon, both in 1989).

Kendall premises his case against impeachment on the idea that only "wrongs committed against our system of government" are impeachable. He cites Alexander Hamilton's *Federalist* 65, which describes impeachment as the Constitution's remedy for "the abuse or violation of some public trust," and constitutional scholar Charles L. Black Jr.'s 1974 book, *Impeachment: A Handbook,* which says impeachment is warranted only by "serious assaults on the integrity of the processes of government" or "such crimes as would so stain a president as to make his continuance in office dangerous to public order."

But Kendall loses this argument even on his own terms. To the extent that his point is that Clinton should not be impeached for having a tawdry affair with a 22-year-old intern in the Oval Office, he'll get no argument from me. But it *is* a grave "abuse or violation of some public trust" for the president—whom the Constitution mandates "to take care that the laws be faithfully executed"—to violate those laws *and* to use government personnel and resources in an effort to make sure that the laws are *not* faithfully executed.

Clinton's lesser abuses are also of some relevance as aggravating factors. They include using his government-paid subordinate Lewinsky as "special assistant to the president for [oral sex]" (in her words), using his government-paid secretary as a kind of Oval Office sex facilitator, and using his U.N. ambassador as a girlfriend-outplacement service.

Clinton's defenders gloss Framers' discussions of the presidency: the emphasis by James Madison and others on the need for people of "virtue" in high office. Madison saw impeachment as an indispensable remedy for, among other things, "the negligence or perfidy of a president." Perfidy, anyone?

## CLINTON AS VICTIM?

President Clinton and his defenders have suggested that the issue should not be his own conduct but that of his adversaries. But Starr's report is persuasive in addressing Clinton's invasion-of-privacy complaint:

"All Americans, including the President, are entitled to enjoy a private family life, free from public or governmental scrutiny. But the privacy concerns raised in this case are subject to limits, . . .

"The first limit was imposed when the President was sued in federal court for alleged sexual harassment. The evidence in such litigation is often personal. . . . Nevertheless, Congress and the Supreme Court have concluded that embarrassment-related concerns must give way to the greater interest in allowing aggrieved parties to pursue their claims. . . .

"The second limit was imposed when Judge Wright . . . specifically ordered the President, on more than one occasion, to provide the requested information about relationships with other women, including Monica Lewinsky.

---

## ■ 'IT DEPENDS ON WHAT THE MEANING OF "IS" IS'

When the Monica Lewinsky scandal first broke in January, President Clinton was asked, in a television interview, whether he had had a sexual relationship with the former White House intern. After he replied that "there is not a sexual relationship," reporters jumped on his use of the present tense. Was this a Clintonian loophole? Was the president slyly denying sex with Lewinsky only at that moment in time, not in the past? This prompted cries of cynicism from Clintonites, with one White House aide accusing the press of indulging in a "bizarre Talmudic analysis." But the Starr report makes it clear that journalists were right to wonder.

The report notes that when Clinton was asked during his grand jury testimony about a statement that his lawyer Robert S. Bennett had made during the Jones deposition, "the President contended that when Mr. Bennett said, 'There *is* absolutely no sex of any kind,'" Mr. Bennett was speaking only in the present tense and thus was making a completely true statement. The president further stated: *"It depends on what the meaning of the word 'is' is,"* and that, "actually, in the present tense that is an accurate statement."

Clinton also told the grand jury: "If 'is' means is and never has been, that is not—that is one thing. If it means there is none, that was a completely true statement. . . . Now, if someone had asked me on that day, are you having any kind of sexual relations with Ms. Lewinsky, that is, asked me a question in the present tense, I would have said no. And it would have been completely true."

—**Burt Solomon**

# ■ THE DEVIL IS IN THE FOOTNOTES

A few choice items from the fine print in the Starr report:

### THE NARRATIVE

44. After the President's August 1998 speech acknowledging improper conduct with Ms. Lewinsky, she testified that she was no longer certain of her feelings because, in her view, he had depicted their relationship as "a service contract, that all I did was perform oral sex on him and that that's all that this relationship was. And it was a lot more than that to me. . . ."

126. Ms. Tripp produced to the Office of the Independent Counsel 27 tapes (four of which proved inaudible or blank) of her telephone conversations with Ms. Lewinsky. . . . According to a preliminary FBI examination, several of the 23 tapes containing audible conversations exhibit signs of duplication. . . . These preliminary results raise questions about . . . the accuracy of Ms. Tripp's testimony regarding her handling of the tapes. The Office of the Independent Counsel is continuing to investigate this matter.

479. A fragment of a deleted file recovered from Ms. Lewinsky's home computer apparently refers to the President's May 24 announcement: " . . . I don't care what you say, but if you were 100% fulfilled in your marriage I never would have seen that raw, intense sexuality that I saw a few times—watching your mouth on my breast or looking in your eyes while you explored the depth of my sex."

### THE GROUNDS:

31. As Ms. Lewinsky departed, she observed the President "manually stimulating" himself in Ms. Hernreich's office.

258. Ms. Currie testified that she was taking Saint-John's-wort to try to remember, but it was not helping.            **—Shawn Zeller**

. . . Perjury and attempts to obstruct justice can never be an acceptable response to a court order, . . .

"The third limit is unique to the President. . . . In view of the enormous trust and responsibility attendant to his high Office, the President has a manifest duty to ensure that his conduct at all times complies with the law of the land."

Starr has also been criticized, with a bit more reason, for having laid out so many sordid details of Lewinsky's testimony as to suggest an agenda of humiliating the president. But Starr's report plausibly argues that considerable detail was necessitated by Clinton's persistence during his grand jury testimony that he had been "legally accurate" in his Jan. 17 deposition. Given that, "the detail is critical" to providing Clinton's perjuries, Starr argues, because it "provides credibility and corroboration" for the Lewinsky testimony contradicted by Clinton.

## HAS HE EARNED FORGIVENESS?

President Clinton has admitted an "inappropriate" relationship and has sought forgiveness from just about everybody in the country except Starr and Linda Tripp. But his admissions and apologies have been extracted from him, bit by bit, first by the accumulation of evidence, such as Lewinsky's famous DNA-stained dress, and since then by Clinton's growing realization that his defiant Aug. 17 speech was a disaster.

Clinton will not earn forgiveness from the public unless and until he has, at the very least, stopped lying. He hasn't done that—and it appears he won't. His current defense rests heavily on asserting that his former girlfriend is lying about the nature of their sex acts, not he. Believe that one?

## WHERE LIES THE NATIONAL INTEREST?

Impeachment is largely a backward-looking exercise. But it has a built-in forward-looking aspect, which should carry some weight with those who are not fully convinced that the president is guilty of "high crimes."

The forward-looking question is whether President Clinton can ever recover his ability to be a credible and effective leader, in either foreign or domestic policy. More and more people seem to think the answer is no. A crippled presidency is danger-ous in many ways. It is bad for the country. For all these reasons, President Clinton should go.

---

*See *Annual Editions* article 15, "The Case Against."

# The Case Against*

## By Kirk Victor

President Clinton and his dwindling number of allies won't have an easy time defending behavior that even yellow-dog Democrats admit is bad. But they must defend it—and they should, because they have quite a powerful case to make.

**THE CASE FOR CLINTON IS SIMPLY THIS: HE TRIED TO KEEP ADULTEROUS SEX A SECRET. THAT DOES NOT WARRANT REMOVING HIM FROM OFFICE.**

What is this that began with the arrival of two vans and 36 boxes at the Capitol last week? It is a constitutional struggle—which is to say that it is a struggle of such weight and danger that it should not even be joined unless what the struggle is about really matters.

And what is this particular constitutional struggle about? It is not about a great disagreement over the fundamental nature of the nation, such as the rancor over Reconstruction that brought President Andrew Johnson within a single Senate vote of being removed from office in 1868. Nor is it about the profound abuses of power that made up Watergate.

The case so painstakingly built by Independent Counsel Kenneth Starr against President Clinton is, as the president's lawyers rightly (if somewhat splenetically) argued in their Sept. 12 response, all about sex.

Sex. The president partook of some he shouldn't have. He did not tell the truth about this. He tried to keep it a secret. Do these acts justify removing from office the elected leader of the executive branch of government? That question is the gist of the case for Clinton, and against impeachment. The crux of the disagreement between Clinton and Starr isn't really over the facts. It's over how important those facts are.

On the facts, the case in Clinton's favor is mixed, at best. His defense against the perjury charges, which rests on a convenient and rather peculiar definition of sexual relations, is—to put it kindly—convoluted. But on Starr's other accusations—of obstruction of justice, witness tampering and abuse of power—Clinton has a stronger defense to mount.

And Starr's report is remarkable for what it doesn't address. In 453 pages, Starr says virtually nothing about his original point of investigatory departure four years ago—the so-called Whitewater affair and the allegedly illegalities committed by Bill and Hillary Rodham Clinton in their 1970s dealings with a corrupt Arkansas savings and loan. Nor does his report address the firing of White House travel office employees or Clinton aides' access to hundreds of FBI files about their Republican predecessors. Starr is still expected to file a separate report on these matters to the three-judge panel that oversees the independent counsels, but that report clearly will not implicate Clinton in the commission of a crime. By omitting these issues from his congressional report, Starr has already, if implicitly, admitted that he found no compelling evidence of transgressions that rise to the level of impeachable offenses.

Where Starr's report is extraordinarily—even obsessively—detailed is in describing the sexual activities between Clinton and Monica Lewinsky. Here, it must be said that there's no question that Clinton's alleged behavior, as Lewinsky describes it, was disgusting, indefensible, arrogant. But impeachable? That is another question.

Impeachment is the most awful weapon that the legislative branch has at its disposal against corruption and abuse of power by the executive and judicial branches. The framers were very clear that impeachment should be always regarded as the most rare and extraordinary remedy, justified only by proof of "treason, bribery, or other high crimes and misdemeanors." Impeachment by the House and conviction by the Senate would set aside the people's vote in the 1996 presidential election, a radical step that isn't remotely warranted by charges of lying about sex and trying to conceal those lies. The accusations against Clinton concern, at worst, the lowest of crimes and the least consequential of misdemeanors.

### OBSTRUCT JUSTICE? MOI?

The Starr report argues that Clinton's lies about his relationship with Lewinsky to the public and to Congress, his efforts to cause aides to lie about it, and his attempts

From *National Journal*, September 14, 1998, pp. 22-25. © 1998 by National Journal Group, Inc. All rights reserved. Reprinted by permission.

to invoke executive privilege to conceal his personal misconduct from a grand jury add up to an abuse of power.

But many constitutional scholars view this argument by the independent counsel's office as far-fetched. "Consider the consequences of that [approach]—if you challenge an effort by a prosecutor to put you in jail, you would be abusing your power," said Herman Schwartz, a professor of constitutional law at American University. "The notion that you don't have a privilege to hide lies is nonsense."

Surely the Founding Fathers had no such extravagant claim in mind when they narrowly defined "abuse of power." In the *Federalist Papers,* Alexander Hamilton described such abuse as "the corrupt use of the office for personal gain or for some other improper purpose." Nothing of the sort has been alleged in Clinton's case.

As for lying to the public in denying his relationship with "that woman," Clinton has repeatedly apologized to his family, his friends, Democratic leaders and the country at large; he has taken responsibility for his sins, even bared his soul. In the logic of the independent counsel's office, however, apologies are irrelevant and public officials would be barred from mounting a defense against accusations while they hold office. This is a position that requires, in effect, an immediate admission of guilt.

And this position is typical of the Starr approach. Time and again, the prosecutor has sought to transform personal misconduct into an impeachable offense—a dangerous precedent, if Congress were to acquiesce.

Starr's allegations that Clinton obstructed justice rest chiefly on the notion that Clinton and Lewinsky agreed to jointly conceal the truth about their illicit and potentially ruinous relationship—a proposition that is hardly surprising. And, certainly, this is an effort that falls far short of constituting obstruction of justice.

Moving from the philosophical to the particular, the independent counsel's report itself concedes that Clinton never told Lewinsky to lie. Nor was there anything improper about Clinton's suggestion that Lewinsky file an affidavit in the sexual harassment case brought by Paula C. Jones, in hopes that they might both avoid being called to testify about their relationship. There's no evidence that Clinton told Lewinsky what to say in her affidavit, and even she testified that he turned down a chance to review it. No defendant—no citizen, not even one who happens to be president—has a legal duty to volunteer information that might be used against him or her, or to induce another person (such as Lewinsky) to volunteer such information. Indeed, lawyers commonly prepare witnesses for depositions by reminding them to answer questions as narrowly and literally as they can.

The independent counsel also charges that Clinton failed to correct a misstatement that his lawyer made to a federal judge during the president's deposition in the Jones litigation. But there's no evidence that Clinton was paying attention to what his lawyer was saying. In any event, he had no legal obligation to set his attorney's misstatement straight.

The independent counsel's office also bases part of its case for obstruction on the efforts made to find a job for Lewinsky in the private sector. But the prosecutors have never established a quid pro quo—that she was promised a job in exchange for favorable testimony. Instead, the independent counsel's office has acknowledged that it is relying on "inferences." There was limited presidential involvement—an inquiry into the possibility of a recommendation from the White House legislative office, where Lewinsky had worked. But there is no evidence that Clinton sought special favors for her because of their relationship.

To the extent that Clinton's friend Vernon E. Jordan was involved in Lewinsky's job search—which does lend some credence to the charge of obstruction—it should be noted that it was Clinton's personal secretary, Betty Currie, who sought his assistance, not the president himself. Currie also sought the assistance of U.N. ambassador Bill Richardson in the hunt for a job.

And even if Clinton *did* orchestrate the effort to find Lewinsky an out-of-town job, this may well have been inspired by nothing more illegal than a desire on the president's part to rid himself of a troublesome ex-girlfriend—who was pestering him for this very favor. Indeed, the effort to line up a job for Lewinsky in New York City occurred months before Clinton was questioned in the Jones case or Lewinsky's name surfaced as a possible witness.

The independent counsel's report is just as weak on another part of its claim that Clinton obstructed justice, the part regarding Clinton's efforts to conceal gifts he had given to Lewinsky. After he offered the ex-intern holiday and going-away gifts when she visited the White House last Dec. 28, according to Lewinsky's testimony, she suggested putting the gifts outside her apartment or giving them to Currie. She later testified that Clinton responded inconclusively, saying "I don't know" or "Hmmm"—ambiguous utterances that hardly support a charge of obstructing justice.

Currie and the president echoed each other in testifying that Lewinsky asked Currie to retrieve the gifts that the former intern possessed and to keep them. Currie did pick up a box of gifts, but Lewinsky kept other gifts—a decision that flies in the face of the argument that she was trying to get rid of all of his gifts so that she wouldn't have them in her apartment when she gave her deposition.

Starr's report alleges that the president had tampered with a witness—namely, Currie—when he asked her a series of leading questions in an effort to influence her testimony so that it would jibe with his. Clinton's lawyers have described this as "a transparent attempt [by Starr's office] to draw the most negative inference possible about lawful conduct"—to criminalize a private conversation between two citizens. When Clinton compared recollections with Currie, he had no reason to suspect that she would be called as a witness in the Jones case.

Finally, Starr's case rests on claims that Clinton committed perjury in the Jones civil case and before the grand jury, in denying having had sexual relations with Lewinsky. To make their case, the prosecutors must show that Clinton knew he was wrong and intended to lie. But in fact, Clinton responded to imprecise questions with narrow answers based upon his interpretation of the definition of "sexual relations" as applied in the *Jones* case.

So Starr's perjury charges are shaky. But even if, for the sake of argument, one were to accept them, they hardly rise to the level of an impeachable offense. Prosecutors, after all, don't treat all lies the same. There are lies that matter, such as those about bribery or campaign dirty tricks. Others, such as lying about one's sex life, don't—or at least, not to the level of prosecutable offenses.

## PROSECUTORIAL DISCRETION

Some prosecutors just shake their heads as they discuss the progression of the independent counsel's case. Former Independent Counsel James C. McKay, a Democrat, is astonished at what has come to pass. Noting that the present case against Clinton began with allegations of lies in a civil deposition in a sexual harassment case, McKay flatly says he would not have pursued it.

In cases like that, "you will find that people are not telling the truth, and it happens almost daily," McKay said in an interview. "In every contested divorce case, probably somebody is lying. And it just seemed to me that this was not material in the first place. To have built an entire case, which had such a destructive effect on so many people— and also the country and the world, for that matter—it just seems to me that the whole thing has been blown completely out of proportion. Starr seems to have lost his perspective as to what he is doing."

Paul Bender, a former dean at Arizona State University Law School, agrees. "This is not an important lie," he said. "It didn't change anything. It is mostly about personal conduct for which you don't normally prosecute people. . . . I have never heard of a perjury prosecution for that kind of a perjury."

Consider how McKay proceeded in his investigation of then-Attorney General Edwin Meese III in 1987. Meese allegedly had used his influence improperly to win federal contracts for a New York City defense contractor. In addition, McKay had evidence that the attorney general may have violated the Foreign Corrupt Practices Act. Despite his belief that he could probably win guilty verdicts on a number of counts, McKay decided against putting the nation's top law enforcement official on trial.

The reason: prosecutorial discretion. McKay decided to pass up the hot case, out of fear it would cause the nation too much trauma. "We had made our case," he recalled. "We had sent the message, and we didn't feel that anything would be particularly gained by going through with a prosecution, so we decided not to recommend an indictment by the grand jury."

As for Clinton, McKay said, "the president has already admitted [his affair]. It seems to me that the point could well have been made without the inclusion of this kind of X-rated pornographic material. My stomach would not have permitted me to do that."

## A CAP PISTOL

Many lawyers and constitutional scholars say they're dumbfounded that the country is on the brink of impeachment proceedings over a president's sexual escapades. "The impeachment of President Nixon was supported by taped conversations of Nixon, regarding the payment of hundreds of thousands of dollars in laundered campaign hush money," recalls a former solicitor general and former House deputy general counsel, Charles Tiefer, a Democrat. "Compared to those smoking guns, Starr doesn't even have a cap pistol."

In 1974, as it pondered the case against Nixon, the House Judiciary Committee decided that a high threshold must be met before it would try to topple a duly elected president. "Clearly," the committee concluded, "the impeachment process was intended to be used only in cases of grave abuse of the power entrusted to the president by the people."

The language of the Constitution itself makes this intention clear by coupling the words "high crimes and misdemeanors" with "treason" and "bribery." That language means that for the impeachment process to sweep the president from office, he must be "unfit to be president— not a bad person, not a person who has done bad things, but [one who has committed grave crimes such as] treason—acting against the interests of the United States—and bribery or corruption—taking money to make decisions," Bender said. "It goes to the core of whether the person is capable of serving in the office."

Bruce Ackerman, a Yale University law professor, worries that, with the Starr precedent, "impeachment can be turned into an all-purpose tool," and he adds: "We have to define 'high crimes and misdemeanors' in a way that's narrow, so as not to constitute a precedent for the destruction of the separation of powers."

The prospect of national trauma weighs heavily against a willingness to proceed with an impeachment of Clinton. Other remedies, including censure and the judgment of history, are surely severe enough.

Impeachment would also fly in the face of public opinion. And this is one time when governance should take its lead from the opinion polls. To remove an elected president whom the voters wish to keep in office is to do a fundamental violence to democracy. That hardly seems a price worth paying to punish a bit of sinning and a mess of lying.

---

\*See *Annual Editions* article 14, "The Case for Impeachment."

---

\*\*Editor's note: On Saturday, December 19, 1998 President William Jefferson Clinton was impeached by the House of Representatives for perjury and obstruction of justice, and a trial in the Senate began on January 7, 1999. This was the first time a U.S. President faced an impeachment trial since Andrew Jackson was tried 130 years ago. As the trial progressed, it became obvious that the Senate was divided along party lines, and on February 12, 1999, President Clinton was cleared of both articles of impeachment with the Senate could not muster two-thirds of their members, or 67 votes for impeachment.

## Unit Selections

## Key Points to Consider

❖ Read Articles I, II, and III of the U.S. Constitution to get a picture of the legislative, executive, and judicial branches as painted by the words of the Framers. How does that picture compare with the reality of the three branches as they operate today?

❖ How might the presidency and Congress change in the next 100 years?

❖ What advantages and disadvantages do each of the following have for getting things done: The president? The vice president? A cabinet member? The Speaker of the House of Representatives? The Senate majority leader? The chief justice? A top-ranking bureaucrat in an executive branch agency? A congressional aide?

❖ Which position in American government would you most like to hold? Why?

❖ Do you think Bill Clinton has been a successful president in getting things done? A *good* president? Why or why not?

❖ Do you think it makes sense for a president to emphasize economic and domestic concerns over foreign policy, as Bill Clinton promised during his initial campaign for the presidency in 1992? Defend your answer.

 **Links** **www.dushkin.com/online/**

10. **Department of State**
*http://www.state.gov*
11. **Federal Reserve System**
*http://woodrow.mpls.frb.fed.us/info/sys/index.html*
12. **Policy Digest Archives**
*http://www.public-policy.org/~ncpa/pd/pdindex.html*
13. **Supreme Court/Legal Information Institute**
*http://supct.law.cornell.edu/supct/index.html*
14. **United States House of Representatives**
*http://www.house.gov*
15. **United States Senate**
*http://www.senate.gov*
16. **The White House**
*http://www.whitehouse.gov/WH/Welcome.html*

These sites are annotated on pages 4 and 5.

James Madison, one of the primary architects of the American system of government, observed that the three-branch structure of government created at the Constitutional Convention of 1787 pitted the ambitions of some individuals against the ambitions of others. Nearly two centuries later, contemporary political scientist Richard Neustadt wrote that the structure of American national government is one of "separated" institutions sharing powers. These two eminent students of American politics suggest an important proposition: the very design of American national government contributes to the struggles that occur among government officials who have different institutional loyalties and potentially competing goals.

This unit is divided into four subsections. The first three treat the three traditional branches of American government and the last one treats the bureaucracy. One point to remember when studying these institutions is that the Constitution provides only the barest skeleton of the workings of the American political system. The flesh and blood of the presidency, Congress, judiciary, and bureaucracy are derived from decades of experience and the shared expectations of today's political actors. A second point to keep in mind is that the way a particular institution functions is partly determined by those who occupy relevant offices. The presidency operates differently with Bill Clinton in the White House than it did when George Bush was president. Similarly, Congress and the Supreme Court also operate differently according to who are serving as members and who hold leadership positions within the institutions. There were significant changes in the House of Representatives after Republican Newt Gingrich succeeded Democrat Tom Foley as Speaker of the House in 1995, and lesser changes in the Senate after Trent Lott replaced fellow Republican Bob Dole as majority leader in mid-1996. With Speaker Dennis Hastert succeeding Gingrich in January 1999, we can again expect changes in the way the House of Representatives functions.

The first subsection contains articles on the presidency. After 12 straight years of Republican presidents (Ronald Reagan and George Bush), Democrat Bill Clinton assumed the presidency in 1993. For the first 2 years of his presidency, the Democrats also held a majority of seats in the House of Representatives and Senate. But in the 1994 and 1996 congressional elections, Republicans won control of the House and Senate, a development that led to changes in the way Clinton functioned as president. An important point to remember is that neither the presidency nor any other institution operates in isolation from the other institutions of American national government.

The second subsection addresses Congress. The legislative branch underwent substantial changes in recent decades under mostly Democratic control. Reforms to the seniority system and the budgetary process in the 1970s brought an unprecedented degree of decentralization and, some would say, chaos to Capitol Hill. In addition, during the 1970s and 1980s, both the number of staff and special-interest caucuses in Congress increased. The Republican takeover of the House of Representatives as a result of the November 1994 elections brought even more changes to that body. Compared with his Democratic predecessors of the past few decades, Republican Speaker Newt Gingrich consolidated power within the House and become a prominent figure on the national scene. But 1998 brought the downfall of Gingrich as a result of the November elections and, for the second time in history, impeachment of the president. These events will likely affect the functioning of Congress (and the presidency) for some time to come.

The Supreme Court sits at the top of the U.S. court system and is the main topic of the third subsection on the structures of American politics. The Court is not merely a legal institution; it is a policymaker whose decisions can affect the lives of millions of citizens. Like all people in high government offices, Supreme Court justices have policy views of their own, and observers of the Court pay careful attention to the way the nine justices interact with one another in shaping decisions of the Court.

The bureaucracy of the national government, the subject of the fourth and last subsection in this unit, is responsible for carrying out policies determined by top-ranking officials. The bureaucracy is not merely a neutral administrative instrument, and bureaucratic waste and inefficiency often seem excessive. On the other hand, government bureaucracies also share credit for many of the accomplishments of American government. Most presidents claim that they will make the bureaucracy perform more efficiently, and President Clinton is no exception in this regard. Vice President Al Gore's National Performance Review of the federal bureaucracy is an example of this effort.

For many readers, the selections in this unit will probably rank among the most enjoyable in the book. Not surprisingly, most of us are more comfortable on familiar territory, and the separate branches of government are likely to be familiar from earlier study in school or from media coverage of politics. Nevertheless, the selections in this unit should provide additional and more sophisticated insights into how the institutions of American national government actually work.

# Structures of American Politics

# The Separated System*

## Charles O. Jones

*Charles O. Jones is Hawkins Professor of Political Science, University of Wisconsin-Madison. A former president of the American Political Science Association, he is author of* The Presidency in a Separated System. *In the fall 1995 he delivered the Rothbaum Lectures on Representative Government at the University of Oklahoma.*

Shortly after his inauguration, President Bill Clinton reiterated an extravagant campaign promise, accompanied by a dramatic announcement:

> As a first step in responding to the demands of literally millions of Americans, today I am announcing the formation of the President's Task Force on National Health Reform. Although the issue is complex, the task force's mission is simple: Build on the work of the campaign and the transition, listen to all parties, and prepare health care reform legislation to be submitted to Congress *within 100 days of our taking office.* This task force will be chaired by the First Lady, Hillary Rodham Clinton.

The effect was to draw accountability clearly and unmistakably to the White House, indeed, into the residence itself. The president and his partner by marriage would be held directly accountable for what happened. Yet as political scientist Hugh Heclo observed, "Never in the modern history of major social reform efforts had a president with so few political resources tried to do so much."

Ours is not a unified political and governmental system. Setting ambitious goals, promising swift action, and assuming complete management for dramatic change, taken together, represent a huge political gamble for a leader in a government of truly separated institutions. To do so having won 43 percent of the popular vote is surely an instance of derring-do. By drawing accountability to himself, Clinton accentuated a problem inherent in a separated system. A prime challenge to presidents is to manage the often-lavish expectations of their accountability under conditions of distributed power. A necessary background for my assessment of the Clinton presidency, therefore, is an understanding of the diffused accountability inherent in our system.

## Accountability in a Separated System

Though a government of separated institutions sharing or competing for powers has many virtues, *focused responsibility is not one of them.* Accountability is highly diffused by dint of the dispersal that is characteristic of separationism. And though some observers argue that to have accountability everywhere is to have it nowhere, that is not so. A system like ours has substantial *individual accountability* but limited *collective accountability.* The reasons why are clear enough to those familiar with constitutional history.

Operationally, formal accountability for presidents is primarily rhetorical. Presidents speak of representing the public. The media often act as enforcers, holding presidents accountable to an inexact public-interest standard. Presidents are held answerable for actions within the government, and yet the precise manner of holding them to account is rather indistinct. This reality is central to the governing strategy of modern presidents. They should be aware that they will be held responsible for that over which they have only limited control. At the very least, they must avoid contributing further to this tendency by guaranteeing grand results.

In brief, the White House cannot depend for support on what happened in the last election but must account for how the members' policy preferences relate to the next election. The president must develop and redevelop policy strategies that acknowledge the ever-shifting coalitional base. Serious and continuous in-party and cross-party coalition building thus typifies policy making in the separated system.

* Forum essays are slightly revised versions used by permission from the Spring 1996 issue of *Extensions,* a copyrighted publication of the Carl Albert Congressional Research and Studies Center, University of Oklahoma. Charles O. Jones's essay is a version of his discourse in the 1995 Julian J. Rothbaum Distinguished Lecture in Representative Government.

From *Society,* September/October 1996, pp. 18–23. © 1996 by Transaction Publishers. All rights reserved. Reprinted by permission.

## Bill Clinton's ambition is for a kind of greatness that is defined by approval. He wants to do good things for many people.

The defining challenge for a new president is to capitalize on his freshness without elevating further the lofty expectations of his position. The president is well advised to resist the efforts by others, or himself, to assign him the heady charge of being the commander of government.

## Managing High Expectations

Imagine that the fires of ambition burn so strongly that sleep is your enemy. Success by most measures comes easily, but it does not provide solace. The need to do more is all-consuming. There is no reward great enough; an obstacle overcome is less valued than the identification of a new challenge.

Conceive, if you can, the challenge involved in making everyone happy, then in getting credit for having done so and you will understand why there is little time or patience for sleep. Meet Bill Clinton, "first in his class"; bound to be president.

Bill Clinton's ambition is for a kind of greatness that is defined by approval. He wants to do good things for many people. He is a talker, engaged in a gamelike process of exploration. As such, he is puzzled by listeners who hear the talk as commitment. Talkers find satisfaction in the immediate response. They are unlikely to make a strong distinction between campaigning and governing. Nor are they likely to be intrigued by the intricacies of the lawmaking process. Bill Clinton is the quintessential campaigner as president. He most assuredly is not a lawmaker president in the Lyndon Johnson mold; had he been so, he may have had a more successful first two years. What follows, then, is a description and analysis of a presidency increasingly at risk, one persistently "on the edge," as Elizabeth Drew entitled her book on the Clinton administration, yet one prepared as few have been to seek reelection.

The 1992 campaign and election were bound to encourage a parliamentary-style accounting. A new-generation Democrat won after twelve years of Republican dominance of the White House. He promised to work hardest at economic recovery, as well as acting on a number of other issues generally acknowledged to form the contemporary agenda. One party would now be in charge of both ends of Pennsylvania Avenue. The gridlock that was presumed by many to have prevented the proper functioning of government was judged to be over.

Additionally, there was the sheer energy and excitement conveyed by the youthful Clinton-Gore team. It would require a substantial degree of self-discipline to ensure that post-election enthusiasm did not overreach and contribute to inflated expectations as to what could be achieved by the 103rd Congress.

Contributing to high expectations were political analysts, especially those who adhere to the perspective on national elections that I term "unitarian" (as opposed to "separationist"). At root, the unitarians disagree with the separation of powers concept. They propose reforms designed to ensure one-party government so as to achieve collective accountability. For the unitarian the best possible election result is that in which one political party wins the White House and majority control of both houses of Congress. That party is then expected to display unity on policy issues and to produce a record for which it can be held responsible at the next election. Though I cannot produce an exact count, I would wager that most political analysts are unitarians.

In contrast, the general voting public and most members of Congress are practicing "separationists." For the separationist the best possible election result is one that reinforces the legitimacy of independent participation by each branch. Party leaders, including presidents, are then expected to build cross-partisan support within and between the elected branches whether or not one party has majorities in Congress and a president in the White House. A separationist perspective of the 1992 election would have stressed the rejection of George Bush without identifying a mandate for Clinton. By this view, voters continued to split their tickets, albeit in new and interesting ways, making it difficult to spot a "mandate."

Evidence for this separationist interpretation abounds. There is the substantial vote garnered by Ross Perot, the most for an independent or third-party candidate since Theodore Roosevelt ran in 1912. A president won in a three-way contest by designating a credible agenda and projecting a sufficiently moderate policy posture as to be reassuring to just over half of the Ronald Reagan (1984) and Bush (1988) voters who were disillusioned with the Bush presidency. Clinton's campaign strategy was, by William Schneider's view, to "convince middle-class voters that Democrats could work within the Reagan-Bush consensus." Moreover, House Republicans had a net gain of ten seats and received 46 percent of the national vote for the House, compared to Bush's 37 percent of the national vote for president.

It follows from these assertions that a partisan, unitarian approach was unlikely to succeed. Yet that is the approach Clinton employed. Not only that, but Clinton's activist style drew accountability to himself. A book of promises, entitled *Putting People First,* was published during the campaign; it was bound to raise hopes while defining awesome challenges and providing a scorecard for the media. In reading from this text of pledges, little was to be left untouched by a Clinton-Gore administration—it included 35 proposals for the "national economic strategy" and 577 proposals for "other crucial issues."

Lacking was an understanding of how ours is truly the most elaborated lawmaking system in the world. It does not submit to enthusiasm alone. Effective leadership starts with knowing how the system works. The 1992 election produced exceptionally challenging conditions for lawmaking, requiring extraordinarily sensitive strategies for producing cross-party majorities on Capitol Hill. Bill Clinton lacked the skills for devising these strategies and therefore had to learn them or, like Reagan, rely on those who did have that competence.

---

**Perhaps most stunning as a measure of political mismanagement was the fact that by raising expectations, inviting responsibility, and yet failing to produce, the president and his leaders in Congress deflected criticism of Republicans for having obstructed much of the president's legislative program.**

---

It is with the understanding of the centrist underpinnings of Clinton's electoral and preinaugural support that one comes to understand the problems the new president faced during the first two years of his presidency. For the actions that could be taken early in order to demonstrate momentum—executive orders regarding abortions performed in military hospitals, federal funding of fetal tissue transplant research, the importation of abortion pill RU-486, and ending the ban on gays in the military—were likely to project a substantially more liberal cast than could be justified by public opinion as expressed either in the election or in subsequent polls.

Moreover, actions that were more moderate-to-conservative in nature—reducing the federal workforce, terminating advisory committees, seeking to make government more efficient—were overshadowed at the start by the more liberal actions cited above. Why? They were noncontroversial, not newsworthy, and therefore unavailable as ballast to the liberal tilt on controversial issues.

As if these developments were not sufficient to ensure Republican unity, Democrats in the House of Representatives used the rules of that chamber to prevent Republicans from effective participation in the amending process. Senate Republicans were in a substantially stronger position than their colleagues in the House due to the fact that they had sufficient numbers to prevent the closing of debates, and advantage used early against the president's economic stimulus package and late in 1994 to kill much of the president's program.

With all of these problems and miscalculations, Clinton's first year was moderately productive under contentious political circumstances in which partisan lines hardened substantially. Several bills vetoed by Bush were passed again and signed by the president, a deficit-reduction package was enacted by Vice President Gore's tie-breaking vote in the Senate and two votes in the House, NAFTA was approved with the crucial support of Republicans, and the president got a modified version of his National Service Program.

However, many of the most contentious issues were carried over to the second session. As a result, the second year was among the least productive of major legislation in the post-World War II period. Of the ten presidential priorities mentioned in the State of the Union Message, four became law—the GATT (again with Republican support in a special session), Goals 2000, an anticrime package, and community development loans. Each was important, but none was as important for the president as the proposal to reform the health care system—a matter that dominated the politics of the year. "We will make history by reforming the health-care system," was the president's promise in his January 1994 State of the Union Address. Yet by September 26, 1994, Senate Majority Leader George Mitchell had issued the last rites.

Perhaps most stunning as a measure of political mismanagement was the fact that by raising expectations, inviting responsibility, and yet failing to produce, the president and his leaders in Congress deflected criticism of Republicans for having obstructed much of the president's legislative program. As was noted in a *New York Times* editorial, Republican cooperation "was never part of the original promise." Democratic leaders had informed the president that they could deliver without Republican support. Republicans were content to be excluded. In the end it permitted them to avoid the accountability that was solicited by the administration.

---

**Bill Clinton has a number of weaknesses. He had never held a position in the federal government. While governor, he worked with a Democratic legislature, seldom having to take Republicans into account or to display the kind of lawmaking prowess of a governor from a state with a more competitive two-party government.**

---

Clinton's personal strengths are many. He is a superb campaigner—an effective and empathetic communicator with the public and a man with an "upbeat personality." He is, unquestionably, highly intelligent, possessed of an extraordinary capacity to identify and explore public policy issues. We also know from David Maraniss's fine biography, *First in His Class,* that he knows how to cram for an exam—a characteristic displayed in playing his role in lawmaking, as he often waits to the last minute to engage the issue to the extent of making a choice.

## The Midterm Earthquake

But Bill Clinton also has a number of weaknesses. He had never held a position in the federal government. While governor, he worked with a Democratic legislature, seldom having to take Republicans into account or to display the kind of lawmaking prowess of a governor from a state with a more competitive two-party government. As with most governors, he lacked direct experience in foreign and national security policy. He is an admitted "policy talk wonk" who finds it difficult to concentrate on a limited agenda. And there is ample evidence that Bill Clinton lacks direct experience in forming and accommodating to an effective staff. Clinton's strengths are more intellectual than managerial.

---

## Bill Clinton was still president, but he was not leader of the Democrats in any serious or meaningful sense.

---

Moreover, instead of compensating for his weaknesses, Clinton preferred to capitalize on his strengths. He sought to govern by campaigning, not lawmaking, virtually melding the two in his own mind and in his behavior. In his first two years the president visited 194 places, making 264 appearances (excluding foreign travel, visits to Arkansas, and vacations). Bill Clinton is the most traveled president in history, exceeding even President George Bush. One effect was to reinforce the distorted view of the president as the government, with the effect of holding him accountable for what is and has ever been a separated system of diffused accountability. As a consequence, Bill Clinton became a major issue in the midterm election. The result was to produce a very different presidency for this second two years in office.

It is standard wisdom that congressional elections are state and local events, albeit with important national effects. In 1994, however, there were two bids to nationalize the midterm elections: one by the president, who seemingly could not resist joining the fray, and one by Newt Gingrich, the House Republican Leader in waiting, who had national, crusadelike ambitions.

As the election approached, the president might well have followed the advice given Harry Truman by the Democratic National Committee Chairman in 1946—that is, stay out of midterm politics! Truman, whose standing in the polls was at 40 percent, accepted this advice. "He kept silent on politics." Few, if any, Democratic candidates invoked his name.

Clinton was in a similar situation, with approximately the same poll results. And in fact his pollster, Stanley Greenberg, issued a memorandum to Democratic candidates advising that they run on their own accomplishments, not on those of the president. "There is no reason to highlight these as Clinton or Democratic proposals. Voters want to know that you are fighting to get things done for them, not that you are advancing some national agenda."

A flurry of foreign and national security policy decisions on North Korea, Haiti, and Iraq—all judged to be successful—resulted in a boost in the president's approval rating to 50 percent, exceeding his disapproval rating for the first time in six months. That was the good news; the bad news was that the good news encouraged him to reenter the campaign. He launched a last-minute, furious schedule of appearances, drawing attention to his record and attacking the Republican "Contract *on* America," as he called it. By campaigning so energetically in the last week, the president naturally attracted press attention to himself as an issue. The effect was to ensure that dramatic Republican gains would be interpreted as a rejection of Clinton's presidency, whether or not that conclusion was merited in terms of actual voting behavior.

The other half, or more, of the nationalization of the 1994 elections is explained by what the Republicans did. As political scientist Gary G. Jacobson pointed out: "All politics was *not* local in 1994. Republicans succeeded in framing the local choice in national terms, making taxes, social discipline, big government, and the Clinton presidency the dominant issues." The Republicans tied "congressional Democrats to Clinton, a discredited government establishment, and a deplorable status quo."

Gingrich, too, deserves notice for his daring strategy of committing Republican candidates to a bold midterm party platform, the "Contract with America." It is true that most voters knew little or nothing about the contract. But the act of getting over three hundred Republican candidates to commit themselves in a media show at the Capitol on September 27 had profound effects on how the election results would then be interpreted.

The new Republican leaders were also not in the least bothered by Democratic claims that the contract tied "Republican candidates back into their congressional leadership." That was precisely the point. Gingrich and company would be strengthened in their effort to establish firm control of the agenda if the new members supported them. Meanwhile, the Democrats were in considerable disarray. Bill Clinton was still president, but he was not leader of the Democrats in any serious or meaningful sense. One study concluded that "the more the Democratic incumbent voted to support the president's policies, the more likely he or she was to be defeated."

Justified or not in terms of what the voters actually wanted, a new agenda had been created. "Change isn't Bill Clinton's friend anymore," is how two reporters put it. A *Washington Post* editorial referred to a "sea change," pointing out that "this was not just an 'anti-incumbent' vote. The incumbents who were defeated this year were Democrats—and in particular Democrats in Congress . . . the change called for went almost uniformly in one direction, and that was against liberalism and toward the right." A mandate had been declared, centered in just one of the three elected branches—the House of Representatives. Meanwhile, defeated or not, Bill Clinton remained in office, now freed from the responsibilities of leading Congress, for which he seemed ill-suited anyway.

## Reclaiming Leadership

How then did this policy-ambitious president—one who wanted government to do more, not less, and to do it better, not worse—how did he respond to dramatically new political conditions? I have made the point that Bill Clinton is not a lawmaker president. Yet there are functions that cannot be avoided, choices that have to be made—notably whether to sign or to veto a bill, to let it become law or to let it die without his signature. How did the president cope? He altered his governing style from that of a *campaigner* to that of a *prospector,* searching for a role compatible with the unusual politics of the time. The strategy devised in 1995 contained these tenets:

- Associate the president with the change seemingly demanded by the voters.
- Remind the public that the president was there first with many of the issues in the Contract with America.
- Argue that the Republicans are going too far. It is not necessary to destroy programs to improve government. Be the voice of moderation against the extremist Republicans. "I'm for that, but not so much."
- Search for high-profile issues subject to executive order, pushing the limits of that power (as with the anti-teenage smoking measures and barring government contracts with firms replacing strikers).
- Await the completion of lawmaking, then exercise the veto while imploring Republicans to meet on "common ground." Avoid specifics in favor of a "no, that's not it" response.
- Travel, taking your presidency to the people, posturing as the voice of reason, the interpreter of change, the preserver of values.
- Take full advantage of the uniquely presidential status in foreign and national security issues and disasters.

Taken as a whole, this strategy was defensible and rational given the president's political status. It permitted him to turn full attention to raising money and creating an organization for re-election while Republicans were absorbed with the difficult and often unrewarding exercises of balancing the budget and reforming social programs. Lacking an opponent, the president was able to rise above the fray, even calling for a moratorium on politics as usual. Republicans, on the other hand, were engaged in a hotly contested nomination battle in the early months of 1996, with the winner, Bob Dole, then held responsible for leading the Congress that was taken from the president in 1994. Until he announced his resignation from the Senate, Dole found himself battling surrogate campaigners—Tom Daschle, Ted Kennedy, and Chris Dodd—rather than the president.

## Clinton in Historical Perspective

Bill Clinton joins others whose presidencies have been at risk. Indeed, the imbalance between expectations and authority perpetuates political peril for presidents.

I stressed earlier that Bill Clinton amplified the inherent risk for the president by raising expectations despite weak political advantages. He invited accountability for the failures that, given the overreaching that characterized his early months in office, were likely to come. A dramatically new politics was created as a result.

---

**The reports of his political demise were premature. Once more, Bill Clinton demonstrated his capacity for political regeneration.**

---

Freed from the exacting demands of his original ambitious agenda by the 1994 elections, the president settled into the role of moderating the striking, even threatening, policy changes proposed by Republicans. Though not a leadership role, it is a mode that becomes him. As the nation's moderator in the serious policy debates at hand, he can justify the travel and public exposure that he finds personally and intellectually rewarding. He displayed patience in 1995, permitting Republicans to dominate the agenda and awaiting the time when his veto power would inevitably attract their lawmaking efforts—inexorably drawing them into the public arena where he excels. At last the campaigner could reinsert himself into the policy process. But having been more an observer than participant during the active congressional session, it was no simple matter for President Clinton to reconnect with the lawmaking process. Therefore, negotiations with congressional leaders have been protracted and disorderly, with the Republicans of the 104th Congress having drawn to themselves precisely the large measure of accountability that the White House invited in the 103rd Congress. Given his experience, President Clinton was more than happy to oblige in holding Republicans responsible for, among other things, shutting down the government.

Control of his political destiny was taken from the president in the 1994 elections, and so he positioned himself to take advantage of what others did or failed to do. The reports of his political demise were premature. Once more, Bill Clinton demonstrated his capacity for political regeneration. Perhaps even he would agree, however, that the separated system works best when success is measured less by recovery than by effective participation by the president throughout. It is exceptional to be the "Come Back Kid" over and over again. Yet it is substantially more imposing as president not to require recuperation.

## SUGGESTED FURTHER READING

David W. Brady, John F. Cogan, and Douglas Rivers. "How the Republicans Captured the House: An Assessment of the 1994 Midterm Elections." Stanford, Calif.: Hoover Institution, Stanford University, 1995.
Bill Clinton and Al Gore. *Putting People First: How We Can All Change America.* New York Times Books, 1992.
Elizabeth Drew. *On the Edge: The Clinton Presidency.* New York: Simon & Schuster, 1994.
Gary C. Jacobson. "The 1994 House Elections in Perspective." In *Midterm: The Elections of 1994 in Context,* Philip Klinker, ed. Boulder, Colo.: Westview Press, 1996.
David Maraniss. *First in His Class: A Biography of Bill Clinton.* New York: Simon & Schuster, 1995.

# Hooked on Polls

### By Carl M. Cannon

In 1992, Ross Perot brought a radical idea to American presidential politics: the real-time plebiscite. In Perot's world, decisions on the great issues of the day, from federal budget policies to war-making, could be reached instantaneously by the American people through the use of high-tech referendums conducted by telephone or the Internet. This voting would follow televised presentations on the issues in which various policy options would be explained to the public.

**THEY'RE BEING USED LIKE NEVER BEFORE. WHATEVER HAPPENED TO REPRESENTATIVE GOVERNMENT?**

Perot called his concept the "electronic town meeting," but what he really was describing was elevating the public opinion polls to the status of a kind of super-Congress and president-in-chief that would trump the desires and machinations of Washington's elected leaders.

"With interactive television every other week, we could take one major issue, go to the American people, cover it in great detail, have them respond, and show by congressional district what the people want," Perot explained. "If we ever put the people back in charge of this country and make sure they understand the issues, you'll see the White House and Congress, like a ballet, pirouetting around the stage getting it done in unison."

Perot placed a lot of faith in "experts" to explain to the public what needed to be done, but most experts in politics and government tended to view his electronic town hall idea as simplistic and unworkable, if not an affront to the Constitution.

"It just gives me the shudders, the potential for manipulation, the one-sidedness, that a thing like this could do," said Norman Bradburn, director of the polling center at the University of Chicago.

Vice President Dan Quayle asserted that Perot's plan entailed nothing less than "nullifying representative democracy with a bizarre scheme of government by polls." And President Bush said Perot "was out of touch with reality" when he suggested Bush could have used the electronic town hall to build a mandate for liberating Kuwait.

Perhaps most scathing was liberal journalist Sidney Blumenthal, who now works in the Clinton White House. "Thus the Madisonian system would be replaced by the Geraldo system; checks and balances by applause meter," Blumenthal wrote.

In hindsight, however, the most instructive response to Perot's idea was the one offered by the Democratic presidential nominee in 1992. Asked about Perot's electronic town hall ideas—on CNN's *Larry King Live*, fittingly—Bill Clinton replied, "Oh, I think it's a good idea." Clinton went on to make the obligatory comments about how polls don't absolve elected officials from their responsibilities, but the most animated part of his answer was this: He took credit for holding electronic town hall meetings before Perot did.

Today, barely six years after the putative rise and demise of Ross Perot, polls are being used more aggressively than ever before by the president and his loyalists, he and they, both, endless consumers and endless peddlers of polls. "They become addictive," said a former White House official. "They work once, and then they become a crutch; you don't do anything without them."

As president, Clinton has commissioned polls on issues ranging in gravity from whether he ought to stop genocide in Bosnia (the public gave a qualified thumbs-up) to whether it was better public relations to vacation in Wyoming or Martha's Vineyard (voters preferred he go out West). It is now common for polling results to be offered

From *National Journal*, October 17, 1998, pp. 2438-2441. © 1998 by National Journal Group, Inc. All rights reserved. Reprinted by permission.

as validation in themselves, an argument—sometimes the primary argument—for such disparate positions as whether tax cuts are warranted, what an independent counsel should properly investigate, what the president's legal strategy should be, whether he should apologize for having sex with an intern, how much coverage the media should devote to the topic, and, of course, the dominant political question of the day: whether Bill Clinton should be impeached.

"On [impeachment], polls are our religion," said a Clinton loyalist. "We cite them, we flog them, we beat people over the head with them." Some Democrats, in fact, say polling numbers are more definitive than election returns. This postulate was advanced by the president and his press secretary as recently as Oct. 7. That day, the president said on the question of his own impeachment that "ultimately, it's going to be up to the American people to make a clear statement there."

Hours later, at the regular White House briefing, Clinton spokesman Joe Lockhart reiterated this point. Lockhart was asked if he and the president had the upcoming November elections in mind. Oh no, Lockhart said, adding that congressional elections are usually decided on local considerations. So then, Lockhart was asked, was he talking about the public opinion polls? "Yes," he replied. "People in Congress, people in elective office do, properly, stay in touch with their constituents."

One member who seems to have taken this doctrine literally is Rep. Ted Strickland of Ohio, one of the 31 Democrats who voted for the sweeping GOP impeachment inquiry. "It was not a particularly courageous vote," he told *The Washington Post*. "I think I did what my constituents wanted me to do."

How did he know what they wanted him to do? He commissioned a poll.

It's almost impossible to resist comparing this approach with the stance taken by Sen. Edmund G. Ross of Kansas in 1866 as pressure mounted on him back home to vote for conviction in the impeachment proceedings against President Andrew Johnson. No scientific public opinion surveys existed back then, but public opinion certainly did, and on the eve of Ross' fateful vote, he received this telegram from well-connected Republicans back home:

*Kansas has heard the evidence and demands the conviction of the President. [signed] D.R. Anthony and 1,000 Others.*

The morning of the vote, May 16, 1866, Ross sent a telegram back:

*To D.R. Anthony and 1,000 Others: I do not recognize your right to demand that I vote either for or against conviction. I have taken an oath to do impartial justice according to the Constitution and laws, and trust that I shall have the courage to vote according to the dictates of my judgment and for the highest good of the country. [signed] E.G. Ross.*

To David W. Moore, a Gallup Organization vice president and political scientist by training, the dichotomy of their two approaches has echoes in the venerable civics debate over how much pure democracy a representative form of government ought to have. Are the voters back home supposed to choose representatives whose judgments they trust, and who are then free—indeed, obligated—to exercise their wisdom as they see fit? Or are officeholders bound to vote the prejudices, viewpoints and passions of the majority in their districts?

> **MARK PENN:**
> At a Tuesday morning staff meeting, he assured everyone that Clinton's Lewinsky speech had struck just the right tone.

"In political science, we call these two approaches the 'trustee model' and the 'delegate model,' " notes Moore. "I would be perfectly willing to debate either side of the question."

But there are several possible problems with the 'delegate model.' One is that despite the mythic faith pollsters and political consultants put in polls, they aren't infallible. They are also often misinterpreted and misused. And, finally, there are times when leadership is needed, not polls.

## How Accurate?

Today polls are taken on subjects ranging from the profound to the profoundly silly. Is O.J. Simpson guilty or innocent? Whom do you want to break Roger Maris' home run record? Would a woman rather be married to a man who looked like Danny DeVito and did the dishes or a man who looked like Robert Redford and did no dishes? Do you approve of Monica Lewinsky?

But polling's origins, and its bread and butter, have always been the business of predicting elections. The question traditionally asked is basic: "If the election were held today, would you vote for x or for y?" The tricky part is ensuring that question is asked of a representative sample. Since the Truman-Dewey debacle of 1948, polling firms, led by the Gallup Organization, have refined their techniques for gathering this information to a fine art and have compiled an impressive record for accuracy. In the early 1990s, however, venerated California pollster Mervin Field began to notice a troubling trend: the plummeting response rates in his polls.

This phenomenon seems to be caused by a variety of factors, including the availability of call-screening devices, the fact that polling is not a novelty anymore and, probably more than anything else, the vast increase in telemarketing that has left the public surlier and less cooperative. With response rates dipping below 40 percent—half what he sought when he started out—Field said he feared that eventually the industry was going to be simply wrong about an election.

That election happened, in 1996, though nobody seemed to notice. As late as Oct. 23 of that year, the major polling organizations said Clinton had a huge lead over Bob Dole that ranged from the mid-teens to nearly 20 percentage points. The final numbers were 49 percent for Clinton, 41 percent for Dole and 8 percent for Perot. The only pollster who was right was an unknown named John Zogby, who polled for Reuters. For his efforts, Zogby found his methods harshly attacked—he is still attacked to this day—by the pollsters he'd embarrassed.

The 1996 results were hardly in the league of 1948—at least the pollsters picked the right winner—but they sent alarm bells ringing at Gallup, which concluded that it had waited far too long to start polling only "likely voters" instead of registered voters.

But was this lesson really learned?

In recent months, the airwaves have been inundated with polls showing a significant majority of the American people do not want Bill Clinton impeached over lies he told about Monica Lewinsky. From that fact, all kinds of other theories emanate: that the Republicans are overplaying their hand, that Clinton is out of the woods, that this issue will actually work in Democrats' favor in the upcoming elections.

But a closer examination of the numbers, what pollsters call the "internals," raise doubts. For starters, who is being polled? Well, it turns out that it is not likely voters or even registered voters, but the general public. This is quite relevant. Zogby, who polls only likely voters year-round, consistently finds an approval rating for Clinton that's 10 points lower than the other major polls find. "The demographics of all adults is very different from the demographics of likely voters," Zogby says.

Underscoring this point is a new Gallup poll in which the impeachment question is broken down by likely voters. The results are interesting: Whereas the general population opposes impeachment 62 percent to 34 percent, the likeliest voters are against it only 54 to 42. If you add party affiliation to the mix (registered Republicans *favor* impeachment by more than 2-to-1) one can see how unlikely it is that a Republican candidate in a solidly Republican district could be hurt by making Clinton's life difficult.

Take another frequently bandied-about poll number—Clinton's approval rating. Gallup and others have this figure in the mid-60s. Assume for a moment that number is accurate. What does it really tell us? Well, it's 10 points higher than Clinton's normal number, even when things are going well. Not to put too fine a point on it, but even White House officials concede privately that nothing Clinton has done in the policy arena in his second term can really explain the upward spike in support that came after the Lewinsky story broke.

So here's a postulate: It's no coincidence that the approval rating and the anti-impeachment numbers are virtually the same; voters are substituting one question for the other because they know how polls are used today to try to win debates.

## USE AND ABUSE

The day after Clinton's disastrous pseudo-apology on the Monica Lewinsky matter, Clinton Pollster Mark Penn assured everyone at the Tuesday morning staff meeting that the president had struck just the right tone—because 58 percent of those polled in Penn's surveys told him this, according to one participant in the session.

But those polls didn't take into account—and couldn't, really—a host of other factors, including that Clinton's new story meant he had personally lied to the very Democrats who could give him cover, including Cabinet members and Capitol Hill leaders. In other words, as every reputable pollster readily admits, there are limits to what polling can tell us. "There are just things you can't poll," said one White House aide, with a laugh. "But we try."

They aren't alone. The last president who didn't employ polling was Herbert Hoover. Jimmy Carter actually began the tradition of having an in-house pollster, and Ronald Reagan's extensive polling operation was the model for the Clinton White House.

The first president to study polls, to commission his own private polls and, ultimately to ignore the polls, was Franklin D. Roosevelt. In 1940, FDR desperately wanted to help Britain stave off Nazi aggression, but Americans were in an isolationist mind-set. According to Robert Eisinger, assistant professor of political science at Lewis & Clark College, Roosevelt began quietly obtaining poll data from Gallup and another Princeton pollster with ties to Gallup named Hadley Cantril.

Roosevelt consulted polls on everything from support for Lend-Lease to whether Catholic voters would be offended if strategic bombing by the Allies harmed religious sites in Italy. In the end, however, Roosevelt scholars say that FDR set his own course. "I don't think there's any evidence that he relied on polls," said Eisinger. "They are feeding into his policy decisions, but they are not driving them."

Two, more recent, examples of presidents and polls are also instructive. In 1990, after Iraqi tanks overran Kuwait, polls showed Americans overwhelmingly opposed to the idea of American ground troops being deployed to the Arabian peninsula. But President Bush, asserting that national security was at stake, decided to send troops anyway. The following winter, 10 days before the ground war began, only 11 percent of Americans were in favor of launching one. A month later, this figure was closer to 90 percent—and so was Bush's approval rating.

A third example is Clinton's 1995 decision to send troops to the Balkans to halt ethnic genocide. After ago-

**DICK MORRIS:**

"You don't use a poll to reshape a program, but to reshape your argumentation for the program so the public supports it."

nizing over this issue for a year, Clinton finally decided to act. Deeply concerned about public opinion polls that were running 2-to-1 against committing American ground troops, the White House pollsters delved deeply into exactly what the public would accept. Clinton pollster Dick Morris insists that the purpose of these polls was to know how to explain the Bosnian commitment to the public, but it also seems that the American public helped set the parameters of the military mission. The public told Clinton's pollsters it didn't want American troops scouring mountainsides looking for war criminals or disarming the Bosnian militias, and that it wanted a firm timetable for withdrawal. All these elements ultimately became conditions of the deployment.

"Clinton does polls to decide what to do," says Republican pollster Frank Luntz, who tested the GOP "Contract With America" in surveys. "That's not what they should be used for. When we did the contract, we used polls to decide what to say, not what to do."

Morris insists that this is what Clinton does as well.

"A misuse of polls is when a politician switches positions because of a poll," Morris said. "You don't use a poll to reshape a program, but to reshape your argumentation for the program so that the public supports it and it works." Morris points out that Bosnia was not the first time Clinton bucked the polls, and he rattles off a litany of issues, ranging from the International Monetary Fund bailout and the rescue of the Mexican peso to support for late-term abortion and affirmative action.

Clinton also uses polls to tell people what they want to hear about a policy—sometimes even when the language doesn't actually describe the policy. In the case of affirmative action, for instance, Clinton's polling told him what to say—"mend it, don't end it"—and he said it, but he made no real changes in policy.

Lawrence Jacobs, a political scientist at the University of Minnesota, says this example highlights the real abuse of polling. Jacobs argues that since 1980, presidents and members of Congress have charted their courses mostly on the basis of special-interest pressure, campaign contributions and ideology, while using polls to help them put a (sometimes false) face on their policies. "They use polls to learn how to manipulate the language and to employ buzzwords and symbols," he says. Thus voters get the worst of both worlds. They don't believe their elected officials are listening to them, and when the politicians pretend to listen, it's merely to learn how to fool them.

So where does this leave us on impeachment?

One possible answer is that on this issue, the public knows it has a right to be consulted and is taking back some of the power of politicians, pollsters and the media to spin.

Republican House members keep stressing "the rule of law," and holding out hopes that they can bring public opinion along with them. But this issue is not as remote as understanding the menace of the Third Reich—or even of Saddam Hussein. Infidelity (and lying about it) is domestic policy, literally, and the public seems to believe it knows as much about it as do members of Congress, the media and these lawyers who keep popping up on television. "I'm not saying we should have a national referendum on it, clearly that's not what the Constitution and the Founders had in mind," White House Press Secretary Joe Lockhart said in an interview. "But the public ought to be heard on this, on what constitutes an impeachable offense. They have a right to be heard."

Certainly the facts are in the public domain—Independent Counsel Kenneth W. Starr and the Republicans made sure of that—and on this issue, at least, the polls are probably accurate. "If there's one clear message in all this data," said Gallup's David Moore, "it's that they don't want him impeached."

---

*Sydney J. Freedberg Jr. contributed to this report.*

# The Governor-President

## Bill Clinton

invented a new way to use the Oval Office, and not just for tawdry sex. Like Andrew Jackson and Franklin Roosevelt, he has changed the very nature of the American Presidency. They enlarged it, necessarily. He has shrunk it, necessarily—and made a legacy for himself that could supersede the Monica mess. **By Jacob Weisberg**

As a 10-year-old glued to the TV through the summer of Watergate, I remember the air of gravity that hung over the proceedings, the sense that it was a dreadful necessity to put a President on trial. I don't recall authority figures having to explain that it was a national crisis—even to a kid, that was pretty obvious. One of the oddest things about the impeachment weekend just before Christmas was the constant stream of reminders that the country was again experiencing such a crisis. Throughout the ordeal, legislators and commentators tried to come up with more dramatic ways to frame the events taking place. Bill Clinton was about to become only the *second* President ever impeached. He would be our *first elected* President ever impeached. All through the holidays and on into January the tone remained the same: we were having the first Senate trial of a President in 130 years. Watching TV was like having someone grab you by the lapels and shout, Don't you understand this is supposed to be historic!

Bill Clinton's impeachment is historic in the sense of it being an event historians will puzzle over in decades to come. But what those historians will have to ponder is not how it shook the country, but why it didn't. they will have to explain how the country experienced the form of

a constitutional crisis without the content of one, how an impeachment could drive a President's approval rating up instead of down. They may be better disposed than contemporary observers of the Clinton scandal to look beyond the Dow Jones industrial average for an explanation. For Clinton's weathering of the Lewinsky scandal represents something that is truly historic—a break in the way the American Presidency functions.

For the 60 years or so that preceded Clinton's election in 1992, the nation lived through what might be described as the heroic phase of the American Presidency. Not that all modern Presidents have been heroes, of course. But beginning in the late 1920's, the country was enveloped in a succession of crises—the Great Depression, the Second World War and the cold war. We measured our Presidents against their roles in these great events. Thankfully, we're not living in different times. The nation is at peace and growing more prosperous, not merely or even mostly as a consequence of executive decision-making, but as a backdrop to it. This places a different and in some way more difficult burden on the leader of the free world. An American President now has a more diffuse and bewildering job. He must focus on a series of comparatively minor problems at home, make sense of international confusion and compete for the public's attention with more captivating forms of entertainment.

Clinton has not failed to keep his public entertained. To some it has seemed like a tragedy, to others a sitcom.

*Jacob Weisberg is a contributing writer for the magazine. His most recent article was about Treasury Secretary Robert Rubin.*

From *The New York Times Magazine*, January 17, 1999, pp. 31-35, 41, 52, 65. © 1999 by The New York Times Company. Reprinted by permission.

Following the pattern of his career in Arkansas and of his accident-prone 1992 campaign, Clinton as President has repeatedly toyed with ruin, practically digging his own grave, only to pop back up, Houdini-like, after everyone thought he could no longer be breathing. With his impeachment on charges of perjury and obstruction of justice, his dialogue with disaster has reached what is likely to be its final phase (though another eruption is always possible). The debate is no longer over Clinton's continued viability as a politician, because he faces no more elections. The stain of impeachment cannot be washed away by what he does in his remaining time in the White House, because part of what his impeachment means is that the House of Representatives is no longer much interested in doing business with him. A conviction in a Senate trial would make Clinton history sooner rather than later, but whether he is convicted, acquitted or censured as a result of some Senate-White House deal, it does not seem too soon to try to characterize his Presidency. Bill Clinton is the President who, for better and worse, turned the White House into a governor's mansion.

BILL CLINTON WAS WORRIED ABOUT HIS LEGACY LONG BEFORE HE learned, a year ago, that the world was about to learn about Monica Lewinsky. In his hook, "Behind the Oval Office," Dick Morris described a Sunday morning phone conversation in August 1996 on the topic of how Clinton would rate in the history books. Clinton agreed he wasn't a top-tier President, but wondered what he could do to make it into the ranks of Morris's second tier, with Harry Truman, Theodore Roosevelt, Andrew Jackson and Ronald Reagan. (Morris said he'd have to do three big things: make welfare reform work, balance the Federal budget and smash international terrorism, on top of some littler things.)

Though the word "legacy" has a positive cast, Presidential historians often use it to convey a more neutral meaning. A legacy is properly understood as a mark left on the country for good or for ill. Popular democracy is Andrew Jackson's legacy. The national park system is part of Theodore Roosevelt's. The New Deal, which molded the modern Federal Government, is F.D.R.'s. Watergate is Nixon's. There are legacies of neglect, like Ronald Reagan's bequest to his successors of a vast Federal budget deficit (offset by his affirmative legacy of drawing the cold war to a surprising and successful close). Gerald Ford, Jimmy Carter and George Bush, to name three of our last five Presidents, arguably left no major legacy at all. The same is true of the late-l9th-century Presidents who populate the murk between Lincoln and Teddy Roosevelt.

We know something else about Presidential legacies. Matters that loom large now will diminish in retrospect. Clinton's popularity, and by extension his survival as President, do rely heavily on the extraordinary strength of the economy, now in the eighth year of what will soon be-

come our longest known peacetime expansion. But over time, even that impressive statistic is likely to fade in importance. A lousy economy can define a Presidency, as it did for Herbert Hoover. But the simple fact of a good economy tends not to make a legacy. If it did, Eisenhower, Johnson and Nixon would be considered greater Presidents than F.D.R. and Truman.

There is already a rough consensus among historians that Clinton is a significant President. He stands to be remembered, most obviously for causing a big scandal and getting impeached, but also for getting re-elected, something no Democrat since F.D.R. had done. But Clinton, I think, will also be remembered for reforming the Federal Government and for reshaping his party. Most strikingly Clinton, like Andrew Jackson and F.D.R., has changed the very nature of the American Presidency. Where those two Presidents expanded the role and importance of the Presidency, Clinton has downsized the office, both in the negative sense of stripping away some of its dignity and in the positive one of making adjustments demanded by the historical moment.

Coming to the White House from the governor's mansion in Little Rock, Clinton has recast the Presidency on the more modest model of his previous job. Unlike Presidents, governors have few opportunities to be visionaries. Instead, they do what Clinton has done—a job of crisis management, political accommodation and governmental reform.

In one way the public doesn't expect much from a governor; in another way it expects a great deal. A governor is expected to address whatever issues arise, from upgrading the skills of his state's work force to reducing traffic congestion on its highways. Financial constraints deny governors the possibility of grander schemes. Within the confines of balanced and limited budgets, however, they can distinguish themselves with creative social policy ideas. In smaller states, the governor is a familiar figure whose blunders and foibles are as well known as his cartoon caricature. If the governor proves himself intelligent and capable, people tend to be willing to indulge a fair amount of rascality on his part. As flawed as he may be, he's all that protects them from a Legislature that's inevitably far worse than he is.

GOVERNORS, OF COURSE, DON'T SHAPE FOREIGN POLICY. There's no doubt Clinton will be remembered as primarily a domestic President and perhaps the first in a line of domestic Presidents who followed the cold war. Clinton ran on domestic and economic issues in 1992, in answer to George Bush's international focus. His platform, "Putting People First," the most detailed policy statement ever issued by a candidate, elaborated a series of ideas about how to make government more effective. Clinton has improved a range of Federal agencies and programs. But what may stand as most significant is not just that he mended broken policies, but that he restored the feeling that domestic government could work.

From his first Presidential campaign, Clinton was guided by a revised philosophy of government's role. Probably the most underappreciated thing Clinton did during his first year was expanding the Earned Income Tax Credit, a program by which the Federal Government supplements the income of low-wage workers. Clinton's notion was that if you work full time, you shouldn't have an income below the poverty line. A government commitment to this principle exemplified his reform liberalism. As a successor to the New Deal-Great Society archetype of ever-expanding social benefits, Clinton proposed a more modest, reciprocal model, one based on what he has described as an exchange of opportunity for responsibility, and hence a model based on more limited expectations of what the Federal Government can do. During his 1992 campaign, Clinton characterized this notion, in a phrase coined by Will Marshall of the Progressive Policy Institute, as the "New Covenant."

Clinton's subsequent successes, like national service and welfare reform, have come from applying this notion of a limited social contract. His early failures occurred when he strayed from it, relapsing into the older pattern of delivering new Federal benefits from on high. Most notable was his failure in health care.

It's possible that a better-designed and more politically astute plan could have placed his Presidency on stronger footing. But Clinton botched the design and marketing of his plan, setting himself at odds with moderates in both parties whose support he needed. Considering himself a centrist reformer, Clinton didn't see the potential for his "managed competition" scheme to be portrayed as an oldfangled liberal spending program.

What Clinton didn't yet get was the depth of the discontent with the way government was working. When he took office, trust in government had been steadily eroding for a quarter century. In 1964, 76 percent of Americans told pollsters they thought they could trust government to do the right thing all or most of the time. In 1994, the year Clinton's plan for health-care reform fizzled, the number who said they trusted government bottomed out at 15 percent. The nature of this disillusion is a debate of its own, but it was based at least in part on the failures of government in welfare and public housing, in worsening crime and deteriorating public education.

This loss of confidence easily attached itself to Clinton's attempt to award the Federal Government another vast responsibility. Clinton was regarded as someone who had promised change and failed to deliver; This frustration came to fruition in 1994. Not until the ascendancy of the Gingrich Congress did Clinton fully grasp the depth of disenchantment with Washington. But from that point on, Clinton began to understand that he had to grapple with this corrosive skepticism. Michael Waldman, Clinton's chief speech writer, remembers sitting with him in the White House residence working on last year's State of the Union address. At one point, according to Waldman, Clinton paused and remarked that "F.D.R.'s mission was to save capitalism from its excesses. Our mission has been to save government from its own excesses so it can again be a progressive force."

The idea of Clinton as the savior of liberal government will strike many as perverse. Following the 1994 election, Clinton faced tremendous criticism, not just from Republicans but also from Democrats who felt he was trying to jettison, in an effort at conciliation, the party's bedrock beliefs. The lightning rod for this anger became his nefarious political consultant Morris, whom Democratic traditionalists saw as pulling Clinton not in the direction of reform, but toward a dead centrism derived from opinion poles. Clinton was much ridiculed for proposing microinterventions like free walkie-talkies for neighborhood watch groups.

But what Clinton was beginning to understand was that government's failures weren't arcane managerial issues; they were questions of public trust. While devising gubernatorial-scale programs that encapsulated his New Covenant approach, he proceeded to address the two biggest causes of that mistrust. First, Clinton agreed to the Republican goal of a balanced budget. But where the G.O.P. long supported a balanced budget as a means of downsizing government, Clinton saw it as a way to reinvigorate government. From his first economic plan in 1993, Clinton regarded the deficit as a problem serious enough to warrant putting many of his pet projects on hold. What he subsequently discovered was that by operating within the context of a balanced budget, he could argue for expanding spending in certain areas, like school construction or national service, without being accused of fiscal irresponsibility. The Federal budget had become like a state budget. Only if government was convincingly limited in size could it hope to get away with activism.

His second and arguably more important decision was following through on his campaign promise to end welfare "as we know it." Many liberals mistook Clinton's interest in the subject as political; they saw the subtext as race baiting. In fact, Clinton saw welfare as disruptive of the proper relationship between government and its citizens. The system's unpopularity was not just because of its being counterproductive or a waste of resources, but because it offered something for nothing.

Members of Clinton's cabinet objected strenuously to his decision to accept a modified Republican bill based on the idea of block grants, and a few of his own policy makers resigned in protest over the issue. The smoke of battle obscured the fact that Clinton was following through on his New Covenant notion of welfare reform and not merely acceding to a punitive rollback. Clinton could also see that the country's governors, already embarked on a variety of welfare-reform experiments, were in the best position to know how the system might be fixed. Only in

# Clinton

is now and probably forever our priapic President, who takes his place alongside our drunken President, Ulysses S. Grant, our napping President, Calvin Coolidge, and our treacherous President, Richard Nixon.

the last year has it become evident that Clinton did reform welfare largely in the way he said he would with pretty much the results he anticipated. Welfare rolls have declined from five million families in 1995 to three million in June 1998. A downturn in the economy could curtail this progress by making it harder to place people in jobs, but at the moment the national picture is one of drastically declining levels of dependency with scant evidence of increased misery.

These promising signs have been accompanied by progress in other areas in which government has failed. Under Henry Cisneros, the Department of Housing and Urban Development actually began breaking up pockets of concentrated poverty by tearing down parts of the worst urban housing projects and moving to voucher-based subsidies. Cities have also benefited from two changes that may have been largely incidental to Clinton's agenda—a big drop in crime and the end of a long-term increase in out-of-wedlock births. Together these developments have begun to have a tipping-point effect for America's urban centers. It's too early to say that these improvements have restored the 30-year slide in faith in government. But from its low in 1994, confidence in government had recovered more than 20 points by early 1998. Impeachment has driven it down a bit—but to nowhere near its lowest level.

AS COLLECTIONS OF DISPARATE INTERESTS AND IDEOLOGIES, political parties are never fully agreed or united. But there are times when disagreement within parties is stimulating and productive rather than harmful. Unresolved differences get put aside for the sake of more important common goals and are subsumed under the aegis of a popular and effective leader. In recent years, we have seen this happen twice, once to the G.O.P. in the 1980's under Ronald Reagan and again to the Democrats in the 1990's under Bill Clinton.

Before Clinton was elected in 1992, conventional wisdom held that the Democrats faced a crisis. After 12 years of G.O.P. White House rule and defeat in five of the previous six Presidential elections, the party had seemingly ceased to become competitive at the Presidential level. Peter Brown's 1991 book, "Minority Party: Why Democrats Face Defeat in 1992 and Beyond," was one of several arguing the thesis. White working-class and suburban middle-class voters, according to the conventional wisdom, were abandoning the party in droves because of its excessively liberal positions on crime, welfare, foreign policy and "values" issues. How could the Democrats become politically competitive again in an era when what the party once stood for—an expanding Federal role—was proving less and less popular? The party itself was deeply divided over how and whether it should evolve. On one side was a group of centrist reformers clustered around the Democratic Leadership Council. On the other was a rump of liberal traditionalists, including labor unions and minority groups who viewed D.L.C. positions as treasonable to their basic beliefs.

Clinton has faced the problems of his party—at least at the Presidential level—methodically, systematically and effectively. To a remarkable degree, he has succeeded in making once seemingly incurable ailments vanish, while giving back to the Democrats the kind of well-oiled national political machine they had before 1968.

His first task was pulling thorns from the party paw. Asked which party did a better job handling crime, voters chose the G.O.P. by a margin of 18 points in 1991. Clinton reversed this pattern by jettisoning Dukakis-era positions like opposition to the death penalty while exploiting the one aspect of the issue where public opinion diverges from the dictates of G.O.P. interest-group politics: gun control. Clinton doesn't have much of a basis for claiming that it's his policies that have reduced crime rates over the past several years, but he has put away the charge that Democrats don't like punishing criminals. Recent surveys show the parties polling essentially even on the issue.

What's most remarkable is not that Clinton has taken crime and other reliable wedge issues away from Republicans. It's that he has done so while unifying a party that was itself divided over these issues. In 1992, both the New Democrats and the traditionalists supported Clinton in the belief that he was, at heart, one of them. Perhaps

# The President's

### screw-ups are a reminder that he isn't any better than the rest of us and doesn't think he is . . . He has devised an entirely idiosyncratic populism, based on the sense of him as a personally flawed but public-spirited and highly intelligent leader.

inevitably, both sides were disappointed in the way he governed. For much of his first term Clinton was out of favor with the center or the left of the party, or both at the same time. In his first two years, the D.L.C. saw Clinton as swinging left with his health-care plan and tax increase. In his second two years, liberals griped over Clinton's accession to a balanced budget and welfare reform. But by the time of the 1996 election, Clinton had again forged an alliance.

Many people are puzzled about how Clinton has been able to appease liberal constituencies while flouting their principles—confronting unions with Nafta, poor blacks with welfare reform, teachers with charter schools and feminists with Paula Jones. The simplest explanation is that he has restored a model last seen among Democrats during the Presidency of Lyndon Johnson, when those joining his coalition get to experience victory and taste power. Clinton has created a sense of partisan pride powerful enough to quell the narcissism of small differences. This thrill of putting up a good fight against a common enemy—something Presidents as different as Reagan and F.D.R. have created and used—has overcome ideological and sometimes moral scruples. Democratic activists have taken the advice he gave a group of them in 1981: 'When someone is beating you over the head with a hammer . . . take out a meat cleaver and cut off their hand."

It hasn't always been pretty, or even, perhaps, ethical. Since 1992, Clinton's style has been to dispense with qualms and play politics in as ruthless and relentless a way as the G.O.P. In the 1980's, Reagan and Bush were charged with relying on polling to an unprecedented degree; Clinton has gone them one better, market-testing his rhetoric then deploying it with a numbing repetitive precision. He answered the slick fabrications of Michael Deaver with the more subtle and compelling mythography of Harry Thomason and Linda Bloodworth-Thomason. He

dug deeper for dirt on his opponents, devised more effective 30-second attack ads and showed great ingenuity in exploiting loopholes in the campaign finance law.

The biggest change is financial. In the l980's, the G.O.P. advantage in fund-raising was as high as 5 to 1. In the 1992 election cycle, Clinton and Ron Brown, then chairman of the Democratic National Committee, whittled it down to 3 to 2. In 1996, Clinton and Harold Ickes nearly caught up in the chief corporate category, so-called soft money, bringing in $123 million to the G.O.P.'s $138 million. They did this with willful blindness about the sources of these funds. Clinton's attitude is that because the rules aren't enforced and Republicans are preventing him from creating a level playing field he is free to fight as dirty as they do.

SINCE THE LEWINSKY SCANDAL, VARIOUS SECTORS OF THE ideologically disgruntled Democratic "base"— those who might be thought to be less than keen about Clinton's small-bore, poll-driven, corporate-friendly centrism—have been the President's staunchest supporters. Black leaders disappointed with Clinton over matters ranging from the balanced budget to welfare reform have flocked to his defense. Among blacks, Clinton's approval rating remains as high as Ronald Reagan's rating was among conservative Republicans. This is a testament in part to the real feeling Clinton evinces over racial issues, as well as to black sensitivity to prosecutorial unfairness and sympathy for victims of persecution. But it also speaks to a different kind of party, one in which members are willing to settle for half a loaf.

Republicans, on the other hand, now face the problem of a radical base that has lost its willingness to postpone gratification. The adage that Democrats look for heretics while Republicans seek converts has ceased to apply. To a remarkable degree, the parties have switched places.

Clinton's political formula is now almost universally regarded as a winning one for Democrats. All of the serious contenders for the 2000 Democratic nomination have indicated their desire to continue in the same basic direction. Al Gore, Bill Bradley and John Kerry have all positioned themselves as Clinton Democrats. The potential contenders who do not fit this profile—Paul Wellstone and Jesse Jackson—are running as protest candidates. Clinton's "Third Way" formula has an international following as well. From a historical viewpoint, the question is whether a Democratic successor will be able to carry off Clinton's balancing act within the party. There is a worrisome analogy in the G.O.P. where Reagan became a successful two-term President by appeasing the religious right while reaching out to moderate voters. George Bush's efforts to sustain this equilibrium made the Republican right truculent to the point of self-destructiveness. Today the G.O.P. remains badly divided, looking back to the Reagan years as an irretrievable golden age. Clinton's successor, almost certain to lack his political gifts and perhaps his ruthlessness, faces an enormous challenge in maintaining the Clinton coalition. Yet it is what happens to his party after he leaves the scene that will determine whether remaking it constitutes a major aspect of Clinton's legacy.

CLINTON'S POLICY AND POLITICAL SUCCESSES WILL STILL HAVE TO BE weighed against his personal reputation. Even if his impeachment continues to be seen as disproportionate punishment, it will be remembered that Clinton gave his enemies the sword they used against him. Assuming he is not convicted by the Senate and finishes his term, impeachment will still be in the first paragraph of Clinton's obituary.

At some level, Clinton can't escape becoming a historical joke. He is now and forever our priapic President, who takes his place alongside our drunken President, Ulysses S. Grant, our napping President, Calvin Coolidge, and our treacherous President, Richard Nixon. Whatever else he does in office, Clinton will not be able to keep this out of his capsule biography: he's the one who had oral sex with a 21-year-old intern in the Oval Office, got caught, lied, caused a national spectacle and saw it undermine his second term. This story line may be tempered with sympathy. In a longer view, Clinton's libido may not differentiate him from Franklin Roosevelt (who died with his mistress, not his wife) or John Kennedy (who arranged orgies in the White House swimming pool). But it will be hard to avoid the view that there was something more reckless about Clinton, because he had no basis for thinking the press would protect him, as it did his predecessors.

Nor can Clinton escape his reputation for being slippery. He is not the first President to lie, or lie under oath. But he will surely be remembered as someone who habitually played games with the truth. Clinton is the President who said he never inhaled, who told a national audience, "I did not have sexual relations with that woman" and considered it true because his definition of sexual relations did not include receiving oral sex. The most evasive of these lines, like "It depends on what the meaning of the word 'is' is," are destined for inclusion in Bartlett's. Clinton is to hairsplitting legalisms what Yogi Berra is to tautological absurdities; he seems nearly to have invented the form.

It will also be recalled that he was disloyal to friends and took advantage of people who worked for him. Early in his Presidency, Clinton failed to stand by nominees in trouble, even when they were old friends like Zöe Baird. He has taken advantage of faithful aides, using and disposing of them when convenient, as with Harold Ickes, whom Clinton threw overboard after Ickes finished the dirty work involved in getting him reelected. His sexual incontinence was itself a betrayal of people who spent years working for him, some of whom faced their own legal problems because they helped protect him. He led subordinates like his former press secretary Michael McCurry to damage their own professional reputations by amplifying his lies. Clinton will be remembered as, among other things, a cad.

But more significant than what the impeachment episode says about Clinton's character may be what it tells us about national mores at century's end. Contrary to the prediction of many reporters, myself included, the scandal not only did not end his Presidency; it actually made a President reelected on a "values" agenda more popular. When the scandal first broke a year ago, Washington reporters were still dealing with the issue of whether to protect the public from information they assumed it was too unsophisticated to handle. Few suspected how much the rest of the country had changed in the previous decade. The America of today is no longer the America of 1987, the year that Gary Hart was driven from a Presidential race by the Donna Rice scandal and that Clinton decided not to go for the nomination after his aide Betsey Wright presented him with a list of ex-lovers capable of sabotaging his candidacy.

Clinton is not simply the beneficiary of the arrival of a more tolerant moral standard; he is personally responsible for its application to politics. He was the first Presidential candidate to publicly acknowledge that he had committed adultery. Some have argued that, based on the famous "60 Minutes" appearance, in which he acknowledged causing pain in his marriage, there was an implicit bargain between Clinton and the voters. If we elected him, he promised to sin no more. But the real proposition was direct and explicit: Clinton stood for office on the basis of what he could do rather than who he would be. Unlike previous Presidents, he proposed to be hired on the basis of his abilities and his approach to government, not his qualities as a moral exemplar. He was promising to be a good governor.

Such a promise is built into Clinton's own view of government. The notion of a New Covenant implies a transformation in expectations. Washington no longer delivers solutions to our problems; it merely helps us to solve them. Not looking to government as an all-purpose savior implies no longer putting politicians on a pedestal. To perform their new role, leaders don't have to be ideal human beings, superior projections of ourselves. They merely need to understand our problems and help us grapple with them. If they hold up their end of the bargain, by governing well, we won't go beyond ours by judging them harshly for inevitable human failings. While he has surely tested our commitment to this pact, Clinton has held up his end of it.

The compact that Clinton embodies has emerged as our country's de facto standard of political morality. We are still less dismissive of marital infidelity than, say, the French. But like the Europeans and Canadians, we now distinguish public from private in the lives of our leaders, and forbear from judgments about the latter. The new rules have not taken hold everywhere yet. Much of the press has yet to assimilate the concept that most of the public no longer considers intrusive reporting about private lives relevant to democratic decision-making. Nonetheless, a President with a rare ability to compartmentalize his psyche has ratified a new attitude toward the private lives of public figures.

You can go further than that and say that the Lewinsky scandal says something not just about the development of American political morality, but also about American morality in general. A quick survey might leave one with the impression that the 1990's were the decade that Puritanism died. Since Clinton has been President, homosexuality has gained public acceptance; legal gambling has swept the country; pornography has become ubiquitous; and vice has been redefined as disease. Meanwhile, the public has become unshockable about sex and unconcerned about Presidential adultery. These changes imply that traditional morality has receded.

But something more complicated is going on. The same public that has forgiven Clinton his trespasses holds to a strict personal morality and has endorsed Clinton's emphasis on "values" in government programs—what Prof. Michael Sandel of Harvard calls Clinton's repudiation of "moral neutrality" in public policy.

The harmonization of these seeming contradictions may be arising from the increasingly subtle distinction Americans are making between the public and private realms. One striking thing the sociologist Alan Wolfe shows in his book "One Nation, After All" is that while American suburbanites are far from relativistic in their own moral views, they shrink from judging the private behavior of others, and dislike moralizing when they see it practiced. At the same time, they want government policy to support their values.

The Lewinsky scandal writes these distinctions large. Few approve of Clinton's behavior. Yet the vast majority object even more to casting stones at the President for mistakes in an area where he is answerable to his family and his God, not to voters or the media. Though these mistakes may make it impossible for Clinton to talk about values any longer, voters care more about how he applied his views in public—welfare reform, for example—than how he violated them in private. Clinton didn't devise this ethic, but his election and survival encapsulate it. He leaves behind an electorate that wants its values embedded in public policy, but that no longer moralizes about private behavior.

ONE HISTORICAL ISSUE ABOUT CLINTON'S IMPEACHMENT may be a simple extension of the current mystery: why a Republican Congress pursued it. Scholars of the 21st century will recall that removing a popular President from office was very unlikely, that it wasn't dictated by the Constitution and that demanding it was obviously harmful to the G.O.P.'s public standing. The episode will undoubtedly be measured, as it already has been, against Andrew Johnson's impeachment in 1868. A historical consensus now views Johnson's impeachment largely as a mistake that grew out of the aggravated passions of the Reconstruction Era. The deeper fight was over the terms under which the Southern states would be readmitted to the union. In 1999, we have a similarly overheated political environment, yet it's hard to see what the fuss is really about.

This time, the prime motivating factor in impeachment seems to be personal. There's a simmering hatred of Clinton, which has boiled hotter and hotter through his time in office and bears little relation to the passions people ordinarily bring to politics. What explains it? Historians examining this phenomenon years hence might ask first if Clinton-hating came from interests threatened by his policies, following the pattern of F.D.R. But Clinton has hardly been a foe to the moneyed classes. On policy grounds, Republicans might be expected to embrace a President who shares their views on big issues including free trade, balancing the Federal budget, crime and welfare.

THE MOST COMMON EXPLANATION IS THAT HATRED FOR CLINTON IS an expression of "a culture war." The idea here is that in their strenuous dislike of the President; conservatives are fighting a battle over the 1960's and its legacy. Clinton is the first baby-boomer President, the first who dodged the Vietnam draft and admitted to smoking marijuana. His conservative opponents, including many members of the same generation, see such a figure as a threat to the moral order. During the impeachment fight, Tom DeLay, the House Republican whip, described it as "a debate about relativism versus absolute truth."

But the culture-war argument doesn't do justice to an antipathy that goes back to Clinton's candidacy. I think there are three separate psychological profiles of Clinton-hating, which have blurred together at times. The first type of Clinton-hater liberal, and he does derive his hatred from the 60's. His is the view that Clinton is a fundamentally disingenuous and inauthentic person who uses public interest as a cover for private ambition. This opinion, which is manifest in much of Clinton's press coverage, does not draw a line between the personal and the political. The problem isn't that Clinton committed adultery or that he lied about adultery. Indeed, these lapses have inclined liberal critics to support him. What they object to is that Clinton cares about winning more than he cares about principles; that he has thrown overboard such worthy causes as civil liberties; intervention in Bosnia, human rights in China and campaign finance reform.

A second kind of hostility to Clinton is neither liberal nor conservative but comes from the Washington establishment. Sally Quinn, the journalist and Washington hostess, has written that the Clintons "dissed" Georgetown society—a culture she approaches not merely as an anthropologist—by neglecting its advice and avoiding its company. This is true, but the falling out goes well beyond a mere social snub. By downsizing the Presidency and ushering in an era of a less ambitious Federal Government, Clinton has made Washington and its establishment less important. By turning away from both foreign affairs and big-ticket domestic programs, Clinton has made Washington less central to the concerns of the nation than it was in the days of SALT treaties. Turning the Presidency into the country's biggest governor's job is contrary to the political establishment's sense of the office and their relation to it. By allowing the Lewinsky scandal to happen, Clinton has turned the American Presidency (and by extension those who feed off it) into an international laughingstock. "Clinton acted . . . as if he does not recognize what it means to be President of the United States," wrote David Broder, a Washington Post columnist, after Clinton's first nationally televised mea culpa.

The third and most potent kind of Clinton-hating is conservative, but is related to the liberal kind in its aversion to a Democrat who plays politics to win. Instead of being pleased that Clinton has enacted parts of their agenda, Republicans are furious at him for co-opting the best bits of it. With the end of their monopoly on such issues as crime, welfare and balancing the budget, Republicans are forced to contend with Democrats over issues where their positions are distinctly less popular: education, the environment, Social Security and social issues like abortion and homosexuality. Clinton's seizure of the center has driven the G.O.P. to the right, empowering the radicals who want either to legislate on the basis of a narrow moral code or drastically curtail the Federal Government's role, or both. To conservatives, Clinton didn't win the center legitimately. He stole it from them.

Clinton himself is most focused on the Republican opposition. A year ago, he invited a group of historians to meet with him for a private talk. This was just before he was to give his deposition in the Paula Jones case. After a discussion about the Progressive Movement and past Presidents, Clinton held forth to a smaller group clustered around him. The right, he inveighed, controlled most of American politics, They had both houses of Congress, the

think tanks and the big money. He was all that stood in the way of conservative control over the whole apparatus of government. Republicans would never accept him as legitimate, one of the participants remembers the President thundering at nearly midnight, because he was blocking their ascent to power. A few weeks later, the First Lady described her husband's opponents as "a vast right-wing conspiracy."

The question of Clinton-hating finally transcends conventional political analysis. It's personal and aggravated. Destestation of the President is worsened by the phenomenon of sustained public support for Clinton, which his opponents find baffling. Why does this man's approval rating rise in the teeth of humiliation? At one level, Clinton's supporters have made a pragmatic judgment that he governs in their interest. But at another level, he draws on a reservoir not of love, not of respect even, but of identification.

This identification works in two directions. It is partly the public's identification with Clinton, the perpetual underdog who refuses to ever quit fighting. To a public that consumes quantities of confessional entertainment and self-help advice, Clinton's turmoil seems not bizarre, but familiar. His cyclical progress through stages of sin, denial, contrition and forgiveness has humanized him like no previous President. To a public that had already accepted Clinton with his faults, the Starr report arrived not as a shocking indictment, but as a juicy soap opera with footnotes. As with other celebrities, Clinton's screw-ups are a comforting reminder that he isn't any better than the rest of us and doesn't think that he is.

But possibly more important is the way Clinton himself identifies with regular people. No one who has ever seen him work a rope line or entertain questions at a town meeting can fail to be impressed by the way that he engages with ordinary people. In public forums, Clinton is not just indefatigable, requiring his aides to forcibly pull him away from people who want to shake his hand at the end of an evening. He is, unlike any other politician of this generation, in his element with a crowd—black, white, religious, academic—it almost doesn't matter. Clinton moves an audience by empathizing with its feelings and concerns. The way he draws sustenance by relating to strangers is part and parcel of his political talent.

Clinton-haters of all kinds often describe the President's caring about the problems of regular folk in terms of fakery. They think his "I feel your pain" act is exactly that, a fraud, rather than an expression of natural sympathy. There is in their anger at him something of the mystification with which the liberal intelligentsia beheld Reagan's popularity with the rest of the country. It's as if Clinton's bond with the public was based on some kind of black art. In Reagan's case, this was chalked up to the mesmeric power of his acting (a power never attributed to him during his screen career). With no ready explanation of how Clinton does it, conservatives like William Bennett have often taken the route of becoming infuriated with the public for falling for such a charlatan.

In both the popular defense of Clinton and the elite attacks upon him, one hears the echoes of the passions evoked by two former Presidents: Andrew Jackson and Franklin Roosevelt. Jackson, like Clinton, was twice elected President on the basis of a powerful mutual identification with the public. Conservatives suspected and feared Jackson's popularity, because it represented a different version of democracy from the one the founders had envisioned, a kind they saw as close to mob rule. F.D.R. had a similar bond with ordinary people, which opened up a well of class resentment. People who called Roosevelt "that man" felt that as a patrician populist he was a phony and an opportunist. Many of Clintons critics see him likewise as a beneficiary of meritocratic privilege who has seduced the heartland. They fear him, as they feared Jackson and F.D.R., as a demagogue.

Clinton's bond with the public is based less on economic unfairness than was Jackson's or Roosevelt's and more on a kind of post-ideological pragmatism. He has devised an idiosyncratic populism, based on the sense of him as a personally flawed but public-spirited and highly intelligent leader ready to fight to his last breath for the people who elected him.

REDEFINING GOVERNMENT'S ROLE WILL NEVER MAKE CLINTON beloved in the way F.D.R. is beloved. But he may well be remembered as a President who squarely faced the big problem presented to him with the resources at his command. Someday the loathing that Clinton provokes may be understood in the context of his role in creating a post–cold-war Presidency. Americans may recognize that liberals objected to a narrower role for government, that the Washington establishment resisted his diminishing its stature and that conservatives objected to his substituting prudent downsizing for radical deconstruction.

Knowing Clinton as it has known no other incumbent President, the public has nonetheless refrained from judging him—or at least has been willing to judge him in his complexity, separating his private behavior from his record. I expect historians will continue to draw the distinction in one way or another. Clinton is likely to remain an equivocal figure, a man of significant accomplishments and flawed character, who created gratuitous troubles but defined a social transformation in surviving them. He may come to be remembered as the most paradoxical President: an undisciplined man who reformed government and in so doing restored trust in it, while inspiring almost none in himself.

# There He Goes Again: The Alternating Political Style of Bill Clinton

**Fred I. Greenstein,** *Princeton University*

Some political leadership styles are of a piece. Jimmy Carter's is a case in point. Both in the comments he privately jotted on the margins of memos from his aides and in his public discourse, Carter exhibited a common concern for detail and insistence on the correctness of his own positions. Other styles are layered, as in that of Dwight Eisenhower, whose apolitical public demeanor concealed an analytically detached political sophisticate who obtained results by indirection (Greenstein 1982).

The political style of President Bill Clinton is neither unitary nor layered. It alternates. The tempest over whether Clinton was involved in a dalliance with a White House intern is a reminder of his tendency to oscillate between an uninhibited, anything-goes approach to leadership and a more measured operating mode in which he sets attainable goals and proceeds skillfully in his efforts to realize them.

The pattern is recurrent. After his election as governor of Arkansas in 1978, Clinton instituted a substantial increase in automobile licensing fees, peopled his administration with bearded political activists, and other-

wise failed to conform to the political mores of his state. As a result, he was voted out of office two years later. He then spent the next two years stumping the state and promising to remedy his ways. He was returned to office, serving from 1983 to 1993 and establishing a reputation as a pragmatic and effective state executive (Maraniss 1995).

Similarly, the initial phase of the Clinton presidency was an exercise in excess. Having promised to "focus like a laser," Clinton hit Washington with a splatter of controversial initiatives—gays in the military, problematic cabinet nominations, and a controversial, closed-door health-care task force headed by his wife (Drew 1995; Johnson and Broder 1996; Woodward 1994). His public approval rating at the hundred-day mark set a record low for that point in a presidency. In the words of *Time,* his was an "amazing shrinking presidency."

But he then made an abrupt correction, signaling his willingness to adhere to the norms of the policymaking community. He further improved his performance when the Republicans took control of Congress

in 1996, using his Capitol Hill adversaries as a foil to increase his own public support, and went on to become the fourth of the ten post-World War II chief executives to win reelection.

## Anatomy of a Political Style

Underpinning Clinton's political style is a constellation of traits that vary in their ascendancy depending upon the circumstances in which he finds himself. The traits themselves are not unique, but their pattern is.[1]

### 1. Preoccupation with Policy

Clinton's most unusual quality is his deep absorption in public policy, particularly domestic policy. Most chief executives have broad programmatic aims, but, more so than any other president, Clinton is an aficionado of policy *qua* policy.

### 2. Political Passion

Clinton also is striking in the extent to which he is a political animal, although his passion for politics

From *PS: Political Science & Politics,* June 1998, pp. 179-181. © 1998 by Fred I. Greenstein and the American Political Science Association. Reprinted by permission.

stands out less than his fascination with policy in a universe that includes Franklin Roosevelt, Lyndon Johnson, and Richard Nixon. As a compiler of reminiscences about him by citizens of his native state puts it:

> He had what seemed to be a compulsive need to meet people, to know them, to like them, to have them like him. These are the instincts of the calculating politician, but they long preceded Clinton's political impulses. Bill Clinton's is the case where a man's deepest human instinct perfectly matched, maybe even gave rise to, his most abiding ambition. (Dumas 1993, xvi)

## 3. Verbal Facility

The link between Clinton's policy preoccupation and his political proclivities is his capacity to pour out words. The record abounds with evidence of his ability to expatiate on his policies with modifications from audience to audience. He effortlessly spins out statements of prodigious complexity, as in this 101-word utterance on health care:

> The people who say that if I want to go to a four-year, phased-in competition model and that won't save any tax money on the deficit in the first four years, but will save huge tax money on the deficit in the next four years, miss the main point, which is that if we have a system now which begins to move health care costs down toward inflation, and therefore lowers health care as a percentage of the GNP in the years ahead, the main beneficiaries by factor of almost two to one will be in the private sector. (Clinton 1992)[2]

## 4. The Not-So-Great Communicator

But Clinton's astonishing fluency serves him badly. He finds it too easy to deluge the public with details and is less-than-adept at conveying the principles behind his programs. In this he is the antithesis of Ronald Reagan, who was notoriously lacking in information, but gifted at evoking larger themes.

## 5. Charm

In spite of being thin-skinned, Clinton has proved to be one of the more ingratiating occupants of the Oval Office. But his charm, like that of Franklin Roosevelt, can lead those who consult with him to believe he has accepted their views when he means only to acknowledge that he has heard them.

## 6. Dynamism and Good Cheer

Other elements in the amalgam are Clinton's preternatural optimism, energy, and ebullience. Even when he is deeply beleaguered, as in the controversies that bedeviled him during the 1992 New Hampshire primary and the Monica Lewinsky episode, Clinton has an ability to appear up-beat that also is reminiscent of FDR.

## 7. Lack of Self-Discipline

Then there is his lack of self-discipline and imperfect impulse control. Herein is a major source of his troubles, whether in the form of a tendency to overload the policy agenda, or to give excessively long speeches, or to be scandal-prone in his private life.

## 8. Insensitivity to Organization

Clinton's talents cry out for management, but he is insensitive to the need to back himself up with a well-ordered support system. He has acknowledged that he entered the presidency without attending closely to how to organize his White House (Nelson and Donovan 1993), and his initial team was short on political skill and Washington experience. Then his well-known learning curve manifested itself, and he took on such able, seasoned aides as David Gergen, Leon Panetta, and Michael McCurry.

## 9. Resilience and Capacity to Take Correction

Finally, there is his uncommon ability to rebound in the face of misfortune and his readiness to admit his own failings, qualities that account

for the claim that he is incapable of sustained error.

## The Two Syntheses

Under some circumstances, Clinton's attributes combine to contribute to his anything-goes approach to governance; under others, they converge in his more measured and effective style. His second mode often does not come into play until outside forces have constrained him. Thus, he was far more surefooted after the Republicans won control of Congress in 1994 than before, and he delivered a bravura State of the Union address in the midst of the media barrage about Ms. Lewinsky.

It is not clear why someone as intelligent and politically adept as Clinton should be so dependent on external correction. As is often pointed out, he is the step-son of an alcoholic; and the children of alcohol abusers exhibit a wide variety of behavioral difficulties (Kaufman and Pattison 1982; Cruse 1989). He also was raised by a doting mother, whose strong point was not setting limits, and his high aspirations in themselves are an invitation to overreaching himself.[3]

Clinton's outward characteristics seem to place him in James David Barber's active-positive character category, but he clearly has inner complexities that do not figure in Barber's classification (Barber 1992). More to the point may be the writings of Richard Neustadt (1960), which address the political requirements of presidential effectiveness. In addition to his formal powers, the president has two resources with which to accomplish his purposes, Neustadt argues. One is his reputation in the policy-making community as a skilled, determined player and the other is the perception of other policymakers that he has the support of the public.

When he has his act together, Clinton can be impressively successful in meeting Neustadt's criteria, but there is no guarantee that he will not slip into his alternate mode. Stay tuned!

## Notes

1. For an earlier attempt to take Clinton's measure, see Greenstein (1993–1994).
2. It is less clear how good Clinton is at making the balanced judgments that are referred to by the term "common sense," or whether he thinks critically about the validity of the formulations he verbalizes with such ease.
3. For an examination of Clinton through a psychoanalytic prism, see Renshon (1996).

## References

Barber, J. D. 1992. *The Presidential Character: Predicting Performance in the White House.* 4th ed. Englewood Cliffs, NJ: Prentice Hall.

Clinton, W. J. 1992. "Excerpts from the Interview with President-Elect Clinton." *Wall Street Journal,* December 18.

Cruse, S. W. 1989. *Another Chance: Hope and Health for the Alcoholic Family.* Palo Alto, CA: Science and Behavior Books.

Drew, E. 1995. *On the Edge: The Clinton Presidency.* New York: Simon and Schuster.

Dumas, E. 1993. *The Clintons of Arkansas: An Introduction by Those Who Knew Them Best.* Fayetteville, AR: University of Arkansas Press.

Greenstein, F. I. 1982. *The Hidden-Hand Presidency: Eisenhower as Leader.* New York: Basic Books.

___. 1993–1994. "The Presidential Leadership Style of Bill Clinton: An Early Appraisal." *Political Science Quarterly 108* (Winter): 589–601.

Johnson, H., and D. Broder. 1996. *The System: American Politics at the Breaking Point.* Boston: Little, Brown.

Kaufman, E., and E. M. Pattison. 1982. "The Family and Alcoholism." In *Encyclopedic Handbook of Alcoholism,* ed. E. M. Pattison and E. Kaufman. New York: Gardner Press.

Maraniss, David. 1995. *First in His Class: The Biography of Bill Clinton.* New York: Simon and Schuster.

Nelson, J., and R. J. Donovan. 1993. "The Education of a President: After Six Months of Quiet Success and Loud Failure, Bill Clinton Talks About the Frustrating Process of Figuring Out His Job." *Los Angeles Times Magazine,* August 1.

Neustadt, R. E. 1960. *Presidential Power: The Politics of Leadership,* New York: Norton.

Renshon, S. A. 1996. *High Hopes: The Clinton Presidency and the Politics of Ambition.* New York: NYU Press.

Woodward, B. 1994. *The Agenda: Inside the Clinton White House.* New York: Simon and Schuster.

## About the Author

**Fred I. Greenstein** is professor of politics and director, Woodrow Wilson School Research Program in Leadership Studies at Princeton University.

# BEYOND MONICA: THE FUTURE OF CLINTON'S PAST

The Clinton presidency may have two years to run, but after the events of these past few weeks it seems fair to wonder whether, substantively speaking, it is already over. Without making the mistake of underestimating the President, The Nation is taking a step back this week to ask just what—besides his job—he is fighting so hard to save. Will there be a Clinton legacy beyond an exploding stock market (though even that could turn nasty) and an imploding welfare state? The following is one of seven assessments.*

—The Editors

## Robert B. Reich

I was there for the first four years, there even before the beginning. I could give you a catalogue of worthwhile things that have been done, and some not so worthwhile. Yet I fear none will be remembered nearly as much as the viciousness of these years: the virulent spins and counter-spins, the war rooms, the deadly battle over healthcare, the government shutdown and the stream of allegations over the White House travel office, Vince Foster's suicide, Whitewater, illegal fundraising, and Gennifer, Paula, Kathy and Monica.

It was a time in America when politics became the crudest of spectator sports, and few Americans bothered to vote. Why? The first post–cold war presidency could never find its point. With the disappearance of the "evil empire," the background condition that had automatically legitimized presidential power for more than half a century was now gone, and there was no moral authority to replace it. Absent a superpower challenging the American creed, the nation no longer understood what it was about. Bill Clinton occasionally tried to tell us, but he wasn't bold enough or consistent enough; he seemed to compromise and weasel too much, and thus America never trusted him enough.

Universal healthcare was centrally important for two years, and then, when the bill ran aground, almost nothing was heard

of it again. Large-scale investments in education and job training (I was in the middle of this one) crested and then vanished amid V-chips and school uniforms, and then rose slightly again. Reform of campaign finance was vitally important at one time, and then less so. Nothing rivaled protecting American kids from cigarettes, but when the legislation fizzled a few months ago, that objective seemed to vanish as well. A national dialogue on race was critically important one day, then seemed to disappear for want of clarity and boldness. Early on, the earned-income tax credit was expanded and then the minimum wage was raised, but almost nothing was said about the continued stagnation of median earnings. The most important goal, for a time, was to reduce the budget deficit, then to eliminate it altogether. Then, just as suddenly, the central goal became saving Social Security.

What are we about, anyway? What is the core narrative? How do we define ourselves, as global capital erases national borders? What is it that deserves our passionate, relentless, unswerving commitment? In the absence of a coherent answer, the public arena has become a vacant lot, open to all sorts of wacky squatters: Newt Gingrich, Rush Limbaugh, right-wing pundits from the Cato Institute and, from under other right-wing rocks, Ken Starr, Dick Morris, Phyllis Schlafly, Linda Tripp, Matt Drudge, editorial writers and columnists for the

---

*Robert B. Reich, University Professor of Social and Economic Policy at Brandeis and the author of* Locked in the Cabinet *(Knopf), was Secretary of Labor in the first Clinton Administration.*

[*See *The Nation,* September 7–14, 1998, pp. 13–18, for the other assessments. *Editor*]

*Wall Street Journal*, the *Weekly Standard*, the *Washington Times*, religious nuts, conspiracy crazies, racists, Hillary-haters. And all the while, a baby boomer President who could charm snakes has tried to charm America and only infuriated the snakes.

Legacy? I feel Bill Clinton's pain. The presidency is a Jerry Springer show. The public is variously entertained, appalled and titillated by the smallness and coarseness of it all. Americans' daily working lives have been transformed by the flows of global capital, by Alan Greenspan's Federal Reserve and by the wonders of the Internet. But in the evenings, when the work is done, we're transfixed by the perils of Bill Clinton. News has become an Entertainment Division, a diversion from the daily grind. No matter that Asian economies are imploding, the world's poor are expanding, more than a fifth of our own children are impoverished, American schools are falling apart, a record 41 million of us lack health insurance and the nation is experiencing the widest divergence of income, wealth and opportunity in five decades. It is more fun to ponder semen stains. There was even a Web site, firstpenis.com. It wasn't worth the visit.

This political obituary is premature, of course. The presidency has more than two years to go, and we have learned never to count Bill Clinton out. But the swirl of meanness and pettiness will last, I'm afraid, unless, or until, he fills the public arena with something larger and nobler, on the scale of the true challenges facing the nation. Even if a virulent Republican Congress blocks all such measures, there is profound value in laying down markers for the future. The end of the cold war, a time of overall prosperity, should be an era when we roll up our sleeves and get on with it. There are budget surpluses as far as the eye can see. And even if the economy were to grow only 1 percent more productive each year, as it has over the past thirty, by the time Social Security is projected to run into trouble (in 2032) there would be enough additional wealth to allow every American at least 25 percent more purchasing power than today. In short, we can afford it.

At the close of his confessional, Bill Clinton asked us to put Monica behind us because "we have important work to do." That is precisely the issue. The failure on his part to chart any such bold course, leaving the public arena to be filled instead by debris and distraction, would be the most tragic legacy of all.

# IMPERIAL CONGRESS

## JOSEPH A. CALIFANO JR.

*Joseph A. Califano Jr., an attorney, is chairman and president of the Center on Addiction and Substance Abuse at Columbia University. He was President Lyndon Johnson's top assistant for domestic affairs and Secretary of Health, Education and Welfare under President Jimmy Carter.*

Congress has become the King Cong of Washington's political jungle, dominating an executive branch that can no longer claim the coequal status that the Founding Fathers saw as crucial. Those who blame Bill Clinton for this sorry imbalance of power fail to take into account the stunning ascendancy of Congressional clout since the years of Lyndon Johnson.*

In the 1960's, Democratic members of Congress not only depended on Lyndon Johnson. Many owed their seats to him. The 89th Congress of 1965–66—the only time in this century when a liberal majority ruled both House and Senate—was a tribute to Johnson's walloping 61-to-39-percent margin over Barry Goldwater. Johnson never let those young Senators and Representatives forget that he

had carried their states and districts by margins wider than their own.

Even members who didn't owe their victories to L. B. J. needed him to raise money for their campaigns. Johnson was quick to accommodate those who supported his programs with appearances at fund-raising events and donations from his own political bankroll.

Members of Congress also needed Johnson for political patronage. In those days the President controlled jobs even as menial as that of local postmaster and had discretion to decide where to build roads, sewerage systems, hospitals and courthouses.

The executive branch had the staff to draft legislation, and Congressional committees depended on executive departments to write their bills. We in the Johnson Administration were happy to oblige; that way we could provide plenty of room for executive action.

When we wanted to close post offices, consolidate regional centers or shut down military bases, we did it. L. B. J. stiff-armed Congressional attempts to trim our efforts, vetoing legislation to limit his power to close bases as an unconstitutional intrusion on Presidential prerogatives. When Johnson wanted to step up military action in Vietnam, he had Congress pass the sweeping Gulf of Tonkin Resolution which he (and later Richard Nixon) used as authority to wage a full-scale war without asking Congress to declare one.

But the next 20 years saw a steady erosion of executive power as Congress moved to center stage. The triple hit—escalation of the Vietnam War, the Watergate scandal and President Nixon's refusal to carry out civil rights laws and spend money appropriated for Great Society programs—bred in the Congress a profound distrust of the Executive that persists to this day. As a result, Congress began writing

---

*This article first appeared almost a year before the Republicans' startling takeover of both houses of Congress in the November 1994 elections. The author served in two Democratic administrations (Lyndon Johnson and Jimmy Carter) during which Democrats were also in majority control of both houses of Congress. Since President Johnson left office in 1969, however, there have usually been Republican presidents (Richard Nixon, Gerald Ford, Ronald Reagan, and George Bush) at the same time Democrats controlled both houses of Congress. In 1995 and 1996, the reverse has been true: Democratic President Bill Clinton will have to contend with Republican majorities in both houses of Congress. Under these new circumstances, it should be particularly interesting to observe the shape and direction of congressional-presidential power relations and to consider whether Califano's notion of an "imperial Congress" remains valid. **Editor**

laws in excruciating detail on the premise that the executive branch would try to circumvent them.

**B**Y THE 1990's, CONGRESS HAD NOT only knocked the crown off the imperial Presidency. It had legislated itself into a position of independent power, shedding its reliance on the White House.

First and foremost, members no longer need the President to raise money for them. Congress has given itself the power to raise its own campaign funds by legalizing political action committees and by creating enough committees and subcommittees (more than 100 in the Senate; almost 150 in the House) so that virtually every Senator and most Representatives can have a senior position. Congressional leaders can assign members to committees that oversee well-heeled private interests. Committee chairmen can provide funds to a junior member's re-election campaign out of war chests they amass from their perches of power.

Nor do members any longer need the President to dole out patronage. Congress has increased its work force from about 22,000 in 1960 to 37,000 today, giving each member plenty of jobs to fill. Personal staffs of House members have jumped from 2,500 in 1960 to more than 7,000 in 1992; in the Senate personal staffs have more than tripled, from 1,200 in 1960 to more than 4,000 in 1992.

## It has tripled its own payroll, abandoned its deference to the President and tilted, alarmingly, the scales of constitutional power.

A new President goes to Washington, as Clinton did, with only a handful of loyal aides. He usually has his cabinet and key members of his White House staff on board within a week of his inauguration. But it takes more than a year to choose most remaining Presidential appointees. Many of them, new to the ways of political Washington, face off against a Congress that is already well staffed with experienced institutional partisans. While the President struggles to find hundreds of appointees to fill the geographic, ethnic and political commitments of his campaign, Congress is already moving *its* agenda forward.

Not content with its own patronage positions, Congress has assumed greater control over executive branch personnel. In 1960, there were 149 Presidential appointments that required Senate confirmation. Today there are 310. And the Senate has abandoned the deference accorded Presidential nominations in the 1960's.

At the flood tide of Great Society legislation in 1965–66, Congress passed laws totaling 2,912 statute book pages. Most observers thought the nation would never again see such a flurry of Congressional activity. But Senators and Representatives have come to revel in the power of patronage gained from a prolific legislative pen. Despite numerous vetoes by President George Bush, in 1991–92 the Congress enacted laws, totaling 7,544 pages.

Such laws claim for Congress a host of powers that are truly executive. The tax committees legislate in such detail that lawyers go to staffers on the Senate Finance and House Ways and Means Committees with matters that, 20 years ago, they could have resolved only with the Internal Revenue Service. In fiscal 1993, Congress earmarked $763 million—triple the 1988 amount—for specific projects on more than 200 college campuses, like a $76,000 University of Georgia study of urban pests. Congress has legislated that the Interior Department maintain 23 positions in the Wilkes-Barre, Pa., office of anthracite reclamation and that the Secretary of Health and Human services hire "six medium sedans" for transportation. This trespassing occurs in lengthy reconciliation and appropriations bills that the President must veto in their entirety if he wants to challenge the intrusion.

As a result, King Congress has become the throne before which most governors and mayors plead for Federal bounty. Congress has learned that it's better to give out the goodies directly than to let the President get the credit. State and local officials who once prowled the corridors of executive departments and the White House now crowd the anterooms of representatives and senators.

**W**HEN I REORGANIZED the Department of Health, Education and Welfare in 1977, Congress made it more difficult for my successors to take similar actions. When President Clinton lifted the ban on gay soldiers, Congress legislated a narrower change, assuring that any future moves would require legislation rather than simply executive action. The foreign policy ax of Congress has chopped off Presidential moves in Bosnia, Haiti and Somalia.

Democratic members of Congress, confident of perpetual control of the legislative branch, are not as concerned about who sits in the Oval Office as they were a generation ago. The barons of Capital Hill make it clear to any incoming Administration where the true power resides. Cabinet officers and agency heads spend far more time testifying before Congressional committees and visiting their members and staffs than they do with the President, while their subordinates prepare the battery of reports Congress demands of them—some 5,000 last year.

Clinton's situation is aggravated by the fact that he was elected with only 43 percent of the popular vote, less than the margins by which incumbent Representatives and Senators carried their districts and states. When the President submitted his stimulus package, these members ridiculed and killed it. When he proposed his deficit reductions, Congress returned essentially the same budget cuts it had shipped to George Bush the year before, knowing that this President had to take whatever they sent him and declare victory.

Health care reform offers a quintessential example of the fundamental shift of power in the capital. The President has spoken in broad principles, assuming the role of cheerleader to arouse the citizenry. When he finally sent Congress draft legislative language, he stressed his willingness to compromise on just about everything. Clinton knows that Congress will draft the reforms in detail unthinkable even for executive branch regulations 25 years ago. Congress knows that the President will, again, have to sign whatever it sends him and, again, declare victory.

It won't be easy to reset the scales of constitutional power, but it is as critical to try today as it was to bring the imperial Presidency down to size in the early 1970's. Congress has enormous difficulty making coherent policies (conservative or liberal) that complex problems like economic development and urban decay require. Individual members tend to ricochet from the demands of their constituents to the interests served by their committees and caucuses.

Congressional muscle is most easily flexed in obstructionist ways. The members' ability to fudge individual accountability licenses them to play political games—sending President Bush a campaign reform bill they knew he'd veto; refusing to send President Clinton the same bill because they know he'll sign it.

Where Congress takes the initiative, it tends to write laws with a little bit for everyone who has votes to barter or bucks to donate, at the expense of a focused national policy. Thus, it pours money into tobacco, sugar and dairy subsidies as it promotes free trade and tries to cut health care spending. A proposal to test a model program in a few cities quickly becomes a national undertaking with something for every state and enough Congressional districts to muster a House majority.

The Nafta battle underscores this point. While no President in this century has lost a legislative contest over trade, none had to pay so much in the way of tribute to Congress: hundreds of millions in subsidies for fruits and nuts, lower cigarette tax increases and barrels of other pork.

To help put Congress back in its constitutional place will require significant campaign finance reform with public financing, and a Presidential line-item veto. Campaign finance reform is critical to give the President more power to assert the national interest over the special interests that prevail on Capital Hill. The line-item veto is essential to end the Congressional blackmail contained in lengthy bills the President is forced to sign in order to keep Government functioning.

Such steps are only a beginning. But they can help a President, even one elected by a minority, reclaim coequal status as the Founding Fathers intended.

# THE TOWN THAT ATE ITSELF

*The rise of tabloid politics began with Newt Gingrich, but the causes
went much deeper. How did the Republicans and the Democrats confuse
scandalmongering and endless prosecutions with governing?*

## BY JOE KLEIN

LATE in the afternoon of May 15, 1984, Speaker of the House Thomas P. (Tip) O'Neill, a politician known for his even-tempered charm, publicly and unexpectedly blew his stack. The moment was astonishing for several reasons. Speakers of the House rarely set aside the gavel and step down to take the microphone in the well; when they do, it usually is to provide a dignified conclusion to a debate of national import. But this was a spontaneous moment of rage. O'Neill rumbled down the center aisle of the chamber, seized the lectern, and began to excoriate a fellow-representative—an obscure backbencher, at that—for what he believed to be a severe breach of decorum. His face lobster-red and his finger wagging, O'Neill began to yell, over the derisive hoots of the Republican opposition, at a junior member from Georgia. It should

come as no surprise that the member who had provoked O'Neill to such unseemly rage was Newt Gingrich.

"It was Newt's first big victory," Vin Weber, a former Republican representative from Minnesota who was a close Gingrich ally, said recently. "And it was a huge mistake on Tip's part." It was also one of the first significant skirmishes in the present era of personal political assault—an era that some observers hope may be coming to an end with Gingrich's departure as the current Speaker, his replacement by Bob Livingston*, and Bill Clinton's settlement of the Paula Jones sexual-harassment case.

O'Neill had been boggled by three developments that were to become prominent features of today's political landscape: a new generation of abrasive, disrespectful baby-boom politicians from the suburbs (O'Neill was, of course, a titanic ur-

ban anachronism from the Boston area); a more partisan and ideological Republican Party, with a rising crop of Southerners to lead it; and the arrival within the halls of Congress of a disruptive new medium—television.

In point of fact, O'Neill had gone berserk over the Republicans' use of C-SPAN. A week earlier, Gingrich had made a late-night speech in which he seemed to question the patriotism of several Democrats, by name. The chamber was virtually empty, but his real audience was cable-TV viewers across the country. With the camera fixed, by House rules, on the orator, he was able to challenge the Democrats to defend their votes against defense spending. There was no way for the audience to know that the Democrats could not respond. O'Neill decided to change the C-SPAN rules without consulting the Republicans: he would allow cameras to pan the empty chamber. Gingrich rose to protest the "unilateral" decision—which led to O'Neill's angry response. "You deliberately stood in the well of this House and took on these members when you knew they would not be here," the Speaker shouted at Gingrich. "It's un-American. It's the lowest thing that I've heard in my thirty-two years here."

Chaos ensued. Representative Trent Lott, of Mississippi, the deputy Republican leader, demanded that O'Neill's comments be "taken down," since they violated House rules prohibiting derogatory remarks about fellow-members, and Representative Joseph Moakley, of Massachusetts, an O'Neill protégé, who had taken the chair, reluctantly was forced to agree. The Republicans, downtrodden after thirty years in the minority, were stunned and delighted: one of their most outspoken and least popular members had humiliated the Speaker of the House. Gingrich was given a standing ovation as he took his seat.

"That was the opening shot in the war," Weber recalled. "I guess I have mixed feelings about it now. I'm not ashamed of the things I said." Weber had contributed to the mayhem, calling O'Neill "one of the cheapest, meanest politicians to occupy that office in this century," but he'd said it off the House floor, and therefore free from the shackles of parliamentary language. "The Democrats were arrogant to the point of corruption," Weber added, "and Newt's idea was to expose the arrogance and corruption for what it was. It was guerrilla war, and I don't think we could have won the House in 1994 without those sorts of tactics. But the victory came at a price, and the price was a loss of civility. And we are paying for it now."

Indeed, a sustained, ever-deteriorating culture of personal assault was institutionalized in Washington well before the discovery, last January, that Monica Lewinsky delivered pizza to her President. It was not merely Gingrich's doing, either. The political atmosphere had turned ran-

cid with hearings and investigations and special prosecutors and accusations and diatribes directed against public figures. The accusations and diatribes were nothing new, of course; but now they were accompanied by endless legal procedures. "There have always been political scandals," said Gordon S. Wood, the Pulitzer Prize-winning Brown University historian. "There have been periods of severe partisanship and vitriolic rhetoric. But I don't think we've ever had a time in American history like this one, with so many prominent figures facing legal action, and with politics criminalized."

In the past decade, scandals—sometimes over the most niggling misdemeanors—have become the defining events of public life, often far more compelling and significant than elections. In Washington, there has been a fierce, undeclared war between the two parties over what has come to be called "ethics" but has usually been something less than outright illegality; rather, it has been "The Appearance of Impropriety"—to quote the title of a recent book by Peter W. Morgan and Glenn H. Reynolds. The Clinton impeachment fiasco is only the latest in a series of public carnivals, orchestrated by furious partisans of both parties and cheered on by a happily voracious media. Two Speakers of the House, Gingrich and Jim Wright, of Texas, have been investigated (and Wright was forced to resign) because of ethical questions. Independent Counsels are now chasing two current and two former members of the Clinton Cabinet, as well as the President himself; a fifth investigation was curtailed when its target, Commerce Secretary Ron Brown, died. Three Republican Supreme Court nominees—Robert Bork, Clarence Thomas, and Douglas Ginsburg—have been subjected to severe ideological and personal assault. A slew of Cabinet-level nominees—from John Tower to Anthony Lake—have been shot down, for reasons either trivial or incomprehensible and in any case long forgotten. And, just below the level

of media attention, hundreds of other government officials have been investigated on charges—often frivolous complaints, filed anonymously—that were brought to the attention of the Inspectors General of the various Cabinet departments. At the moment, the nomination of Richard Holbrooke to the post of United Nations Ambassador is being held up by an anonymous conflict-of-interest complaint made to the State Department's Inspector General.

All this in a Washington that is, by most accounts, far less corrupt than it has ever been. "Compare this Congress to the one in 1950, during the era that many of the old-timers consider the golden age of civil discourse," Senator Joseph Biden, Democrat of Delaware, says. "Those guys were taking handouts, honoraria, junkets. When I came here, in 1973, Jacob Javits—a distinguished senator—was making money from a private law practice. You don't think he'd be under investigation today? By comparison, these new guys are squeaky clean. I can't stand most of the S.O.B.s—they're ideologues, they practice Khmer Rouge politics—but they are the cleanest bunch of politicians this capital has ever seen."

The phenomenon of constant prosecutions and investigations may be more damaging to the country's political future than any of the charges that have been brought, and this year's electoral reaction may finally compel the contending parties—the politicians, the prosecutors, and the press—to attend to the essential wisdom of the public revulsion against their behavior. But a change in the culture won't come easily: contentiousness and partisan legal harassment have become industries in Washington, providing crude entertainment and satisfying careers for thousands of short-sighted practitioners.

P eople around here think the Clinton thing is an aberration," Alan Simpson, the former Republican senator from Wyoming and now the director of the Institute of Politics at the Kennedy School of Government, at Harvard, told me several days before the election. He reasonably argued that the President's recklessness and brazen untruthfulness were not common to most politicians; that the Starr investigation was justified by the extraordinary circumstances. But after an hour spent reviewing the sordid history of the past fifteen years—particularly the Robert Bork and Clarence Thomas hearings, which Simpson had witnessed at first hand as a member of the Judiciary Committee, and the successful campaign to oust his friend Bob Packwood, Republican of Oregon, from the Senate after a long record of sexual peccadilloes—I asked Simpson if he really thought that the Clinton case was an aberration. He laughed. "No, I guess there's been a sedimentary encrustation of these things," he said. "It might not be happening if all those other things hadn't happened."

The Clinton impeachment debacle is part of a pattern and a pathology in a political system infected by the unintended consequences of affluence, technology, and mangled reform. There are a great many opinions about how the trouble began; there is near-unanimity that the atmosphere must change; but there is not much hope that it can or will.

The trouble began when we political scientists finally got our wish—'responsible' political parties instead of broad, nonideological coalitions," Nelson Polsby, the Berkeley political scientist, says. "The idea was, of course, completely nuts from the start."

As long as the South was solidly Democratic, the two political parties remained broad coalitions. The Democrats were a mixture of conservative Southerners and urban Northerners (both groups supported Franklin Roosevelt's populist economic activism, but they agreed on little else); the Republicans repre-

sented Wall Street and Main Street, the Eastern élite and the Western middle class (who agreed on a preference for limited government, and little else). In the fifties and the first half of the sixties, the Southern Democrats—who by seniority controlled many of the significant congressional committees—joined with Republicans to prevent much of anything from happening except appropriations for highways and defense.

But the solid South shattered over civil rights. When Northern Democrats decided to support desegregation, a new generation of Southerners emerged within two decades and became Republicans. At the same time, many of the liberal children of the Eastern Republicans élites joined the Democrats, as did Southern blacks when they gained the right to vote. As the parties grew more ideologically "responsible," debate became more abrasive and partisan. In the House of Representatives, Democrats—stoked by moral outrage over segregation, Vietnam, and Watergate, and made complacent by their seemingly permanent majority—became far less tolerant of the Republican minority. The musty, ornate rituals of collegiality, the respectful parliamentary language, the staff and privileges granted the minority, were gradually abandoned or severely modified to the Republicans' disadvantage.

Tip O'Neill got his revenge against Gingrich and the Republicans with an outrageous episode in 1985. A very close congressional race in Indiana, between the Republican Rick McIntyre and the Democrat Frank McCloskey, had been decided, on a recount, in favor of McIntyre by Indiana's Republican Secretary of State; McCloskey protested to the House of Representatives, which decided to investigate. O'Neill chose a three-member commission, composed of two Democrats and a Republican. Not surprisingly, the Democrats voted to seat McCloskey—and the entire Republican caucus walked out of the House chamber in protest. "That was Newt's second big victory," Vin We-

ber says. "People began to think, Well, if the Democrats are going to be like that, maybe Newt's right. We might as well blow up the place."

Gingrich, empowered, continued his guerrilla warfare. In 1987, he brought ethics charges against Jim Wright, O'Neill's successor as Speaker of the House. The charges were flimsy and confusing at best: Wright was guilty of fairly standard political shenanigans—selling to lobbyists mass copies of a campaign book he had written; a slightly too cozy relationship with a local businessman—and most members of Congress figured Gingrich's campaign would be no more than a minor form of harassment. But the Wright case had an unanticipated aspect that raised the ante considerably and exacerbated the war between the parties: the House Ethics Committee appointed a Special Counsel, a Chicago Democrat named Richard Phelan, to investigate Wright. A year later, Phelan was still digging, and Wright was forced to resign. "I was worn out, completely spent," Wright told me recently. "I couldn't sleep. I could see this thing dragging on another year or two and costing me a million dollars. I couldn't afford that. I gave a speech denouncing the 'mindless cannibalism' that was consuming the Congress and I figured my resignation would so shock and shame the members that they'd end the war. That turned out to be a miscalculation on my part, of course. Things only got worse."

By 1989, when Wright resigned, it was clear that the ethics war had reached a new level of intensity; each side was using high-powered legal weapons to hurt the other. The weapons were of recent vintage—the product of a historic government-reform effort that came after the Watergate scandal. "We were going to reform the system," says Joseph Biden, referring to his arrival in Congress. "But we created more problems than we solved. The campaign-finance laws, the Independent

Counsel statute—nothing turned out the way it was supposed to."

Biden might have added the Ethics in Government Act of 1978; the reforms of the Presidential-primary selection process and of the congressional seniority system; the limitations on Presidential war and budgetary powers; the "whistle-blower" reforms that enabled disgruntled government employees everywhere to bring anonymous complaints against their bosses; and the establishment of independent Inspectors General to process the whistle-blower complaints—a forest of new regulations which sprouted up in the years after Watergate. Much of it was the work of the forty-three additional Democrats elected to the House in 1974—the first major infusion of baby-boom politicians into the Congress. "They came to Congress wanting to end the war in Vietnam," says Jim Thurber, a political-science professor at American University, who was an aide to Hubert Humphrey in the seventies. But the war ended four months after they arrived, "and the question was, What else could they do?" Thurber says. "One thing they all agreed on was the need to reform government."

Unquestionably, the reforms curtailed some egregious practices, but the powerful new ethics weapons were also put to trivial, partisan political use: the first investigation under the Independent Counsel statute, in 1979, was of Jimmy Carter's chief of staff, Hamilton Jordan, for alleged cocaine use. The second was of Carter's campaign manager, Timothy Kraft, also for alleged cocaine use. No charges were filed in either case. When Reagan came to power, the Democrats returned the favor by investigating Labor Secretary Raymond Donovan, Attorney General Edwin Meese, and the Presidential aides Michael Deaver and Lyn Nofziger—with only Deaver pleading guilty to an unrelated infraction. Indeed, when Donovan was finally cleared after a grueling investigation, he asked the memorable question "Which office do I go to get my reputation back?" The

only Reagan-era investigation that transcended political pettiness had to do with the Iran-Contra scandal—the plan to sell arms illegally to Iran and use the proceeds to fund anti-Communist Nicaraguan rebels.

Along with the political reforms came an army of political reformers and a new industry, the ethics establishment. "I remember working as a congressional aide in the late sixties," says Norman Ornstein, a resident scholar at the American Enterprise Institute. "Across the street from our office was a building—the Methodist Building—that was filled with antiwar activists. And I remember thinking, What are these people going to do when the war is over? They had learned a skill—political organizing—and they put it to use. There was an explosion of 'public interest' activist groups in the early seventies, and they had a significant impact not just on political reforms but also on environmental and consumer regulations. Then, in the late seventies, there was an explosion of industry groups and trade associations to counteract them."

The various interest groups exerted a centrifugal pull on the Democrats and the Republicans, moving them to their respective extremes, where the most passionate advocates were festering. The trade associations formed political action committees, which brought enormous amounts of money into the system—especially after the Federal Election Campaign Act was amended, in 1979, to permit unlimited contributions to the national political parties (the source of "soft" money, as opposed to the "hard" money contributed to specific candidates). The money was used to pay for advertising on television, which expanded in frequency and ferocity as the eighties began. For many Democrats, the "war" actually began in 1980, when the National Conservative Political Action Committee (NCPAC) ran a scurrilous television campaign against six liberal senators, four of whom were defeated—

which returned control of the Senate to Republicans for the first time in twenty-six years. "You can't underestimate the impact that the rise of vicious, false, distorted negative advertising had on the members of Congress," says Warren Rudman, a Republican who left the Senate in disgust in 1992. "For example, I had a hard time getting to like Joe Lieberman when he came to the Senate, because the campaign he ran against Lowell Weicker, who was a good friend of mine, was disgraceful. Eventually, we became friendly, because Joe's a terrific guy. But a lot of people don't get over those things. It makes it a lot harder to work together—a lot harder to do anything. You're always wondering whether this or that vote is going to be distorted in some crummy ad in the next campaign."

If Democrats point to NCPAC and Newt Gingrich as the root causes of the incivility, Republicans point to the liberal activists' campaign, in 1987, against the nomination of Robert Bork to the Supreme Court—and particularly to the hyperbolic speech Ted Kennedy made on the floor of the Senate, less than an hour after the nomination had been announced, about the various terrible things, like "back-alley abortions," that would happen in "Robert Bork's America."

"All of us sort of stunned our colleagues by going off the deep end at one point or another during one of these circuses," Alan Simpson says. "Teddy did it with his Bork speech. Sam Nunn did it with his campaign against John Tower. I did it with Clarence Thomas, when I went ballistic over this 'sexual harassment' crap. I'll tell you, you get so wrapped up in the moment, your mind sometimes comes unhinged."

The anti-Bork campaign and hearings seem decorous compared with the crude personal assaults that came to characterize later witch-hunts. Bork was a distinguished academic but an ideological bomb thrower; an argument could plausibly be made that he was not merely a conservative but a radical reactionary, who sought to overturn many of the precedents set by the liberal Warren Court. The leaders of the anti-Bork coalition decided to have the argument made substantively, by constitutional scholars, rather than emotionally; activists like Ralph Nader and Molly Yard, of the National Organization for Women, were persuaded not to testify. "Nader came to me before the hearings began," Joe Biden, then chairman of the Judiciary Committee, recalls, "and said the Bork hearings should be a constituency-building exercise. He wanted to do what all these groups do—send out mailings, raise money. I told him no, and I'm proud of the way those hearings were run." (Nader says he told Biden that the hearings could be a "public-education medium.")

But the battle over the Bork nomination proved to be an escalation in the ethics war for two reasons. It was the first time a coalition of ideologues had mounted an activist campaign—including grassroots organizing, opposition research, and even a television commercial (featuring the voice of Gregory Peck)—to oppose a Presidential nominee. This became a fixture of the post-Bork prosecutorial scene, with activist groups using ethics targets—ranging from Clarence Thomas to Bill Clinton—as a means of raising "awareness" and, more important, money from their supporters. "One of the things Ralph Nader taught us was to demonize the opposition," said Mike Pertschuk, a consumer advocate and Nader protégé, who wrote a book about the Bork campaign, and who now, like Vin Weber, has mixed feelings about the harsh tactics used. "And, you know," he added, "it's a very effective tactic—but there's a terrible cost to that."

Another notable feature of the Bork campaign was the invasion of the nominee's privacy—particularly the attempt to investigate Bork's video-store records by a reporter for the Washington *City Paper*, an alternative weekly. Only a few months earlier, reporters from the Miami *Herald* had waited in the bushes outside the town house of Gary Hart, the Democratic Presidential candidate, to catch him in an adulterous liaison.

The press, of course, has been a crucial, omnivorous, and obnoxious component of the machinery of scandal. Watergate made heroes of the Washington *Post* reporters Bob Woodward and Carl Bernstein, but it also caused a serious distortion in the culture of journalism: elected officials were now, routinely, presumed guilty. There was a gleeful quality to much of the reporting, and especially to the new, witlessly contentious television sound-bite shows: "Groups" and "Gangs" of journalists screaming at each other and making facile judgments about complicated issues. There was considerable peer pressure to stay cynical: reporters who wrote favorably about politicians were considered to be "in the tank."

"Over the last two decades, political reporters have become more concerned with how *other* political reporters judge their work," I was told by Bill Kovach, the curator of Harvard's Nieman Foundation. "Not wanting to look soft leads to a negative spin: no matter what position is taken by a politician, the journalistic tendency is to examine it in a negative light—to emphasize political calculations rather than the substance."

Tom Patterson, a professor at Harvard's Kennedy School of Government, has numbers to back up Kovach's analysis: in the 1960 Presidential election, three-quarters of the references to the candidates which could be characterized as positive or negative were positive; in the last three Presidential elections, the proportion had shifted to sixty per cent negative. Furthermore, Patterson cited a study that calculated that stories emphasizing conflict among politicians had increased three hundred per cent from the early seven-ties to the late eighties. "The Watergate investigative model was very scrupulous," Patterson said. "By the late seventies, that had changed—'investigative' reporting became getting on the phone and finding someone to attack someone else. The purpose wasn't to find things out but to bring things down."

It is difficult to overstate the ire that most politicians—even those who have had good relations with the press—now feel toward journalists. "The media love hate," says Representative Barney Frank, Democrat of Massachusetts, a homosexual whose private life was the subject of a breathless exposé in 1989. "In Washington, excessive cynicism is the most prevalent form of naïveté. I just wish reporters were as skeptical about bad news as they are about good news."

By 1989, the rigorous standards of Woodward and Bernstein's Watergate reporting had been long forgotten, even in much of the élite press. The enduring impact of George Bush's failed attempt to appoint the former Texas senator John Tower as his Defense Secretary was to take mainstream journalism to an ever more squalid level. The Washington *Post*, for example, published raw data from the F.B.I.'s investigation of Tower, including an unreliable account of two drinking-and-fondling incidents at an Air Force base—reported, as it happens, by Bob Woodward. The Tower case was bizarre and terrifying to many elected officials: no one could remember the last time a former senator had been denied a Presidential appointment by his colleagues in the Senate. But Senator Sam Nunn, Democrat of Georgia and a respected defense expert, was a very credible leader of the opposition, arguing that even the possibility of heavy drinking would be intolerable in a Secretary of Defense. Jim Wright told me, "I liked Tower. We were friends, fellow-Texans, and I thought he'd been treated unfairly. But it was clear, after that, that the Republicans were going to demand retribution. On

Texas Independence Day, March 2nd, that year, a Republican told me the caucus was energized to come after me now. I said, 'What is this? An eye for an eye?' And he said, 'No, a Texan for a Texan.' "

Wright and Tower had several things in common: neither was well liked, and neither had committed anything resembling a crime. "I disagreed with Newt about going after Wright," Vin Weber says. "In fact, Newt didn't have very much support at all in the Republican conference. But, when Wright was forced to resign, that was Newt's third big triumph—and the Republican conference looked at Newt and said, 'He's been right all along.' "

On May 15, 1984, the day Newt Gingrich successfully confronted Tip O'Neill and received a standing ovation as he took his seat, one Republican did not join in the applause: Robert Michel, of Peoria, Illinois, the House Minority leader. Michel was, in many ways, Gingrich's opposite. He had grown up poor, the son of an immigrant factory worker; he worked three paper routes during the Depression. After Pearl Harbor, he joined the infantry, rose to the rank of sergeant, and was seriously wounded in the Battle of the Bulge. When Michel was first elected to the House, in 1956, he had a mission that he believed was the essence of conservatism: he wanted to give his fellow-G.I.s and their families a period of peace and quiet. He wanted government kept under wraps; his goal was stability.

"I still think I had a more conservative record than Newt. The media called me a 'moderate,' because I talked with Democrats, but that was the way things were when I was coming up," Michel told me, speaking slowly, his voice deep and pleasant and unpretentiously mid-American. He was sitting behind his old congressional desk, which he had moved to his Washington, D.C., law office. "Those were happy days," Michel said. "My district rep-

resented Hiram Walker's distillery. A lot of members would come by the office for a snort, and we'd gas about this and that. When we had committee meetings, we'd sit at long tables, the majority and minority across from one another, and so we'd have to talk and work things out. Now they have these long daises, with the majority on one side and the minority way over on the other, and no one gets to know one another."

Newt Gingrich arrived in 1979, a professor and political activist who had only read about the wartime horrors that Bob Michel had seen. Gingrich was obsessed with books about military tactics and had become something of a reverse Clausewitz: he considered politics the extension of war by other means. Michel was appalled. He figured politics was the opposite of war. "I don't think you can underestimate the generational aspect of this situation," Vin Weber says. "Our generation came in, and we had absolutely no respect for any of the traditions—not the Speakership, not the Presidency, not bipartisanship. We thought the parliamentary language was stuffy and silly. We thought hypocrisy was the only sin. Bob Michel's generation—they wanted to make life less political for the returning veterans. We wanted to politicize everything. Remember the slogan 'The personal is political'? That was the feminists, right? That became us, too."

In the early nineteen-nineties, both the Gingrich Republicans and the feminists had their moments. The 1991 campaign against Clarence Thomas's nomination to the Supreme Court was far more personal and extreme than the campaign against Robert Bork had been. Members of the civil-rights establishment set the tone by calling Thomas a variety of despicable names because he disagreed with the prevailing wisdom about affirmative action. Then the feminists came to the fore with the appearance of Anita Hill, who accused Thomas of offensive rib-

aldry when he was her boss at the Equal Employment Opportunity Commission; she was questioned intensely and skeptically by Simpson and several other Republicans on the Judiciary Committee. A delegation of feminists visited Joseph Biden, just as Ralph Nader had done four years earlier. "They wanted the committee to expose the fact that Thomas watched pornographic films," Biden recalled. "But I told them that if he did, it wasn't material. It was private." (Of course, the media were happy to provide all the relevant details to a soap-opera-loving public.) The incredible ugliness that both Thomas and Hill were forced to suffer—the grotesque invasion of their personal lives—was becoming part of the price paid by public servants. Any future Presidential nominee could expect to have his or her closet emptied—as Zoe Baïrd and Kimba Wood soon would for alleged improprieties associated with the employment of immigrant babysitters. A businessman who had declined Bill Clinton's offer to join the Cabinet told me, "And go through *that*? What did I need that for?"

Meanwhile, Gingrich's demolition work in the House proceeded apace. The end of the Cold War meant that political anarchy could flourish in placid times. In the early nineties, hundreds of members were tainted by their misuse of the House bank and post office (the latter operation resulted in a jail term for Dan Rostenkowski, the chairman of the House Ways and Means Committee); even the prices charged by the barbershop were called into question. At the same time, Gingrich expanded his operation and took on his President, George Bush: in 1990, when Bush broke his "No new taxes" pledge by cutting a budget deal with the Democrats, Gingrich challenged the result and forced a renegotiation—the first sign that the weakened President might not be invincible in the 1992 elections.

Bob Michel, who had supported the Bush budget deal, knew that he was going to be Gingrich's next target. "I could see what was happening behind my back," Michel told me. "Newt was coming along. He was going to challenge me for the leadership in 1994. It would have been a bitter challenge." He paused a moment. "I might have lost. I decided that I'd had enough." He brightened and added, "I'm so *happy* I'm out."

The Clinton era has been marked by dense, endless, and almost always peripheral scandals, pursued by a battalion of prosecutors who have spent years and millions of dollars to very little effect. Whitewater—the failed Arkansas land deal that initiated the prying into the President's past and private lives—has always seemed a remarkable waste of time and money, a trivial investigation, based on the testimony of unreliable witnesses, of activities that had nothing to do with Bill Clinton's performance in federal office. The subsequent investigations by Kenneth Starr's prosecutorial team—the Travel Office firings, the F.B.I. files mistakenly ordered by Security Office incompetents, and, of course, the Lewinsky perjury entrapment—uncovered poor judgment (and, in the Lewinsky case, spectacularly louche behavior) on the President's part, but seem more a sort of political harassment than the pursuit of serious legal or ethical lapses. Webster Hubbell, the former Associate Attorney General who went to prison for crimes unrelated to Clinton, was indicted yet again by Starr, on perjury and other charges, last week. (An earlier indictment, for tax evasion, had been thrown out by a federal judge.) The other Independent Counsels assigned to Clinton Cabinet officers have managed to isolate such threats to the republic as petty gift-taking (former Agriculture Secretary Mike Espy), understating the amounts paid to an ex-mistress (former Housing Secretary Henry Cisneros), and choosing a politically friendly Indian tribe's position over that of a less friendly tribe in a casino dispute (Interior Secretary Bruce Babbitt).

To the great glee of many Democrats, there also was a Gingrich scandal. It was another in the series of incomprehensible technical violations of ethics rules. In 1997, Gingrich agreed to pay a three-hundred-thousand-dollar fine for using a tax-exempt fund for political purposes. There was an Al Gore scandalette, too. It was an even more trivial brush with the fund-raising regulations, in which a rarely used hundred-year-old statute—pertaining to shakedowns of government employees on government property—was mobilized after Gore was found to be making fundraising calls from his White House office. No doubt there will be George W. Bush scandals in the months to come: the Governor of Texas, who is the front-runner for the Republican nomination in the year 2000, has admitted to a misspent youth that lasted well into adulthood. If Bush, or any other Republican, is elected President in 2000, he can expect the same sort of treatment from the ethics police—and from the Democrats in Congress—that Bill Clinton has received from the Republicans.

"I don't know where the bottom is," said Harvard's Tom Patterson, speaking of the press, but his concern easily could extend to the other parties to the scandal-making process—the politicians and the prosecutors. "I don't think this sort of negativity can be sustained in the long run."

There is talk of new reforms. The Independent Counsel Act will probably be abandoned—or, at the very least, severely modified—when it comes up for renewal in 1999. The system of political finance may be modified again. There will be a more vigorous effort to ban "soft" money in the next Congress, especially after the noble victory of Wisconsin's Senator Russell Feingold, who nearly lost his seat on a point of principle: he insisted that his campaign be run according to the finance laws he wants to see enacted. But the impact of any new reforms is likely to be minimal. As long as there is a First Amendment, people with money will find a way to get their messages across.

And the media are likely to remain negative and increasingly unaccountable. Internet gossip will continue to wend its way into the mainstream; the pressures of deadline and market share—and the promise of television appearances and lecture fees—will cause reporters to bend the rules to retail sensational tidbits. "I think there's an answer to that," says Alan Simpson, smiling wickedly. "Some politician is going to turn to a reporter who asks an ugly, invasive, disgusting personal question and say, 'I'll answer that if you will. Tell me what you did. Did you ever use cocaine? You're a public figure. You're on TV all the time. The public has a right to know. What gives you the moral authority to ask that question? Who gave you your Jesus shoes?' "

It is possible that Newt Gingrich's departure from public life will be a turning point—the moment when comity began to be restored. But I suspect not. In the weeks before the election, many of the old-timers I interviewed about the deteriorating political atmosphere seemed to yearn for such an epiphany. More than a few of them cited Joseph Welch, the Boston lawyer who, in 1954, finally punctured Senator Joseph McCarthy's balloon with a simple question: "Have you no sense of decency, Sir, at long last?"

McCarthy was already heading for trouble, having overreached by taking on the apparition of Communism in the United States Army. His moment onstage was ending, and Welch provided the appropriate exit line. The current moment is far more complicated. When the Welch scenario came up in interviews, I'd usually ask, Who would have the moral authority to do something like that now? Whom would he address his remarks to? Depending on your point of view, a latter-day Welch might credibly speak those very words—"Have you no sense of decency?"—to Ken Starr, Bill Clinton, Newt Gingrich, or to any of the special-interest extremists of the left and right, or to any member of the press. Or all of the above.

And although it might be argued that the American people—in a sweet, Frank Capra sort of way—finally chose to play the Joseph Welch role themselves in this past election, one wonders how effective the defenestration of Newt Gingrich will be. Gingrich wasn't the sole dispenser of the poison that has consumed public life; he simply exploited the noxious atmosphere more persistently than anyone else. He was a creature of the phenomenon, not the phenomenon itself. The fundamentals of contentiousness remain in place. The special-interest groups will be more than ready to exploit the next public drama that comes along. There are journalists ready to write the stories, politicians who'll be anxious to make the headlines, political consultants who'll be more than happy to make the ads, and an ethics industry on alert for the next chance to prosecute.

Washington's partisans continue to see each new prosecution as separate and unique—as justified or improper, according to political taste—rather than as part of a disorder that has done significant damage to the public's faith in politics. The myopia is often stupefying. A few years ago, I had dinner with Newt Gingrich. He was in the midst of his own ethics travails, and was clearly in some pain. I asked him if he had more sympathy now for Jim Wright. Gingrich bristled. "Absolutely not!" Then he said, "There's no comparison. What Wright did was criminal."

---

*On January 6, 1999, Representative J. Dennis Hastert of Illinois replaced Representative Livingston as Speaker of the House.

# IN THE MONEY: A CONGRESSMAN'S STORY

*Former United States Representative Dan Hamburg served in Congress as a California Democrat from 1993 to 1995. He is now executive director of VOTE Action Committee and a member of the Green Party.*

My wife and I have a favorite saying about the choices we make in our lives: "It's not the money." To me, getting money to make my first run for Congress in 1992 was simply something I needed to do to win. I certainly never intended to become the least bit impressed with it or driven by it. After getting elected, I was sure I could be a free-wheeling progressive. Joining what I believed would be legions of my kind in the new Congress and a Democratic administration, we would begin to put the country right.

Before I ran for Congress, I had never raised more than $15,000 for a political race. But I knew that congressional seats didn't come cheap, so I contacted an old supporter, musician Bonnie Raitt, and asked her to help me raise money for my campaign. To my elation, she said yes, and I was off and running.

Bonnie did several concerts for me in early 1992, raising a total of about $60,000. It turned out, incredibly, that no one challenged me in the spring primary. I remember thinking that the money would now flow like wine. It was exciting. I had already caught money fever. But by June of that year, I was broke, my campaign-management team having used virtually all of the money for their salaries and expenses. My campaign manager put it this way: "As a candidate you have two jobs—carry the message and raise money." It was time to raise more. I was learning my job.

I raised another $800,000 or so for the general election. Bonnie helped raise a chunk of that by doing a blockbuster concert with Jackson Browne on the driving range of a Napa country-club golf course. Where did the rest of the money come from? Environmentalists. Labor. Women. Peace and justice organizations. That was my mantra whenever anybody asked me where the money was coming from. I said it with pride, as if cool people got cool money and everything was cool.

Pretty quickly I lost track of where much of the money was coming from. I was far too busy trying to cover my sprawling seven-country district and secure the funds needed to keep an ever-expanding campaign team in place. Some money came from wealthy individuals who were known to me simply as "major donors," some from state and national parties, some from Democratic incumbents hoping to maintain a majority in the House. And of course some—about a third of it—came from PACs. At one point, at the urging of Democratic Representative Bill Brewster, I found myself talking to the NRA about giving me money because my opponent had voted to restrict sales of automatic weapons. Ultimately they did not offer me any money but agreed not to fund my opponent either.

By the time I won the general election that November, the campaign was in debt about $80,000 and I was personally in debt another $40,000. But hell, I'd raised nearly a million and now I was the incumbent, so no sweat! Still, it took nearly all of 1993 to clear my '92 campaign expenses, since in off years (years in which there is not a House election) much of the fund-raising has to be done at in-district events where supporters pay to hear the incumbent expound on the political wars in D.C.

In September 1993, I went to the White House to see the President and Vice President. This was a small meeting, which also included about eight members of Congress, George Stephanopoulos, and David Gergen. The day before, I had been at the annual picnic of the Operating Engineers, a union that had "maxed out" to me ($5,000 each for primary and general elections). At the picnic, several of the union leaders spoke to me about a problem they were having—getting

the go-ahead for a freeway-widening project in the district. I said I'd do what I could. The next day, there I was at the White House, arguing for more money for "infrastructure," including, of course, the project the Operating Engineers were pushing.

This is the kind of thing members of Congress do routinely. After all, this is how the system is supposed to work. The member goes out into the district, talks to his constituents, finds out what they need, and then fights to get it, especially if it's for a group that's good for $10,000 in the next election. I knew lots of reasons that the widening project was a bad idea, at best unnecessary. In fact, as a county official, I had voted against it several times. But it wasn't hard to conjure up reasons to be *for* it either: primarily, jobs and campaign money.

Since a "successful politician" is a politician with a healthy bankroll, behaviors that one might think of as degrading to the profession or detrimental to democracy are to the politician both legitimate and necessary. All the rewards come with raising tons of money—pundits laud your "prolific fund-raising," colleagues have confidence in your viability (i.e., re-electability) , staff members need not fear for their jobs.

Members of Congress spend hours each week and, during campaign season, hours each day, making fund-raising calls from private offices on Capital Hill. "Making your calls" is a basic responsibility of the job. And despite all the whitewash, the fact is that campaign fund-raising calls are routinely made from federal offices. (When I entered Congress, I was advised that while it was illegal to make such calls from my congressional office, it was legal to accept return calls. Of course, even this phony line is frequently crossed.)

The unending hunt for money also shapes relations between individual members once they are in Congress. Many long-term incumbents are not only able to fund their own reelection campaigns; they also manage to establish their own PACs to give money to other members. This is another way, besides the seniority system, that established politicians influence less established politicians. Several times I went to the floor of the House to seek out members (whose names I had typed on an index card) who were known to have money to hand out. These members might be ideological allies or

might simply have ambitions to move up through the system by handing out $1,000 checks.

At the end of my first term, it was no secret in the House that Charlie Rose of North Carolina intended, in the next term, to challenge Dick Gephardt for Democratic leader. His plan was to run against Gephardt during the party organizational period just before the 104th Congress commenced. I had an important bill before one of Rose's subcommittees, so I felt the need to have him as a friend. After all, he could kill my bill on a whim anytime he desired. Instead, Charlie took me under his wing and helped guide my bill toward passage. He also gave me $1,000 from his personal PAC to help me in an unexpected primary I faced in the spring of '94, a race in which my challenger spent at least $250,000.

The next time I asked Charlie for money it was for the November general election. In the meantime, I had decided to support Gephardt, mostly because of his strong stance against NAFTA and his generally more liberal politics. I also knew that I was facing another million-dollar race. When I approached Charlie for money, his response was, "Son, you better get on over with your friend Gephardt. You won't see any more money coming from me." I felt so awkward and silly. Here I was, a grown man, a congressmen, getting blown off for a lousy $1,000.

Now that I am out of Congress, I watch both parties mired in controversy over the sources of campaign funds, and I view the events with a sense of familiarity. Money has been the dominant player in yet another election, and, as usual, there's been no accounting for it. And as I hear politicians speak of the need for campaign-finance reform, I wonder: Just what are they talking about? What are they prepared to do? Turn off the spigot or, with much fanfare, simply redirect the flow?

The issue of campaign finance points to a deeper problem in U.S. politics: the subservience of all other issues of representation to economics. The real business of our nation's government is all too clearly dominated by large corporations. Fostering a secure environment in which corporations and their investors can flourish has long been the paramount objective of both parties. We ought to use the campaign-finance reform debate to consider how money works to place and keep in office those who willingly reproduce this culture.

# Few in Congress Grieve as Justices Give Line-Item Veto the Ax

## Law failed to live up to expectations as pet projects continued to abound; Congress appears unlikely to surrender such power of the purse again soon

*By Andrew Taylor*

When historians evaluate Congress' uneasy experiment with the line-item veto, they will examine a law that failed to live up to its advance billing. Under President Clinton, the budget-cutting tool was neither the pork-slashing sword envisioned by proponents nor the presidential club opponents feared would beat Congress into following White House orders.

Nor did the law appear to have an effect on Congress' appetite for parochial pet projects.

Even some Republicans who eagerly voted for the law in 1996 breathed a sign of relief June 25 when the Supreme Court struck it down in a 6-3 ruling.

Others immediately proffered new bills aimed at giving the president some ability to curb congressional spending. They conceded that these bills had poor prospects. Now that the budget deficit is just a memory, Congress appears less likely to volunteer again to give away part of its cherished power of the purse—which means congressional porkbusters will have to police their colleagues, which they have done previously with limited success.

The court, accepting arguments that opponents had voiced from the onset of debate in 1995, said the law (PL 104-130) was unconstitutional because it permitted the president to rewrite bills he had already signed into law.

> **Even some Republicans breathed a sign of relief when the Supreme Court struck down the line-item veto law. Others immediately proffered new bills aimed at giving the president some ability to curb congressional spending. But Congress appeared unlikely to volunteer again to give away part of its power of the purse.**

"If the Line-Item Veto Act were valid, it would authorize the president to create a different law—one whose text was not voted on by either House of Congress or presented to the president," Justice John Paul Stevens wrote for the court. "If there is to be a new procedure in which the president will play a different role in determining the final text of what may 'become a law,' such change must come not by legislation but through... amendment." (*Excerpts, p. 1748*)

The law's opponents were jubilant. Sen. Robert C. Byrd, D-W.Va., who rarely holds a news conference, summoned reporters to declare: "This is a great day for the Constitution of the United States of America.... The liberties of the American people have been assured. God save this honorable court!"

Byrd and other opponents had fought for years to block the line-item veto, saying it would shift far too much power from Congress to the president, an argument echoed by Justice Anthony M. Kennedy in a concurring opinion: "Separation of powers was designed to implement a fundamental insight: Concentration of power in the hands of a single branch is a threat to liberty."

The court's decision gave Byrd a victory it denied him a year ago

From *CQ Weekly*, Vol. 56, No. 26, June 27, 1998, pp. 1747-1749. © 1998 by Congressional Quarterly, Inc. Reprinted by permission.

when it threw out Byrd's challenge to the law, saying he did not have legal standing to sue because he had not been directly harmed by the law. (*Ruling, 1997 CQ Weekly, p. 1498*)

But after Clinton used the power to "cancel" from last year's twin tax and budget laws (PL 105-33, PL 105-34) two narrowly targeted tax breaks and a "direct spending" provision to

help the state of New York finance its Medicaid program, two other lawsuits (*Clinton v. New York* and *Snake River Potato Growers Inc. v. Rubin*) were filed by plaintiffs who had been injured by the vetoes. U.S. District Judge Thomas F. Hogan ruled the law unconstitutional in February; his colleague Thomas Penfield Jackson had ruled in Byrd's favor in 1997 before being reversed by the Supreme Court. (*Lower court rulings, CQ Weekly, pp. 380, 120*)

In defending the law's constitutionality, the government argued that Congress was delegating to the president additional discretion to enforce laws, not ceding any lawmaking power. And the president has long had the authority to impound or refuse to spend money appropriated by Congress, although such authority was curtailed in 1974 in response to President Richard M. Nixon's provocations. (*1974 Almanac, p. 145*)

Joining Stevens and Kennedy in striking down the law were Chief Justice William H. Rehnquist and Justices David H. Souter, Clarence Thomas and Ruth Bader Ginsburg.

Justices Antonin Scalia, Stephen G. Breyer and Sandra Day O'Connor dissented. Scalia, reading his dissent from the bench, said the veto power was "entirely in accord with the Constitution." He wrote: "There is not a dime's worth of difference between Congress's authorizing the president to *cancel* a spending item and Congress's authorizing money to be spent on a particular item at the president's discretion."

Presidents dating back to Ulysses S. Grant have yearned for the line-item veto, which permits the executive to strike individual items from bills without having to veto the entire measure. Forty-four governors have the power.

The strongest recent call came from Republican President Ronald Reagan, who complained of having to accept wasteful spending in huge appropriations bills that he had to sign. The veto was a dead letter as long as Democrats controlled Con-

## Excerpts From the Opinions

The Supreme Court ruled 6-3 on June 25 that the 1996 line-item veto law (PL 104-130) is unconstitutional. The court said it violated Article I, Section 7 of the Constitution, which says, in part, that every bill "which shall have passed the House of Representatives and the Senate, shall, before it becomes a Law, be presented to the President of the United States; If he approves he shall sign it, but if not he shall return it." The following are excerpts from the majority opinion, written by Justice John Paul Stevens, and from the opinion of Justice Antonin Scalia, who dissented:

### From Justice Stevens:

"There is no provision in the Constitution that authorizes the President to enact, to amend, or to repeal statutes. Both Article I and Article II assign responsibilities to the President that directly relate to the lawmaking process, but neither addresses the issue presented by these cases." [Article I allows the president to veto a bill; Article II allows the president to recommend legislation.]

"There are important differences between the President's 'return' of a bill pursuant to Article I, Section 7, and the exercise of the President's cancellation authority pursuant to the Line Item Veto Act. The constitutional return takes place *before* the bill becomes law; the statutory cancellation occurs *after* the bill becomes law. The constitutional return is of the entire bill; the statutory cancellation is of only a part.... The Constitution ... is silent on the subject of unilateral Presidential action that either repeals or amends parts of duly enacted statutes.

"There are powerful reasons for construing constitutional silence on this profoundly important issue as equivalent to an express prohibition. ... Our first President understood the text of the Presentment Clause as requiring that he either 'approve all the parts of a Bill, or reject it in toto.' What has emerged in these cases from the President's exercise of his statutory cancellation powers, however, are truncated versions of two bills that passed both Houses of Congress. They are not the product of the 'finely wrought' procedure that the Framers designed."

"The Line Item Veto Act authorizes the President himself to effect the repeal of laws, for his own policy reasons, without observing the procedures set out in Article I, Section 7. The fact that Congress intended such a result is of no moment. Although Congress presumably anticipated that the President might cancel some of the items in the Balanced Budget Act and in the Taxpayer Relief Act, Congress cannot alter the procedures set out in Article I, Section 7, without amending the Constitution.

"Neither are we persuaded by the Government's contention that the President's authority to cancel new direct spending and tax benefit items is no greater than his traditional authority to decline to spend appropriated funds. ... The critical difference between this statute and all of its predecessors ... is that unlike any of them, this Act gives the President the unilateral power to change the text of duly enacted statutes.

"If the Line Item Veto Act were valid, it would authorize the President to create a different law—one whose text was not voted on by either House of Congress or presented to the President for signature."

### From Justice Scalia:

" ... The President's discretion under the Line Item Veto Act is ... no broader than the discretion traditionally granted the President in his execution of spending laws."

" ... there is not a dime's worth of difference between Congress's authorizing the President to *cancel* a spending item, and Congress's authorizing money to be spent on a particular item at the President's discretion. And the latter has been done since the Founding of the Nation."

gress, but the idea was a key plank in the House GOP's 1994 "Contract With America," and Republicans overcame their qualms about giving it to Clinton. It was among the few contract items on which Clinton and Congress wholly agreed.

"The decision is a defeat for all Americans," Clinton said. "It deprives the president of a valuable tool for eliminating waste in the federal budget and for enlivening the public debate over how to make the best use of public funds."

## Enhanced Rescissions

Giving the president a true line-item veto would require amending the Constitution, which proponents believe is not politically viable. Instead, Republicans devised a procedure in which they significantly strengthened the president's power to rescind spending that he has already approved.

Under this "enhanced rescissions" framework, within five days of signing a bill the president sends a list of proposed rescissions of spending items in appropriations bills or cancellations of narrowly focused tax benefits and new entitlement spending. These cuts automatically take effect unless Congress passes a bill to reverse them. The president can veto such a disapproval bill.

That is exactly what happened after Clinton killed 38 projects worth $287 million last year on the fiscal 1998 military construction law (PL 105-45). Congress overturned the vetoes, many of which were based on out-of-date or faulty information from the Pentagon. (*Override, CQ Weekly, p. 506*)

After taking a scalding from lawmakers in both parties, Clinton used the new power much more tentatively, vetoing only projects that seemed difficult to defend, such as $1.9 million to dredge a Mississippi lake for a private marina and conference center.

Clinton and his aides also refrained from threatening members' projects to get them to vote for his

priorities, such as his failed bid to renew "fast track" trade negotiating authority. "The potential was there" for such threats, said a senior aide to House Minority Leader Richard A. Gephardt, D-Mo., "it just wasn't used." (*Fast track, p. 1787*).

Nor was there any horse trading on spending decisions. When former Office of Management and Budget Director Franklin D. Raines offered during negotiations on the fiscal 1998 defense spending bill (PL 105-56) to forgo any vetoes in exchange for funding of administration priorities, he was rebuffed. (*Defense, 1997 CQ Weekly, p. 2979*)

"We basically kind of dismissed them and said, 'Go ahead, make our day,' " recalled House Appropriations Committee Staff Director James W. Dyer. "This is a law that really did not make a significant contribution to reducing the deficit and was poorly handled to the point it was an embarrassment to the administration and the Hill both."

Although most members were unaffected by the line-item veto, several of those who got hit by the veto were outraged. Even conservatives such as Sen. Larry E. Craig, R-Idaho, did quick about-faces after losing home state projects. Craig also was a sponsor of one of the tax provisions that Clinton killed last August. It aimed to make it easier to sell food processing plants to farmer-owned cooperatives.

Supporters of the line-item veto vowed to rejoin the battle.

"This is a temporary defeat for the American people, for fiscal responsibility," said Sen. Daniel R. Coats, who co-sponsored the law with Sen. John McCain, R-Ariz. "But . . . this is one battle in a war to address the issue of fiscal responsibility and to represent the American taxpayer so that the light of day can be shed on the way in which the Congress spends their money."

McCain and Coats immediately introduced an alternative bill (S 2221) under which Congress would pass appropriations bills as it does now, but the bills would then be un-

bundled with each item sent to the president as a separate bill to be signed or vetoed. The Senate took this approach in 1995 when it originally passed the line-item veto. (*1995 Almanac, p. 2–40*).

This separate enrollment approach—the version of the veto filibustered to death in 1985—was revived in 1995 not because line-item veto proponents thought it was a good idea but instead to head off a collision in Senate GOP ranks between McCain and old-timers such as Budget Chairman Pete V. Domenici, R-N.M. At the time, Domenici and Ted Stevens, R-Alaska, supported a milder "expedited rescissions" framework in which Congress would vote on proposed presidential rescissions but be able to reject them by majority vote, instead of the two-thirds required to override a veto. (*1985 Almanac, p. 468*)

Privately, McCain and Coats acknowledge that sending the president hundreds or thousands of separate bills is logistically unworkable, and the Senate quickly ceded that issue to the House during conference talks in 1995–96.

In the House, Budget Chairman John R. Kasich, R-Ohio, said the best response to the court's decision would be a constitutional amendment, but he conceded that it was unlikely to pass. Kasich reintroduced an expedited rescissions bill (HR 4174) similar to bills that passed the House in 1994, 1993 and 1992. But it is unlikely any scaled-back measure could become law this year. Under existing rules, the president can request rescissions, but Congress can ignore him. (*1994 Almanac, p. 87*).

The court decision capped a frustrating period for McCain, a former prisoner of war who was also the chief GOP advocate of the now-dead anti-smoking bill (S 1415). "This has been a wonderful two weeks for me personally," McCain said. "I really haven't had quite so much fun since my last interrogation in Hanoi."

# THE REHNQUIST REINS

*The Chief Justice has brought order to the Court and won striking support for judicial restraint. But Anthony Kennedy turns out to be the decisive voice.*

## David J. Garrow

*David J. Garrow is the author of "Liberty and Sexuality" and "Bearing the Cross," which won the Pulitzer Prize in 1987. He wrote about Justice David H. Souter for the Magazine in 1994.*

WHEN THE SUPREME COURT RECONVENES TOMORROW morning, William H. Rehnquist will mark his 10th anniversary as the 16th Chief Justice of the United States. The Rehnquist Court's first decade may best be remembered for such surprisingly "liberal" decisions as the 1992 reaffirmation of Roe v. Wade and this year's vindication of gay rights in a case from Colorado. In both exceptional cases, Rehnquist was in dissent on the losing sides, but those outcomes are unrepresentative of his winning record in crucial, if less publicized, areas of the law.

Rehnquist's most far-reaching triumphs have come in cases raising fundamental questions of federalism, involving the distribution of power between the Federal Government and the states. One year ago, in United States v. Lopez, for the first time in 58 years a court majority restricted Congress's ability to expand Federal authority after it enacted an anti-gun-possession law. This June, in the otherwise unsung death penalty case of Felker v. Turpin, Rehnquist ratified a significant victory in a long-standing war over the power of Federal courts to review and potentially reverse state inmates' criminal convictions. This seemingly abstruse battle over greatly truncating Federal courts' habeas corpus jurisdiction demonstrates how successfully Rehnquist has extended his own staunchly conservative, lifelong beliefs into a judicial agenda that has significantly remade major portions of American law.

But as decisions like Romer v. Evans, the Colorado gay rights case, and 1992's reaffirmation of Roe in Planned Parenthood of Southeastern Pennsylvania v. Casey exemplify, the "Rehnquist Court" is only sometimes the Rehnquist Court. That's true only when the Chief Justice is able to win the determinative fifth vote of the one crucial Justice who most oftentimes is the deciding voice whenever the Court is split 5 to 4—Anthony Kennedy. When he chooses to side with the High Court's four moderates, the "Rehnquist Court" is turned into the "Kennedy Court." In the meantime, Rehnquist will no doubt continue his drive to shrink the influence of Federal courts in American life.

MONDAY MORNING, JUNE 3, 1996, MARKED A POTENTIALLY CULMINATING moment for the 72-year-old Chief Justice.

Just as it will be tomorrow, the court's magisterial courtroom is packed to capacity. United States Senators and members of the House sit toward the front. Former clerks to several Justices have come from as far away as California just to watch; senior members of the Court's press corps squeeze into two tightly packed wooden benches on the left. Members of the marshal's staff shush tourists in the rear of the intimate chamber.

At precisely 10 A.M., a marshal brings the courtroom to its feet as the nine Justices emerge from behind the velvet curtain to take their seats on the elevated bench. Chief Justice Rehnquist declares that several decisions are ready for announcement, and in quick succession the authors of the majority opinions offer brief summaries of the new holdings.

Only at 10:28 A.M. does Rehnquist reach the event the capacity crowd has come to see. "We'll hear argument now in No. 95-8836, Ellis Wayne Felker v. Tony Turpin." The Chief Justice, too, has been waiting for this opportunity for a long time.

The Court's regular argument calendar ended more than five weeks earlier, on April 24; for all of May and June, the Justices normally would have devoted themselves simply to finishing up their opinions in cases that had been argued during the standard October-through-April schedule. However, on that very same April 24, President Clinton signed into law a new statute awkwardly titled the Antiterrorism and Effective Death Penalty Act of 1996.

Long under consideration by Congress, the new law includes a host of provisions intended to reduce and hasten Federal court review of criminal offenders' challenges to the finality of their state court convictions—including challenges by convicted murderers sentenced to death. Prisoners have an initial right to appellate court review; those who fail can pursue subsequent challenges by filing petitions for writs of habeas corpus—literally "you have the body" but in essence a Federal court order overturning a state court conviction. The new law imposes stringent limits on *any* Federal court consideration of a *second* or additional habeas petition from a convict. Death-row prisoners often file petition after petition, thereby delaying their executions even if their sentences are never overturned; some noncapital felons file such papers year after year.

Opponents of the new law argued that, if allowed to stand, it would eventually open the floodgates to speedier executions of the 3,153 prisoners now on death row nationwide. For Rehnquist, however, the limiting of Federal habeas corpus reflects not some sort of personal blood lust for the death penalty. It instead bespeaks his commitment to a federalism-centered view of American politics and government, which encompasses many other issues in addition to Federal court respect for the finality of state court criminal convictions. "The core" of Rehnquist's theory, one scholar has written, "is the idea of state sovereignty," above and beyond Federal Government control.

Testifying at his 1986 confirmation hearings for promotion to Chief Justice, Rehnquist acknowledged that "my personal preference has always been for the feeling that if it can be done at the local level, do it there. If it cannot be done at the local level, try it at the state level, and if it cannot be done at the state level, then you go to the national level."

Rehnquist strongly opposed an expansive habeas role for the Federal courts even long before President Richard M. Nixon nominated him to the Supreme Court in the fall of 1971. Then a 47-year-old Assistant Attorney General, Rehnquist had joined the Justice Department in 1969 at the behest of his fellow Arizonan, Deputy Attorney General Richard G. Kleindienst, whom he had come to know during 15 years of law practice in Phoenix. But 1969 hadn't marked Rehnquist's first job in Washington, for way back in 1952 and 1953—just after he had graduated first in his class from Stanford Law School—young Rehnquist had served for 18 months as one of two law clerks to the highly regarded Supreme Court Justice Robert H. Jackson. Rehnquist had enjoyed his clerkship immensely, but when he himself was nominated to the High Court in 1971, his work for Jackson generated a major controversy when a

Rehnquist memorandum arguing *against* any Supreme Court voiding of segregated schools and *for* a continued endorsement of the old doctrine of "separate but equal" was discovered in Jackson's file on Brown v. Board of Education. Rehnquist unpersuasively insisted—as he would again during his 1986 confirmation hearings for Chief Justice—that the memo represented an articulation of *Jackson's* views rather than his own. The Senate nonetheless confirmed him on a vote of 68 to 26.

Jackson's papers also contain a Rehnquist memo with a minority view on *another* Brown case, Brown v. Allen, a 1953 ruling little known to the general public but justly famous among criminal law practitioners as the modern fount of an expansive approach to Federal courts' habeas jurisdiction. In that memo, Rehnquist argued that Federal courts should not grant habeas petitions involving any issue that had been considered by a state court unless the defendant had been denied the right to counsel. In 1953, that recommendation had no more impact than did Rehnquist's advice in the other Brown case, but three decades later, once he sat on the High Court in his own right, habeas excesses reappeared as a subject of his special concern. In a 1981 opinion involving a death-row petitioner, Coleman v. Balkcom, Rehnquist complained that in light of habeas's "increasing tendency to postpone or delay" death-penalty enforcement, "stronger measures are called for" beyond the Court's simple denial of repeated death-row appeals.

Reminded of his Jackson clerkship memos in a 1985 interview with this Magazine—the last such interview Rehnquist has granted—he frankly acknowledged that "I don't know that my views have changed much from that time." Four years later, Chief Justice Rehnquist vented his continuing anger at repetitive filings in a 5-4 majority opinion rebuffing an application from an ostensibly penniless petitioner named Jessie McDonald. "Since 1971," Rehnquist observed, McDonald "has made 73 separate filings with the Court, not including this petition, which is his eighth so far this term." Rejecting the solicitude of four dissenters who objected to the majority's order instructing the clerk's office to reject any further unpaid filings from McDonald, Rehnquist emphasized that "every paper filed with the clerk of this Court, no matter how repetitious or frivolous, requires some portion of the institution's limited resources."

A few months later, Rehnquist took up his capital habeas cudgel in his role as head of the Judicial Conference, the administrative arm of the Federal judiciary. Failing in an effort to obtain majority support for a recommendation calling upon Congress to limit Federal habeas jurisdiction, Rehnquist nonetheless forwarded a report to the Senate Judiciary Committee. In an unprecedented public letter, 14 of the conference's 26 other members objected to the Chief Justice's action. Rehnquist refused to back down.

Congress did not act, but in April 1991 Rehnquist achieved much of his legislative goal *judicially* in a 6-3 court ruling that starkly limited successive habeas petitions and vindicated his 1981 call for action in Coleman. Decrying "the abusive petitions that in recent years have threatened to undermine the integrity of the habeas corpus process," the majority stressed that "perpetual disrespect for the finality of convictions disparages the entire criminal justice system."

But even that ruling in McCleskey v. Zant did not set as high a hurdle to successive petitions as Rehnquist sought. Warning that America cannot afford "the luxury of state and Federal courts that work at cross purposes or irrationally duplicate" each others' efforts, the Chief Justice continued to emphasize that "capital habeas corpus still cries out for reform." Come April 1996, after 24 years on the court and 10 years as Chief Justice, it seemed with the Felker case that Rehnquist's wish had finally come true.

WHEN REHNQUIST WAS NOMINATED TO SUCCEED THE RETIRING Warren E. Burger as Chief Justice by President Ronald Reagan in 1986, his colleagues were unanimously pleased and supportive. Fourteen years of working together had built good personal relations even between Rehnquist and his ideological opposites, William J. Brennan and Thurgood Marshall. Brennan startled one acquaintance by informing him that "Bill Rehnquist is my best friend up here," and a Washington attorney, John D. Lane, who privately interviewed all seven other Justices on behalf of the American Bar Association's Committee on the Federal Judiciary, informed the Senate Judiciary Committee that Rehnquist's nomination was met with "genuine enthusiasm on the part of not only his colleagues on the Court but others who served the Court in a staff capacity and some of the relatively lowly paid individuals at the Court. There was almost a unanimous feeling of joy."

Rehnquist's colleagues looked forward to his installation as "Chief" in part because they welcomed the departure of his overbearing, manipulative and less-than-brilliant predecessor, Burger, who had succeeded the legendary Earl Warren 17 years earlier. Reporters always stressed that Burger *looked* the part of Chief Justice of the United States, but among his fellow Justices there was virtually unanimous agreement that his skills at leading the Conference—the Justices' own name for their group of nine—had been woefully lacking. John Lane told the Judiciary Committee that one Justice said that "he looks for a tremendous improvement in the functioning of this Court" under Rehnquist. Based upon all the Justices' comments, Lane reported, "I came away with a very strong opinion that Justice Rehnquist will make an excellent Chief Justice."

Much of the 1986 debate over Rehnquist's promotion focused upon newly augmented allegations that 20-odd years earlier he had taken part in Republican Party efforts to intimidate black voters at Phoenix polling places. The charges were not provable, but the final Senate confirmation vote of 65 to 33 was closer than Rehnquist's backers had expected and in its wake the new Chief Justice privately told friends that he felt the Judiciary Committee hearings had treated him very badly. "He took it somewhat

personally," one acquaintance remembered, but within the Court there was immediate agreement that Rehnquist was far superior to Burger in leading the Conference's discussion of cases.

Ten years before, in a 1976 law review essay on "Chief Justices I Never Knew," Rehnquist had stressed the importance of firmly run sessions in which each Justice, speaking in order of seniority, stated his views succinctly and without interruption: "A give and take discussion between nine normal human beings, in which each participates equally, is not feasible." He also acknowledged how a "Chief Justice has a notable advantage over his brethren: he states the case first and analyzes the law governing it first. If he cannot, with this advantage, maximize the impact of his views, subsequent interruptions of colleagues or digressions on his part or by others will not succeed either." Citing Harlan Fiske Stone and Felix Frankfurter as brilliant Justices of the past whose efforts to influence their colleagues had generally failed, Rehnquist added that "the power of persuasion is a subtle skill, dependent on quality rather than quantity."

In his 1987 book, "The Supreme Court," Rehnquist gently noted that "I have tried to make my opening presentation of a case somewhat shorter than Chief Justice Burger made his." Justice Harry A. Blackmun often disagreed substantively with Rehnquist, but he was quick to praise Rehnquist's management skills. "The Chief in conference is a splendid administrator," he told one semiprivate gathering. Unlike the Burger years, "we get through in a hurry. If there's anything to be criticized about it, he gets through it in too much of a hurry at times."

Warren Burger was seen by his colleagues as a Chief who often abused his power to assign the writing of majority opinions whenever he was not in dissent. One Rehnquist clerk from the mid-1970's still recalls how Burger, unhappy with the political humor of a Rehnquist-produced skit at the Court's 1975 Christmas party, the next month assigned Rehnquist only one opinion, in an Indian tax case. Most Justices expected Rehnquist to eschew such gamesmanship, and the record of the past decade generally bears that out. Some former clerks contend in private that in recent years Anthony Kennedy has fared far better in receiving important assignments from Rehnquist than other Justices, but Rehnquist as Chief is far more concerned with maximizing the speed and efficiency of the Court's opinion-writing than with playing favorites.

In a 1989 memo to his colleagues, Rehnquist divulged that "the principal rule I have followed in assigning opinions is to give everyone approximately the same number of assignments of opinions for the Court during any one term." But, he warned, any Justice who failed to circulate a first draft of a majority opinion within four weeks or who failed to circulate the first draft of an anticipated dissent within four weeks of the majority opinion or who had not voted in any case in which both majority and dissenting opinions had circulated would now be looked upon less favorably. "It only makes sense," he asserted, "to give some preference to those who are 'current' with respect to past work."

Rehnquist's announcement provoked an immediate objection from John Paul Stevens, now the second-most-senior Justice to the Chief himself. An iconoclastic and generally liberal thinker, Stevens in recent years has outpaced all of his colleagues in his number of individual dissents and concurrences. Reminding Rehnquist that "too much emphasis on speed can have an adverse effect on quality," Stevens warned that it "may be unwise to rely too heavily" on rigid deadlines, especially when a Justice's investment in a major dissent, or a handful of dissents, might create a lag. "I do not think a Justice's share of majority opinions should be reduced because he is temporarily preoccupied with such an opinion, or because he is out of step with the majority in a large number of cases." Rehnquist remained largely unmoved, chiding his colleagues just a few weeks later about several decisions that were running behind schedule. "I suggest that we make a genuine effort to get these cases down 'with all deliberate speed.' "

EIGHT DAYS AFTER PRESIDENT CLINTON SIGNED THE NEW HABEAS legislation into law, a three-judge panel of the Court of Appeals for the 11th Circuit applied the statute in denying

# ONE ANGRY MAN

## Antonin Scalia's Decade

William Rehnquist's 10th anniversary as Chief Justice is also Antonin (Nino) Scalia's 10th anniversary as an Associate Justice. Nominated to Rehnquist's seat when Rehnquist was promoted to replace Warren Burger, Scalia—a four-year veteran of the United States Court of Appeals for the District of Columbia Circuit—faced no opposition. He was confirmed, 98-0, after less than five minutes of Senate floor discussion.

During Scalia's first few years on the Court, commentators wondered whether his combination of intelligence and gregariousness would make him into the Rehnquist Court's real intellectual leader. As Laurence H. Tribe, a Harvard law professor, told The Boston Globe in 1990: "There is no question Scalia is brilliant. What remains to be seen is if he is wise."

Six years later, the verdict is all but unanimous: Scalia is rash, impulsive and imprudent, a Justice who in case after case would rather insult his colleagues' intelligence than appeal to them. Judge Alex Kozinski, a conservative member of the United States Court of Appeals for the Ninth Circuit, pronounced his judgment as early as 1992: "Commentators said, 'This is the guy who, through his charm and intellect, will forge a conservative consensus.' He hasn't done it." The New Republic's Jeffrey Rosen, contending that Scalia "has intellectual contempt for most of his colleagues," suggests that the relatively young Justice—Scalia is now 60—calls to mind the sad career of another brilliant judicial failure, Felix Frankfurter.

One former Scalia clerk insists that the Justice is "100 percent impervious" to public criticism. But Scalia is hardly ignorant of his bad-boy reputation; three years ago, he insisted to one Washington audience that "I am not a nut." In comments to the Supreme Court Historical Society, Scalia observed that dissenting opinions "do not, or at least need not, produce animosity and bitterness among the members of the Court." But even more revealing was a statement Justice Sandra Day O'Connor made to a Ninth Circuit judicial conference. Reminding her audience of the old saying that "sticks and stones will break my bones but words will never hurt me," O'Connor added, "That probably isn't true."

A colleague confirms that O'Connor has been "deeply wounded" by the insults Scalia has sent her way, starting in 1989 in the abortion case Webster v. Reproductive Health Services. O'Connor analysis, Scalia wrote there, "cannot be taken seriously."

A former Scalia clerk acknowledges that Scalia "completely alienated" O'Connor and "lost her forever," and a former Rehnquist clerk notes how O'Connor's "personality is in many ways just the opposite of Justice Scalia's. She's very willing to build consensus on opinions." But Scalia, says another ex-clerk, is not only "in love with his own language," he also believes that "what he's doing is a matter of principle. He knows how right he is."

On the next-to-last day of the 1995–96 term, Scalia turned his rhetorical guns on Rehnquist, who had committed the grievous sin of concurring with the Court's 7-1 majority in striking down the Virginia Military Institute's exclusion of women from a state institution. In his lonely, splenetic dissent, Scalia called the majority's equal protection analysis "irresponsible" and mocked Rehnquist's separate views as "more moderate than the Court's but only at the expense of being even more implausible." Saying Rehnquist erroneously suggested that Virginia "should have known . . . what this Court expected of it" because of an earlier Court ruling, Scalia truculently asserted that "any lawyer who gave that advice to the Commonwealth ought to have been either disbarred or committed."

Scalia's characterization of the Chief Justice's views represented the first time in memory that one member of the Court had suggested that another might be better situated in a nonjudicial institution, but virtually nothing that Scalia might say could worsen the reputation he has made for himself among students of the Court. Harvard's Laurence Tribe decries Scalia's "extreme stridency and disrespect for opposing views." Another well-known law professor, far less liberal than Tribe and a social colleague of several Justices, ruefully looks back on the Senate's 1987 rejection of Supreme Court nominee Robert H. Bork and concludes that Bork would have been more civil and more broad-minded than Scalia by a long shot." Indeed, Scalia, he contends, "has become precisely what the Bork opponents thought Bork would be."

—D.J.G.

a request from a Georgia death-row inmate, Ellis Wayne Felker, to file a successive petition. Convicted 13 years earlier of murdering a 19-year-old woman soon after being released from prison on a prior felony conviction, Felker now was finally facing actual execution; three times before, the Supreme Court had turned aside appeals. Later that very same day, May 2, Felker's attorneys asked the High Court to review how the new law prohibited Felker from appealing the circuit court's refusal.

Less than 24 hours later, the Supreme Court granted Felker's request for a hearing and set oral argument on his challenge to the new law for exactly one month later. The Court's swift action—the first such accelerated hearing in six years and the fastest grant of review since the famous Pentagon Papers case, New York Times Co. v. United States, a quarter-century earlier—brought a cry of protest from the four least conservative Justices, John Paul Stevens, David H. Souter, Ruth Bader Ginsburg and Stephen G. Breyer. Formally dissenting, they called the majority's action "both unnecessary and profoundly unwise" and declared that review of the new law "surely should be undertaken with the utmost deliberation, rather than unseemly haste."

One question posed by Felker was whether the new limits on appeals involving second or successive habeas petitions represented a Congressional diminution of the Supreme Court's own appellate jurisdiction. That would be a constitutional issue of the highest order; not since the Civil War era had the Court directly confronted it. Felker's lawyers, focusing on an avenue Congress had failed to address, noted in their brief that the new law did not expressly affect the Court's authority to consider "original" habeas petitions filed directly with it. Conceding that the High Court's use of "original habeas" would be "exceptional and discretionary," Felker's attorneys nonetheless acknowledged that "no unconstitutional interference with this Court's appellate jurisdiction exists if Congress merely eliminates one procedure for review but leaves in place an equally efficacious alternative."

Henry P. Monaghan, a Columbia University law professor and an experienced Supreme Court advocate, spoke for Felker when oral argument got under way on June 3. The present-day Rehnquist Court is as vocal and energetic a nine-member bench as any attorney could imagine confronting (only Justice Clarence Thomas is usually silent, but the liberal icons William Brennan and Thurgood Marshall were likewise generally quiet), and Rehnquist himself—along with Justices Souter, Breyer, Ginsburg and Antonin Scalia—is an outspoken questioner, as both Monaghan and his opponent, Senior Assistant Attorney General Susan V. Boleyn of Georgia, soon found. "Why shouldn't we just try to apply the statute as written?" asked Rehnquist with some exasperation. "I mean, rather than trying to torture some meaning out of it that's not there?" Monaghan tried to demur, but drolly conceded that "this statute passed by Congress with respect to second petitions is not the work of Attila the Hun."

Susan Boleyn, however, faced a far tougher grilling. "That's not a very specific position, Ms. Boleyn," the Chief Justice interjected before she had uttered her fourth sentence. Peppering her with questions, Rehnquist asked how she would distinguish a 19th-century decision, Ex Parte Yerger. Boleyn struggled. "Well, I think that this Court has recognized exceptions to its jurisdiction both in the constitutional venue under Article III—." An unhappy Rehnquist cut her off. "Are you familiar with the Yerger case?" "Yes, Your Honor, but I'm not familiar with what exactly you're asking me to respond to."

It only got worse. Breyer, telling her, "I'm sorry, I don't understand," asked Boleyn a fast-paced hypothetical and demanded an answer. "Do we have jurisdiction to hear it? Yes or no." Boleyn said no, but Breyer objected: "I thought from your brief the answer was yes."

Asked in 1992 by C-span's Brian Lamb whether he could tell if attorneys are nervous during oral argument, Rehnquist jocularly replied that "I assume they're all nervous—they should be." Occasionally—most often in the months before his wife's slow death from cancer in October 1991—Rehnquist has rebuked or snapped at lawyers who have been unprepared or who have committed the tiny but grievous sin of calling him Judge rather than Chief Justice.

---

*Not long after Ellis Wayne Felker finally goes to the electric chair, the pace of death-row executions across America will pick up substantial speed. Rehnquist's victory may not yet be 100 percent complete; his triumph nonetheless is impressive, and still growing.*

---

The day after the Felker argument, the Justices met in private conference to discuss the case. The substance of that meeting isn't likely to be known for a long time; accounts of conference discussions generally become available only years after the event, with release of the handwritten notes of one or more Justices. Even then, some Justices' papers—Thurgood Marshall's are the most recent example—shed next to no light on conference discussions, for not all Justices take notes. Those of William O. Douglas and Brennan offer reliable guides to the 1960's, 70's and 80's, but every modern Court scholar knows full well that the ultimate treasure trove for the years 1970 through 1994 will, in time, be the conference notes of now-retired Justice Blackmun.

In his own chambers, Rehnquist instructs each of his three clerks to have their first drafts of his opinions ready for his review within 10 to 14 days. Some wags insist that Rehnquist has three clerks—seven other Justices now have four, Stevens has three—primarily to ease the arrangements for his weekly tennis-match doubles, but Rehnquist treats his young aides in a warm, low-key manner. He revises their drafts by orally dictating amended wording into a recorder, and he volunteered in his 1987 book that "I go through the draft with a view to shortening it, simplifying it and clarifying it."

In Rehnquist's first 15 years on the Court, commentators praised his writing as "clear, lucid, brief and mercifully free of bureaucratese." One commended "the somewhat peculiar references to history, the classics and gamesmanship with which Rehnquist likes to sprinkle his opinions"—this June a Rehnquist concurrence included a passing reference to "Grover Cleveland's second inaugural address"—but since 1986 such acclaim has gradually diminished, with critics noting "the characteristic terseness of a Rehnquist opinion" and journalists labeling his prose "dry and to the point."

Rehnquist's June 28 opinion announcing the Court's *unanimous*—including the four Justices who had protested the accelerated hearing—resolution of Felker v. Turpin manifested all these traits. Back in 1987, Rehnquist acknowledged how "the Chief Justice is expected to retain for himself some opinions that he regards as of great significance," but Rehnquist traditionally has written a disproportionate number of criminal law rulings. The 12½-page Felker decision had been written, edited and circulated for other Justices' comments and agreement in little more than three weeks' time, and the substance of Rehnquist's—and the Court's—holding followed closely from the implications of the questions Rehnquist had put to Monaghan and Boleyn back on June 3.

The new statute "makes no mention of our authority to hear habeas petitions filed as original matters in this Court" and thus, fully in keeping with Ex Parte Yerger, it "has not repealed our authority to entertain" such petitions. Therefore, Rehnquist held, "there can be no plausible argument that the Act has deprived this Court of appellate jurisdiction in violation of Article III." No constitutional collision thereby occurred, and the new statutory restrictions on Federal court consideration of successive habeas petitions could remain fully in place. Convicts and death-row prisoners *could* send "original" petitions directly to the High Court, but—just as Felker's lawyers had conceded in their brief—only in a rare instance of "exceptional circumstances" would such an appeal be granted.

Felker's own habeas request was denied; Georgia has not yet set a new date for Felker's execution.

Some habeas specialists, pointing back to Rehnquist's earlier 1991 judicial breakthrough in McCleskey, dismiss

Felker's actual holding as "relatively insignificant." They emphasize that several pending challenges to other particular provisions of the new law, including Lindh v. Murphy, a case that was decided by the Court of Appeals for the Seventh Circuit in Chicago in late September, are likely to force Rehnquist and his colleagues to revisit the habeas battlefield sometime in 1997.

But such characterizations unintentionally minimize the extent and scale of Rehnquist's long-term agenda and long-term victory. Federal habeas jurisdiction is now only a shadow of what it was when Rehnquist first joined the Supreme Court, and what in 1981 in Coleman was a lonely individual call for action has now won decisive support from a solid Court majority and from bipartisan majorities in both houses of Congress as well as an ostensibly liberal Democratic President. Not long after Ellis Wayne Felker finally goes to the electric chair, the entire pace of death-row executions all across America will pick up substantial speed as one habeas petition after another is quickly cast aside by the courts. Rehnquist's victory may not yet be 100 percent complete; his triumph nonetheless is remarkably impressive and still growing.

**F**ELKER IS THE LATEST IN A LINE OF FEDERALISM CASES THAT FOR Rehnquist began with a 1975 solo dissent in Fry v. United States, an opinion that directly foreshadowed the landmark 5-4 majority victory he would win exactly 20 years later in United States v. Lopez. In 1975, writing

---

*In 1986, Rehnquist had volunteered that a one-third decline in the Court's annual caseload from 150 to 100 would be 'unseemly,' but by the 10th anniversary of his statement, the Court had reduced its annual workload by more than half—from 151 to 75.*

---

only for himself, Rehnquist had advocated "a concept of constitutional federalism which should . . . limit federal power under the Commerce Clause." In Lopez, writing on behalf of a 5-vote majority, Rehnquist dismissed the Justice Department's defense of the Federal anti-gun-possession law and declared that "if we were to accept the Government's arguments, we are hard-pressed to posit any activity by an individual that Congress is without power to regulate."

As early as 1982, a Yale Law Journal analysis of Rehnquist's jurisprudence by H. Jefferson Powell (now a high-ranking Clinton Justice Department appointee) cogently identified "federalism's role as the organizing principle in Rehnquist's work" and persuasively concluded that "Rehnquist's federalism does form a consistent constitutional theory."

More than 10 years later, in one of the three most important decisions of the 1995–96 term, Seminole Tribe of Florida v. Florida, another 5-vote Rehnquist majority forthrightly declared that "each State is a sovereign entity in our Federal system." Dissenting vigorously, Justice Souter protested how Rehnquist was deciding "for the first time since the founding of the Republic that Congress has no authority to subject a State to the jurisdiction of a Federal court at the behest of an individual asserting a Federal right." Souter's objection brought him a harsh rebuke from the Chief: the dissent's "undocumented and highly speculative extralegal explanation . . . is a disservice to the Court's traditional method of adjudication."

One core principle of Rehnquist's federalism, as the habeas battle has reflected, is a firm belief in a modest—some would say *excessively* modest—political and supervisory role for the Federal courts. Back in the early 1980's, the annual docket of the Supreme Court itself—the number of cases it chooses to hear, not the thousands upon thousands it turns aside—had grown to a peak of 151. Many voices, including both Burger and Rehnquist's, called unsuccessfully for the creation of a new, nationwide court of appeals to ease the pressure on the High Court's docket, but the idea died aborning and in recent years has completely vanished from both public—and private—discussion.

At his 1986 confirmation hearings, Rehnquist told the Senate Judiciary Committee that "I think the 150 cases that we have turned out quite regularly over a period of 10 or 15 years is just about where we should be at." Addressing whether that load might be too great and noting how the caseloads of Federal district and appellate courts were increasing rapidly, Rehnquist said that "my own feeling is that all the courts are so much busier today than they have been in the past, that there would be something almost unseemly about the Supreme Court saying, you know, everybody else is deciding twice as many cases as they ever have before, but we are going to go back to two-thirds as many as we did before."

A year later, in his 1987 book, Rehnquist cited the 150 figure and observed that "we are stretched quite thin trying to do what we ought to do." Privately, inside the Court, Rehnquist brooded about the annual "June crunch" of backlogged decisions awaiting finished opinions and suggested to his colleagues the "desirability of cutting down the number of cases set for argument in April," toward the end of the Court's year. But year by year the Court's annual caseload has shrunk further and further: from 132 cases in 1988–89 to 129 in 1989–90, to 112 in 1990–91, to 108 in 1991–92, to 107 in 1992–93, markedly to 84 in 1993–94, then to 82 in 1994–95 and finally to 75 in the just-completed term of 1995–96.

In 1986, Rehnquist had volunteered that a one-third decline in the Court's annual caseload from 150 to 100 would be "unseemly," but on the 10th anniversary of his statement, the Court had reduced its annual workload by more than half—from 151 to 75. Granted, a 1988 statute had virtually eliminated some mandatory appeals that the Court previously had been obligated to hear, whether or not a minimum of four Justices voted to accept the case, but the issue of the "incredible shrinking docket"—what Court watchers call it—has been one of the most striking developments of the Rehnquist years.

The Court, of course, issues no explanations for even so momentous a trend, but in April 1995, at the Third Circuit's annual dicial conference in White Sulphur Springs, W.Va., Justice Souter spoke extemporaneously about the docket shrinkage in remarks that were virtually unprecedented in their public frankness. Referring back to the early 1980's, when he was still an obscure New Hampshire state judge, Souter recalled that in reading Supreme Court opinions at the time, it "seemed to me . . . some of those opinions had the indicia of rush and hurriedness about them." Now he realized, given the caseloads of those years, that those shortcomings "could not have been otherwise and the remarkable thing is that the number of really fine things that came down in that period was as high as it was."

Souter said he was "amazed" that the docket annually had continued to shrink throughout the 1990's, but he stressed that "nobody sets a quota; nobody sits at the conference table and says: 'We've taken too much. We must pull back.' . . . It simply has happened." Identifying a host of contributing factors, Souter noted the "diminishing supply" of new Federal statutes in the late 1980's and early 1990's, and how "not much antitrust work" and "not much civil rights" work, beyond voting cases, had been generated by the Reagan and Bush Administrations' Justice Department. In the criminal area, "drug prosecution does not make for Supreme Court cases these days" because of how Fourth Amendment search-and-seizure standards have "been pretty much raked over. . . . The basic law, the basic standards which have been governing and do govern most of the appeals that people want to bring to us are products of the 60's and the 70's and the 80's. There hasn't been an awful lot for us to take."

In addition, Souter added, according to a comprehensive account of his remarks in the Pennsylvania Law Weekly, 12 years of Reagan-Bush judicial nominations had produced "a relative homogeneity" and "a diminished level of philosophical division within the Federal courts." But, he emphasized, "I know of no one on my court who thinks that we're turning away cases which by traditional standards . . . we should be taking. In fact, it's just the contrary."

Once, he confessed, when the numbers were declining, "I said out loud as well as to myself that if that continued,

I was going to start voting to take interesting Federal questions whether there was a conflict [among lower Federal courts] or not." However, Souter went on, "those were rash words," for "as it turned out, I didn't have to make good on that" because more cases began attracting 4 or more affirmative votes. "About 100 a year is about right," Souter concluded, and the number for the upcoming 1996–97 term seems destined to rise from this past year's remarkable minimum of 75.

With a total caseload of 75 (34 of which were decided unanimously), there are not all that many opinions to spread out over nine months of work for nine Justices—and 34 law clerks. The image of clerks working seven-day-a-week, 12-hour-a-day jobs is a polite fiction of the past, and—though it is considered rude to mention it—many Court observers know that a typical at-the-office workday for the Chief Justice of the United States often stretches from about 9:10 A.M. to 2:30 P.M. Some Justices—Souter, Kennedy and Stevens among them—work decidedly longer hours, but Rehnquist's crusade to shrink the role and responsibilities of the Federal courts has definitely born fruit right at home.

Rehnquist has certainly registered historic doctrinal achievements—in habeas law, in United States v. Lopez, in Seminole Tribe and in the 1994 "takings clause" decision in Dolan v. City of Tigard, but there is no denying Rehnquist has been on the losing side in the two most important, highly visible constitutional holdings of the last five years: 1992's vindication of abortion rights in Planned Parenthood v. Casey and, just a few months ago, the remarkable voiding of a homophobic, antigay Colorado state constitutional amendment in Romer v. Evans. The 6-3 Romer ruling, in which two swing Justices, Anthony Kennedy and Sandra Day O'Connor, sided with the "liberal" foursome of Stevens, Souter, Ginsburg and Breyer rather than with Rehnquist, Scalia and Thomas, was without doubt the most important and symbolically momentous decision of the 1995–96 term.

Romer's majority opinion, written by Kennedy, featured a rhetorical verve rare for the High Court. The Colorado amendment "seems inexplicable by anything but animus toward the class that it affects," Kennedy explained, and "disqualification of a class of persons from the right to seek specific protection from the law is unprecedented in our jurisprudence." Declaring that "it is not within our constitutional tradition to enact laws of this sort," Kennedy pointed out that a statute "declaring that in general it shall be more difficult for one group of citizens than for all others to seek aid from the government is itself a denial of equal protection of the laws in the most literal sense." The state amendment "classifies homosexuals not to further a proper legislative end but to make them unequal to everyone else. This Colorado cannot do. A State cannot so deem a class of persons a stranger to its laws."

In a style and tone to which his colleagues have become all too well accustomed, Scalia angrily and vituperatively dissented. Joined by both Rehnquist and

Thomas, Scalia protested that the majority's holding "places the prestige of this institution behind the proposition that opposition to homosexuality is as reprehensible as racial or religious bias." Avowing that his fellow Justices have "no business imposing upon all Americans the resolution favored by the elite class from which the Members of this institution are selected," Scalia alleged that "our constitutional jurisprudence has achieved terminal silliness" and complained of how Kennedy's opinion was "so long on emotive utterance and so short on relevant legal citation." Declaring that Colorado's action was "eminently reasonable" since citizens are "entitled to be hostile toward homosexual conduct," Scalia maintained that "the degree of hostility reflected by" the state enactment was "the smallest conceivable." His final blast was explicitly contemptuous: "Today's opinion has no foundation in American constitutional law, and barely pretends to."

**B**UT THE MOST IMPORTANT JUSTICE ON THE 1996 REHNQUIST court is not the angry Antonin Scalia; it's the man who ascended to the Court in the wake of Robert H. Bork's rejection: Anthony Kennedy. A quiet and thoughtful Californian, Kennedy throughout his eight-year tenure has been both the crucial fifth vote for virtually all of Rehnquist's major victories *and* the decisive vote and voice when Rehnquist has suffered historic defeats in cases like Casey and Romer. Occasionally apologetic in tone ("sometimes we must make decisions we do not like," Kennedy volunteered in the 1989 flag-burning decision, Texas v. Johnson), Kennedy term after term has been the balance wheel of the Rehnquist Court. Early on, in 1988–89, when Rehnquist and the now-retired William Brennan disagreed in *every one* of that year's 31 5-4 outcomes, Kennedy was with Rehnquist 29 times. (Johnson was one of the two exceptions.) In 1991–92, when Kennedy dissented from only 8 of the term's 108 decisions, his crucial "liberal" votes in both Casey and an important school prayer decision, Lee v. Weisman, drew intense flack from conservative critics.

The following term, 1992–93, Kennedy dissented in only 5 of 107 cases, and the year after that, when he was in the majority in *every one* of the term's 14 5-4 decisions, he again dissented in only 5 cases out of 84. In 1994–95, Kennedy was in the majority in 13 of the term's 16 5-4 cases, including both Lopez and the highly publicized Congressional term limits decision, and in the just-completed 1995–96 term, Kennedy again was the Court's least frequent dissenter (in just 5 of 75 cases) and was in the majority in 9 of the 12 5-4 outcomes.

Now Kennedy is again under fire from extreme conservatives for his memorable majority opinion in Romer (National Review magazine labels him "the dimmest of the Court's intellectual lights"), but among serious Court watchers the impression is growing that Kennedy has more than found his footing. David O'Brien of the University of Virginia calls Kennedy "more principled, less of a pragmatist" than other Justices. Peter J. Rubin, a Washington attorney and a former two-year High Court clerk, points out that Kennedy "understands the moment of what he's doing" and stresses how there can be "no question after Romer about his integrity and courage."

Legal historians sometimes wonder whether the "Brennan Court" and the "Powell Court" might actually be more accurate monikers for the 1960's, 70's and early 80's than the "Warren Court" and the "Burger Court." And in that same spirit, Peter Rubin readily agrees that, yes, "it's the Kennedy Court." But, Romer and Casey notwithstanding, in most other particulars the court of 1996 is indeed the "Rehnquist Court," and it is likely to stay the Rehnquist Court for longer than most commentators now think.

Prior to the death of his wife, Nan, in October 1991, most people who knew Rehnquist expected him to step down as Chief Justice sooner rather than later. In July 1991, Rehnquist apologetically turned down the newly retired Thurgood Marshall's request for home-to-office transportation in a court car, while adding that "in all probability I will be in the same boat you are within a couple of years." Eleven months later, Rehnquist told C-Span's Brian Lamb that while he enjoyed his job, "I wouldn't want to hold it forever." In September 1995, when he underwent major back surgery to remedy a long-festering problem that had suddenly mushroomed into crippling pain, what Tony Mauro of Legal Times called

Rehnquist's "rumored plan for retiring from the Court after the next Presidential election" looked all the more certain.

But a wide sample of former Rehnquist clerks say "not so" and predict against any Rehnquist retirement in the summer of 1997, especially—as some of them hesitantly volunteer—if Bill Clinton is re-elected this November. The Wall Street Journal columnist Paul Gigot has slyly pronounced Rehnquist's scheduled departure, but a former clerk says the Chief already has begun hiring the clerks who will join him next summer.

"I think he's too committed and too interested in winning the battles he's been fighting to retire during the Presidency of a Democrat," says one Court insider with a high personal opinion of Rehnquist. He adds, with emphasis, that the Chief is "extraordinarily politically savvy" and that Bill Rehnquist "plays for the long, long, long run," as his entire career consistently demonstrates.

"He's more inclined to stay," says another former Rehnquist clerk who keeps in regular touch and who feels that the Chief does not want to leave during a Democratic Presidency but "would never say it."

"He enjoys his work," this clerk states. "He never expected to be in the majority as much as he is now," and the ongoing victories—like Lopez and Seminole Tribe on federalism, and in the habeas arena with cases like Felker—all incline him to stay, not retire. "He's fully in stride right now."

# Indicting the Courts: Congress' Feud With Judges

**The latest struggle over the bounds of judicial power is being waged on several fronts**

*By Dan Carney*

**American political history includes a long tradition of attacking the judiciary, but legal scholars on both ends of the political spectrum are concerned that Congress has brought the conflict to a new level. When lawmakers hold up confirmations, assail sitting judges and limit their power, experts say, it upsets the balance of power envisioned by the Founding Fathers.**

It is hard to imagine former Sen. Alan K. Simpson worrying what others might think of him. Here, after all, is a man who proudly calls himself an "old geezer" and penned a book entitled "Right in the Old Gazoo." But the one-time lawyer wonders: What if he were starting out and wanted to be a judge, rather than a politician? Would he be confirmed? What dirt would today's senators have on him?

"Good God," he muses. "I represented murderers, insane people, a guy who bit someone's ear off. What would they do with that?"

The question is not altogether academic. Simpson says he has seen many would-be judges of today turned into "gargoyles" by a process that has gotten out of hand. One can almost imagine the press releases from whatever faction that would want to end his chances: "Al Simpson Coddles Criminals, Defends Weirdos!"

Simpson, who served from 1979–97, is one in a host of former lawmakers, judges and academics who are alarmed by what they see as an increasing hostility on the part of Congress toward the federal judiciary. Fierce attacks on judicial nominees, they argue, are but one front in an extraordinary, escalating war of wills between the legislative and judicial branches of government. This war is being driven in consid-

erable part by politics and mistrust. But it shows more fundamental differences as well, over such matters as the proper balance in a democracy between the rule of law and the rule of popular sentiment, and the proper role and scope of government in general.

Three broad areas of confrontation are at the center of this conflict:

• **Confirmations.** The Senate has turned the process of confirming federal judges into a political sideshow for the two parties to curry favor with their hard-core supporters. In some cases, this has meant distorting the nominees' records. In others, it has meant quietly holding up whole blocks of nominees for months or years at a time. Many Republicans trace this trend to the villainization of Robert H. Bork by Senate Democrats, when they defeated his Supreme Court nomination in 1987. Most Democrats argue that the atmosphere is much worse now that the tables have turned. There are 73 vacancies on the 845-member federal bench. The number passed 100 last year. It is not uncommon for nominees to wait two or three years for confirmation. (*Bork, 1987 Almanac, p. 271*)

• **Attacks on sitting judges.** A number of judges, ranging from District Judge Harold Baer Jr. of New York to District Judge Thelton E. Henderson of California, have come

From *CQ Weekly,* Vol. 56, No. 25, June 20, 1998, pp. 1660-1666. © 1998 by Congressional Quarterly, Inc. Reprinted by permission.

under virulent criticism from members of Congress. House Majority Whip Tom DeLay, R-Texas, has called for widespread impeachments, and individual members have launched rhetorical broadsides: "There is no doubt in my mind that there is a special place in hell for a number of federal court judges . . ." Rep. Jack Kingston, R-Ga., declared in a May 4 floor speech on school prayer.

• **Jurisdiction.** In the past several years, Congress has passed bills to prevent federal judges from hearing cases that could undermine policies advocated by conservative lawmakers. Specifically, they have prevented judges from hearing cases involving prison conditions or appeals from immigrants about to be deported. At the same time, it has forced the courts to participate in a cause very popular in Congress—prosecuting crime at the federal level. This intrusion into an area previously left to state courts has loaded the federal dockets, crowding out other important cases.

The courts' harshest critics argue they are merely preventing the worst judicial abuses. Simpson and his compatriots say such attacks on the judiciary threaten its very independence and ultimately could upset the system of checks and balances envisioned by the Founding Fathers.

"The erosion of the independence of the judiciary is not something absolutely dramatic," said Sheldon Goldman, a political scientist at the University of Massachusetts. "It's an incremental thing. It's a cancer on the American constitutional framework. Someday we may wake up to find a very different United States."

### A Long Tradition

Attacking the judiciary is an old tradition in American politics. The biggest actual threats to the courts came in the early years of the republic, the Civil War era, and during Franklin D. Roosevelt's New Deal, when he demanded the chance to

pick six additional Supreme Court justices.

Sharp verbal criticism of the federal judiciary has been particularly popular among presidents and members of Congress with a populist bent. The notion of an unelected group of powerful jurists serving for life, and accountable to virtually no one, has been an irresistible target for politicians ranging from President Andrew Jackson to Wisconsin Sen. Robert M. LaFollette Jr. (1925–47), leader of the Progressive movement in the 1920s. A few Supreme Court rulings—most notably the landmark 1954 desegregation case *Brown v. Board of Education*—have produced an avalanche of hostility to the federal courts.

Today's generation of court critics is led by DeLay in the House and John Ashcroft, R-Mo., in the Senate. While the Democrats held up some Republican judges and passed legislation unpopular with the third branch, most legal scholars agree that the relationship between Congress and the courts has deteriorated since the GOP took control in 1995. Many Republicans see some sitting judges as arrogant, unresponsive to the public and prone to "activist" rulings that overstep their constitutional role of applying, rather than creating, the law.

"There is an activist judge behind each of most of the perverse failures of today's justice system," DeLay said in a floor speech April 23. "When judges legislate, they usurp the power of Congress. When judges stray beyond the Constitution, they usurp the power of the people."

One of the most often-cited examples is Missouri District Court Judge Russell Clark, who forced $1.8 billion in tax increases in Kansas City to fund court-ordered improvements to inner-city schools. (*Judges*, p. 1664)

Also cited are several judges who have struck down public referendums that won popular majorities, such as a California vote to limit affirmative action (Proposition 209) and a 1992 Colorado proposition to

---

## Confirmations in the Clinton Era

President Clinton's nominees for district and circuit courts were confirmed at a quick pace when Democrats controlled Congress but slowed after Republicans took control.

• In the 103rd Congress, 141 nominations were received; 127 were confirmed.

• In the 104th Congress, 105 nominations were received; 73 were confirmed.

• In the 105th Congress, as of June 1, 108 nominations were submitted, 61 were confirmed.

Source: Congressional Research Service

---

limit civil rights protections for homosexuals. Judges who are considered soft on crime are highly unpopular with conservatives, as are those who impose a rigid church-state separation.

Much of the criticism of the courts centers on their interpretation of the Constitution. For instance, when Rep. Ernest Istook, R-Okla., is asked why Republicans are so quick to propose amendments to the Constitution, he responds that the courts do it all the time. Istook, sponsor of a proposal (HJ Res 78) that would expand rights of religious expression, argues that the Supreme Court has perverted the First Amendment through a series of church-state rulings in the past three decades.

DeLay argues that such rulings indicate the judicial branch has exceeded its authority. "The system of checks and balances so carefully crafted is in serious disrepair and has been for years," he said.

Others criticize the expansive role of government advocated by some judges. Judge Clark's rulings in Kansas City have been attacked not just for their activism but for their liberalism. The notion of transferring almost $2 billion to inner-city schools strikes many conservatives as an exercise in social engineering reminiscent of President Lyndon B. Johnson's Great Society or of the New Deal.

In essence, many Republicans see themselves using pressure on the courts to undo what Roosevelt may have done in part through pressure in his day. Even though Roosevelt's bid to "pack" the Supreme Court failed because Congress would not allow it, it apparently had an impact.

For reasons that are still being debated by legal scholars, the Supreme Court began a shift to the left not long after the episode in 1937. Initially, this appeared to be driven by a switch in positions by sitting members, though by 1941, the trend had been accelerated by a string of seven Roosevelt appointments in just four years.

This shift represented the beginning of a major expansion of the federal government's size and function. Subsequent courts championed integration, and later busing; created a limited constitutional right to abortion; took officially sanctioned prayer out of schools; and made other rulings opposed by conservatives.

Today's criticisms of the federal judiciary are not merely an inside-the-Beltway spat between two branches. They have broad resonance among religious conservatives, libertarians and populists.

Sitting judges are a regular target of conservative talk radio shows. Blocking pending nominees is also a popular topic. President Clinton has already appointed almost a third of the federal bench, and he will get more opportunities as judges retire.

Supporters of a more independent judiciary argue the judiciary is being dragged into a fight between the two other branches. Furthermore, they argue, it is Congress, not the courts, that is jeopardizing the balance of power envisioned by the Constitution.

## Out of Balance

The judicial branch "is beyond comparison the weakest of the three departments of power," Alexander Hamilton wrote in Federalist Paper Number 78. " . . . It can never attack with success the other two; and all possible care is requisite to enable it to defend itself against their attacks."

That the judiciary is the weakest branch is evident in Article III of the Constitution, which makes its very existence subject to the good will of the two other branches. The Senate could strangle it by refusing to confirm judges. The president could do the same by not nominating any. Congress could refuse to fund it, or even abolish all but the Supreme Court, which is created by the Constitution.

Last year, DeLay proposed widespread impeachments, naming three district court judges he thought were ready to be taken on immediately: Henderson, who blocked California's referendum limiting affirmative action; Baer, who dismissed key evidence in a drug case; and Fred Biery, in Texas, who refused to seat a Republican sheriff and county commissioner because of controversy over absentee ballots.

In Tennessee, the ouster of District Court Judge John T. Nixon has become a crusade of victims' rights advocates. His decisions blocking executions has enraged them to the point of bringing a judicial misconduct suit and persuading the state legislature to pass a resolution asking Congress to impeach him.

Baer's case may be the most illustrative because of the 1996 presidential campaign and its aftermath. GOP candidate Bob Dole made Baer, and his evidentiary ruling, the centerpiece of his criticism of Clinton appointees. Not wanting to be outflanked, Clinton joined the criticisms.

Under attack from both sides, Baer reversed his decision. Regardless of the merits of his original ruling, and his switch, champions of an independent judiciary are horrified by the possibility that a judge changed his opinion under political pressure.

"After taking a battering in the press for some days, he reviewed his decision and altered it," said former New York Democratic Gov. Mario M. Cuomo. "He altered it into a form that was acceptable to the people who were criticizing him. . . . And no one but God knows exactly why he did that."

Cuomo has joined with Simpson and a number of other former lawmakers and legal experts to form a group called "Citizens for Independent Courts." The group will argue that granting the courts considerable autonomy is in the nation's best interest.

The judiciary is designed to be the only branch of government that does not respond to political pressure. The Constitution gives judges lifetime tenure so they can make rulings based solely on the law, as informed by their legal education and experience. If parties in lawsuits believe that rulings are made on the basis of polls, popular sentiment or political pressure, it undermines judges' authority, said William S. Sessions, a former district judge and FBI director from 1987–93.

"Having judges rule on the basis of law is a tremendous advantage to society," Sessions said.

Another function of a strong independent judiciary is to check the excesses of the other two branches. When Roosevelt attempted his court-packing scheme, he was, in essence, trying to take over all three branches of government. Thanks to huge Democratic majorities in both houses of Congress after the 1936 election, he had control of two but mused over a recalcitrant court that blocked many of his early legislative proposals. He looked at the three branches not as autonomous entities striving to check each other, but as a team of horses that should function together, with the president as driver.

"Two of the three horses are pulling in unison," he said in a radio ad-

# A Gallery of Controversial Judges

A number of the 845 members of the federal bench have been criticized by conservative lawmakers for being "activists," liberals or soft on crime. Many are so labeled on the basis of one or two rulings, while others have earned their reputation over a career.

Conservative lawmakers such as House Majority Whip Tom DeLay, R-Texas, argue these types of judges are evidence of the need to speak out against the judiciary, cast a wary eye on pending nominees and sometimes even impeach sitting judges.

Advocates of leaving the courts alone say many of the rulings have a legitimate basis in law, and are merely disliked by conservative lawmakers. In the cases of rulings that are genuinely bad, they argue that the appeal process, rather than beating up on the federal judiciary, is the appropriate antidote.

Among the most commonly cited judges are:

• **Harold Baer Jr., District Court, New York.** Baer became Exhibit A in Bob Dole's election-year criticism of President Clinton's judicial selections after he dismissed all of the evidence (75 pounds of cocaine and a videotaped confession) in a drug trafficking case on the grounds that the defendant had been arrested improperly. After criticism from Dole, Clinton joined in, calling the ruling "wrongheaded" and even threatened to ask Baer to give up his lifetime appointment. On further consideration, Baer reversed his ruling.

• **Rosemary Barkett, 11th Circuit Court of Appeals.** A former nun who became Florida's first female Supreme Court justice before being tapped for the federal bench, Barkett is considered an exceptionally good judge by some legal experts. Dole and other conservatives have criticized her position on crime, such as a 1992 dissent she joined calling for life imprisonment, rather than death, in a racially motivated murder. She is also cited for a case in which she reinstated a sexual harassment suit brought by a fifth-grade student.

• **Russell G. Clark, District Court, Missouri.** From 1977 through 1997, Clark took over considerable control of the Kansas City school district. Hoping to stem the decline of inner-city schools, he forced the city to raise an additional $1.8 billion in taxes, more than doubling the assessment on local property, to pay for a host of improvements, including a model United Nations and a 2,000-square-foot planetarium.

• **Stewart Dalzell, District Court, Pennsylvania.** Dalzell served as the central focus of a video by the conservative group Judicial Selection Monitoring Project. The purpose of the video was to raise money to oppose judicial activism and Clinton's nominees to the bench (Dalzell was actually appointed by President George Bush.) Dalzell garnered national attention when he released a convicted murderer six years into her prison term, declaring she was the victim of a terrible miscarriage of justice. He said he found 25 instances of prosecutorial misconduct, and prohibited local officials from retrying her. Dalzell's ruling was reversed by the 3rd Circuit Court of Appeals and the woman went back to jail after 10 months of freedom.

• **Ira DeMent, District Court, Alabama.** DeMent is reviled among religious conservatives for ordering a school in DeKalb County to stop conducting prayers on the public address system in the morning and before football games. When the school resisted, he sent monitors, who were dubbed the "prayer police."

• **Thelton E. Henderson, District Court, California.** Henderson blocked implementation of California's Proposition 209, which bans discrimination or special treatment on the basis of race or gender in state hiring, contracting and school admissions. Henderson's ruling was overturned by the 9th Circuit in an unusually strongly worded opinion saying, "as a matter of law, Proposition 209 does not violate the United States Constitution." The Supreme Court let the 9th Circuit ruling stand without comment.

• **M. Blane Michael, 4th Circuit Court of Appeals.** Michael is often cited for his dissenting opinion in a case involving a letter bomb sent to a prosecutor. Michael concluded this bomb, which did not explode, was not a deadly weapon since it was so poorly made.

• **John T. Nixon, District Court, Tennessee.** Nixon has angered victims' rights groups by his frequent reversals of death sentences, and by the years he sometimes takes in considering death row appeals. The state legislature asked Congress to begin impeachment proceedings. And a group brought a judicial misconduct suit against him on the grounds that he once accepted an award from a ministers' group. Neither action produced any results. But Tennessee lawmakers inserted two provisions pertaining to his case into a bill (HR 1252) to curb federal judges' powers. The bill would prohibit a judge from repeatedly delaying an inmate's execution. And it would require that judicial misconduct cases be heard in a different part of the country from where the judge in question sits. (*House passage of HR 1252, CQ Weekly, p. 1074*)

• **Stephen Reinhardt and Betty Binns Fletcher, 9th Circuit Court of Appeals.** Both are criticized for a range of rulings considered liberal and both have a record of being overruled by the Supreme Court. Reinhardt is a frequent target of Senate Judiciary Committee Chairman Orrin G. Hatch, R-Utah. Fletcher's son, William A. Fletcher, has been nominated for a position on the same court. (*Fletcher, CQ Weekly, p. 1399*)

—Dan Carney

dress advocating his plan. "A third is not."

The courts routinely rule on congressional and presidential powers and prerogatives. The Supreme Court has recently struck down a number of public laws on the grounds that they represented an overstepping of congressional authority. A unanimous court in 1974 forced President Richard M. Nixon to release his White House tape recordings, precipitating the end of his presidency. And Judge Norma Holloway Johnson has ruled against President Clinton, who sought to shield his aides from having to testify in the ongoing investigation by Independent Counsel Kenneth W. Starr. (*Starr, p. 1686*)

Defenders of the courts say the judiciary needs its independence to serve as a counterweight to the other branches. Attacking it, they say, could come back to haunt conservatives.

"A true conservative would want to maintain the independence of the judiciary, because it is the last best break on a runaway executive," said Sen. Patrick J. Leahy, D-Vt.

### A New Level

After being virtually shut down in 1996 and 1997, the pace of confirmations has picked up this year, partly because of some pointed complaints from Chief Justice William H. Rehnquist (who even took the unusual step of attending a Democrats-only luncheon in the Senate). Also, Senate Judiciary Committee Chairman Orrin G. Hatch, R-Utah, has been willing to stand up to pressure from other committee members who want to block the nominees.

Certain courts have been hit harder than others by this slowdown. The San Francisco-based 9th Circuit Court of Appeals, which has a reputation for liberalism and a knack for being reversed by the Supreme Court, had 10 open slots out of 28 at the end of last year. This shortfall of judges has meant lengthy delays in trials, and considerable haste when they do come up,

said Chief Judge Proctor Hug Jr. Struggling to keep up with his caseload, he has had to bring some judges out of semi-retirement and import others from other regions.

"We have made superhuman efforts," said Hug. "I have pleaded with our judges to take more than they otherwise would. I've noticed there is a real burnout level in the judges. There's a feeling we just need more time with these cases."

A debate rages over whether these types of holdups are merely Republicans retaliating for the Bork affair, or whether they are so widespread that they represent an entirely new level of partisan judicial politics.

Democrats tended to go after high court judges such as Bork and a select few lower court judges. Their strategy was to publicly attack them to build enough votes to defeat the nominations.

"Before my eyes, they turned [Bork] into a gargoyle—a sexist, racist, invader of the bedroom, violator of women," said Simpson. "That was repugnant to me."

Republican senators who were elected in 1994 have not had a crack at a Clinton nominee to the Supreme Court yet. But in lower court positions, their main strategy in the past three years has been to hold up scores of nominees, preventing them from even coming up for a floor vote. Groups such as the Judicial Selection Monitoring Project, a division of the conservative Free Congress Research and Education Foundation, have mounted a full court press against Clinton nominees. (*Groups, p. 1663*)

"We want to make sure that the Senate does not underestimate how strongly the American people feel about standing up to judicial activism," said project director Thomas L. Jipping.

The Senate has responded to this pressure not so much by defeating nominees as delaying them. If and when nominations do reach the floor and are openly debated, they usually pass with relative ease. For instance, Margaret M. Morrow, a

corporate lawyer from Los Angeles, saw her nomination to a district court judgeship held up for nearly two years amid intense criticism that she was an activist in waiting. When she finally got a vote Feb. 11, she was approved 67–28.

"You have extremely good people who are held in limbo for year after year," said Leahy. "If you are a woman or a minority, you are held longer. It may be coincidental but it's what happens. It's demeaning to the court, and it's demeaning to the Senate."

### Issues of Jurisdiction

Starting when the Democrats controlled Capitol Hill, but picking up considerably under Republican rule, Congress has been keen to tell the courts what they can and cannot rule on.

The 1996 immigration bill (PL 104–208), for instance, contains a section saying certain deportation orders issued by the Justice Department are "not reviewable in a court of law." A similar provision, included in a portion of the 1996 omnibus spending bill, was designed to limit prison inmates' ability to file grievance cases in federal courts (PL 103–134). Another measure (PL 104–132) would significantly limit the ability of prisoners to use habeas corpus appeals to federal judges to question the constitutionality of their convictions. These appeals are often used by death row inmates to have their executions delayed or blocked entirely (*Immigration, 1996 Almanac, p. 5–3; prison litigation, p. 10–5; anti-terrorism death penalty, p. 5–18*)

Not surprisingly, these types of limitations enrage civil rights groups, which say Congress is imposing its ideology on the courts by preventing them from ruling on certain issues.

"When Congress selectively removes particular issues, then it is in effect prescribing the outcome," said Nadine Strossen, national president of the American Civil Liberties Union.

Limiting the jurisdiction of federal judges was the purpose behind a bill (HR 1252) the House passed April 23. In its original form it would have prevented any judge from issuing an order that forced a local jurisdiction to raise taxes. It also would have allowed civil litigants to reject the first judge assigned to them. (*CQ Weekly, p. 1074*)

Although these two provisions were dropped, the measure still included jurisdictional limits and an overall tone expressing a lack of confidence in the courts. It would strengthen provisions in earlier laws limiting federal court involvement with prison crowding issues. And it would further limit habeas corpus appeals.

The bill would also attempt to protect public referendums from judges such as Henderson by stipulating that they could be struck down only by a three-judge panel. The measure would take a swipe at the judiciary's ability to police itself by requiring that judicial misconduct cases be automatically transferred to another part of the country. (The provision arose from the Nixon case in Tennessee, after judges there quickly dismissed a misconduct case against him.)

At the same time that Congress has limited federal court involvement in liberal causes, it has greatly increased its role in dealing with crime. As Congress has passed numerous bills creating new federal offenses, it has not only increased the workload for the Justice Department and the FBI but also for the federal courts that must now hear all these cases. Since criminal defendants have a constitutional right to a speedy trial, this onslaught of cases means important civil cases are often put on the back burner or not heard, because the litigants do not think it worth the wait.

This trend has not only come under attack from liberal groups, which see it as more evidence that Congress is attempting to legislate judicial output by dictating input. It has also been sternly criticized by Rehnquist.

In a May 11 speech, the chief justice complained bitterly about expanded federal authority in pending juvenile crime legislation (HR 3, S 10). Rather than focus the burden on the courts (which he has cited before), Rehnquist spoke in terms designed to capture the attention of congressional Republicans. He said the juvenile crime bills are hardly conservative, because they involve a vast expansion of the federal government's role in crime fighting. Indeed, he said, they represent a fundamental violation of federalist principles developed by some of the party's brightest lights—namely Abraham Lincoln and Dwight D. Eisenhower.

He suggested Congress was unwittingly erecting a government not unlike the highly centralized system in France.

"How much of the complex system of legal relationships in this country should be decided in Washington, and how much by state and local governments?" he asked. "Do we really want to move forward into the 21st century with the prospect that our system will look more and more like the French government?"

### A 'Three Bowler' Issue

Criticizing judges and nominees is fairly easy. And passing bills limiting their jurisdiction wins plaudits from conservative groups. In contrast, advocates of a more independent judiciary, such as Cuomo and Simpson, find themselves dealing with a very dry and complicated issue when they start talking.

Charles Geyh, a professor at Case Western Reserve University in Cleveland and a consultant to the American Judicature Society, an organization of legal professionals, calls it a "three-bowler" issue. This means that even if he can get a newspaper writer to tackle the issue, it usually results in little more than a series of sleep-induced splashes.

"Your face falls into the cereal bowl three times before getting through the article," he said.

Be that as it may, defenders of an independent judiciary say it is vital that the issue be raised. Judges do not feel it appropriate to publicly defend themselves, their rulings or the institution they represent. Rehnquist's comments are considered by many to be extraordinary, even though they are couched in measured and legalistic terms.

Because judges usually steer clear of political debate, it is vital that someone speak up on behalf of the judiciary, said Sessions.

"We should be very concerned about this," he said. "It is very easy in this day and time to destroy a perfectly valid judge. Similarly, it is possible to attack the judiciary broadly and take away respect for the rule of the law."

*Edited by Susan Benkelman*

## 'WE ALL (PARTICULARLY POLITICIANS AND THE MEDIA) NEED A CIVICS LESSON.'

# A Judge Speaks Out

## H. LEE SAROKIN

*Democracy in America today faces many seemingly intractable problems—inequality, corruption, political disengagement—but is equally threatened by discrete official acts that eat away at its core institutions. Jesse Helms autocratically denies William Weld a hearing to be ambassador to Mexico. Janet Reno stubbornly drags her feet on appointing an independent counsel on campaign finance abuses. House majority whip Tom DeLay callously calls for impeachment of federal judges who heed a legal "technicality" called the Bill of Rights. These actions feed mistrust of government and must be loudly condemned, as they often are. But in the case of the assault on judicial independence by DeLay, Senator Orrin Hatch and others—which was ramped up during the 1996 elections and continues in an unprecedented stonewalling of President Clinton's nominees to the federal bench—the people who could fight back most eloquently, the judges themselves, are bound by a code of silence.*

*Judges should be loath to enter the fray, but there are extraordinary circumstances where their rebuttals are warranted, even necessary. When Bob Dole and Newt Gingrich threatened Judge Harold Baer with impeachment in March 1996 because of his decision to suppress evidence in a routine drug case (a decision that, under pressure, he later rescinded), it was inspiring to see four appellate judges publicly proclaim that the criticism had gone too far.*

*Now, we have the first riposte from one who was a target. Judge H. Lee Sarokin, a courageously independent federal trial and appellate judge for seventeen years in Newark, was for years a favorite scapegoat of those on the right. Last year, battered by increasingly malicious and distorted assault, Sarokin left the bench, saying he no longer wanted his rulings to be fodder for their twisted campaign. While we regretted his decision, we respected it and urged him to break the silence and explain just how corrosive these attacks have become [see "Gavel-to-Gavel Politics," July 1, 1996]. Here is his response.*
*—The Editors*

---

*H. Lee Sarokin is a retired judge of the United States Court of Appeals.*

I retired from the federal bench not because my opinions were being criticized but in protest over the politicization (what I characterized as the "Willie Hortonizing") of the federal judiciary. Politicians increasingly mischaracterize judicial opinions and then use them against those who nominated, appointed or voted to confirm the judges involved (like blaming a governor for crimes committed by a paroled prisoner). Not only do such tactics threaten the independence of the judiciary but, more important, they have a corrosive effect on the public's confidence in our judicial system and those who implement it. This is the toll when respected persons in high office constantly contend that judges are not following the law but rather are pursuing their own private agenda. I thought that by stepping down from the court and making my concerns public, I would convey the gravity of this dangerous course.

Now, a year later, I concede that my grand gesture was a complete fizzle, and indeed, rather than dissuade the practice, seems to have emboldened it, since it has been followed by demands, led by Representatives Tom DeLay and Bob Barr, to impeach judges for unpopular decisions. Although the election has ended, the political rhetoric attacking the judiciary has not.

Admittedly, from time to time there will be judicial decisions with which many will not agree. All too often that disagreement arises from the mischaracterization of the opinion and focuses on its result rather than its reasoning. But the validity of a judicial opinion cannot rest on its popularity. Resisting the pressure to please the majority is the strength of the judiciary, not its weakness. Judges who invoke the Constitution to protect the rights of people charged with crimes are not "soft on crime." Judges who declare that a statute or a public referendum violates the constitution are not "legislating" from the bench or "thwarting the will of the majority." They are carrying out their oath of office and following the rule of law.

The verdict in the Oklahoma City bombing trial may have restored some confidence in our judicial system. But a different scenario might illustrate the dangers of the current political vilification of judges and the resulting erosion of respect for our judicial system. Assume that prison guards, angered over the 168 deaths caused by the bombing of the Murrah Federal Building and frustrated by the lack of cooperation from those arrested, decided to beat one of those charged in order to obtain a confession.* As a result, they obtained a statement with sufficient detail so that there could be no doubt as to the knowledge and guilt of the confessor. Furthermore, these details led to the gathering of additional evidence regarding the source of the materials utilized in the making of the bomb, how they were transported, where they were stored, how the bomb was made and how it was ultimately delivered and detonated and by whom.

There are those who would argue, quite reasonably, that the guards should be punished, but that the evidence should be utilized. However, there are some protections that we view as so precious that nothing can be gained from their violation. Under existing law, the confession would not be admissible. In all probability, neither would any of the details, evidence and corroboration obtained as a result. Indeed, the taint of the illegally obtained confession and the fruits thereby gained might have led to an acquittal or dismissal of the charges. One can well imagine and understand the public outrage at such a result. Conservative politicians would be elbowing one another aside to reach microphones to lambaste the "liberal judge" who made such a ruling and decry the use of the "technicality" that made it possible—another example of a judicial system run amok, although there probably is not a judge in the country who would rule otherwise.

But suppose we were to change the above hypothetical scenario as follows: The guilty person beaten by law-enforcement officers was not the first but the tenth. Seven did not confess, because they were not guilty; two other did, even though they were not, just to bring the beatings to an end. One can imagine and hope for an equally vociferous outcry. If public confidence is essential to the maintenance of our judicial system—and it is—what lesson is to be drawn from these two hypothetical instances? What people really desire is two sets of rules and rights: one for the guilty and one for the innocent. People do not want criminals to gain advantage from the assertion of constitutional rights. On the other hand, they want those rights available to and enforced for the innocent. The problem with such an approach is that the determination of constitutional violations is frequently made by a judge before there is a determination of guilt or innocence. Furthermore, for the pre-

*There is no suggestion that any guard would engage in such conduct. The discussion is for illustrative purposes only.

sumption of innocence to have any meaning, a determination of guilt must await a final verdict.

So if it is impossible or impractical to preserve the Bill of Rights for the innocent and deny it to the guilty, should the constitutional protections extended to those accused of crimes be repeated? Has crime become so prevalent and the need to combat it so great that we are willing to sacrifice some of our fundamental rights in order to win this battle? For both practical and principled reasons, the answer should be "no," even if the present atmosphere makes such amendments to the Constitution seem politically possible.

First, we all (and particularly the politicians and the media) need a civics lesson. Have we forgotten our history? The Fifth Amendment is not a "technicality." The right against self-incrimination was considered fundamental and essential to our freedom. Likewise, the restriction on searches and other government intrusions into our private lives was of sufficient importance that our forefathers were prepared to die for it.

Even if one is unmoved by the historical significance of these rights, their enforcement has virtually no impact on crime in this country. If the Bill of Rights were repealed tomorrow, insofar as its protections extend to those accused of crimes, it would not make the slightest ripple in the amount or nature of crime in this country. Law-enforcement officials themselves have repeatedly stated that enforcement of the Bill of Rights has not impeded them, and criminals hardly sit around a kitchen table and say: "If we are apprehended we can invoke our right against self-incrimination, and thus we shall go ahead and rob the corner candy store." They may be street-smart and "know their rights," but that knowledge is neither the catalyst nor cause of their unlawful activity. It probably never enters their thinking, assuming that there is much forethought given to the commission of most crimes.

Most significant, and contrary to the vision portrayed by conservative politicians and media, there is not a group of loony liberal judges out there leaping at the chance to set criminals free. The idea that any judge relishes ruling in favor of a person charged with a crime in the face of evidence of guilt, and particularly after a finding of guilt, is utter nonsense. Those rulings are made with great reluctance, but done because the law compels it. The suppression of the confession referred to earlier in this article would have to be made by any and every judge confronted with those facts. Furthermore, the number of such rulings is minuscule. Roughly, between 5 and 10 percent of all criminal cases are actually tried. In those that are tried, motions to suppress evidence are routinely denied every day, in every court in every state in this country. A dismissal of charges following the granting of a motion to sup-

> *The validity of a judicial opinion cannot rest on popularity. Resisting pressure to please the majority is judicial strength, not weakness.*

press evidence is as rare an event as Senator Orrin Hatch recommending a liberal for a seat on the Supreme Court.

When motions to suppress are granted, those who wish to capitalize on such rulings invariably discuss the heinous nature of the crime or the long criminal history of the defendant, if one exists, neither of which is relevant to the question of whether the defendant's constitutional rights have been violated. Here again, we do not and cannot have two sets of rules—one for bad crimes and criminals and another for those less offensive. The exercise I posed above was chosen because there has been no more horrific crime in the history of this country than the Oklahoma City bombing; but the rights afforded by the Constitution cannot be reduced as the severity of the crime increases.

The law and those who administer it are not perfect. Mistakes are made. That is why we have courts of appeal. But it is essential that the public understand that in large measure the guilty are convicted (indeed, most plead guilty), the innocent are protected and the judicial system and its judges are devoted and dedicated to fairness and justice. Criticism has its place, but truth must have some role in the dialogue. (My nomination to the Court of Appeals was opposed on the basis that I "had a long history of freeing criminals in disregard of the rights of their victims." In fifteen years on the bench two people are free as a result of my rulings—Rubin "Hurricane" Carter, a decision affirmed by the Court of Appeals and left standing by the U.S. Supreme Court after review, and James Landano, who is still awaiting retrial while on bail—hardly a "long history of freeing criminals.") Indeed, granting a writ of habeas corpus orders a new trial and does not free the petitioner unless the state elects not to retry.

The Bill of Rights is meant to protect us all. If in the process a criminal benefits, we must decide whether that detriment outweighs the benefits and freedoms we all enjoy. It is ironic that the criticism leveled at the Bill of Rights and the frequent characterization of its parts as "technicalities" come from conservatives, since the rights enunciated are the embodiment of the conservative philosophy. They codify the fundamental conservative principle of excluding unwanted and unwarranted government intrusion in the private lives of citizens.

Although the critics of "judicial activism" insist that neither the result nor the identity of the judge is what motivates them, the evidence suggests otherwise. There are many former prosecutors who now sit on the judicial benches of this country who were strong advocates of the death penalty. When they rule in favor of capital punishment, none of these critics claim that the judges involved are "activists carrying out their own agendas"; but the personal motives or background of those who vote against the death penalty in a given case invariably becomes relevant. When the Chief Justice of the United States wrote an opinion declaring unconstitutional an act of Congress that prohibited guns within 1,000 feet of schools, there was no cry of "thwarting the will of the people"; if I had authored that opinion, *The Wall Street Journal* editorial world have read: "Sarokin Rules Schoolchildren Can Have Guns!"

The independence of the judiciary is essential to our democracy. Those who seek to tamper with it to gain a momentary political victory for themselves will cause a greater and more lasting loss to the public, and to the confidence in our judicial system, without which the rule of law cannot survive.

# Gaveling Back the Imperial Presidency

*From Watergate to Paula Jones, the Supreme Court*
*has reminded the White House of its limits*

## By Joan Biskupic

The case riveted the nation. The president was trying to avoid a trial, and he had taken his constitutional argument all the way to the Supreme Court. The rebuff was unanimous, with the president's own appointees voting against him. The president of the United States, the justices said, is not beyond the law's reach.

That was the court's answer to Nixon tapes case in 1974—and to the Paula Corbin Jones case two weeks ago.

Although the two rulings have important differences, they represent the modern legacy of judicial limits on presidential power. The sensational lawsuit brought by Jones against Clinton for alleged misconduct while he was Arkansas governor and she was a low-level state employee now becomes part of a small but mighty set of decisions curtailing the prerogatives of the nation's chief executive. The underlying message is one that ratifies a fundamental premise of American democracy: Despite the president's extraordinary responsibility, he is ultimately an ordinary citizen.

"The notion that the president would be like a king was implicitly rejected in our founding documents," says Harvard law professor Laurence H. Tribe. "Complaints about royal prerogatives helped to fuel the revolution. The concern was that the King of England was deemed something more than an ordinary human, that his mandate came from God."

With unusual unanimity, the court rejected Clinton's claim that, while in office, he is immune from being sued for personal conduct. The ruling allows Jones's allegations—that Clinton sought sexual favors from her in a Little Rock hotel room—to move forward.

"This opinion is very much in the post-Watergate, post-Vietnam tradition of extremely strong skepticism of the so-called imperial presidency," observes Yale University law professor Akhil Amar.

"It's in that same particular vein of the Nixon tapes case: Even the president comes under the law. We have the right to every person's evidence," says University of Illinois law professor Ronald Rotunda.

The Clinton administration has aggressively asserted various special prerogatives over the years, for example, claiming executive privilege in refusing to give Congress documents on the firings at the White House travel office. In some instances the White House relented and a compromise was reached, reflecting how much privilege disputes tend to be resolved at a political level. In the past, privilege cases have tended to be about matters of national security. The Nixon tapes case still stands as the only modern instance of a president pushing the matter of privilege to the Supreme Court.

YET ANOTHER TEST OF THE STRENGTH OF EXECUTIVE branch prerogatives could come in a pending case involving notes taken by White House lawyers of conversations with first lady Hillary Rodham Clinton. Whitewater independent counsel Kenneth W. Starr is seeking these notes. Both sides have cited the Nixon tapes case, with Starr saying the ruling means the notes must be surrendered and White House lawyers saying it does not. The Paula Jones ruling—focusing on presidential immunity, rather than a privilege to withhold information—offers scant clue on how the justices might ultimately resolve the notes case.

What is clear, however, is that the Supreme Court is prepared to question and even take a tough line on presidential prerogatives.

In the tapes episode 23 years ago, Watergate prosecutors wanted to use recorded conversations between the president and his aides as evidence in a criminal trial of former Nixon aides charged with attempting to obstruct justice. The aides were accused of covering up the break-in at the Democratic National Committee headquarters in the Watergate building.

Nixon claimed executive privilege to avoid relinquishing the recordings.

But the court said the president's broad assertion of privilege must yield to the need for evidence in a criminal trial. It ordered Nixon to provide the subpoenaed material, and he resigned shortly after.

In the large scheme of things, a president is more likely to claim a privilege to withhold records, documents or conversations than he is to assert immunity from lawsuit for his personal actions. (The Jones-Clinton case is the first of its kind to reach the courts.) So the Nixon ruling was much more momentous constitutionally and politically.

Nonetheless, the two cases effectively pitted the chief executive against the judiciary. In the court's ruling in *Clinton v. Jones*, Justice John Paul Stevens referred to *United States v. Nixon* and said, "[I]t is . . . settled that the president is subject to judicial process in appropriate circumstances." The court rejected Clinton's contention that a 1982 court case finding that presidents are immune from civil damages lawsuits for their official actions should cover personal conduct as well.

Though it is unlikely that the ruling would undercut the central power of the presidency, Justice Stephen G. Breyer raised serious concerns in a separate opinion about whether the ruling could lead to interference by the courts in executive business and diminish the president's ability to control his time and energy.

IN BOTH THE TAPES AND JONES CASES, TRIBE NOTES, the justices showed "they are not blind to the fact that the presidency is a unique office with unique responsibilities. But in both instances, they said the president is answerable to the law, [a view] that is much more predictable in the post-Watergate era than before."

Indeed, the court showed it was aware of the need to shield the president to some extent. "The high respect that is owed to the office of the chief executive, though not justifying a rule of categorical immunity, is a matter that should inform the conduct of the entire proceeding," the court noted. The ruling said a trial judge still must be sensitive to the president's schedule.

Along those lines, the court in *Jones* referred to Justice Robert H. Jackson's description of the presidency in the court's first great reversal of executive power this century, a 1952 case rebuffing presidential war powers and Harry S. Truman's seizure of the nation's steel mills. Executive authority, Jackson said, is concentrated "in a single head in whose choice the whole nation has a part, making him the focus of public hopes and expectations."

THE COURT HAS TAKEN ITS OWN STANDING INTO account as well, as evidenced by the unanimous decision. Past cases make clear that the justices realize the importance of speaking with one voice in highly politicized cases affecting the balance of powers as unanimity no doubt raises public confidence in the ruling.

The justices's internal papers from *United States v. Nixon* reveal how vigorously they worked to avoid dissent during the Watergate crisis and a time of great constitutional uncertainty. The vote was 8–0. (William H. Rehnquist did not participate because he had previously worked for one of the White House aides.)

Similarly, the justices must have seen the fractious Jones matter the same way. During oral arguments last January, the justices had appeared quite divided over who should win and on what basis. The 9–0 vote was startling when Stevens announced it from the bench.

Individual justices decided it was in the great national interest to compromise. In 1974, three Nixon appointees (Chief Justice Warren Burger, Harry Blackmun and Lewis F. Powell Jr.) voted against the president. In the Jones case, Clinton appointees (Breyer and Ruth Bader Ginsburg) similarly overcame any political allegiance toward their patron.

The rare challenges to presidential prerogatives demand a rare closing of ranks.

*Joan Biskupic covers the Supreme Court for The Washington Post.*

# Census: A Political Calculation

## From courts to congressional committees, battles rage over the 2000 count

*By Charles Pope*

As famed as the Bureau of the Census is for collecting the statistical strands of American life, it has never tabulated one important detail—the number of angry words exchanged over how the head count is conducted.

Even without an official tally, the number is immense. And the fight over the 2000 census may become the most bruising in recent history. That is no small achievement given the level of controversy surrounding almost every census since the first one was conducted in 1790.

Nearly two years before the next count is to begin, the battle over the 2000 census has already spawned two lawsuits, delayed passage of a disaster relief bill in 1997 (PL 105–18) because it contained a rider prohibiting the Census Bureau from using statistical sampling, and, in recent weeks, fueled an increasingly abrasive stream of words over the bureau's plan for conducting the census. Many believe the fight will continue even beyond April 1, 2000, when the count is to officially begin. (*Disaster relief, 1997 CQ Weekly, p. 1362*)

"It shouldn't be a surprise to anyone that the census is contentious because it's at the core of political representation. But the tenor of the debate has become more harsh," said TerriAnn Lowenthal, an independent consultant on census issues and former staff director of a House oversight panel on the 1990 census.

The latest twist occurred June 24 when a House Appropriations subcommittee approved a bill that would stop funding for the Census Bureau on March 31, 1999, unless a dispute is resolved over how the census will be conducted. (*CQ Weekly, p. 1769*)

The agency proposes using statistical sampling on a large scale for the first time to improve the accuracy of the count. Critics, including many Republicans, vehemently oppose such a step, arguing that it would not necessarily improve accuracy and that the numbers could be manipulated. So broad are the differences that census officials are concerned the stalemate could directly affect the census by disrupting funding and distracting bureau officials with political concerns.

Commerce Secretary William M. Daley urged the House on July 8 not to allow political differences over the use of statistical sampling to interfere with the census, though he conceded that the battle lines are so hardened that his plea will likely be ignored.

"The success of census 2000 absolutely requires that there be no interruption in full funding," Daley said, noting that important preliminary work will begin this fall.

"This kind of living with a sword over the Census Bureau's head does not lend well to long-term planning. ... If Congress is going to have a fight and vote over what method

ought to be used ... they should not hold hostage the census," Daley said.

And he said that if Congress failed to heed his warning, he would recommend that President Clinton veto not just the Census Bureau's $4 billion spending plan, but the entire fiscal 1999 $33 billion appropriations bill for the departments of Commerce, State and Justice that contains the funding for the decennial count.

Republicans, most of whom oppose a census using sampling, are unlikely to be swayed by such threats. "It's very irresponsible to use a plan that is unproven and which has failed in the past," said Rep. Dan Miller of Florida, chairman of the House Government Reform and Oversight subcommittee on the census, who holds a doctorate in marketing and statistics.

Miller, like many of his Republican allies, objects to sampling on several levels. It is unconstitutional, he said, and it is too complicated to carry out on a large scale. Most important, it can be manipulated for political gain by a Democratic administration, he said.

"This should not be a partisan issue," Miller said. "But it is the administration that wants to make a change after 200 years that will benefit them."

From *CQ Weekly,* Vol. 56, No. 28, July 11, 1998, pp. 1873-1876. © 1998 by Congressional Quarterly, Inc. Reprinted by permission.

## History of Controversy

By now, however, the Census Bureau should be accustomed to living under a sword that has been dangling precariously for more than 200 years.

In 1792, George Washington issued the first presidential veto in history because he disagreed with the way Congress decided to apportion itself based on the 1790 census which put the population at 3.9 million.

According to the General Accounting Office, the experience in 1790 set the stage for the next two centuries.

"Ever since George Washington questioned the results of the first census in (1792), the accuracy of any given census has been in question," said a GAO report issued in May. "The questions have always been legitimate: The census has never counted 100 percent of those it should, in part, because American sensibilities would probably not tolerate more foolproof census-taking methods."

There are ways to ensure a better count using traditional practices, experts say, but Americans, not to mention Congress, would never accept the conditions that would have to be imposed. The census could be made precise if people were required to register with the government. Or, the country could follow the example set by Turkey, where a 14-hour mandatory curfew was imposed in December 1997 so census canvassers could easily count people.

## Chronic Undercount

Doubts and disputes about the census have surfaced with regularity every 10 years, with much of the attention focused on the size of the undercount.

As the GAO report pointed out, "The debates over the years about methods of apportionment focused on mathematics, but the crux of the matter was political power."

The pressure became even more acute in 1911 when Congress set the number of representatives at 435. After that action, a gain of representation in any one state came only at the loss of representation in another.

Concerns about the accuracy of the census crystallized in 1941 when the number of men turning out for the wartime draft was considerably higher than the number anticipated by the 1940 census.

There have been more recent controversies, too. Several states and cities sued the government in 1991 when Commerce Secretary Robert A. Mosbacher refused a Census Bureau request to adjust the 1990 census to compensate for an undercount. The case ended in 1996 when the Supreme Court ruled against the suit. (1996 Almanac, p. 5–52)

But this year, criticism has spilled beyond questions of how the count will be conducted to the motives of key officials to charges of racism from both sides.

The fights, says historian Margo J. Anderson of the University of Wisconsin at Milwaukee, "are structural to the process. The decision over how to count can be dressed up as science over politics, but the bottom line is, one side usually ends up with the advantage."

The struggle for advantage is being played out in full fury in the House where Democrats support the proposal as the best way to count every American, including minority populations that traditionally have been undercounted.

Embarrassed by missing an estimated 4 million Americans in the 1990 census, the Census Bureau recommended that statistical sampling be used in 2000 to ensure a more accurate count. Under the bureau's proposal, at least 90 percent of the people in every census tract (a geographic area) would be physically counted.

Sampling would then be used to fill in the statistical holes. Census officials insist sampling is a valid approach that will yield a more accurate census at a lower cost. Republicans, however, claim the technique is unconstitutional and open to political manipulation.

# Up in Smoke

A 1921 fire that started in a storage room of the Commerce Building on Pennsylvania Avenue wiped out or damaged much of the 1890 census.

When the smoke cleared on Jan. 10, 1921, it was a disaster for historians.

Officials determined that about 25 percent of the completed census surveys had been destroyed, and half of the remaining surveys had been damaged.

Although the 1890 data had been analyzed by statisticians, the original questionnaires were irreplaceable. It was the first time questions had been asked about such issues as race, homeownership, ability to speak English and service in the Civil War.

The questionnaires were stacked outside a vault containing other census records. But as fate would have it, they were directly in the path of firefighters.

The cause of the three-alarm fire was never determined. Many suspected it was caused by a cigarette.

The disaster heightened awareness among researchers and historians of the need for formal archiving procedures to prevent destruction of valuable documents. The public furor that ensued over the Commerce building fire led to the 1933 construction of the National Archives building to protect national documents.

In 1938, the Census Bureau took other steps to protect the census, copying completed questionnaires onto microfilm.

The microfilmed records are open to the public after 72 years, a waiting period that became law in 1978 (PL 95–416). (178 Almanac, p. 815)

While the National Archives felt access to the schedules would benefit historians, the Census Bureau wanted to preserve the confidentiality of all those surveyed.

—Vanita Gowda

"It is a very risky approach," Miller said, voicing concerns by some statisticians that the Census Bureau may not have enough time to develop a fail-safe sampling program.

The Senate, meanwhile, has shown no interest in the debate.

"We represent the same amount of people, no matter how they count them," said Sen. Judd Gregg, R-N.H.

### Money and Politics

The view is far different in the House, where the fight is being fueled by two of the most powerful forces in Washington—money and politics.

Census results help determine how $180 billion annually in federal spending is distributed through 20 grant programs, including such important ones as Medicaid and educational assistance to poor children.

And, most important for the political landscape, the results form the basis for redrawing boundary lines for congressional districts as well as those for state legislatures.

The Census Bureau, Miller said, "is one institution of government that should be above politics. Most elected officials in this country are dependent on a fair and accurate census, and if people don't trust it, it is a real threat to our democratic process."

With such high stakes comes sharp rhetoric.

One particularly acerbic display occurred June 23, when Miller derided Kenneth Prewitt, Clinton's choice to head the agency, as an academic who is ill-equipped to manage the logistics of the massive undertaking.

"The bureau needs a Gen. [H. Norman] Schwarzkopf, not a Professor Sherman Klunk, to save the census," Miller said on the House floor. "So why did the president nominate an academic? Because of politics."

That same day, Loretta Sanchez, D-Calif., proclaimed on the House floor:

"The Republican leadership of House fails to match their rhetoric

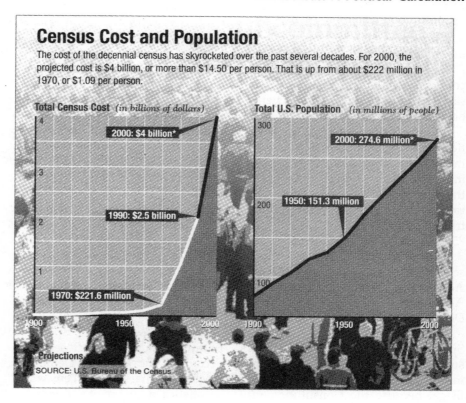

**Census Cost and Population**

The cost of the decennial census has skyrocketed over the past several decades. For 2000, the projected cost is $4 billion, or more than $14.50 per person. That is up from about $222 million in 1970, or $1.09 per person.

Total Census Cost *(in billions of dollars)*

2000: $4 billion*
1990: $2.5 billion
1970: $221.6 million

Total U.S. Population *(in millions of people)*

2000: 274.6 million*
1950: 151.3 million

Projections
SOURCE: U.S. Bureau of the Census

in favor of a colorblind America with deeds. . . . We who oppose government-sanctioned racism will not be silenced by these attacks. We will stand in this well as long as it takes to shed light and bring honest debate about the merits of an accurate census. . . . Race became an issue by those who have turned this process into a fight over raw political power."

Two weeks earlier, on June 11, when a Republican-sponsored court challenge to the bureau's plans for the 2000 census was heard in U.S. District Court in Washington, D.C., Democrats had first unleashed their own tough talk.

"Shame on Newt Gingrich and other Republican extremists who want to pursue another racially exclusionary and inaccurate census in the year 2000," said J. Gerald Hebert, counsel to the Democratic Congressional Campaign Committee.

Driving the fight is the bureau's plan to break from tradition by using statistical sampling on a large scale to augment the physical count of the population.

Without sampling, supporters say, the 2000 census will be less accurate than the one conducted in 1990, which was the most inaccurate in decades. The 1990 census, which cost $2.6 billion, earned the dubious honor of being the first census in modern history to be less accurate than the one preceding it.

The 2000 census, by comparison, is projected to cost $4 billion if sampling is used. That is nearly twice the $2.6 billion spent in 1990 and four times the $1.1 billion cost in 1980. With costs so high, census officials say they feel pressure to deliver the most accurate count possible.

"You could end up spending $4.7 billion and have a worse census than you had in 1990," Daley said.

### Counting Heads

The Census Bureau, backed by the National Academy of Sciences, proposed to increase accuracy by augmenting the traditional count with statistical sampling. Under the Census Bureau's proposal, most Americans would be counted the traditional way by tabulating surveys returned in the mail and follow-up interviews by census-takers for those who did not respond.

Even with such arduous work, census officials and other experts say it is impossible to count everybody using those methods.

Sampling would use the information gained from physically counting at least 90 percent of the people in a given census tract and project the remaining population. The accuracy of the projections would be buttressed by a separate survey of 750,000 households nationwide.

That approach has been deemed scientifically valid by the National Academy of Sciences, the General Accounting Office and the Commerce Department's inspector general.

But House Republicans, led by Speaker Gingrich, R-Ga., filed a lawsuit in U.S. District Court in Washington, arguing that sampling is illegal because the Constitution requires an "actual enumeration" every 10 years.

A second lawsuit was filed with a special three-judge federal panel in U.S. District Court in Alexandria, Va., on behalf of several plaintiffs led by Matthew Glavin, president of the Southeastern Legal Foundation of Atlanta. Both cases are pending.

When the Constitution was written, Maureen E. Mahoney, a lawyer representing House Republicans, told a special three-judge panel at the U.S. District Court in Washington on June 11, "The word 'enumerate,' in every dictionary at the time, said to count one-by-one or reckon singularly."

In other words, Mahoney said, the Constitution requires the census to be based on a physical counting of the population and not statistical extrapolation.

No matter what the court rules, an appeal to the Supreme Court is a virtual certainty, Republicans and Democrats agree.*

Outside the courtroom, however, the legal arguments are supplanted by political realities. Democrats believe a more accurate count would help them because minorities, who tend to vote for Democrats, are the most-often-missed group. Republicans recognize the same phenomenon and charge that a census with sampling would be flawed.

"Having the power to define population as the basis both for representation and for federal funding is an enormous concentration of power," Gingrich wrote in his most recent book, "Lessons Learned the Hard Way."

In addition, Gingrich pointed out, the Census Bureau is part of Daley's Commerce Department. Daley is the son of the late mayor of Chicago Richard Daley, famed for creating a Democratic machine often accused of using unorthodox methods to ensure victory.

Gingrich wrote, "The specter of putting someone so closely connected to the Chicago Democratic machine in charge of the census with a statistical adjustment was too chilling even to contemplate."

Daley is fully aware of the tumultuous history of the census, but he believes the debate has gone beyond the normal bounds.

"People's motives are being questioned; [critics ask] how are you going to politically cook the books? It's ridiculous," he said in a July 8 interview.

"This is a career operation; we have more monitoring and oversight, and the idea that somebody is going to go in some room and cook some numbers just feeds an attitude, a cynicism that is distressing," Daley added.

Republican political operatives warn that sampling could make vulnerable 24 Republican House seats, a distressing prospect for a party with a thin, 228–206 majority.

Historians and other analysts, however, believe that number exaggerates the threat. Historically, about 10 seats shift after each census, but even that is a rough estimate.

"What the census does is count people. It has no correlation to voters," said Anderson, who wrote a respected history of the census. "The census does not count only the politically active."

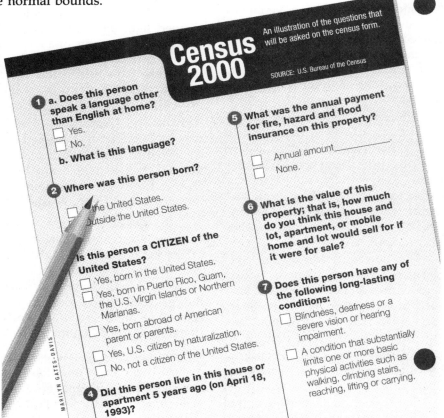

Census 2000

An illustration of the questions that will be asked on the census form.

SOURCE: U.S. Bureau of the Census

MARILYN GATES-DAVIS

1 a. Does this person speak a language other than English at home?
☐ Yes.
☐ No.
b. What is this language?

2 Where was this person born?
☐ In the United States.
☐ Outside the United States.

Is this person a CITIZEN of the United States?
☐ Yes, born in the United States.
☐ Yes, born in Puerto Rico, Guam, the U.S. Virgin Islands or Northern Marianas.
☐ Yes, born abroad of American parent or parents.
☐ Yes, U.S. citizen by naturalization.
☐ No, not a citizen of the United States.

4 Did this person live in this house or apartment 5 years ago (on April 18, 1993)?

5 What was the annual payment for fire, hazard and flood insurance on this property?
☐ Annual amount_____
☐ None.

6 What is the value of this property; that is, how much do you think this house and lot, apartment, or mobile home and lot would sell for if it were for sale?

7 Does this person have any of the following long-lasting conditions:
☐ Blindness, deafness or a severe vision or hearing impairment.
☐ A condition that substantially limits one or more basic physical activities such as walking, climbing stairs, reaching, lifting or carrying.

She and others point out that it would be difficult to tilt the numbers even if the Census Bureau wanted to do so. And that's unlikely, Democrats said, because the bureau has only two political appointees out of a work force of over 10,000.

Republicans, however, have focused most of their criticism on fears that a Democratic administration would use the census to benefit its party and candidates.

"Our Constitution calls for an actual enumeration of citizens, not just an educated guess by Washington bureaucrats," Rep. John A. Boehner, R-Ohio, said.

"The American people deserve to be properly represented. Sampling corrupts a basic sense of fairness by treating people as numbers that can be estimated, rather than individuals who have a right to be counted. . . . Sampling is very simply an attempt by a politics-obsessed White House to politicize this important individual right and constitutional obligation," he added.

Democratic Rep. Carolyn B. Maloney of New York worries, like Boehner, that a flawed census could undermine democracy. She argued that an inaccurate census could benefit the Republicans.

"The sad truth is that the Census Bureau has developed a plan that will count everyone who lives in America, including blacks and Latinos and the poor and Asians and whites, everyone," she said on the House floor June 23. "But some members of Congress do not want that to happen. Why? Because they believe not counting certain minorities and the poor is to their political advantage."

Back and forth it goes with almost no movement or compromise. Anderson predicts a more subtle result, one deeply rooted in census history.

If the Republicans prevail, she said, "We may end up with crummy data, and we, as a society, will have to live with that."

---

*Editor's note:* In January 1999, the U.S. Supreme Court rejected the federal government's plan to use "statistical sampling" in the 2000 census.

## Why I Do What I Do

# HOWARD SMITH, I.R.S. AGENT

For the tax collector, every month is the cruelest month.

## By Michael Winerip

THEY ARE THE MOST ABUSED, THREATENED AND ASSAULTED workers in the entire Internal Revenue Service. The revenue officers. The Office of Personnel Management identifies them as G.S.–1169's. For short, they call themselves R.O.'s. But in plain English, they are the Federal Government's bill collectors, the men and women dispatched when all else fails to bring in those overdue taxes, even if it means seizing a business to auction its assets. "I don't know how they do it," says David Sullivan, a Federal prosecutor in New Haven. "I work with F.B.I., D.E.A., Customs, Postal, but the I.R.S. collection guys, without doubt, have *the* most difficult, *the* most thankless job."

According to I.R.S. S.P.D. No. 91450E, Section 9: "The Revenue Officer must be capable of functioning effectively under high stress. . . . Potentially dangerous and/or life-threatening situations may typically induce a range of disturbing emotional as well as physical reactions."

This, in a nutshell, has been Howard Smith's life. "It's no fun seizing a business," says Smith, a revenue officer for 24 years. "Your palms are sweaty, your heart rate's up, you feel apprehensive. You're taking away something someone spent a lifetime building."

For such dangerous or life-threatening situations, Smith is equipped with a Government-issued laptop and a calculator. Revenue officers work civil cases and are not permitted to carry weapons. Even quick getaways are problematic. Revenue officers are usually not supplied with a Government vehicle, and Smith is no Rockefeller. Most days he can be found in his '87 Bronco, which has 137,000 miles on it. "I've been having trouble starting it lately," he says.

And yet the revenue officer, according to I.R.S. S.P.D. No. 91450E, Section 5, must always be friendly and well mannered: "The R.O. is responsible for providing courteous, fair, prompt, accurate and thorough service." It's a challenge. Irate taxpayers often do not feel bound by I.R.S.

S.P.D. No. 91450E, or most other generally accepted codes of behavior. Smith has had taxpayers pull guns and knives on him; he has been choked and chased by junkyard dogs; he has had a large sandwich hurled at him. "I can still see that grinder flying by," he says.

In one case, after repeated visits, Smith told a machine-shop owner that the Government—i.e., Smith—was going to seize his business. "He reached into his drawer," recalls Smith, "and pulled out this gun. He's waving it around. I'm thinking, This is not a good situation—my life is in peril. He yelled, 'O.K., this is it!'" At such times, Smith thinks of his wife and son spending Christmas alone. "He's got the gun pointed at me, and he tells me: 'Take this gun and shoot me. I have nothing to live for!'"

In some ways, that was a pleasant turn of events for Smith, though assisted suicide is no bargain, either. "I said: 'Let's calm down. We have to figure this thing out.' I didn't take the gun. I said, 'Let's put it down—relax.' I said, 'Why don't we call my office and talk to my supervisor?' I figure that way, somebody else knows the situation and where to look for the dead body. I put him on the phone to my manager. All of a sudden he throws the phone down and

## 'He reached into his drawer and pulled out this gun. He's waving it around. I'm thinking, This is not a good situation.'

runs out. I figure it's a good time to exit. I'm about to leave. He picks me up and throws me in a chair. It didn't seem like a good thing to resist at that point. I figure we'll go with the flow, see how it turns out. He went on for about 15 minutes and then he let me leave. A lot of times, you just have to let people vent."

There are 7,500 revenue officers, 7 percent of the I.R.S.'s national work force of 102,000. They make about 10,000 seizures a year, which does not win them friends; revenue officers account for two-thirds of the agency's reported assaults and threats. "A lot of people do this job a few years, then go into management," Smith says. "They don't like confrontation. To me, this is the genuine function of the agency—to come in contact with the most difficult collection cases. I like that I'm not tied to a desk, I'm out meeting all kinds of people. I don't know where the time goes. I look up, the day's over. I look up, the week's over. It's been 24 years—it flew!"

Smith, who is based in New Haven, tries to win over taxpayers by being low-key. "Good morning. Howard Smith. I have an appointment," he said to a receptionist during a recent visit to a trucking company. While the woman got her boss, Smith whispered, "Notice, I don't flash my badge—I don't think that's a good way to build a relationship." The majority of Smith's cases involve businesses that fail to pay the Government the Federal wage and Social Security taxes they are withholding from workers. Usually, Smith says, the owner is in trouble and trying to buy time by giving himself a cash infusion. So often, lurking just below the failed business is a human being coming unglued—it can be gambling, alcohol, a health problem, a chatty mistress.

Smith is part social worker, part financial adviser to the taxpayer, trying to keep the business afloat so the Government can get its money. "I go home nights trying to figure out how to work out these difficult situations," he says. For months, he tried to help save a construction company, but couldn't. "The day of seizure, the wife brought me a platter of chocolate-chip cookies. It made the seizure a little harder."

It took several visits to the trucking company, but Smith was finally able to get the owner to reveal where he stashed his 18-wheelers so Smith could assess their value. "He had them hidden all over Connecticut," Smith says. "It took a couple days to find them all."

Doing the job so long, Smith has picked up certain tricks, like never letting the taxpayer sit between him and the door. Also, if you're seizing a restaurant, do it early in the day: "You don't want to interrupt someone's lunch, make a big thing out of it."

Even some of his targets speak well of him. "Howard's been fair," said the owner of a small private school who is $83,000 behind in taxes. "It's not personal. If Howard wants to keep his job, he has to do these kinds of things to people." During a visit to the man's office, Smith displayed his special brand of cheery tenacity. The owner

had pledged to keep up with his current withholding while also paying back his overdue taxes.

"How's your wife?" Smith asked.

"A lot better," the owner said.

"You're not keeping current," Smith said.

"I know, Howard," the man said.

"You owed $63,000, now it's $83,000," Smith said. "Those darn penalties and interest."

"Didn't we agree to $3,000 a month?"

"Let me just check," Smith said, pulling out his laptop. "No, $5,000. It's right here—you want to look?"

"I know, Howard. There's nothing more humiliating than telling you I can't pay you." He explained that he had done well with other businesses, including construction. "Even built my own house. It's real nice, probably worth $300,000 plus change today."

Smith brightened. "Anything we could do with that?"

"Oh, no," the man said. "No, no. We're maxed out on the mortgage."

A revenue officer in Connecticut starts at $21,792 a year; with seniority, Smith earns $60,000. To make ends meet, he works a security job weekends. "I could make more preparing tax returns or selling real estate, but I'm not allowed to under our ethics code," he says.

After last year's Senate hearings on I.R.S. abuses, the agency became a juicy target. Last month, the Democrats, fearful that Republicans were becoming the party that hated the I.R.S. most, unveiled their own reforms. "To be honest, it hurts," Smith says. "If there's wrongdoing, it should be stopped, but I hope they look and see all the good things being done. The one thing I always liked about this job, you had the aura of integrity. When I hear them use the word 'corrupt'—I mean, we don't even accept a cup of coffee from a taxpayer."

His hardest moment as a revenue officer involved a foundry owner who owed about $200,000 and offered him a bribe. "Our training is to be noncommital," Smith says. "I said, 'I'll get back to you.'" Smith called the I.R.S.'s inspection services. They wired him, and on his next visit, he accepted a $1,000 bribe. "I was so nervous," Smith says. "I kept thinking he was going to find the wire. You know you're doing right, but you feel dirty."

Rudy Riddick pleaded guilty and was sentenced to three years' probation. "It wasn't really publicized," Smith says, although the I.R.S. did recognize his efforts. "Somebody important came from our New York office and gave me a plaque."

**Unit 3**

## Unit Selections

## Key Points to Consider

❖ How "democratic" is the American political system compared with others?

❖ Do the Republican and Democratic parties offer the American people alternatives that amount to a meaningful choice?

❖ How do the political views of young people compare and contrast with those of their parents?

❖ If you were running for office, would you use public opinion polls? Focus groups? Talk radio? If so, how?

❖ Do American citizens have satisfactory ways of getting information about their government that do not involve news media?

❖ What effects do you think running for and holding political office have on the individuals involved?

❖ Who do you think are likely to be major candidates for the presidency in 2000 and thereafter? Do you think that the kinds of backgrounds from which future presidential candidates come will be much different from those of recent candidates? Why or why not?

❖ Do you think that our current procedures for choosing the president are good ones? Explain your answer.

 **Links** **www.dushkin.com/online/**

These sites are annotated on pages 4 and 5.

According to many political scientists, what distinguishes *more* democratic political systems from *less* democratic ones is the degree of control that citizens exercise over government. This section focuses on the institutions, groups, and processes that are supposed to serve as links between Americans and their government.

Political parties, elections, pressure groups, and news media are all thought to play important roles in communications between people and government in the American political system. Changes that are occurring today in some of these areas may affect American politics for decades to come, and these changes are the focus of many of the readings in this section.

The first and second subsections focus on politicians, parties, money, and elections. One of the legacies of the Watergate scandal of the early 1970s was the passage of new laws to regulate campaign financing, followed by extensive debate about the impact of the reforms. Violence and controversy relating to the 1968 Democratic nominating convention led to a series of changes in the procedures that both parties use to select their candidates.

In the 1980s, candidates increasingly used focus groups, political consultants, and public opinion polling to shape expensive advertising campaigns, and many observers thought that negative television ads played a particularly prominent role in the 1988 presidential campaign. In 1992 more changes in campaign tactics and techniques appeared, including numerous appearances by presidential candidates on television talk shows and a half dozen or so 30-minute paid "infomercials" by Ross Perot. In the 1994 congressional elections, Republicans were generally successful in "nationalizing" the competition for 435 House and 30-odd Senate seats, apparently belying the adage that "all politics is local" and winning control of both houses of Congress for the first time since 1954. In 1996, apparently unprecedented amounts of "soft" money from questionable sources fueled President Clinton's reelection campaign, and campaign finance practices became the target of much criticism. All these developments and more underlie the selections in the section.

The third subsection treats the roles of interest groups in the American political process and their impact on what government can and cannot do. While "gridlock" is a term usually applied to inaction resulting from "divided government" in which neither major party controls the presidency and both houses of Congress, it seems clear that

"gridlock" also results from the interaction of interest groups and various government policymakers. The relative weakness of parties is almost certainly responsible for the great strength of interest groups in the American political system, and one can wonder whether a possible new era of stronger, more disciplined parties in government will contribute to weakening interest groups.

The fourth subsection addresses news and other media, which probably play a more active role in the American political system than their counterparts do in any political system in the world. Television news broadcasts and newspapers are not merely passive transmitters of information. They inevitably shape—or distort—what they report to their audiences. They also greatly affect the behavior of people and organizations in politics. As previously noted, in recent years, especially during the 1992 and 1996 presidential campaigns, less traditional media forums have begun to play bigger roles in politics. Radio and television talk shows and 30-minute "infomercials" entered the political landscape with considerable effect. Selections in the fourth subsection provide coverage of how media can shape or distort political communication and the behavior of political actors.

# Process of American Politics

# RUNNING SCARED

### by ANTHONY KING

*Painfully often the legislation our politicians pass is designed less to solve problems than to protect the politicians from defeat in our never-ending election campaigns. They are, in short, too frightened of us to govern*

To an extent that astonishes a foreigner, modern America is *about* the holding of elections. Americans do not merely have elections on the first Tuesday after the first Monday of November in every year divisible by four. They have elections on the first Tuesday after the first Monday of November in every year divisible by two. In addition, five states have elections in odd-numbered years. Indeed, there is no year in the United States— ever—when a major statewide election is not being held somewhere. To this catalogue of general elections has of course to be added an equally long catalogue of primary elections (for example, forty-three presidential primaries last year). Moreover, not only do elections occur very frequently in the United States but the number of jobs legally required to be filled by them is enormous—from the presidency of the United States to the post of local consumer advocate in New York. It has been estimated that no fewer than half a million elective offices are filled or waiting to be filled in the United States today.

Americans take the existence of their never-ending election campaign for granted. Some like it, some dislike it, and most are simply bored by it. But they are all conscious of it, in the same way that they are conscious of Mobil, McDonald's, *Larry King Live,* Oprah Winfrey, the Dallas Cowboys, the Ford Motor Company, and all other symbols and institutions that make up the rich tapestry of American life.

To a visitor to America's shores, however, the never-ending campaign presents a largely unfamiliar spectacle. In other countries election campaigns have both beginnings and ends, and there are even periods, often prolonged periods, when no campaigns take place at all. Other features of American elections are also unfamiliar. In few countries do elections and campaigns cost as much as they do in the United States. In no other country is the role of organized political parties so limited.

America's permanent election campaign, together with other aspects of American electoral politics, has one crucial consequence, little noticed but vitally important for the functioning of American democracy. Quite simply, the American electoral system places politicians in a highly vulnerable position. Individually and collectively they are more vulnerable, more of the time, to the vicissitudes of electoral politics than are the politicians of any other democratic country. Because they are more vulnerable, they devote more of their time to electioneering, and their conduct in office is more continuously governed by electoral considerations. I will argue that American politicians' constant and unremitting electoral preoccupations have deleterious consequences for the functioning of the American system. They consume time and scarce resources. Worse, they make it harder than it would otherwise be for the system as a whole to deal with some of America's most pressing problems. Americans often complain that their system is not sufficiently democratic. I will argue that, on the contrary, there is a sense in which the system is too democratic and ought to be made less so.

Although this article is written by a foreigner, a Canadian citizen who happens to live in Great Britain, it is not written

---

**Anthony King,** a political scientist who teaches at the University of Essex, and an elections analyst for the British Broadcasting Corporation, is a regular contributor to *The Economist.*

in any spirit of moral or intellectual superiority. Americans over the years have had quite enough of Brits and others telling them how to run their affairs. I have no wish to prolong their irritation. What follows is the reflections of a candid friend.

## FEAR AND TREMBLING

**P**OLITICS and government in the United States are marked by the fact that U.S. elected officials in many cases have very short terms of office *and* face the prospect of being defeated in primary elections *and* have to run for office more as individuals than as standard-bearers for their party *and* have continually to raise large sums of money in order to finance their own election campaigns. Some of these factors operate in other countries. There is no other country, however, in which all of them operate, and operate simultaneously. The cumulative consequences, as we shall see, are both pervasive and profound.

The U.S. Constitution sets out in one of its very first sentences that "the House of Representatives shall be composed of members chosen every second year by the people of the several states." When the Founding Fathers decided on such a

*INDIVIDUALLY AND COLLECTIVELY AMERICAN POLITICIANS ARE MORE VULNERABLE, MORE OF THE TIME, TO THE VICISSITUDES OF ELECTORAL POLITICS THAN ARE THE POLITICIANS OF ANY OTHER DEMOCRATIC COUNTRY.*

short term of office for House members, they were setting a precedent that has been followed by no other major democratic country. In Great Britain, France, Italy, and Canada the constitutional or legal maximum for the duration of the lower house of the national legislature is five years. In Germany and Japan the equivalent term is four years. Only in Australia and New Zealand, whose institutions are in some limited respects modeled on those of the United States, are the legal maximums as short as three years. In having two-year terms the United States stands alone.

Members of the Senate are, of course, in a quite different position. Their constitutionally prescribed term of office, six years, is long by anyone's standards. But senators' six-year terms are not all they seem. In the first place, so pervasive is the electioneering atmosphere that even newly elected senators begin almost at once to lay plans for their re-election campaigns. Senator Daniel Patrick Moynihan, of New York, recalls that when he first came to the Senate, in 1977, his colleagues when they met over lunch or a drink usually talked about politics and policy. Now they talk about almost nothing but the latest opinion polls. In the second place, the fact that under the Constitution the terms of a third of the Senate end every

two years means that even if individual senators do not feel themselves to be under continuing electoral pressure, the Senate as a whole does. Despite the Founders' intentions, the Senate's collective electoral sensibilities increasingly resemble those of the House.

Most Americans seem unaware of the fact, but the direct primary—a government-organized popular election to nominate candidates for public office—is, for better or worse, an institution peculiar to the United States. Neither primary elections nor their functional equivalents exist anywhere else in the democratic world. It goes without saying that their effect is to add a further dimension of uncertainty and unpredictability to the world of American elective politicians.

In most other countries the individual holder of public office, so long as he or she is reasonably conscientious and does not gratuitously offend local or regional party opinion, has no real need to worry about renomination. To be sure, cases of parties refusing to renominate incumbent legislators are not unknown in countries such as France, Germany, and Canada, but they are relatively rare and tend to occur under unusual circumstances. The victims are for the most part old, idle, or alcoholic.

The contrast between the rest of the world and the United States could hardly be more striking. In 1978 no fewer than 104 of the 382 incumbent members of the House of Representatives who sought re-election faced primary opposition. In the following three elections the figures were ninety-three out of 398 (1980), ninety-eight out of 393 (1982), and 130 out of 409 (1984). More recently, in 1994, nearly a third of all House incumbents seeking re-election, 121 out of 386, had to face primary opposition, and in the Senate the proportion was even higher: eleven out of twenty-six. Even those incumbents who did not face opposition could seldom be certain in advance that they were not going to. The influence—and the possibility—of primaries is pervasive. As we shall see, the fact that incumbents usually win is neither here nor there.

To frequent elections and primary elections must be added another factor that contributes powerfully to increasing the electoral vulnerability of U.S. politicians: the relative lack of what we might call "party cover." In most democratic countries the fate of most politicians depends not primarily on their own endeavors but on the fate—locally, regionally, or nationally—of their party. If their party does well in an election, so do they. If not, not. The individual politician's interests and those of his party are bound together.

In contrast, America's elective politicians are on their own—not only in relation to politicians in most other countries but also in absolute terms. Party is still a factor in U.S. electoral politics, but it is less so than anywhere else in the democratic world. As a result, American legislators seeking re-election are forced to raise their own profiles, to make their own records, and to fight their own re-election campaigns.

If politicians are so vulnerable electorally, it may be protested, why aren't more of them defeated? In particular, why aren't more incumbent congressmen and senators defeated? The analysis here would seem to imply a very high rate of turnover in Congress, but in fact the rate—at least among incumbents seeking re-election—is notoriously low. How can this argument and the facts of congressional incumbents' electoral success be reconciled?

This objection has to be taken seriously, because the facts on which it is based are substantially correct. The number of incumbent congressmen and senators defeated in either primary or general elections *is* low. But to say that because incumbent members of Congress are seldom defeated, they are not really vulnerable electorally is to miss two crucial points. The first is that precisely because they are vulnerable, they go to prodigious lengths to protect themselves. Like workers in nuclear-power stations, they take the most extreme safety precautions, and the fact that the precautions are almost entirely successful does not make them any less necessary.

Second, congressmen and senators go to inordinate lengths to secure re-election because, although they may objectively be safe (in the view of journalists and academic political scientists), they do not know they are safe—and even if they think they are, the price of being wrong is enormous. The probability that anything will go seriously wrong with a nuclear-power station may approach zero, but the stations tend nevertheless to be built away from the centers of large cities. A congressman or a senator may believe that he is reasonably safe, but if he wants to be re- elected, he would be a fool to act on that belief.

## HOW THEY CAME TO BE VULNERABLE

AMERICAN politicians run scared—and are right to do so. And they run more scared than the politicians of any other democratic country—again rightly. How did this come to be so?

The short answer is that the American people like it that way. They are, and have been for a very long time, the Western world's hyperdemocrats. They are keener on democracy than almost anyone else and are more determined that democratic norms and practices should pervade every aspect of national life. To explore the implications of this central fact about the United States, and to see how it came to be, we need to examine two different interpretations of the term "democracy." Both have been discussed from time to time by political philosophers, but they have never been codified and they certainly cannot be found written down in a constitution or any other formal statement of political principles. Nevertheless, one or the other underpins the political practice of every democratic country—even if, inevitably, the abstract conception and the day-to-day practice are never perfectly matched.

One of these interpretations might be labeled "division of labor." In this view, there are in any democracy two classes of people—the governors and the governed. The function of the governors is to take decisions on the basis of what they believe to be in the country's best interests and to act on those decisions. If public opinion broadly supports the decisions, that is a welcome bonus. If not, too bad. The views of the people at large are merely one datum among a large number of data that need to be considered. They are not accorded any special status. Politicians in countries that operate within this view can frequently be heard using phrases like "the need for strong leadership" and "the need to take tough decisions." They often take a certain pride in doing what they believe to be right even if the opinion of the majority is opposed to it.

The function of the governed in such a system, if it is a genuine democracy, is very important but strictly limited. It is not to determine public policy or to decide what is the right thing to do. Rather, it is to go to the polls from time to time to choose those who will determine public policy and decide what the right thing is: namely, the governors. The deciding of issues by the electorate is secondary to the election of the individuals who are to do the deciding. The analogy is with choosing a doctor. The patient certainly chooses which doctor to see but does not normally decide (or even try to decide) on the detailed course of treatment. The division of labor is informal but clearly understood.

It is probably fair to say that most of the world's major democracies—Great Britain, France, Germany, Japan—operate on this basis. The voters go to the polls every few years, and in between times it is up to the government of the day to get on with governing. Electing a government and governing are two different businesses. Electioneering is, if anything, to be deplored if it gets in the way of governing.

This is a simplified picture, of course. Democratically elected politicians are ultimately dependent on the electorate, and if at the end of the day the electorate does not like what they are doing, they are dead. Nevertheless, the central point remains. The existing division of labor is broadly accepted.

The other interpretation of democracy, the one dominant in America, might be called the "agency" view, and it is wholly different. According to this view, those who govern a country should function as no more than the agents of the people. The job of the governors is not to act independently and to take whatever decisions they believe to be in the national interest but, rather, to reflect in all their actions the views of the majority of the people, whatever those views may be. Governors are not really governors at all; they are representatives, in the very narrow sense of being in office solely to represent the views of those who sent them there.

In the agency view, representative government of the kind common throughout the democratic world can only be second-best. The ideal system would be one in which there were no politicians or middlemen of any kind and the people governed themselves directly; the political system would take the form of more or less continuous town meetings or referenda, perhaps conducted by means of interactive television. Most Americans, at bottom, would still like to see their country governed by a town meeting.

## WHY THEIR VULNERABILITY MATTERS

IN this political ethos, finding themselves inhabiting a turbulent and torrid electoral environment, most American elective officials respond as might be expected: in an almost Darwinian way. They adapt their behavior—their roll-call votes, their introduction of bills, their committee assignments, their phone calls, their direct-mail letters, their speeches, their press releases, their sound bites, whom they see, how they spend their time, their trips abroad, their trips back home, and frequently their private and family lives—to their environment: that is, to their primary and overriding need for electoral survival. The effects are felt not only in the lives of individual officeholders and their staffs but also in America's political institutions as a whole and the shape and content of U.S. public policy.

It all begins with officeholders' immediate physical environment: with bricks, mortar, leather, and wood paneling. The number of congressional buildings and the size of congressional staffs have ballooned in recent decades. At the start of the 1960s most members of the House of Representatives contented themselves with a small inner office and an outer office; senators' office suites were not significantly larger. Apart from the Capitol itself, Congress was reasonably comfortably housed in four buildings, known to Washington taxi drivers as the Old and New House and Senate Office Buildings. The designations Old and New cannot be used any longer, however, because there are now so many even newer congressional buildings.

Congressional staffs have grown at roughly the same rate, the new buildings having been built mainly to house the staffs. In 1957 the total number of people employed by members of the House and

Senate as personal staff was 3,556. By 1991 the figure had grown to 11,572—a more than threefold increase within the political lifetime of many long-serving members. Last year the total number of people employed by Congress in all capacities, including committee staffs and the staffs of support agencies like the Congressional Research Service, was 32,820, making Congress by far the most heavily staffed legislative branch in the world.

Much of the growth of staff in recent decades has been in response to the growth of national government, to Congress's insistence on strengthening its policymaking role in the aftermath of Vietnam and Watergate, and to decentralization within Congress, which has led subcommittee chairmen and the subcommittees themselves to acquire their own staffs. But there is no doubt that the increase is also in response to congressional incumbents' ever-increasing electoral exposure. Congress itself has become an integral part of America's veritable "elections industry."

One useful measure of the changes that have taken place— and also an important consequence of the changes—is the increased proportion of staff and staff time devoted to constituent service. As recently as 1972 only 1,189 House employees— 22.5 percent of House members' personal staffs—were based in home- district offices. By 1992 the number had more than

doubled, to 3,128, and the proportion had nearly doubled, to 42.1 percent. On the Senate side there were only 303 state-based staffers in 1972, making up 12.5 percent of senators' personal staffs, but the number had more than quadrupled by 1992 to 1,368, for fully 31.6 percent of the total. Since a significant proportion of the time of Washington-based congressional staffs is also devoted to constituent service, it is a fair guess that more than half of the time of all congressional staffs is now given over to nursing the district or state rather than to legislation and policymaking.

Much constituent service is undoubtedly altruistic, inspired by politicians' sense of duty (and constituents' understandable frustration with an unresponsive bureaucracy); but at the same time nobody doubts that a large proportion of it is aimed at securing re-election. The statistics on the outgoing mail of members of Congress and their use of the franking privilege point in that direction too. Congressional mailings grew enormously in volume from some 100 million pieces a year in the early 1960s to more than 900 million in 1984—nearly five pieces of congressional mail for every adult American. New restrictions on franking introduced in the 1990s have made substantial inroads into that figure, but not surprisingly the volume of mail emanating from both houses of Congress is still invariably higher in election years.

The monetary costs of these increases in voter-oriented congressional activities are high: in addition to being the most heavily staffed legislative branch in the world, Congress is also the most expensive. But there is another, non-monetary cost: the staffs themselves become one of the congressman's or senator's constituencies, requiring management, taking up time, and always being tempted to go into business for themselves. American scholars who have studied the burgeoning of congressional staffs express concern about their cumulative impact on Congress as a deliberative body in which face-to-face communication between members, and between members and their constituents, facilitates both mutual understanding and an understanding of the issues. Largely in response to the requirements of electioneering, more and more congressional business is conducted through dense networks of staffers.

One familiar effect of American politicians' vulnerability is the power it accords to lobbyists and special-interest groups, especially those that can muster large numbers of votes or have large amounts of money to spend on campaigns. Members of Congress walk the electoral world alone. They can be picked off one by one, they know it, and they adjust their behavior accordingly. The power of the American Association of Retired Persons, the National Rifle Association, the banking industry, and the various veterans' lobbies is well known. It derives partly from their routine contributions to campaign funds and the quality of their lobbying activities in Washington, but far more from the votes that the organizations may be able to deliver and from congressmen's and senators' calculations of how the positions they take in the present may affect their chances of re-election in the future—a future that rarely is distant. Might a future challenger be able to use that speech against me? Might I be targeted for defeat by one of the powerful lobbying groups?

A second effect is that American politicians are even more likely than those in other countries to engage in symbolic politics: to use words masquerading as deeds, to take actions that purport to be instrumental but are in fact purely rhetorical. A problem exists; the people demand that it be solved; the politicians cannot solve it and know so; they engage in an elaborate pretense of trying to solve it nevertheless, often at great expense to the taxpayers and almost invariably at a high cost in terms of both the truth and the politicians' own reputations for integrity and effectiveness. The politicians lie in most cases not because they are liars or approve of lying but because the potential electoral costs of not lying are too great.

At one extreme, symbolic politics consists of speechmaking and public position-taking in the absence of any real action or any intention of taking action; casting the right vote is more important than achieving the right outcome. At the other extreme, symbolic politics consists of whole government programs that are ostensibly designed to achieve one set of objectives but are actually designed to achieve other objectives (in some cases simply the re-election of the politicians who can claim credit for them).

Take as an example the crime bills passed by Congress in the 1980s and 1990s, with their mandatory-minimum sentences, their three-strikes-and-you're-out provisions, and their extension of the federal death penalty to fifty new crimes. The anti-drug and anti-crime legislation, by the testimony of judges and legal scholars, has been at best useless and at worst wholly pernicious in its effects, in that it has filled prison cells not with violent criminals but with drug users and low-level drug pushers. As for the death penalty, a simple measure of its sheer irrelevance to the federal government's war on crime is easily provided. The last federal offender to be put to death, Victor H. Feguer, a convicted kidnapper, was hanged in March of 1963. By the end of 1995 no federal offender had been executed for more than thirty years, and hardly any offenders were awaiting execution on death row. The ferocious-seeming federal statutes were almost entirely for show.

The way in which the wars on drugs and crime were fought cannot be understood without taking into account the incessant pressure that elected officeholders felt they were under from the electorate. As one former congressman puts it, "Voters were afraid of criminals, and politicians were afraid of voters." This fear reached panic proportions in election years. Seven of the years from 1981 to 1994 were election years nationwide; seven were not. During those fourteen years Congress passed no fewer than seven major crime bills. Of those seven, six were passed in election years (usually late in the year). That is, there was only one election year in which a major crime bill was *not* passed, and only one non-election year in which a major crime bill *was* passed.

Another effect of the extreme vulnerability of American politicians is that it is even harder for them than for democratically elected politicians in other countries to take tough decisions: to court unpopularity, to ask for sacrifices, to impose losses, to fly in the face of conventional wisdom—in short, to act in what they believe to be their constituents' interest and the national interest rather than in their own interest. Timothy

J. Penny, a Democrat who left the House of Representatives in 1994, put the point starkly, perhaps even too harshly, in *Common Cents* (1995).

> Voters routinely punish lawmakers who try to do unpopular things, who challenge them to face unpleasant truths about the budget, crime, Social Security, or tax policy. Similarly, voters reward politicians for giving them what they want—more spending for popular programs—even if it means wounding the nation in the long run by creating more debt.

America's enduring budget deficit offers a vivid, almost textbook illustration. For nearly a generation—ever since the early 1980s—American politicians have bemoaned the deficit and exhorted themselves to do something about it. However, they have never done nearly enough, even in their own eyes. Why? Part of the answer undoubtedly lies in genuine ideological differences that make it hard for conservatives and liberals to compromise; but much of the answer also lies in the brute fact that every year in the United States is either an election year or a pre-election year, with primaries and threatened primaries intensifying politicians' electoral concerns. In 1985 Senator Warren Rudman, of New Hampshire, reckoned that he and other senators who had voted for a bold deficit-reduction package had flown a "kamikaze mission." One of his colleagues said they had "jumped off a cliff." Twelve years later, not surprisingly, the federal budget remains in deficit.

## MORE DEMOCRACY, MORE DISSATISFACTION

NUMEROUS opinion polls show that millions of Americans are profoundly dissatisfied with the functioning of their political system. Consequently, there is a widespread disposition in the United States—at all levels of society, from the grass roots to the editorial conference and the company boardroom—to want to make American democracy "work better," and concrete proposals abound for achieving this goal.

The proposed reforms can be grouped loosely under four headings. First come those that if implemented would amount to the creation of electronic town meetings, taking advantage of technological developments such as CD-ROM, interactive cable systems, electronic mail, and the Internet. *The Wall Street Journal* referred in this general connection to "arranging a marriage of de Tocqueville and technology."

Second, and related, are proposals for promoting democratic deliberation and citizen participation. The Kettering Foundation and the Public Agenda Foundation already organize National Issues Forums that embrace some 3,000 educational and civic groups across America. David Mathews, the president of the Kettering Foundation, considers these modern forums to be directly linked to America's ancient "town meeting tradition." Benjamin R. Barber, a political philosopher at Rutgers University, would go further and create a nationwide network of neighborhood assemblies that could take actual decisions on strictly local matters and also debate and lobby on broader national questions. James S. Fishkin, a political scientist at the

University of Texas, likewise seeks to leap the modern barriers to face-to-face democracy by means of what he calls "deliberative opinion polls" (which have been tried, with considerable success, in England).

The third group of proposed reforms is equally radical but more old-fashioned. This group seeks to complete the work of Progressive Era reformers by extending to the federal level the characteristic state-level reforms that were introduced in that period: the referendum, the initiative, and the recall. The political analyst Kevin Phillips, for example, suggests that "the United States should propose and ratify an amendment to the Constitution setting up a mechanism for holding nationwide referendums to permit the citizenry to supplant Congress and the president in making certain categories of national decisions." He would also like to see congressmen and senators be subject to popular recall once they have been in office for a year. Certainly proposals of this kind have broad public support. Depending on the precise wording of the question, more than 50 percent of Americans support the idea of national referenda and more than 80 percent support both the initiative and the recall.

Finally, many commentators—and the majority of the American public—strongly back the newest and most fashionable item on the "making democracy work better" agenda: the imposition of term limits on both state and federal elected officials, notably members of Congress. But the great majority of those who favor term limits, true to the American democratic tradition, are less concerned with good government and the public interest as such than with the present generation of politicians' alleged lack of responsiveness to the mass of ordinary people. At the center of this argument is the idea that the

## WHEN AMERICANS BECOME DISSATISFIED WITH GOVERNMENT, THEY CALL FOR MORE DEMOCRACY. THE MORE THEY CALL FOR MORE DEMOCRACY, THE MORE OF IT THEY GET. THE MORE THEY GET, THE MORE DISSATISFIED THEY BECOME.

United States is now governed by an unresponsive, self-perpetuating, and increasingly remote class of professional politicians, a class that ought to be replaced as soon as possible by "citizen legislators"—men and women who will serve the people simply because they *are* the people. As one advocate of term limits puts it, ordinary people—the proposed citizen legislators of the future—"know things about life in America that people who have lived as very self-important figures in Washington for thirty years have no way of knowing or have forgotten."

Some of the items on this four-part shopping list of reforms are intrinsically attractive, or at least a good case can be made

for them. Nevertheless, taken as a whole, the mainstream reformist agenda, with its traditional American emphasis on agency democracy and its view of politicians as mere servants of the people's will, rests on extremely tenuous conceptual foundations and, more important, is almost certainly inappropriate as a response to the practical needs of turn-of-the-century America. America's problem of governance is not insufficient responsiveness on the part of its elected leaders. On the contrary, America's problem is their hyper-responsiveness. Politicians do not need to be tied down still further, to be subjected to even more external pressures than they are already. Rather, they need to be given just a little more political leeway, just a little more room for policy maneuver. Reforms should seek to strengthen division-of-labor democracy, not to create a still purer form of American-style agency democracy.

### THE USUAL SUSPECTS

IF the reformist prescriptions are bad ones, there may be something wrong with the reformist diagnoses on which they are based. What *are* the principal sources of dissatisfaction with the current state of American democracy?

Many commentators have gotten into the habit of blaming Americans' dissatisfaction, in an almost knee-jerk fashion, on "the Vietnam War and Watergate." It is certainly the case that evidence of widespread dissatisfaction began to appear during and shortly after Vietnam and Watergate. *Post hoc, ergo propter hoc?* Maybe. But in the first place, Vietnam and Watergate led to a flowering of idealism as well as cynicism (and to the election, in 1974, of the "Watergate babies," one of the most idealistic and public-spirited cohorts ever to be elected to Congress). And in the second place, it seems strange to attribute the dissatisfactions of the 1990s to events that took place in the 1960s and early 1970s. That distance in time is roughly that between the two world wars; most of today's college students were not yet born when President Richard Nixon resigned. To be sure, subsequent scandals have undoubtedly (and deservedly) damaged the reputations of the White House and Congress, but at least some of the sleaze of recent years has come about because politicians need such enormous sums to finance their re-election campaigns.

Two other hypotheses can be dismissed, or at least assigned little importance. One is that politicians today are a poor lot compared with the intellectual and moral giants of the past. It probably is the case that having to run scared all the time has tended to drive some able people out of politics and to discourage others from coming in. But the phenomenon is a relatively recent one, and for the time being there is no reason to think that the average congressman or senator is in any way inferior to his or her predecessors. The quality of America's existing political class is at most a small part of the problem.

The same is almost certainly true of the idea that divided government—in which one party controls one or both houses of Congress while the other controls the presidency—is to be preferred. Divided government has characterized America for most of the past thirty years, and it has been associated with some of the more spectacular political and policy failures of that period—the Iran-contra scandal of the 1980s (which arose out of a Republican Administration's desire to circumvent a Democratic Congress), and successive shutdowns of parts of the government as Presidents and Congress have failed to agree on timely taxing and spending measures. Other things being equal, divided government is probably to be regretted.

All the same, it is hard to credit the idea that Americans' disillusionment with their politics would be significantly less today if party control had been mainly undivided over the past thirty years. On the one hand, recent periods in which the government has not been divided (the Carter years, 1977–1980, and the first two Clinton years, 1993–1994) were not notably successful (Carter never surmounted the energy crisis, and Clinton failed to reform America's healthcare system even though that reform had figured prominently in his campaign promises). On the other hand, as David R. Mayhew, a political scientist at Yale University, has shown, periods of divided government have often been extremely productive in legislative terms. On balance, divided government appears to be more of a nuisance and a distraction than a root cause of either the government's difficulties or the public's disillusionment.

The idea that the system suffers from the excessive power of interest groups, however, needs to be taken seriously. Jonathan Rauch, in his recent book *Demosclerosis,* argues persuasively that America's interest groups have become larger, more numerous, and more powerful over the past three decades, to the point that they now have the capacity to prevent the government from doing almost anything that would disadvantage or offend any of the clients they represent—taking in, as it happens, virtually the whole American population.

Rauch is probably right; but one needs to go on to ask, as he himself does, what the power of these pullulating and all-encompassing lobby groups is based on. The answer is straightforward: their power depends ultimately on their money, on their capacity to make trouble for elected officials, on the votes of their members (the AARP has more than 30 million members), and on elective politicians' fear of not being re- elected. The groups' power, in other words, depends on politicians' electoral vulnerability; and America's interest groups are peculiarly powerful in large measure because America's elective politicians are peculiarly vulnerable. It is not quite as simple as that—but almost.

It is also important to note the precise timing of the developments described by Rauch and by almost everyone else who has written on this subject. Nearly all these developments date, almost uncannily, from the past thirty years: the rise in the number of interest groups, the growth in their membership and power, the decline in the public's trust in government officials, and the increased sense among voters that who they are and what they think do not matter to politicians and officials in Washington. In other words, the origins of the present era of democratic discontent can be traced to the end of the 1960s and the beginning of the 1970s. It was then that people began to think something was wrong not with this or that aspect of the system but with the system itself.

What happened at that time? It is hard to escape the conclusion that the crucial developments, largely provoked by the Vietnam War and Watergate, were the attempts from 1968 onward to open up the American system, to make it more transparent, to make it more accessible, to make it, in a word, more "democratic." These attempts led to an increase in the number of primary elections, to a further weakening of America's already weak political parties, to increases in the already high costs of electoral politics, and to the increasing isolation, in an increasingly hostile environment, of elective officials. In short, the post-Vietnam, post-Watergate reforms led, as they were meant to lead, to increased vulnerability to their electorates on the part of individual American officeholders.

The paradox that has resulted is obvious and easily stated. Recent history suggests that when large numbers of Americans become dissatisfied with the workings of their government, they call for more democracy. The more they call for more democracy, the more of it they get. The more of it they get, the more dissatisfied they become with the workings of their government. The more they become dissatisfied with the workings of their government, the more they call for more democracy. The cycle endlessly repeats itself.

## WHAT, IF ANYTHING, MIGHT BE DONE?

**P**RECISELY because American politicians are so exposed electorally, they probably have to display—and do display—more political courage more often than the politicians of any other democratic country. The number of political saints and martyrs in the United States is unusually large.

There is, however, no special virtue in a political system that requires large numbers of politicians to run the risk of martyrdom in order to ensure that tough decisions can be taken in a timely manner in the national interest. The number of such decisions that need to be taken is always likely to be large; human nature being what it is, the supply of would-be martyrs is always likely to be small. On balance it would seem better not to try to eliminate the electoral risks (it can never be done in a democracy) but to reduce somewhat their scale and intensity. There is no reason why the risks run by American politicians should be so much greater than the risks run by elective politicians in other democratic countries.

How, then, might the risks be reduced? What can be done? A number of reforms to the existing system suggest themselves. It may be that none of them is politically feasible— Americans hold tight to the idea of agency democracy—but in principle there should be no bar to any of them. One of the simplest would also be the most radical: to lengthen the terms of members of the House of Representatives from two years to four. The proposal is by no means a new one: at least 123 resolutions bearing on the subject were introduced in Congress in the eighty years from 1885 to 1965, and President Lyndon B. Johnson advocated the change in his State of the Union address in January of 1966.

A congressman participating in a Brookings Institution round table held at about the time of Johnson's message supported the change, saying, "I think that the four years would help you to be a braver congressman, and I think what you need is bravery. I think you need courage." Another congressman on the same occasion cited the example of another bill that he believed had the support of a majority in the House. "That bill is not going to come up this year. You know why it is not coming up? . . . Because four hundred and thirty-five of us have to face election. . . . If we had a four-year term, I am as confident as I can be the bill would have come to the floor and passed."

A similar case could be made for extending the term of senators to eight years, with half the Senate retiring or running for re- election every four years. If the terms of members of both houses were thus extended and made to coincide, the effect in reducing America's never-ending election campaign would be dramatic.

There is much to be said, too, for all the reasons mentioned so far, for scaling down the number of primary elections. They absorb extravagant amounts of time, energy, and money; they serve little democratic purpose; few people bother to vote in them; and they place additional and unnecessary pressure on incumbent officeholders. Since the main disadvantage of primaries is the adverse effect they have on incumbents, any reforms probably ought to be concerned with protecting incumbents' interests.

At the moment, the primary laws make no distinction between situations in which a seat in the House or the Senate is already occupied and situations in which the incumbent is, for whatever reason, standing down. The current laws provide for a primary to be held in either case. An incumbent is therefore treated as though the seat in question were open and he or she were merely one of the candidates for it. A relatively simple reform would be to distinguish between the two situations. If a seat was open, primaries would be held in both parties, as now; but if the incumbent announced that he or she intended to run for re- election, then a primary in his or her party would be held only if large numbers of party supporters were determined to have one—that is, were determined that the incumbent should be ousted. The obvious way to ascertain whether such determination existed would be by means of a petition supervised by the relevant state government and requiring a considerable number of signatures. The possibility of a primary would thus be left open, but those who wanted one would have to show that they were both numerous and serious. A primary would not be held simply because an ambitious, possibly demented, possibly wealthy individual decided to throw his or her hat into the ring.

Any steps to strengthen the parties as institutions would be desirable on the same grounds. Lack of party cover in the United States means that elective officeholders find it hard to take tough decisions partly because they lack safety in numbers. They can seldom, if ever, say to an aggrieved constituent or a political-action committee out for revenge, "I had to vote that way because my party told me to," or even "I had to vote that way because we in my party all agreed that we would." Lack of party cohesion, together with American voters' disposition to vote for the individual rather than the party, means that congressmen and senators are always in danger of being picked off one by one.

## BALLOT FATIGUE

WHAT might be done to give both parties more backbone? Clearly, the parties would be strengthened—and elective officeholders would not need to raise so much money for their own campaigns—if each party organization became a major source of campaign funding. In the unlikely event (against the background of chronic budget deficits) that Congress ever gets around to authorizing the federal funding of congressional election campaigns, a strong case could be made for channeling as much of the money as possible through the parties, and setting aside some of it to cover their administrative and other ongoing costs.

The party organizations and the nexus between parties and their candidates would also be strengthened if it were made easier for ordinary citizens to give money to the parties and for the parties to give money to their candidates. Until 1986, when the program was abolished, tax credits were available for taxpayers who contributed small sums to the political parties. These credits could be restored. Larry J. Sabato, a political scientist at the University of Virginia, has similarly suggested that citizens entitled to a tax refund could be allowed to divert a small part of their refund to the party of their choice. Such measures would not, however, reduce candidates' dependence on donations from wealthy individuals and PACs unless they were accompanied by measures enabling the parties to contribute more generously to their candidates' campaigns. At the moment there are strict legal limits on the amount of money that national or state party organizations can contribute to the campaigns of individual candidates. The limits should be raised (and indexed to inflation). There is even a case for abolishing them altogether.

All that said, there is an even more straightforward way of reducing incumbents' dependence on campaign contributors. At present incumbents have to spend so much time raising funds because the campaigns themselves are so expensive. They could be made cheaper. This, of course, would be one of the effects of making U.S. elections less numerous and less frequent than they are now. Another way to lower the cost of elections would be to provide candidates and parties with free air time on television and radio.

### THE CASE FOR SWANS

CLEARLY, the idea of term limits also needs to be taken seriously. After all, if American politicians are excessively vulnerable at the moment, one way of rendering them invulnerable would be to prevent them from running for re-election—no impending election contest, no need to worry overmuch about the voters.

As is evident, much of the actual campaigning in favor of term limits takes the form of ranting—against big government, against Washington, against "them," against taxes, against the deficit. Much of the rhetoric of term-limiters is sulfurous, and their principal motive often seems to be revenge. They claim that members of Congress are insufficiently responsive to their constituents, when the evidence suggests that, on the contrary, they are far too responsive. The term-limits movement is of a piece with previous outbursts of frustrated American populism, including the Know-Nothing movement of the 1850s—an essay, as one historian has put it, in "the politics of impatience."

Nevertheless, there is an alternate case for term limits, based not on American politicians' alleged lack of responsiveness to the voters but on their alleged overresponsiveness to the voters and interest groups in order to secure their own re-election. The most persuasive and subtle advocate of this line of argument is the political commentator George F. Will. His goal, Will says partway through his book *Restoration* (1992), "is

One way in which term limits might promote deliberation is by causing some incumbent legislators—namely those serving out their final term under term limits—to think, speak, and vote differently from the way they would have thought, spoken, and voted if they had been eligible and running for re-election. In addition, for term limits to affect the behavior not just of certain individuals but of Congress as a whole, it would be necessary for any given Congress to contain a significant number of these final-term members. In other words, congressional lame ducks would have to quack differently from other ducks, and there would have to be a fair number of them on the pond.

It is impossible to be sure, but it seems unlikely that term limits would have significant effects along these lines. In the first place, existing research (along with most human experience) suggests that a final-term congressman or senator, after eleven or twelve years on Capitol Hill, would be unlikely to alter his pattern of behavior in any radical way. He might send out fewer pieces of franked mail and make fewer trips back home, but he would probably not execute many U-turns in the way he spoke and voted. In the second place, although the proportion of senators who would be in their final term under term limits would normally be large (possibly half if senators were restricted to two terms), the proportion of lame-duck congressmen would normally be much smaller (an average of sixty to seventy out of 435 if House members were limited to six terms). The cumulative impact of the lame ducks would thus be much greater in the Senate than in the House, and in both houses it would probably be felt mainly at the margins (though of course the margins can, on occasion, be important).

But those who advocate term limits in fact build very little of their case on the expected future behavior of lame ducks. Rather, they are seeking to create a wholly new class of elected representatives. George Will holds out the prospect that mandatory term limits would have the effect of replacing today's

## THERE IS NO SPECIAL VIRTUE IN A SYSTEM THAT REQUIRES LARGE NUMBERS OF POLITICIANS TO RUN THE RISK OF MARTYRDOM IN ORDER TO ENSURE THAT TOUGH DECISIONS CAN BE TAKEN IN A TIMELY MANNER IN THE NATIONAL INTEREST.

deliberative democracy through representatives who function at a constitutional distance from the people." He reiterates the point about distance in his final paragraphs: "Americans must be less demanding of government. They must give to government more constitutional space in which to think, more social distance to facilitate deliberation about the future."

The case for giving American politicians more space and distance is undoubtedly a strong one, but assuming these objectives are desirable, it is still not clear that term limits are a suitable means for achieving them. Three questions arise. Would term limits achieve the desired objectives? Would they do so at an acceptable cost in terms of other American goals and values? Might the desired objectives not be better achieved by other means? The first question is strictly empirical. The other two mix the empirical and the moral.

political careerists with noncareerists—in other words, of replacing today's ducks with creatures more closely resembling swans. The new legislators, because they were not careerists, would not be driven by the need to secure re-election, and for that reason they would be more likely to concern themselves with the national interest. Also because they were not political careerists, they would be more likely to have some personal, hands-on understanding of America and its real concerns.

The prospect is undoubtedly attractive. But is it realistic? Would term limits in fact diminish the number of careerists and produce legislators who were more national-minded and disinterested?

The most important difficulties with Will's hypothesis are twofold. One is that modern politics at all levels, local and state as well as national, is an immensely time-consuming, energy-consuming activity that demands enormous commitment from those who are attracted to it. Legislative sessions are long, constituents' demands are exigent, policy problems are increasingly complicated. As a result, politics all over the world, not just in the United States, is becoming professionalized. Men and women in all countries increasingly choose a political career at an early age and then stick with it. It seems likely that even under term limits the great majority of congressmen and senators would be drawn from this professional political class, which has not only the commitment to politics but also the requisite patience, skills, and contacts. To be sure, people's political careers would take a different shape; but they would still be political careers.

The other difficulty is the reverse of the first. Just as politics is becoming more professionalized, so is almost every other occupation. As many women in particular know to their cost, it is becoming harder and harder to take career breaks—those who jump off the ladder in any profession find it increasingly hard to jump back even to the level they were on when they left, let alone the level they would have attained had they stayed. For this reason it is hard to imagine that many upwardly mobile corporate executives or successful professionals or small-business owners would take time off to serve in Congress on a citizen-legislator basis. The citizens who sought to serve on this basis would probably be largely the rich and the old.

## VOTER-PROOFING

DESPITE their differences, term limits and the proposals offered here have in common the fact that they seek major changes in America's political institutions—in some cases involving an amendment to the Constitution. But of course America's politicians are free to alter the way they behave in the context of the country's existing institutions. They can try to find alternative ways of insulating at least some aspects of policymaking from the intense campaigning and electioneering pressures they are now under.

Short of taking difficult issues out of electoral politics altogether, there are tactics that could be employed. Most of them are out of keeping with the contemporary American preferences for direct democracy, high levels of political participation, and the maximum exposure of all political processes to the public gaze; but that is precisely their strength. Bismarck is reputed to have said that there are two things one should never watch being made: sausages and laws. Both should be judged more by the end result than by the precise circumstances of their manufacture.

One available tactic might be called "the collusion of the elites." There may be occasions on which the great majority of America's politicians, in both the executive and legislative branches, are able to agree that an issue is of such overriding importance to the nation that it must be dealt with at almost any cost; that the politicians involved must therefore be prepared to set aside their ideological and other differences in the interests of finding a workable solution; and that having found

a solution, they must stick together in presenting it to what may well be a disgruntled or even hostile electorate. In order to be successful, the collusion-of-elites tactic requires not only a substantial degree of bipartisanship (or, better still, nonpartisanship) but also unusually small teams of negotiators, complete secrecy (not a single ray of "sunshine" must penetrate the proceedings), and the presentation to Congress and the public of a comprehensive, all-or-nothing, take-it-or-leave-it proposal.

The number of occasions on which politicians will be prepared to set aside their ideological differences and pool their political risks in this fashion will inevitably be small. There were no signs that such a spirit might prevail when President Clinton and the Republican majorities in Congress wrangled over how to cut the budget deficit last winter. But there have been instances of the successful collusion of elites, even in relatively recent times.

One of them occurred in 1983, when representatives of President Reagan and the two party leaderships on Capitol Hill colluded to save the Social Security system, which at that time was in imminent danger of bankruptcy. Paul Light's classic account of the 1983 Social Security reform, *Artful Work* (1985), is in effect a case study of how to conduct collusion-of-elites politics and of the circumstances in which it may succeed. The so-called Gang of Seventeen that was originally put together to hammer out a deal (and was later reduced to a Gang of Nine) excluded all the more-extreme ideologues and met in circumstances of great secrecy, even using, according to one participant, "unmarked limos."

Of the Gang of Seventeen's activities, Light writes,

> The meetings seemed to inaugurate a new form of presidential-congressional government. The meetings were secret. There were no minutes or transcripts. All conversations were strictly off the record. The gang was free to discuss all of the options without fear of political retaliation. It . . . [existed] completely outside of the constitutional system.

Ultimately, as Light relates, the "secret gang built a compromise, wrapped it in a bipartisan flag, and rammed it through Congress. There was no other way to move. It was government by fait accompli." It was also successful government—and none of the participants suffered electoral damage.

Another possible tactic, with many similarities to the collusion of elites, might be called "putting it into commission." If taking tough decisions is too risky politically, then get someone else to take them. If someone else cannot be found to take them, then make someone else *appear* to take them. The someone else need not be but usually will be a bipartisan or nonpartisan commission of some kind.

Such a commission, the National Commission on Social Security Reform, played a role in the passage of the 1983 act, but an even better example was the procedure adopted by Congress in 1990 for closing redundant military bases. Earlier practice had been almost a caricature of Congress's traditional decision-making process. The Secretary of Defense would propose a program of base closures. Senators and congressmen would immediately leap to the defense of targeted bases in their home states or districts. They of course had the support of their colleagues, who were threatened with or feared base closures in *their* home states or districts. Almost never did anyone manage to close any bases.

Realizing that the process was absurd and that huge sums of taxpayers' money were being wasted in keeping redundant bases open, Congress decided to protect itself from itself. It established the Defense Base Closure and Realignment Commission, which employed an extraordinarily simple formula. The Defense Secretary every two years published a list of the bases he proposed to close, together with a statement of criteria he had used in compiling his list. The commission then examined the list in light of the criteria, held public hearings, and recommended a modified list (with additions as well as deletions) to the President. The President was obliged to accept the commission's list as a whole or reject it as a whole. If, as invariably happened, he accepted it, Congress could intervene only if within forty-five legislative days it passed a bill overriding the President's decision and rejecting the whole list. This it never did.

The formula was a near miracle of voter-proofing. Members of Congress were left free to protest the closure of bases in their home districts or states, but the decision was ultimately taken by the President, who could nonetheless ascribe all blame to the commission, and all Congress had to do for the President's decision to take effect was to do nothing. In the event, hundreds of bases were closed and millions of dollars saved, but no member of Congress ever had to vote—and be seen by his constituents to be voting—in favor of closing a base near home. Beyond any question the results were in America's national interest.

It is not wholly fantastic to suppose that the President in odd-numbered years might, on the basis of advice received from a bipartisan commission, announce a list of "program eliminations," which Congress could countermand only by voting to reject the list as a whole. Presidents would probably prefer to put forward such lists at the beginning of their first term in office—or at any time during their second term—when they, at least, were not up for re-election.

A final tactic, which could also be adopted without major institutional change, might be described as "thinking big." Proposals that are put forward on a piecemeal basis can also be opposed, and in all probability defeated, on a piecemeal basis. In contrast, large-scale, broad-based proposals may have a better chance of success simply by virtue of their comprehensiveness. They can provide something for everyone—conservatives as well as liberals, deficit cutters as well as program defenders, residents of the Sun Belt as well as of the Rust Belt. Gains as well as losses can be broadcast widely. The 1983 Social Security reform and the 1986 tax reform were certainly "big thoughts" of this general type. So, in its way, was the recent base-closure program.

Tactics like these—the collusion of elites, putting issues into commission, and thinking big—all have their virtues, but they also suffer from being tactics in the pejorative as well as the descriptive sense. At bottom they are somewhat cynical devices for getting around the real difficulty, which is the hyper- responsiveness of American politicians that is induced by their having to run scared so much of the time. Although it would be harder, it would be better over the long term to confront this problem directly and try to bring about at least some of the fundamental institutional changes proposed here. The American people cannot govern themselves. They therefore need to find appropriate means of choosing representatives who can do a decent job of governing on their behalf, and that means giving the people's representatives space, time, and freedom in which to take decisions, knowing that if they get them wrong, they will be punished by the voters. In twentieth-century America the airy myths of agency democracy are precisely that: myths. What America needs today, though it does not seem to know it, is a more realistic and down-to-earth form of division-of-labor democracy.

# Lost Opportunity Society

### In 1994, Republicans felt they ruled the world.
### What went wrong?

RICHARD LOWRY

L
ATE on the opening day of the 104th Congress, a packed ballroom of Republican revelers at a Washington hotel strained to see Newt Gingrich onstage through the glare of floodlights and over the heads of fellow partygoers. It was as close to the feeling of a mosh pit as you will experience at a Beltway event, charged with the elation of partisan victory and sheer adulation for this man, Speaker Newt—the Moses, the Solon, the Tony Robbins of House Republicans.

The crowd probably would have charged off a cliff like the Gadarene swine for Gingrich. But soon enough he had them bored. He was holding up into the lights a tiny lapel pin. He was talking—at great length—of the "Earning through Learning" program, a scheme to pay poor children for reading books. In front of an audience so fawningly sympathetic, Gingrich had managed to hit a long, idiosyncratic false note.

It was pure Newt Gingrich. In that moment, it was possible to catch the essence of all the Gingrich missteps to come, from the book deal to his complaint about having to exit through the back of Air Force One. There in the ballroom, as during the Gingrich gaffes to follow, it seemed ungrateful to complain: after all, everyone was present for one reason—Newt. But it didn't lessen the nagging sense of lost opportunity that now, four years later, seems an indelible part of his legacy.

Any evaluation of Gingrich must take account of the qualities Midge Decter writes about below ["Comeback Kid?"]: the intelligence, the optimism, the energy that animated his drive to power and his Speakership. It should also go without saying that historic accomplish-

ments—a GOP House majority, welfare reform, a balanced budget—would have been impossible without him. But since 1994 much has gone wrong for Gingrich and the Republicans, and it is from the mistakes of the Gingrich Majority that Republicans have the most to learn.

After the 1994 election, Republicans rode into Congress on a wave of thoughtless anti-institutionalism. They tried to remake Congress according to populist slogans, rendering it harder for them to run the place. Rather than comfortably reap the staff resources of majority status, they imposed strictures on themselves that would lead to a majority run—in the words of one Hill veteran—by "25-year-old press secretaries." This would put the GOP at a disadvantage when waging high-stakes budget battles with the executive branch. Republicans also promised to hold all debates under "open rules," allowing unrestricted debate on the floor (a promise sensibly and quickly abandoned), and eliminated the convenient "proxy voting" that had made it possible for members to vote in committee even if not present.

Meanwhile, Gingrich centralized power in the Speaker's office, sucking authority from the traditional power centers of the committee chairmen. It seemed the best way to avoid the frustrations of working with the Old Bulls, but also made decision-making too dependent on one man. Still, it was a "revolution." All revolutions have their irrational enthusiasms—and in this one it was passing the "Contract with America" in one hundred days. A spasm of legislative activity was necessary to fulfill this campaign promise, and Republicans ran them-

# Comeback Kid?

The November 16th *Time* magazine cover photo of Newt Gingrich—clearly produced in the first moments after he announced his resignation—is a portrait of someone both very somber and very sad. Now, Newt is by nature and habit neither of those things, neither sad nor somber, and looking at that picture I thought, "So, after all that pummeling, four years of it, night and day without letup and from all sides—from your so-called friends as well as your enemies—you have finally been brought to your knees. Welcome to the human race."

I have known other people who have taken a lot of punishment for the innocent brashness of their ambitions, but I have never seen anyone take what had been so relentlessly dished out to Newt not long before I first made his acquaintance: an enormously expensive campaign of nasty TV commercials, unprecedented in an off-election year, accompanied by the only too predictable game of Gotcha from the press; a series of Mickey Mouse ethics charges intended by the Democrats in the House to bedevil and distract him, and finally levying from him the sum of $300,000 as a repayment for the expense incurred by Congress in pursuing him. Nor had he through all this been lacking in Job's comforters in the conservative community to instruct him in the many different ways he had brought it all upon himself, forgetting that it was his strength for which he was being punished and not his weakness (weakness being something that members of Congress were by tradition only too willing to forgive in one another).

In any case, when I met him, I assumed he would be reeling at least a little from all these assaults—topped off by an attempt on his Speakership

*Miss Decter is an author and social critic whose work has appeared previously in* National Review.

secretly organized by some of the very young Turks for whose presence in Congress he had been so largely responsible. A normal man, I thought, even one long conditioned to the ways of Washington, would at the very least be showing signs of some emotional fatigue. But fatigued, or even just a little off his stride, was the last thing you would have said Newt was. On the contrary, he was cheerfully off on one of his favorite jaunts, i.e., sitting at the kitchen table, word processor at the ready, writing a book. Only hunting dinosaur fossils, it seems, answers more immediately to his thirst for adventure.

Newt writes the way he does most things: speedily, and at full gallop from morning to night. Indeed, Newt at the word processor is a sight to chill the blood of many an author (very much including this one), for he writes as he speaks from the platform, without hesitation and without preening, and hence as fast as his fingers will take him. No doubt he digs for fossils in exactly the same way—and finds them, too, I would bet.

The only other person I have ever met who was quite so exhausting to contemplate was Lyndon Johnson. To be in Johnson's company was like trying to keep on one's feet in a gale-force wind, and so in some sense is the experience of spending time with Newt. The difference is that Johnson's energy was in no small part laced with malignity—as if he were in a constant rage for power and attention—while Newt's is just cheerfully there, bouncing off the walls and demanding little of those present except not to get in the way.

He was also embarked on a project inconceivable not only for Lyndon Johnson but for any other politician in the land: he was writing a book to explain, perhaps to himself as much as to the reader, the various ways in which he had screwed up as Speaker and the lessons he had learned from

doing it. (My own role in helping him in this extraordinary exercise was merely, as an outsider to the ways of Washington, to require that he explain all the details of his story so that any ordinary reader could understand exactly what was going on—a demand he cheerfully answered to).

Moreover, for Newt—again, as for no one else I have ever known—the entire project of confessing error seemed to be a perfectly cheerful undertaking. Indeed, "cheerful" is a rather pale term with which to describe his temper, not because he is any kind of avatar for perfect happiness but because he is a man forever given to looking at, or for, something up ahead. Newt's wife Marianne has said of him that he is like a little boy who gets out of bed every morning expecting to find a plateful of cookies.

In the case of his book, of course, the plateful of cookies he was looking for was a public understanding of what he had been about and what he had been through. But, at least in the oh-so-narrow precincts of Washington, what he sought would not be much in evidence. To put it mildly.

Then in 1998 the question for the Republicans was whether to try to make a deal with Clinton or to try to destroy him. Newt, ever high of heart, tried both and failed at both: the conservatives were against the deal, and the ordinary voters seemed to want no part of any presidential upheaval. So his colleagues and associates laid the full blame for what they felt to be a historic failure upon the back of an all too willing Newt, and fancied that they were sending him out to the wilderness where scapegoats are left to wander.

If I were they, however, I wouldn't be too sure. The efforts to do him down finally paid off, but for how long? Never count yourself rid of an energetic and truly cheerful man.

—MIDGE DECTER

selves into the ground. By the end of the one hundred days, many GOP staffers had literally fallen ill.

And for what? Much of the one hundred-day agenda fell victim to the Senate. But much of it also fell on deaf ears because people don't care about process—about new ethics rules, or staff reductions, or the line-item veto, or even whether an agenda is passed in one hundred

days instead of three hundred. (This is a lesson that Democrats are still learning with campaign-finance reform.) After the frenetic one hundred days—the toughest battle for the party was still ahead.

In the Contract, there was a small deception that in the hothouse of hubris after the 1994 election would grow to overshadow all else: the Balanced Budget

Amendment was said to cost nothing, zero, zilch. Technically, of course, that's right: it doesn't cost anything to pass the amendment. But it does cost something to balance the budget. When Gingrich gathered a small circle of top Republicans together and convinced them to try to eliminate the deficit even after the amendment had failed, that "zero" in the Contract suddenly became a figure in the hundreds of billions of dollars.

## DISHONESTY

Where to go for the money? Instead of talking about tax cuts and "growing our way out of the deficit," Republicans targeted the entitlements, specifically Medicare. During the 1994 campaign, in response to Democratic attacks, Republicans disavowed any intention to touch Medicare. Then, just a few months later, there they were, proposing a major overhaul of the system. During and after the Medicare battle, there would be Republican complaints about the dishonesty of the White House attacks on the GOP Medicare plan. But the real problem was that the White House dishonesty was more believable than the Republican dishonesty.

Republicans had promised to leave Medicare untouched, then did the opposite. They professed only an intention to "save" the program, a touching concern they had never manifested before. And they said the Medicare plan had nothing to do with balancing the budget when, in reality, that was its sole rationale. Surveying this scene at the time, GOP pollster Frank Luntz told one group of conservative activists that, if they did everything exactly right in the Medicare debate, Republicans had a 50–50 chance of *surviving*.

A party that undertakes such a gamble is responding to something other than reality. In the Medicare fight, Republicans mislearned a lesson from the White House, and from their own success with the Contract: that spin and marketing are everything. They aren't. Word choice is important, but it doesn't change reality. Republicans tried mightily to get reporters to say "slowing the rate of growth" instead of "cutting" Medicare, but the fact was that they were still shrinking a popular middle-class program for reasons they weren't willing to own up to.

But if the way Republicans tried to sell their Medicare plan was too cynical, their plan itself was too responsible. Republicans had fallen under the ahistorical delusion that they could govern from Capitol Hill. But the American system has never worked that way. Presidents, not Congresses, strive to pass one hundred-day plans. Gingrich didn't understand that he was elected Speaker rather than Prime Minister (in the early days, he even gave a State of the Union-like prime-time address). The model for his leadership should instead have been Democratic Senate Majority Leader George Mitchell, who worried more about ushering George Bush out of office than about passing legislation.

The Republican drive on Medicare dovetailed into the fateful government shutdowns. A strategic disaster on a par with the Maginot Line, the shutdowns helped create the image of the Republican Party and of Gingrich—harsh and reckless—that clings to them today. Even as Republicans were miscalculating how to bring Clinton to his knees, the President was making a strategic retreat. Rush Limbaugh at the time was playing a hilarious tape showing Clinton reciting an ever-changing number of years—10, 9, 8, 6—for when the budget could be balanced. Republicans assumed these were the risible meanderings of an irrelevant President, when they were really the sound of Clinton finally getting it right.

## Gingrich didn't understand that he was elected Speaker rather than Prime Minister.

What Clinton was slowly concluding is something that Milton Friedman has long maintained: that the size of the budget deficit has nothing whatsoever to do with the size or the nature of the Federal Government. When the shutdowns came, Clinton was ready to accede to what Republicans thought the principle at issue: a seven-year balanced budget. Clinton realized the balanced budget wasn't a matter of principle but of packaging, and—given a steady revenue stream—he could comfortably fit all of his cherished spending inside.

This was a Dick Morris insight, as was the Administration's pivot on cultural issues. In some ways, the White House understood the cultural nature of the Republican victory in 1994 better than Republicans. The line Newt Gingrich repeated most often in the 1994 campaign was, "American civilization cannot survive with 12-year-olds having babies, 15-year-olds shooting one another, 17-year-olds dying of AIDS, and 18-year-olds graduating with diplomas they cannot read." It was a *cultural* indictment, and an implicit rebuke of the nation's ruling elite for not sharing the common-sense values of the rest of the country.

Indeed, in the summer of 1994, Gingrich had won a crucial victory on the GOP's most reliable social issue: crime. He condemned the Administration's crime bill as soft and full of pork and when he defeated the "rule" on the bill on the House floor, he had fired the first shot of the "revolution."

But by early 1996, the White House was saying, Never again. It would run the 1996 campaign from an unassailably centrist position on values issues. Clinton won the endorsement of the Fraternal Order of Police. He endorsed the V-chip and school uniforms, and even bragged of signing the Defense of Marriage Act. Republicans either dismissed these positions as too minor to trouble with or hailed them as their own victories, as still more evidence that history was moving inexorably right, into the Speaker's hip pocket. But, like Clinton's new position on the balanced budget, this repositioning was just a redeployment to more secure ground.

While Clinton dug in, the shutdowns had a devastating psychological effect on Republicans. They couldn't understand how they had failed to march smoothly to victory, let alone how the whole strategy had turned into a rout. Thereafter they would conduct themselves like a blind man in a room where all the furniture has unexpectedly been moved—timid, confused, afraid to take a step lest there be another object to stumble over. This defensiveness would keep Republicans from doing anything bold or creative to counteract the emerging Clinton comeback strategy.

## JUST THE GOOD STUFF

No longer colored by its cultural counterpart—or the red ink of the deficit—Clinton's traditional fiscal liberalism suddenly took on a more attractive glow. The White House could concentrate on just the good stuff, the popular spending programs, the "education, environment, Medicare, and Medicaid" mantra. This spending in itself was sold in terms of values, of "caring," of "the children"—and with the fight over the deficit resolved, Republican opposition seemed less "prudent" and more "mean-spirited."

Meanwhile, increasingly fortified from the usual GOP attacks, the Democrats could turn a traditional GOP wedge issue to their own advantage: crime. Democrats endorsed the death penalty and made an issue of hiring more cops. Then they turned an issue that in the past had seemed a piece of goo-goo naïveté—gun control—into a crime-control issue. Republicans played along by quixotically voting to repeal the assault-weapons ban in the House. Democrats could argue—as they did at their 1996 Chicago convention, with plenty of crime victims as props—that they were just as tough on crime as Republicans, except *they* didn't want Uzis in the hands of gang members.

Democrats also instinctively turned to a different kind of cultural liberalism. The liberalism of "acid, amnesty, and abortion"—the liberalism of license—was out; the liberalism of inclusion and niceness—the liberalism of tolerance—was in. This hits much closer to today's American mainstream and made it possible for Democrats, for a change, to call Republicans "extremists" and have the charge stick (the very act of saying "no" to certain programs, of making firm moral distinctions on issues like abortion, marked Republicans as dangerously "judgmental"). It had seemed that Clinton's affair with Monica Lewinsky might be a reminder of the old kind of cultural liberalism, but, instead, it fit right in with the new (the very act of judging the President made Republicans suspect).

So, Democrats had regained their arguments on spending, found wedge issues of their own, and even discovered a way to marginalize Republicans culturally. But oftentimes in politics, it takes a personality to crystallize a given set of positions—a Michael Dukakis wearing a tank helmet. In Newt Gingrich, relentlessly attacked by the press and by mindless Democratic partisans, Democrats found their persona.

Gingrich suffers from a politician's curse of not being able to seem sincere when he fakes a smile. He is given to harsh-sounding statements, and his tone can sometimes be hectoring. None of this makes him "mean-spirited" or in any way speaks to the nature of his intentions. Yet the Democrats made his name an epithet, and even if this didn't directly sway a single voter, it helped poison the general atmosphere, as Gingrich came to stand for all that was wrong in the Republicans' opposition to spending, the assault-weapons ban, the President, and so on.

In the end, Gingrich wasn't particularly popular with his own colleagues, either. He had consolidated power in the Speaker's office, but also became increasingly isolated there, alienating his colleagues in the leadership, and letting his lack of discipline have free rein. When the November 1998 revolt against Gingrich began in earnest, it had about it an aspect of a reassertion of the *institution* against his aggrandizement. Bob Livingston's quasi-campaign manifesto, a letter to Gingrich, was a brief for giving him more control over his Appropriations Committee—a committee chairman's revenge.

So, 1998 was a world apart from 1994. The lessons of the centrist Clinton campaign in 1992, unlearned in 1993–94, Democrats had recovered, and then some. Gingrich the partisan attacker had seen his targets disappear and himself made the symbol of his own party's vulnerabilities. A changed world indeed. No wonder in a conference call with other Republican leaders after the November election Gingrich confessed to having no idea what to do next. Well, if it's any consolation, Mr. Gingrich, at the moment it's not clear that anyone else in the party does either.

# Democracy v. Dollar

PAUL STARR

Democracy, many people have said, is a matter of faith, but why, dear Lord, must our faith be tested so often? Lately, the role of money in political campaigns has been mocking our civic creed. "Here the people rule," we are taught, and we would like to think so. But if voters (and nonvoters) seem disbelieving, they may merely be acquainted with the material facts of political life. Congressional candidates in this last election cycle raised $1.3 billion, which is a lot of money to change hands with pure intentions. Fiorello La Guardia, New York's reform mayor of the 1930s and '40s, once said that politics requires "supreme ingratitude." That's just the problem. Among those who run for office, ingratitude may not be common enough.

In many respects, the United States is positively fastidious about the influence of money on public officials. Federal employees cannot legally accept even trivial gifts from the public. They risk prosecution if they allow someone to pay for a meal or serve them food that costs more than $20 in the course of a year. During my brief sojourn in government four years ago, I had to listen to a hermeneutic discussion of the donuts-and-coffee exception to this rule (is a bagel a "donut" for purposes of federal law if not in the eyes of cream cheese?). Yet candidates are expected to raise large sums from private contributors, all the while pretending that their constant hunt for money does not influence their views of policy. We might as well make hypocrisy a formal requirement for elected office.

The scandals that have filled the newspapers and airwaves this past year are not just symptoms of the deeper problem; they are also a distraction from it. What a simple issue this would be if the malady could be cured by ensuring that money raised for tax-exempt purposes was kept from partisan political use and that no money came from foreign sources. Of course, those who break the law must be brought to full account. But the real scandal, in Michael Kinsley's aphorism, is what's legal—indeed, what's inevitable under pressures of political competition. And the real story is what hasn't been news: the triumph of money in the 1996 election and the increased financial asymmetry between the parties.

## A MAJORITY OF THE MONEY

Recent reports from the Center for Responsive Politics and Citizen Action on the role of fundraising in the fall election describe a world that does not exactly correspond to our cherished image of popular sovereignty. In House races, the candidate who raised the most money won 92 percent of the time; in Senate races, 88 percent. In effect, we held two elections: the first, a competition for dollars; the second, for votes. Those who won a majority of the money were overwhelmingly likely to win a majority of the votes. To be sure, causation often runs the other way: Likely winners attract contributors. Thus the preponderance of money among the winners does not prove that money made the difference. But even in races that independent analysts rated toss-ups before election day, money was overwhelmingly correlated with victory. And in financial terms, many elections weren't remotely competitive. The fundraising winners often enjoyed so overwhelming an advantage—40 percent of House incumbents outspent their opponents at least ten to one—that the popular election was little more than a charade.

A seat in Congress does not yet carry tenure, but it comes close. According to the Citizen Action report, in the races for the House, only 19 challengers (5 percent) were able to raise more money than incumbents in the 381 districts where incumbents ran. In these 19 races, 8 challengers won, a success rate of 42 percent; but in the remaining 362 races, only 13 challengers won, a success rate of only 4 percent. Thus a challenger who lost the "money" election, as 95 percent did, had slim chance of prevailing in the people's election. This was scarcely surprising since winning incumbents raised an average of $761,000, 3 times the average of $221,000 raised by their opponents. It took an average of over a million dollars to beat an incumbent. Raising that much money is so daunting a task for most potential challengers that the possibility of competitive elections has been effectively nullified in the majority of districts.

In this column in our last issue, I noted that the total national vote for Republican and Democratic candidates for the House in 1996 was almost even, but that Republicans retained a majority in the House because of the way in which votes were distributed. The Republicans won the great majority of tight races, while votes for Democrats were clustered in districts that they won by lopsided margins.* Now that we have the data on campaign spending, the explanation for the Republican success in tight races seems less ambiguous. Here, for example, are three key findings from the Citizen Action report:

- In the 60 congressional seats (41 of them previously held by Republicans) that the Cook Political Report rated "toss-ups" before the election, Republican candidates had an average of 42 percent more money to spend, raising an average of over $1 million per district. Democrats were able to win back only 12 of the Republican seats.
- Republican freshmen defending their seats in 1996 spent almost twice as much as their Democratic challengers.
- In the ten closest races won by Republicans, they held a 56 percent spending advantage.

Before 1994, contributions from political action committees (PACs) were split roughly in half between the two major parties, as congressional Democrats used the advantages of incumbency to offset the affinity of business for Republicans. But after Republicans took over Congress, they garnered two-thirds of PAC contributions. The old balance, never

---

*In reporting preliminary data from the political scientist Martin Wattenberg, I described his criterion for close races as those decided by 2 percentage points or less. In fact, Wattenberg classified as close any race where the winner had 52 percent or less of the *two-party* vote. There were 32 of these races, and Republicans won 23 of them.

ideal since it depended on Democratic incumbency, has disappeared in congressional elections (although it remains at the presidential level because of public funding). The question now is whether reform can not only reduce the power of money, but also bring about a new and more equitable balance between the parties.

## FROM THE BOTTOM UP

Campaign finance reform is the precondition for progress on many other fronts, as environmental and other progressive organizations have increasingly recognized. But in no other area is the path to reform so treacherous. Popular disgust with the present system may someday kindle a political firestorm. The immediate reality, however, is that the forces of reform confront not just the power of money, but also the entrenched self-interest of incumbents in blocking any legislation that lessens their chances of re-election. As if that were not discouraging enough, any reform measures also have to overcome or sidestep the obstacles created by the Supreme Court's decisions in *Buckley v. Valeo* and *Colorado Republicans v. FEC*, which have effectively made it impossible to limit campaign spending by barring any restrictions on "independent" expenditures—even, amazingly enough, by a candidate's own political party.

Moreover, the movement for reform is badly divided and seems likely to dissipate much of its energy in misguided initiatives. Some, for example, are campaigning for a constitutional amendment to undo the Supreme Court's precedents and permit Congress to limit expenditures on political campaigns—a dangerous measure that would invite future restrictions of political speech through overbroad interpretation. If Congress has the authority to limit spending, it may set such low limits that challengers cannot spend enough to become as well known as incumbents. Considering the history of incumbent self-protection, this hardly seems a hypothetical danger.

Other groups, such as Common Cause, want to pass the McCain-Feingold bill, which would eliminate PACs and offer candidates half-price TV advertising time in exchange for voluntary limits on spending and out-of-state contributions. But McCain-Feingold offers no public financing and would force candidates to devote just as much time and energy to fundraising as they do today (except that money would at least nominally have to come from individuals). Much business-related money already comes in the form of individual contributions; business would still be able to use corporate communications to drum up support for political candidates and to elicit contributions from employees concerned about pay and promotions. It's labor that most needs PACs to aggregate small individual contributions. The premise of McCain-Feingold is that individuals should contribute to political campaigns but groups should not—a departure from the basic premise of political pluralism that people should be able to organize as groups to participate in public life. Most likely, however, the whole effort would be pointless: If McCain-Feingold is passed, money will cut a channel right around it.

Since the election, many editorial pages have called on Congress to reform campaign finance, as if the majority were likely to pass a proposal that would give their opponents a better chance to defeat them. Speaker Gingrich has already said that he thinks electoral politics is underfunded and that limits on contributions should be eliminated; last year conservatives were making noises about eliminating public funds for presidential campaigns. If conservatives enact a broad campaign finance measure, they may well use it to take revenge on the AFL-CIO and create a new legal framework that is even more biased in their own favor.

If there is one proposal that might achieve bipartisan support and do some good, it's the idea of free or low-cost TV airtime. Like most people, politicians of both parties might agree that they deserve lower prices. Campaign finance has become a bigger problem today in large measure because of the escalating cost of television advertising. If we could cheapen the cost of campaigns, we could at least get the problem back to a smaller scale. Paul Taylor, a former *Washington Post* reporter, has formulated a proposal for a "broadcast time bank," which would provide candidates and parties with vouchers for airtime, financed by fees on broadcasters. This is public

financing by other means and extends the one successful precedent we have—public funding of presidential campaigns.

In Taylor's proposal, however, the fees that finance vouchers would come from a surcharge on other political advertisements sold at prevailing rates, raising their cost by 50 percent. Taxing independent campaigns at that rate would discourage them, which might seem like a good idea. But it would create a dangerous precedent for discriminatory taxation of political speech that could be used to suppress dissenting opinion. Still, the basic concept of the broadcast time bank is sound.

> Campaign finance reform shouldn't become a backdoor to even stronger incumbent protection.

But the chances of genuine reform passing this Congress are probably about as great as the proverbial camel passing through the eye of a needle. The more promising road to change is the difficult one that Ellen S. Miller described in our last issue ["Clean Elections, How To," January–February 1997]: the development of a grassroots movement in the states, focused on building support for the so-called Clean Money Option recently adopted by popular initiative in Money calls for full public financing of election campaigns. Like the existing system for financing presidential campaigns, it is voluntary for the candidates but once accepted includes spending limits. And rather than banning independent expenditures (which would be overturned by the courts), the Clean Money approach calls for matching public funds for a candidate whose opponent benefits from an independent campaign. The great virtue of Clean Money is that it frees candidates from the demeaning business of raising money, turns their attention back from contributors to constituents, and sufficiently equalizes political resources to encourage people without big financial backers to run for office. The only hope for such a solution is building from the bottom up.

### BREAKING THE POWER OF INCUMBENCY

But there is one further option that reformers need to consider: limiting congressional terms. Popular support for term limits reflects the fundamentally correct judgment that incumbents can too easily consolidate their positions and stifle change—for example, on campaign finance. Representatives who knew that their future as incumbents was limited might be more receptive to reforms that reduced the cost of campaigns and equalized resources.

Seven years ago in these pages ["Can Government Work?" Summer 1990], I wrote in support of term limits for House members only, arguing, "When the control of the House at some point in the future shifts to the Republicans—as it must someday—the Democrats will find themselves as locked out as the Republicans are today. Indeed, the Republicans would then add to their fund-raising edge all the advantages of incumbency that now redound to the Democrats." I suggested that term limits apply to the House but not the Senate in line with the Founders' vision of the House as the branch more responsive to changing public sentiment (although House-only term limits would indirectly spur greater competition for the Senate by denying House members the safe option of keeping their seats).

While proposals for term limits have come mainly from the right, there is no necessary relation between term limits and partisan interests. Some Democrats fear that in view of Republican financial advantages, they would lose a disproportionate number of open seats, but the main evidence for this concern comes from the South, where the partisan realignment has nearly run its course. Despite originally being introduced with conservative support, term limits this year were the key to Democrats' success in recapturing the California Assembly and Maine Senate.

In the form they are currently being proposed for Congress—lifetime limits of 6 or 12 years on service in the House and 12 in the Senate—term limits would too sharply restrict the accumulation of legislative experience. We need a middle ground that limits incumbency but does not preclude the election of experienced legislators. The answer, I suggest, lies in limiting the number of consecutive terms in the House while allowing for re-election after a "time out." A limit of four consecutive terms would significantly increase the number of open seats in any election year and make House elections far more competitive. Some former representatives could retake their seats—and many would, though perhaps only after beating new incumbents under more equal conditions.

If supporters of term limits want congressional approval, they will need support from the center and left. (As I write in late January, term limits are expected to come up for a vote and quick defeat in Congress.) A more modest, House-only limit on consecutive terms ought to be the basis of a compromise and acceptable to those of us who are generally allergic to constitutional amendments.

The system needs shaking up. A broadcast time bank, Clean Money, and limits on consecutive terms in the House would help revitalize the democratic ideas we claim to believe in. Such reforms might enable us to tell our children that ours is indeed a government of the people without the nagging sense that we are only repeating a useful fiction in the hope that it will some day come true.

# CAMPAIGN FINANCING: FOUR VIEWS

## Michael Walzer

All political systems are subject to corruption, but not to the same kind of corruption. The corruptions of American democracy are determined by two things: the radically unequal distribution of wealth in our society and the private financing of political campaigns. We can deal with corruption, then, in two different ways: by radically reducing the inequality and tolerating the private financing or by tolerating the inequality and banning the political use of private money.

I have always preferred the first of these options, a preference that derives in part from my experience of left politics, where we are continually raising money from friends and comrades and judging the strength of their commitment by their readiness to contribute to the cause. We also ask for time and energy, but working people, especially working people with children, don't always have time and energy to spare. A little bit of money ties them to us: it is a sign and a bond.

The case is the same in politics more generally. Time, energy, and money are signs of intensity; they are the media with which we signal to our fellow citizens that this issue or candidate or party means a lot to us, more than a mere vote can indicate. However strongly we feel, we can only "spend" one vote, but we can divide our time, apportion our energy, contribute our money in differentiated ways, which reflect our precise judgments of importance and value. A democratic system ought to be able to register these different judgments, and that requires that just as voting is a private and individual matter, so should contributions be private and individual.

But this will only work as an antidote to corruption if resources are more or less equally distributed among individuals. And that is a fantasy in America today. So the alternative, which is at least a little less fantastic, is public funding of all political campaigns. I think of this as a second-best option because it reduces the possibilities for political participation. The more the state is involved, the less people are likely to act on their own. Even contributions of time and energy will drop, since one of the main activities that require such contributions is fund-raising. Think of the endless parties, benefits, bake sales, raffles, mass mailings, telephone marathons through which money is raised for politics (as for religious institutions, charities, and so on). This is participatory financing, and of course it is eclipsed when the very rich buy themselves a senator (or a president). But won't it also be eclipsed when the state funds everyone's campaign?

But of those last two possible campaign funders, the very rich or the democratic state, we have to choose the second. The courting of the very rich by democratic politicians is obscene (and the obscenity is worse when the politicians are Democrats, because Democrats—no doubt this is a myth but it has sometimes been a useful myth—are supposed to represent the rest of us). So this is a courtship we should ban, even if there are sure to be illicit liaisons: money passed, promises made in the dark. I would only suggest that the public funding not be lavish and that television time, especially, be limited by law. Then parties and candidates will still be forced to mobilize their followers to do something more than vote. They will need people to walk the streets and knock on doors, to organize meetings, distribute leaflets. It's an old-fashioned vision;

I also favor parades and bonfires. The citizens of a democracy should not be allowed to content themselves with the simple act of voting.

We need to avoid the kind of state involvement in political campaigns that reduces corruption by reducing activity and engagement.

## Joanne Barkan

Democratic politics in my version of utopia looks different from Michael Walzer's version in at least one way. When thousands of energetic citizens take part in a presidential or congressional campaign, they might help organize a rally, update a web site, pass out leaflets, or clean up headquarters, but they would not get on the phone to ask for money. Public funds would pay for political campaigns. The contests would be blissfully short, intense, and economically efficient. Television stations would "donate" air time for serious debate. Democracy—including the grassroots participatory kind—would be better off.

Of course, former fat-cat power brokers would miss private fund-raising; they would no longer be able to buy candidates and shape government policies. That's the purpose of public financing. But Michael Walzer says he, too, would miss private fund-raising. He believes grassroots involvement would decline and citizens would lose an important way of indicating the intensity of their support. In his ideal world, he would like to see resources "more or less equally distributed among individuals" and privately funded campaigns.

I don't understand why Walzer sets up the solution to the corruption of American democracy as an either/or proposition: "We can deal with corruption . . . by radically reducing the inequality and tolerating the private financing or by tolerating the inequality and banning the political use of private money." A decent American democracy clearly needs both to reduce inequality and get the private money out of elections. The two go together because a society that remains free and democratic will never achieve a distribution of wealth so equal and so stable as to make the political use of private money unproblematic.

Leftists of the democratic type share a basic definition of the good society: true equality of opportunity. This presupposes equal access to quality health care, education, affordable housing, jobs, pensions, safety-net programs, a clean environment, and so on. Such a profoundly radical vision assumes a commensurately radical redistribution of wealth and restructuring of the economy.

All the while, people in a true democracy are free to make choices: some will be more interested in earning money than others; some will love running a business, others will want to make art; some will be inclined to save their pennies, others won't; some will succeed in their endeavors, others will fail. A progressive tax system and a strong public sector prevent inequalities from increasing to anything even remotely resembling the indecent levels we have today. Moreover, sharp disparities in wealth won't be passed on from generation to generation. Yet enough inequality will remain to corrupt the political process if campaigns are privately funded.

Barred from fund-raising, will citizens languish at home during campaigns, suffocated by a behemoth state which forbids bake sales? Will grassroots participation dwindle? I think not for several reasons:

First, among the myriad activities that make up a campaign, fund-raising is not one of the most enriching in a political sense. This is especially significant if—as Walzer argues—activists spend much of their time and energy raising money. Wouldn't democracy benefit if that time and energy went into analyzing, publicizing, and arguing substantive issues? An hour is better spent defending your candidate's environmental policy than trying to please potential contributors enough to get a few checks. A campaign that organizes five admission-free debates might reach many more citizens than a campaign that turns three of those events into fund-raisers.

Second, once money is no longer a variable in a campaign, other kinds of grassroots activities become crucial. Each candidate has the same funds, so whoever mobilizes more people to put up posters, ring doorbells, and stuff envelopes has an advantage. Finally, who really wants to do grassroots fund-raising anyway? Most folks hate it; many refuse to do it. Campaigns that never ask recruits to make the money pitch might attract more volunteers.

Walzer worries about the people who have no time or energy to work in a campaign. How do they show their strong support beyond a "mere vote"? Many will certainly find themselves with more time or energy during subsequent campaigns. Happily they will live to leaflet another day. Those who are chronically indisposed or unlikely to survive until the next election could at least put in a good word for their candidate to family members and friends. They could also send their checks to an issue organization or charity whose work is compatible with their candidate's views. In the end, I think the benefits of public funding will far outweigh the liabilities.

Moving from utopia to real-time America, Walzer admits that public financing of political campaigns is less of a fantasy than a more equal distribution of wealth. So he supports public funding as a second-best alternative. I believe that all the arguments in favor of public financing in an ideal world make it the best alternative now, too.

Yet even the best alternative brings up both technical questions and an immense political problem. We still have to devise a fair way to distribute public funds and television and ra-

dio time among candidates. Not all the people who declare themselves candidates can, or should, get money and media access. What kind of winnowing process will work best? If Congress enacts a new federal campaign law, how will it survive scrutiny by a Supreme Court that equates money spent and free speech? I think we will eventually need to amend the Constitution to allow government to cut off private campaign funds.

The goal is not impossible. A broad grassroots coalition that included labor unions, environmentalists, and some businesses put a referendum in favor of public funding for campaigns on the ballot in Maine in November 1996. The measure passed with a twelve-point margin. Legislation limiting private funds is making headway in sixteen other states. This nationwide reform effort deserves the left's time, energy, and even enthusiasm. The moment has come for bonfires and parades

---

## Michael Merrill

**T**here are three serious flaws in all the current proposals for campaign finance reform. First, none of them will redress the growing crisis of political representation that leaves most poor and working Americans without an adequate voice in the country's governance. Second, many of them include restrictions on how people can participate in the political system—restrictions that undermine the democracy they are supposedly designed to help save. And, finally, they all require the assent of Congress, or some other group of sitting politicians who, among all the people in the nation, have the least interest in changing the system.

The crisis of political representation is the cumulative effect of many factors. The corrupting influence of money on the political process has a part to play, but it is by no means the lead. After all, corruption has been a persistent concern to democrats since the beginning of the republic and yet for the most part each generation has somehow managed to muddle its way forward to a more democratic and more inclusive political system. Today's crisis of representation runs deeper than money.

First, the continuing growth of the population and of the scale of government has increased the required span of political representation to the point of overload—the ratio of voters to elected representatives in the United States is among the highest in the

world. There is no way that U.S. elected officials can attend to the concerns of everyone they are supposed to represent. Naturally enough, the politicians represent the interests they know, and those excluded from the informal mechanisms that determine who gets listened to rightly feel betrayed and abandoned.

Second, most Americans are still not equal before the law. Wage earners, for example, are routinely denied rights to freedom of association and free speech on the job that wealth holders take for granted. The fact that most of the money in politics comes from wealth holders and not from wage earners helps to explain why this inequality persists, but it is not the only nor even the most important explanation. Restricting the flow of political contributions or financing political campaigns with tax dollars will not ensure wage earners the equal protection of the law.

Finally, the rise of broadcast campaigning and celebrity politics has broken the institutional ties that once bound candidates to constituents in the established mass parties. Historically, political parties have depended on their grassroots membership to get out the vote much more than they do now. Elected officials and party leaders had to be much more directly responsive to the felt needs and interests of that membership. Money was still important. But there was no effective way to appeal over the heads of precinct leaders to the voters themselves. Local party structures helped ordinary Americans feel much more connected to the political system than all the focus groups, talk shows, and town meetings now do—even though it may be the case that modern methods of polling give party leaders a much more nuanced view of public opinion.

Most voters now feel like little more than consumers in a political marketplace, and consumer sovereignty is a feeble lever where the range of goods over which it is exercised is limited. The economy accommodates this weakness by elaborating niches where consumers can express their preferences regardless of what everyone else is doing. But the structure of political representation and choice in the United States presents voters with a very limited range of options that leaves them feeling powerless and unrepresented.

None of the proposals for campaign finance reform addresses any of these problems. They will not alter the structure of representation, ensure equality before the law, or change the balance of power between incumbent politicians and the electorate. So what to do? Changing the way campaigns are financed is neither sufficient nor even, most likely, necessary. What we need are fairer, more open, and more freewheeling political campaigns—ways of ensuring a larger measure of public discussion and genuine political debate—without having to depend upon the incumbents themselves to give it to us.

There are hopeful signs. The print media do a pretty good job of informing the active reading public and encouraging genuine political debate. And even the broadcast media are getting better at providing the public with what they need to know. During the last campaign, television, radio, and on-line services offered access to a wide range of information about the various candidates and their positions. Too much of this information, however, was produced by the candidates themselves—or their consultants—and was, to say the least, self-serving. Most journalists, perhaps for obvious reasons, still preferred to act as if the campaign were something separate from themselves—something they simply needed to report rather than something they had to produce. Fortunately or unfortunately, this is simply no longer the case—as the 1996 Republican and Democratic conventions both revealed. From the run-up to the first primaries to the wind-down before election day, the last presidential campaign was little more than a series of stage-managed photo opportunities

intended to present the candidates talking to the right kinds of people against the most telling backgrounds.

Campaign finance reform won't change the way the politicians conduct their campaigns. It will only change who pays for them. To change the way campaigns are conducted we have to put someone else in charge of producing them. We don't need to take either money or the special interests out of politics. We need to get citizens and the public interest back in it again. The way to do that is for the grant-givers, reformers, pundits, and ex-office holders who claim to care about such things to put their energies and resources where their mouth is and create a nonprofit educational corporation—let's call it "The Real Campaign 2000"—that would immediately set about organizing the events of the next campaign to ensure the most open, the most free-ranging, the most probing discussion possible of all the candidates and issues. Raise the money. (All contributions would be tax deductible). Get the airtime. (The networks might even be convinced to make airtime available at bargain basement rates in return for a greater role in deciding the content of the actual programming.) Start the discussion. (We don't have to wait for congressional approval.) If the media buy is large enough, the candidates will participate, if only to secure the free publicity or to forestall their opponents from getting a leg up on them.

In effect, Real Campaign 2000 would function as the party of all parties, the guarantor of the electoral process as a whole, a new informal fourth branch of government. It would not run candidates, though it would have to establish some threshold rules to determine who gets airtime and who doesn't. Its mission would be to provide every candidate, of whatever party, a chance to state his or her case to the public. And the larger the effort, the more leverage the organizers will have in setting the ground rules. Such leverage is important if Real Campaign 2000 is not to be hostage to incumbents. The goal of an open, freewheeling, genuinely democratic campaign is to make incumbency as insecure and as exposed as possible. The point is not to elect particular people to office, but to make sure that the electorate knows whether those elected actually did what they said they'd do and, if not, give it a chance to know why—so that it can hold the candidates accountable.

Is such a thing feasible? I don't see why not. Indeed, it is little more than the logical extension of recent trends. Since the political parties have started producing media events, it seems perfectly fitting for the media to start producing political events. And since the media love a good argument much more than a sitting politician does, they are much more likely to produce political events that might actually restore serious debate and discussion to the process. Doing it on a nonprofit basis might make it easier to raise the money to finance the effort. But a case could also be made that the networks would make a profit on the whole thing. After all, people are much more likely to tune into something where the outcome is undetermined, and advertisers love an audience. Moreover, if we can't change the way campaigns are conducted, I say let the special interests pay for them. In a few more years, nobody is going to be paying attention anyway.

## James B. Rule

Generating political action from private resources poses some sticky problems for the democratic left. We value grassroots political action—so we like the idea of electoral campaigns and other forms of politicking as populist, participatory activities. But we also deplore the massive inequalities of American society—inequalities of wealth, and hence of all the things that money can buy. In America, that is a lot of things, and political results are obviously among them. Often it looks as though the values of participatory politics and those of creating a level political playing field run in a collision course.

But in fact, the choices are not so stark. One can imagine many innovative arrangements that would countervail against the corrupting role of money in political campaigns, while actually enhancing popular participation.

Contests over the role of money in these settings are largely struggles over *information*—conflicts about what information will be accessible to the public, when, how, and under what auspices. Money would not matter nearly so much in American politics if there were alternatives to high-priced media time as means for conveying information to citizens. The "free market" now prevailing in public communications favors those with the big bucks required to monopolize public attention. The problem is to break that monopoly.

As in many another domain, the "freedom" afforded by today's markets in public communication is spurious. But these markets are not part of some natural order of things. With the right political will, legislation could foster new, and vastly more democratic, markets of political ideas.

Consider the presidential primaries. Here the distorting role of big money is widely acknowledged. Campaigns are wastefully long. Worse, the political possibilities presented to most of the nation's voters are apt to be determined by which candidate can accumulate the biggest bankroll for the February contest in the tiny and atypical state of New Hampshire. By the time most voters get to express their wishes (if indeed they ever do) the terms of public debate will likely have been set by whoever succeeds in establishing early "momentum" in this special contest.

But imagine a radically different set of ground rules for presidential nominations—a two-stage, nationwide primary system. Funding for participation in this primary would be limited to contributions from individual citizens—excluding businesses and all other organizations—with a strict maximum of $1,000 per contributor. Other donations could consist only of citizens' labors. Government subsidies, if permitted, would be in direct proportion to these private contributions.

Note the far-reaching significance of limiting campaign funds to *individual* contributions. A step like this would obviously curtail the political clout of America's most powerful institutions—General Motors, the American Medical Association, the National Rifle Association, and so on. But it would also exclude institutional contributions from the AFL-CIO, the Sierra Club, and Mothers Against Drunk Driving—in short, it would smite the wicked and the righteous with the same sword. The ability of organizations *as organizations* to amass the target financial resources would count for much less—while their ability to inspire their members' active participation would suddenly count for a great deal.

The first of the two ballots in the national primary would be open to a wide variety of candidates—say, to anyone who could amass several hundred thousand voters' signatures collected from anywhere in the country. Candidates would thus presumably range from established professional politicians to leaders of sundry minorities endowed with the determination and donated labor necessary to collect the necessary signatures.

Next, consider a radically new *informational* context for these campaigns. All candidates would be expected to make a basic campaign speech, which would be widely diffused by television and radio (on time furnished in the public interest by all holders of broadcast licenses), as well as print and videotape. Further campaign materials would be prepared at the expense of the campaigns, but disseminated at public expense via libraries, post offices, and the World Wide Web. Candidates would be free to hold public rallies, kiss babies, be interviewed by independent journalists, or engage in any number of other participatory activities available to them today. But they would *not* legally be able to purchase airtime or other forms of publicity beyond that afforded by the budget constraints noted above.

The second phase of the national primaries would be a runoff for those finishing at the top of the first poll. Here new speeches would be solicited and disseminated, and new campaign materials generated. There might be officially sponsored debates—aired again at public expense. As in the first phase, journalistic activity and public rallies would help spread candidates' messages. But the same rigorous limits on cash contributions noted above would apply. The fact that each phase of the campaign involved the entire country at once (rather than just one or a few states at a time) would focus public attention dramatically. And the time required for the entire process could be greatly condensed.

Such innovations would enhance both the interplay of ideas and the dynamism of political participation in the nominating process. Instituting the principles described here would eliminate the advantages of money contributions from single sources—and create strong incentives to broaden the base of political campaigns. Instead of competing to woo big donors, and thereby to dominate the air waves, candidates would be compelled to put their "best shot" in a limited number of campaign communications. In all these matters, having a lot of committed supporters would count for a great deal; access to fat cats and monied interests would count for virtually nothing.

One could (and should) entertain all sorts of tinkering with the details envisaged here. My point is the *kind* of changes required, rather than any version of the fine detail. We urgently need to start considering substitutes for the arrangements that now in effect put the attention of the public up for bid—and which degrade the quality of public discourse in the process.

Needless to say, a proposal like this will not be implemented in the United States, or even widely discussed, any time soon. Those who control our national political life have gained their ascendancy by manipulating the very options that would be curtailed in this plan. They will not willingly yield their advantage to any such populist scheme as this.

Thus my proposal aims to be radical in the best sense of that term—pointing to democratic possibilities that are well removed from current reality, yet eminently feasible.

# Alice

## doesn't vote here anymore.

### When it comes to the way we elect Congress, we're on the wrong side of the looking glass

**by Michael Lind**

O H, MY," SAID ALICE, "IS IT REALLY TRUE THAT THERE ARE elections in Wonderland?"

"Of course, you foolish girl," the Queen of Hearts replied. "This is a constitutional monarchy. The Single Member of the Congress of Wonderland is elected by democratic means. Come, I shall introduce you to the electorate."

Alice followed the Queen to a field, in the middle of which was a table where the Mad Hatter and three of his friends were feasting. "The Mad Hatter's Party, with its four members, is one of the three political parties here in Wonderland," the Queen told Alice. "The other two parties, Tweedledum's Party and Tweedledee's Party, have three members apiece." Sure enough, Tweedledum and Tweedledee stood nearby, each with two followers.

"The electoral system of Wonderland," the Queen continued, "is based on the method of Plurality Voting by Single-Member Districts, sometimes known as Winner Takes All. You understand how that works, of course."

"No," said Alice sorrowfully, "I am afraid I do not."

The Queen shouted, "Off with her head!"

"Please," Alice begged, "I'll do my best to learn about the electoral system of Wonderland, if only you will explain it."

"Very well," the Queen said. "But I must warn you, the more I explain about Plurality Voting, the less you will understand it. For example, the most important part of our system of Plurality Voting by Single-Member Districts is the shape of the district."

"I cannot imagine why," Alice said.

The Queen was shocked. "Have you never heard of the Gerrymander?" At the mention of its name, the Gerrymander— a large and rather fearsome creature somewhat like a cross between a salamander and a Jabberwock—shambled forth. "Go on," the Queen ordered the beast, "draw the Single-Member District for the forthcoming congressional election."

Alice watched as the Gerrymander, dipping its brush in the pot of red paint hanging from its neck, began to outline a square in the grass. Soon the square's borders included the three members of the Tweedledum Party and the three members of the Tweedledee Party. But when it came to the four supporters of the Mad Hatter's Party, the Gerrymander painted a red stripe right down the middle of their banquet table.

"There," the Queen said with satisfaction. "Thanks to the Gerrymander, we now have a Single-Member District with two large parties—those of Tweedledum and Tweedledee— with three voters apiece, and one small party, the Mad Hatter's Party, with only two voters."

"But that isn't right!" cried Alice. She rushed to the Mad Hatter. "Aren't you going to do something?"

"Why on earth should I?" he asked.

"You have the biggest party," Alice replied. "Your party has four members, and the other two parties have only three voters apiece."

"Oh, you silly girl," said the Mad Hatter, pointing to the red stripe bisecting the table. "Can't you see that my party has only two voters eligible to vote in the Single-Member District?"

Alice noticed Tweedledum and Tweedledee handing purses full of coins to the Gerrymander. "Don't you see what they've done to you? They've drawn the Single-Member District to minimize the power of your voters!"

"Of course they have," the Mad Hatter chuckled. "We'd have done the same to them, if we could afford to pay the Gerrymander."

"But it isn't fair to your party! Why don't you protest?"

"Protest!" All four members of his party—the two inside the Single-Member District and the two outside—burst into laughter. "Protest? Why, our elections have always been held this way. To protest would be unpatriotic and vulgar." At this, the Mad Hatter and his friends resumed their banquet.

Alice was thinking very deeply. At length she said, "I have devised a strategy by which your party can maximize its influence—even though the Gerrymander has turned you into a minority party."

The Mad Hatter looked up from the table in annoyance. "Are you still here?"

Alice explained her plan. "The Queen of Hearts said that Wonderland has a Plurality Voting System. Therefore—it is all very puzzling, I admit—the winner needs either a simple majority in a two-party race or less than a majority—a mere plurality—in a three-party race. In a plurality election, the greater the number of parties, the smaller the plurality that is necessary to win."

"Yes, yes, yes," the Mad Hatter said, drumming his fingers on the table. "Is there a point to this tedious lesson in political science?"

"Who can get that plurality is very, very important," Alice insisted. "Your two-person party is too small to win. Therefore you must decide which of the other two parties you prefer."

"Oh, that is easy," replied the Mad Hatter. "The positions of the Tweedledee Party are nearest our own positions, whereas we find the Tweedledum platform positively hateful."

"Well, then," Alice responded, "you must vote for the Tweedledee Party—not for your own."

"Not vote for our own party!" the Mad Hatter exclaimed.

Alice explained: "If you vote for the Tweedledee Party, then it will defeat the Tweedledum Party, by five votes to three. But if you vote for your own party, then you increase the chances that the Tweedledum Party will win. It's only rational."

"It may be rational, but this is Wonderland, and I'll have none of it!" the Mad Hatter declared.

There was no time for further argument, for at that very moment the Queen ordered, "Let the ballasting begin!"

A large balloon appeared above the treetops and drifted over the field. The balloonist shouted down to the Mad Hatter's Party: "How do you want your ballast cast?"

"Two for the Mad Hatter's Party!"

The balloonist tossed down two bags of ballast, which crashed in the midst of the table. Following the instructions of the other parties' voters, he cast three bags of ballast at the feet of Tweedledum and three at the feet of Tweedledee.

"The ballasting is complete," the Queen announced, as the balloon, deprived of ballast, drifted up into the sky and disappeared, taking the panicked balloonist with it.

"The election is a tie," Alice observed. "Tweedledum and Tweedledee each have three votes."

"No matter," said the Queen. "Under our Single-Member District Plurality Voting System, the outcome in a close race is often decided by the way the Swing Vote breaks."

"Who casts the Swing Vote?" Alice asked.

"Why, you do, little girl. Guards!"

Two guards appeared and forced poor Alice to climb up a tree containing an old, rotten, and very unsafe swing. With a great deal of anxiety, Alice sat in the swing and hung on for dear life as the guards gave it a push.

Back and forth Alice swung. As she passed overhead, first the Tweedledum Party and then the Tweedledee Party

## The electoral system of Wonderland is unjust. Unfortunately, that system is our own.

reached up, promising concessions in return for her support. Finally, on the third pass, the Swing Vote broke. Screaming, Alice was hurtled into the arms of Tweedledum.

"I got the Swing Vote!" Tweedledum exclaimed. "I won the election! I won the election!"

"But that isn't fair!" Alice cried. "It isn't fair three ways! It isn't fair the first way because the district was Gerrymandered, so the biggest party, the Mad Hatter's, was turned into a minority. And it isn't fair the second way because the plurality method of voting ensured that either the Tweedledum Party or the Tweedledee Party would win—even though a majority of the voters in the district voted against each party. And it isn't fair the third way because the election was so close that its outcome was settled by a Swing Voter—me—whose views may have nothing in common with what all of the other voters in the district want. It isn't fair at all! It's a travesty of democracy, which means nothing if it does not mean majority rule!"

The Queen gasped. "Little girl, what does democracy have to do with majority rule? In Wonderland, democracy means the Rule of the Largest Minority, helped out by a minuscule Swing Vote, in a Gerrymandered Single-Member District. Majority rule, indeed! Off with her head!"

THE ELECTORAL SYSTEM OF WONDERLAND, AS DESCRIBED ABOVE (with apologies to Lewis Carroll), is—as Alice rightly insists—unjust and perverse. Unfortunately, that electoral system is our own. (Coincidentally, it is one that Carroll himself would not have approved of. A mathematician by training, he was fascinated by voting systems and produced important work on voting theory—including developing elaborate alternative voting procedures that would eliminate bizarre distortions like those in Wonderland—that went completely unnoticed until the 1950s. He used to pass out pamphlets explaining his obscure theories to his Oxford colleagues, none of whom had an inkling as to what he was talking about.)

Plurality voting by single-member districts is how we elect the House, state legislatures, city councils, and other legislative bodies. Our method produces the same undemocratic effects identified by Alice, but they are somewhat less humorous when we tally their political consequences:

• GERRYMANDERING Under the Constitution, state legislatures are permitted to redraw the lines of U.S. House districts every 10 years, following the census. If the Republicans gain control of the statehouses in the midterm elections next November (32 states currently have Republican governors; 18 have GOP-controlled legislatures), this could spell disaster for the Democrats. As Republican National Chairman Jim Nicholson predicts: "The winners are going to determine the political landscape in at least the first decade of the next millennium, because they are the people who are going to preside over the process of reapportionment and redistricting of their respective states as a result of the 2000 census." Because the party of the president usually loses seats in midterm elections, this is an ominous prospect.

And Democrats have good reasons to fear a Republican gerrymander: The current 15-seat Republican majority in the House is largely due to cynical GOP efforts during the last round of redistricting in 1991 to forge what some Democrats have called an "unholy alliance" with black and Hispanic Democrats to carve up racially mixed liberal districts into "safe" black and Hispanic seats and equally "safe" Republican seats. The GOP even went so far as to make expensive redistricting software available to minority activist groups as part of its plan to split up the white liberal vote and ghettoize the nonwhite liberal vote.

As a result, there are only four white Democrats in the House from South Carolina, Georgia, Alabama, Mississippi, and Louisiana combined. In Newt Gingrich's Georgia, before racial gerrymandering, there were nine Democrats (eight white and one black) and only one Republican. Today the Georgia delegation numbers eight Republicans—all white—and three Democrats—all black.

• SWING VOTE A relatively modest swing vote breaking rightward has helped make the South a solidly Republican stronghold. A shift of only a few percentage points can move divided districts from the Democratic to the Republican camp. Where the districts themselves are swing districts, holding the balance of power between the two parties in Congress, the votes of a tiny minority of swing voters in a few districts can create a revolution in national politics. Morton Kondracke, a columnist for *Roll Call,* estimates that less than 12,000 voters nationwide—or six-hundredths of 1 percent of the eligible voting population—swung the vote to the House Republicans in 1996.

• PLURALITY WINNERS The recent rise of third-party politics threatens to strengthen the hold of the two dominant parties in Congress, rather than weaken it. For instance, in a special House election in New Mexico last year, Carol Miller won 17 percent of the vote as the Green Party candidate, splitting the Democratic vote and sending a Republican to Washington to represent a district in which only 42 percent of the voters supported him. She intends to run again in 1998 and is unlikely to fare any better. With more and more Reform, Green, New, and Libertarian party candidates running for congressional seats, perverse results are inevitable: Minuscule returns for a Green Party candidate can throw an overwhelmingly progressive district to the Republicans, just as a spoiler Libertarian Party candidate can ensure the election of a Democrat in predominantly conservative districts. The third-party candidate loses, and the wrong major party candidate wins.

PLURALITY VOTING BY SINGLE-MEMBER DISTRICTS MAY BE CROOKED, but it's the only game in town—isn't it?

No, as a matter of fact it isn't. Most liberal democracies have rejected plurality voting because of its unfair and paradoxical results. Instead, they elect their legislatures by some version of proportional representation by district.

Here's how proportional representation works: Imagine a region with five adjacent single-member congressional districts. In each district, the electorate is divided between Republicans (60 percent), Democrats (20 percent), and Greens (20 percent). Under plurality voting, even though Republicans are only a slight majority of the electorate, they will get 100 percent of the vote. The region will send five Republicans to Congress, no Democrats, and no Greens. Under proportional representation, the five adjacent districts would be consolidated into one five-member delegation, which would send three Republicans, one Democrat, and one Green. This distribution of seats would more accurately reflect the distribution of sentiments in the electorate. In politics, who wins depends upon the rules.

Note that under proportional representation, the Alice-in-Wonderland results of our system—gerrymandering, plurality winners, and swing votes—simply disappear. State legislatures would abandon partisan gerrymandering, because it could no longer effectively prevent the minority from picking up at least a few seats. Racial gerrymandering would no longer be necessary, either. If people wanted to vote along racial or ethnic lines (which is far from a good idea in principle), then members of significant racial or ethnic minorities would be sure to elect one or two members of a multimember district—even if the white majority itself voted along racial lines.

The plurality winner problem would also vanish. A party with 60 percent of the votes couldn't win 100 percent of the seats in a district, only 60 percent of the delegation.

What about the swing vote? It is most troubling in two-party systems, in which the swing voters hold the balance between the parties. The democracies that use proportional representation tend to have multiparty systems, and it is likely that the United States would as well if proportional representation were adopted here. English-speaking populations are not innately more likely to be divided into two parties than are German-speaking populations. A two-party system is an unintended but almost inevitable byproduct of the plurality electoral system.

Such a multiparty system might also help reduce the polarization of American politics. Because a coalition of two or more parties, not just a single majority party, would probably hold power in the House and Senate, a party would gain little political capital by attempting to demonize the president, or to vilify potential coalition partners in the other parties. The rigid connection between lobbies and parties would dissolve as lobbies found it more useful to try to influence two or more parties instead of identifying themselves wholly with one.

Another benefit of proportional representation is that it could abort the otherwise inevitable emergence of a solid Republican South—or any other region that is "solidly" one party or the other. Right-wing Republicans in Cambridge, Berkeley, or New York's Upper West Side might be able to elect at least one or two members of Congress from their own area. Right now, in many districts, the minority party does not even bother to run a candidate. With five-member districts, any party with a chance at winning one-fifth of the vote could run candidates. It would no longer make sense for parties to write off whole districts, or even whole states. All of America would become politically competitive for the first time in history.

AT THIS POINT, THE DEFENDER OF THE status QUO IS CERTAIN to introduce a parade of horribles: for example, the fractionalization of the electorate into too many ineffectual parties, or the tyranny of small, fanatical parties in the multiparty legislature. The first can easily be dismissed: Under proportional representation, interests tend to coagulate into a handful of substantial parties. And we can eliminate the problem of tiny fanatical parties, which has bedeviled Israel, by insisting that no party can get seats in the legislature unless it wins a certain threshold—say, 5 percent—of the national vote. Thus, even if neo-Nazis win a district in Louisiana, they won't be seated in Congress unless they pass the national threshold.

Proportional representation tends to have a stabilizing effect on democracies—usually because a centrist party, such as the Free Democrats in Germany, moderates the extremist tendencies of its coalition partners. By contrast, elections in plurality democracies such as Britain and the United States tend to produce wild shifts in public policy, even though only a small number of swing voters may have changed their votes.

In the United States, the political history of the last quarter-century probably would have been far less turbulent had we adopted proportional representation to elect the House in, say, the 1950s. What would have happened is, of course, anybody's guess. Mine is that three major parties would have emerged from the wreckage of the Democrats and Republicans: An upscale progressive party based in New England and the Pacific Northwest, a conservative party based in the South, and a working-class populist party, with members who were socially conservative but fiscally liberal. On social issues, the House might have had a populist-conservative majority; on economic issues, a populist-progressive majority. The destruction of federal welfare programs and the balancing of the budget through regressive policies—the work of a centrist Democratic president and a right-wing Republican congressional majority—might never have taken place. The far left would have been just as thwarted, but New Deal liberalism—based on an alliance of Northern progressives, Southern populists, and working-class Catholics—might have endured.

What about the executive branch and the Senate? Proportional representation works only with multicandidate districts. For single-candidate offices, a system known as

## Right now, in many districts, the minority party doesn't even bother to run a candidate.

preference voting (also called the "instant runoff") could thwart Wonderland democracy. Where three or more candidates ran for an office such as the presidency, the voter would be instructed to rank the candidates in order of preference. Thus a voter in our imaginary three-party America who prefers the progressive to the populist candidate on social issues, while preferring the populist to the conservative one on economic issues, would assign the following ranking on the ballot: Progressive (1), Populist (2), Conservative (3). If no candidate wins a majority, the second-choice votes are redistributed among the top two candidates. In extreme cases, it might be possible for a candidate who got the most first-preference votes to lose to a candidate who won an overwhelming majority of second-preference votes.

Preference voting makes it almost impossible for a candidate strongly opposed by most voters to get elected in a three- or four-way race. Even more important, the adoption of preference voting for senatorial and presidential races would give candidates an incentive to seek support beyond their own parties. While elections under the plurality system tend to produce rival moderates exaggerating their differences, elections under the preference voting system would encourage candidates from genuinely different parties to reach out to members of other parties. The candidates would campaign not only for the first-preference votes of their party but for the second-preference votes of the parties that were nearest to their positions on particular issues. There might be coalition cabinets and even fusion tickets, with a president from one party and a vice president from another.

Preference voting can also eliminate two potential problems that multiple parties might pose to the American constitutional system. In a separation-of-powers political system like ours, conflict is endemic—particularly when different parties control the branches. If Congress were divided among multiple parties, it could severely weaken its power relative to the presidency. The president could claim to represent "the people," using that as a pretext to get around a Congress split among a number of squabbling parties. Preference voting in presidential elections might reduce that danger by encouraging the candidates, in campaigning for second-choice votes, to promise a multiparty coalition Cabinet.

Second, preference voting might also decrease the likelihood of another catastrophe that can occur from the collision of multiple parties with a plurality electoral system—the minoritarian president. In some countries with presidential systems, political chaos and even civil wars have erupted when a president supported by only a small minority has won election in a multiple-party race. Preference voting would guarantee that the winning candidate would always receive a majority of second-choice (and perhaps third-choice) votes, meaning that voters would never be stuck with their least favorite candidate.

CAN PROPORTIONAL REPRESENTATION EVER BE MORE THAN A fantasy in the United States? It's already used to elect the city council of Cambridge and it was used for many years by the Cincinnati City Council (it was scrapped in the 1950s because it allowed blacks a chance to be elected).

There are no constitutional obstacles to changing our method of voting. The Constitution is silent about electoral systems. Our plurality system was established by statute; it can be replaced by statute. Alternatively, Congress, which has the ultimate say over how its members are elected, might give the states the right to determine how their congressional delegations are chosen. In 1995, Rep. Cynthia McKinney (D-Ga.) introduced the Voters' Choice Act, which would allow states to use proportional representation to elect their congressional delegations.

A supporter of the status quo might argue that our system is somehow uniquely suited to the American character or to our political culture, or that two centuries of tradition have sanctified it. But the Founding Fathers did not actually choose the plurality system in any meaningful sense; they simply adopted the British electoral system they grew up with. No real alternative existed until the 1850s, when an Englishman named John Hare devised one of the first influential versions of proportional representation.

Far from being alien to American society, proportional representation is arguably the only appropriate electoral system for a society as diverse as ours. It encourages social peace by giving every major segment of the population a piece of the action. Proportional representation has proved most successful in ethnically divided societies, such as the Baltic states and South Africa, since it permits every significant minority to elect at least some representatives. The traditional American theory of democracy—majority rule with minority rights—has always been questionable. We cannot count on the federal judiciary to protect the rights of minorities, because its composition, over time, will reflect the partisan majority in the other two branches. Properly understood, democracy means majority rule with minority representation. Under proportional representation, the black or Hispanic or libertarian or socialist or populist minority would have the opportunity to elect the occasional member of Congress, state legislator, or city council member, instead of having to cast a doomed vote.

If the traditionalist argument in support of plurality voting were valid, it ought to be most powerful in Britain, from which the U.S. inherited its archaic electoral method. There, however, Prime Minister Tony Blair made a national referendum on the replacement of plurality voting by proportional representation an important part of his campaign. Australia, New Zealand, and Ireland already have forms of proportional representation in some elections, and Canada recently considered the idea when it attempted to redesign its senate (the plan failed for reasons that had nothing to do with the issue of proportional representation). If Britain and Canada scrap plurality voting, the United States, in a generation or two, might find itself alone among advanced democratic countries in clinging to an electoral procedure rejected as unfair and primitive everywhere else. The "world's greatest democracy" may end up having the least democratic electoral law.

Needless to say, politicians elected under a given voting system are unlikely to change it. In the United States, the best way to force the political class to undertake electoral reform may be to sponsor initiatives in states, such as California, whose constitutions permit this method of direct action. Most electoral reforms, such as the extension of suffrage to women and blacks, were adopted by progressive states before they were enacted by congressional statute or constitutional amendment.

IN THE 1996 ELECTION, LESS THAN HALF OF THE ELECTORATE VOTED. Under the current electoral system, choosing not to vote is a rational decision by people who do not identify with either of the two parties, or who live in congressional districts or states in which one party has an overwhelming majority. When thesystem is rigged against you, a boycott makes perfect sense (international comparisons demonstrate, to nobody's surprise, that voter turnout is far lower in democracies with plurality voting than in multiparty democracies using proportional representation).

Though it may be justified, popular alienation threatens democracy itself in the long run. If people believe—correctly—that they are not represented by the American political elite, they will be drawn to the kind of antipolitics represented on left, right, and center by Jerry Brown, Pat Buchanan, and Ross Perot, respectively. At its worst, antipolitics is the opposite of political reform; its goal is to smash constitutional, representative democracy, not to improve it. As Americans grow more alienated from the two-party system that our antiquated voting scheme encourages, they may be tempted to support a charismatic president who, claiming a popular mandate, promises to get things done, with little regard for constitutional niceties or those crooks in Congress. Only a few years ago, a majority of Americans polled said that they would support Colin Powell for president—knowing almost nothing about his political views. That he wore a uniform was apparently sufficient recommendation. A North American version of Latin American-style Peronism or French-style Bonapartism, disguised as presidential prerogative or direct democracy, is all too conceivable in the 21st century.

Time is running out. Soon, we will have to prove to ourselves that the American political system has not discredited democracy itself—only the democracy of Wonderland.

*Michael Lind is the editor of* Hamilton's Republic. *This is the second in a series of four articles examining the prospects for democratic political reform.*

# March Madness

## *How the primary schedule favors the rich*

### By Walter Shapiro

A SMALL BOAST: I HAVE PERFECTED A QUESTION guaranteed to prompt gape-jawed puzzlement from would-be presidential candidates of both parties. I have not been inquiring about knotty policy conundrums like the economic implications of the Euro or Medicare financing formulas for teaching hospitals. Nor have I invaded marital privacy with one of those snarky have-you-ever queries so favored by the character cops on the political beat. Rather, my question is directly relevant for any long-shot dreamer who fantasizes about taking the oath of office on Jan. 20, 2001.

Here's what I ask: Do you worry that the primary calendar is so rigged that only the best-financed candidates have a shot at winning a presidential nomination? John McCain, the press pack's favorite Republican, confessed that he hadn't thought about the question. Nor had liberal maverick Paul Wellstone on the Democratic side. John Ashcroft, who seems to be the self-appointed candidate of the unborn, ruefully admitted, "It takes wiser heads than mine to figure it out. We've got to play by the rules that they've set up."

Ashcroft talks as if these rules were set down by the Marquess of Queensberry to add a note of gentlemanly fair play to the rough-and-tumble of political combat. In truth, the primary schedule resembles nothing so much as the Mad Tea Party from "Alice in Wonderland." Both parties are likely to select their nominees in 2000 under a hyper-compressed, warp-speed timetable that only money-talks front-runners like Al Gore and 15-year-old computer geeks with joy sticks could possibly love. I know it seems bizarre to brood about the dates for the primaries more than 18 months before the Iowa caucuses, especially with our campaign-finance laws in tatters and the political mood as ugly as the Jerry Springer Show. But I am convinced that the primary calendar, more than any other single factor, unfairly dictates outcomes.

As recently as 1992, the primaries meandered from New Hampshire in mid-February until California in early June. Bill Clinton, for example, uttered his famous I-didn't-inhale puffery in an April TV interview on the eve of the New York primary and didn't silence the doubters in the Democratic Party until he nailed down California. OK, the dour Paul Tsongas, Clinton's last mainstream rival for the nomination, did not survive the daunting gauntlet of mid-March primaries known as Super Tuesday. But this long march to the nomination gave the voters and the press more than enough time to take the measure of Clinton's talents and character, even though some of us may regret our seal of approval.

For reasons that in hindsight defy rational analysis, the GOP establishment in 1996 was determined to nominate septuagenarian Bob Dole or the owlish Phil Gramm. With the Democrats preoccupied with White House coffees, Republicans were free to concoct a cock-eyed rush to judgment, encouraging states to cluster their primaries and caucuses in March. The unspoken logic was to dispense with the messy uncertainties of democracy and coronate a nominee by St. Patrick's Day. California Gov. Pete Wilson, with White House ambitions of his own, joined in this mischief by moving his state's primary to late March. The Republicans held 37 primaries and caucuses, which selected more than 70 percent of the convention delegates, in just five weeks from Feb. 20 to March 26.

Once Gramm dropped out after Iowa, having already lost the Louisiana caucuses that the Texas senator thought

WALTER SHAPIRO, *a contributing editor of* The Washington Monthly, *is a political columnist for* USA Today.

Reprinted with permission from *The Washington Monthly,* June 1998, pp. 24-25. © 1998 by The Washington Monthly Company, 1611 Connecticut Avenue, NW, Washington, DC 20009. (202) 462-0128.

he had rigged, Dole was the inevitable nominee. Even though the Bobster stumbled in Iowa and was upended by Pat Buchanan in New Hampshire, Dole was the only remaining candidate who boasted both the financial and organizational resources to compete over this dizzying terrain. Just 11 days after New Hampshire, with news magazines trumpeting Buchanan's petulant populism still on the coffee tables, Dole became the de facto nominee after sweeping the South Carolina primary.

I recall sitting in an impromptu press room set up in a hotel bar in Columbia, S.C., watching Steve Forbes, Lamar!, Buchanan, and Dole debate right before the primary. The four-way face-off was fast-paced, substantive, and revealing—the kind of event that cried out for a month of sequels. Then, whap, the race was over. When politics outruns even the CNN-style 24-hour news cycle, there is no longer time for reporters to etch delicate candidate portraits, delve deeply into campaign issues, or muse on the political diversity of America. All I managed after New Hampshire were a few hasty columns on the Republicans written on my lap on a campaign plane flying between Who-Can-Remember and God-Knows-Where.

After two decades of trying to live out my childhood Teddy White fantasies, I am sadly accustomed to a cynical political culture that drains content out of campaigns for the voters and the press. But the stacked deck of the breathless primary schedule is worse—it destroys the logic of letting the voters, rather than the party leaders, select the nominee. As Larry Sabato writes in *Toward the Millennium*, a collection of essays he edited on the 1996 campaign, "Front-loading amplified the advantages of the front-runner, leaving little time for his opponents to regroup after the inevitable setbacks." Republican voters in Iowa and New Hampshire performed their proper function by highlighting Dole's weaknesses as a candidate, but the blink-and-it's-over calendar then deprived the GOP of an alternative.

This quadrennial March Madness is particularly cruel to underfunded underdogs because it eliminates what political lingo calls "the reload factor." When a broke but determined Gary Hart stunned the touts in 1984 with a stretch-run victory in New Hampshire, he was able to turn this media acclaim and momentum into campaign cash that fueled his insurgency until the Democratic convention. Had Lamar Alexander, plaid shirt and all, been the surprise 1996 victor in New Hampshire (he finished third in a closely packed field), he wouldn't have even had time to cash the post-primary checks before he was driven out of the race. Under the rules that prevailed in 1996, a candidate needs to raise upwards of $30 million before New Hampshire to have a chance of holding his arms aloft in triumph at his party's convention.

Granted, there is no reason beyond inertia, a never to be underestimated force in politics, why the primary timetable in 2000 must be modeled after the 1996 GOP demolition derby. While nominating Dole amid the syncopated sound-bits in San Diego, the Republicans belatedly conceded the error of their ways by awarding bonus delegates in 2000 to states that hold primaries and caucuses after April 1. A few states have already wisely sounded retreat—Wisconsin, Minnesota, and California among them. (The situation in California is muddled by its bizarre new open-primary law, which may force the state to choose its delegates by the old-fashioned convention system.)

But this small outburst of scheduling sanity is tempered by the irresistible pay-attention-to-us boosterism of states neglected by fly-over primary campaigns. Four small Western states (Utah, Wyoming, Idaho, and Nevada) recently formed a task force to set up a new regional primary in (guess when?) early March, and Arizona and Colorado may join this home-on-the-range alliance. Utah Gov. Mike Leavitt reflected the pressures of front-load fever when he said, "As a function of circumstances, the West has been left out of picking the leader of the free world." Adding to the fast-forward frenzy is the likelihood that politicians will move up primaries in a few states for tactical advantage, as Al D'Amato did last time for Dole in New York. D'Amato was, in fact, such a shameless string-puller that no other Republican was even allowed on the Soviet-style primary ballot.

The two national parties could, in theory, create an orderly sequence of primaries by either enacting explicit rules or simply pressuring governors and state legislatures to fall in line. But the Democrats' lack of interest in helping create a rational primary calendar is a signal that the fix is in for Gore in 2000—and like it or lump it, Bill Bradley, Dick Gephardt, John Kerry, Bob Kerrey, and Paul Wellstone.

President Clinton, piously justifying his unrepentant political buckraking last fall, declared, "I have always been for changing the system. I'm just not for unilateral disarmament." GOP Chairman Jim Nicholson has frequently used the same hackneyed Cold War imagery to explain his party's unrelenting opposition to the McCain-Feingold campaign reform bill. Reforming the presidential primary system is an easy way to lessen the big-money arms race in politics without forcing either party to forsake any partisan advantage. It needs neither congressional legislation nor an FCC ruling. All it requires is for both parties to briefly forsake their habitual cynicism in the name of giving the voters a true voice in selecting the presidential nominees in 2000.

# Demosclerosis

## *The Disease That's Petrifying American Government*

### Jonathan Rauch

*Jonathan Rauch, a contributing editor of* National Journal, *is author of* Demosclerosis: The Silent Killer of American Government, *published by Times Books. Single copies of this book are available from the Democratic Leadership Council.*

In 1991, President Bush appointed Diane Ravitch, a Democrat, to be the Education Department's assistant secretary in charge of research. She had plans and ideas. She got nowhere. Ravitch soon discovered that all but a fraction of the education research budget was assigned, by law, to entrenched recipients with slick lobbyists and protectors in Congress. "The vast bulk is frozen solid," she later said. For instance, a handful of established regional laboratories virtually monopolized a key chunk of the research budget. The laboratories maintained a lobbying group, run by a former aide to a key member of the House Appropriations Committee, which looked after them in perpetuity.

Ravitch, now a visiting scholar at New York University, managed to kill a single tiny program—one that spent only $8 million or so at its peak. Unable to kill anything old, she had neither the means nor the support to create anything new. She had hoped to create videos for parents and a computerized information network for educators. "But there was no interest group for that," she said.

In the end, Ravitch found there were only two ways to do her job. One method was to shovel money out the door to the established lobbies. Her department's clients would all be happy—but the government's education research program would stagnate. The other method was to try to set new priorities—but that would entail trench warfare against the interest groups, a masochistic and probably futile exercise. Some choice.

"At first," Ravitch said of her time in Washington, "I thought it was about people really solving problems. But what it's really all about is people pro-

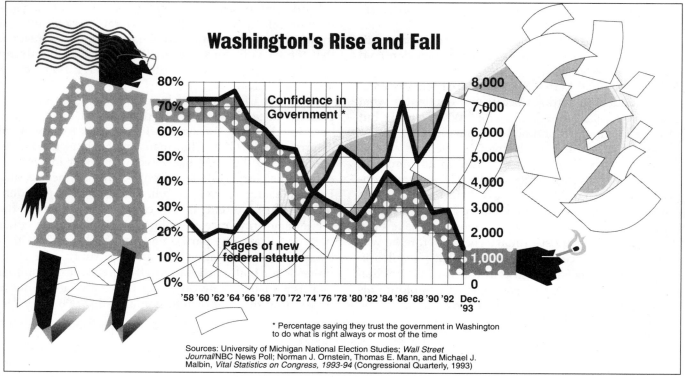

**Washington's Rise and Fall**

Confidence in Government *

Pages of new federal statute

80% — 8,000
70% — 7,000
60% — 6,000
50% — 5,000
40% — 4,000
30% — 3,000
20% — 2,000
10% — 1,000
0% — 0

'58 '60 '62 '64 '66 '68 '70 '72 '74 '76 '78 '80 '82 '84 '86 '88 '90 '92 Dec. '93

\* Percentage saying they trust the government in Washington to do what is right always or most of the time

Sources: University of Michigan National Election Studies; *Wall Street Journal*/NBC News Poll; Norman J. Ornstein, Thomas E. Mann, and Michael J. Malbin, *Vital Statistics on Congress, 1993-94* (Congressional Quarterly, 1993)

ILLUSTRATION BY SAM WARD

tecting their districts and the organizations they're close to. If you don't get the interest groups' support, you can't change anything, but if you change anything, you don't get their support. That's the conundrum.

"At the beginning, I thought I could shape the agency," she continued. "But I couldn't do that. That was already done. My priorities were irrelevant. And that, for me, was a devastating discovery."

Devastating, indeed, Devastating not only for people who work in government but for government itself. Little by little, Washington is turning brittle and rotting, like an intricate machine turning to rust.

Most Americans—and most Washingtonians—assume that Washington's problems lie in partisan feuding or political careerism or George Bush or Bill Clinton or whatever. If only it were that easy. What Diane Ravitch ran up against-and what Bill Clinton is running up against, in a bigger way—is a syndrome that I call demosclerosis: government's progressive loss of the ability to adapt.

Demosclerosis is a slow-acting, cumulative disorder that gradually turns government into a living fossil. In principle, it is treatable. But in practice? Unfortunately, the record so far is discouraging. The cure will have to be more radical than anything anyone in power, or the blowhard Ross Perot, has yet suggested.

To see what demosclerosis is, a good place to begin is with what it emphatically, though subtly, is not: "grid-lock."

In his first press conference after winning the 1992 election, President-elect Clinton declared that his "clear mandate" was to end the gridlock in Washington. His interpretation mirrored the popular wisdom. Things that needed doing supposedly weren't getting done. In response, a whole lot of legislating and policy-making got done last year; President Clinton won a larger share of congressional votes than has any new President since Eisenhower in 1953.

There's something fishy about the "gridlock" story, however. Consider the chart. Americans' confidence in the federal government has fallen dramatically during the past 30 years. In 1958, 73 percent said they trusted the government in Washington to do what's right "just about always or most of the time." In December 1993, only 14 percent did. Today, seven of 10 Americans say government creates more problems than it solves; three-fourths say government wastes "a lot" of their tax money; and so on, and on.

Now, here's the curious thing. Over that same period, government has been anything but gridlocked. Far from declining, the level of activity has risen any way you measure it. One typical yardstick is the number of new pages of federal law added each year. As the chart shows, the more pages of new laws the government passed, the more unhappy people were. Whatever soured people on government, it wasn't gridlock.

Objectively speaking, in fact, *gridlock never happened*. In Washington, things always get done—ever more frenetically, indeed. The Bush years saw passage of the sweeping Clean Air Act and other environmental measures, the almost equally sweeping Americans with Disabilities Act, new money for child care, a major highway bill, a major anti-deficit bill (bigger than Clinton's!), at least 10 piecemeal reforms affecting health care and much else. In the civil rights field alone, the "era of gridlock" produced the Civil Rights Act of 1991, the Voting Rights Language Assistance Act, the Civil Liberties Act Amendments of 1992, the Minority Farmers Rights Act, the Japanese-American Redress Entitlement Programs, the anti-redlining provisions of the banking-reform law, the Hate-Crimes Statistics Act, and the aforementioned Americans with Disabilities Act. Overall, the number of laws and regulations enacted under President Bush remained well in line with the post-1970 norm.

Clearly, something is wrong with the standard analysis of Washington's problems. Maybe this:

The gridlock metaphor implies that traffic isn't moving—a static problem. And therein lies the error. Try, instead, a dynamic metaphor. Imagine that your car's front-end alignment went dangerously askew. This isn't a problem of static immobility but of dynamic imbalance—a very different kind of problem. The last thing you'd want to do about it is to drive faster ("get more done"). On the other hand, driving 10 miles an hour is no answer, either. You need to fix your alignment.

This second, dynamic kind of problem is what's wracking government and infuriating the public. People aren't mad at Washington for not getting enough done; they're mad because what Washington gets done is failing to solve their problems. Government's activity level rises, yet its achievement level falls. The wheels spin faster, yet the car shakes, lurches, veers randomly. Why?

Imagine a rocket ship with three thrusters headed for Jupiter. Now imagine that the thrusters are slightly out of balance. At first, you might not notice. After a while, though, the rocket would be a little off course, then a lot off course, then hurtling aimlessly into deep space. To maintain control, you would constantly need to fight the rocket's tendency to drift. And if you didn't fight hard enough, the whole mission would end in disaster.

A modern democracy faces a similar problem. It's difficult for government to do things, but that's as it should be. The founders made the American system change-averse on purpose, which is why we have competing power centers and the Bill of Rights. The trouble is that everything is not *equally* difficult to do. To create a subsidy or program is hard. To reduce an existing subsidy or program is much harder. And to completely eliminate a subsidy or a program is hardest of all.

This imbalance is fundamental to the way democracy works. Inherently, democracy allows people to form groups—lobbies—to seek benefits from the government. Those groups, of course, can do good as well as harm. The problem comes from a side effect of groupism: Once you create a benefit or program, its beneficiaries organize to protect it, and once that happens, getting rid of either the program or the group is almost impossible.

The Clinton Administration's own "reinventing government" report put the problem well. Government, said the report, "knows how to add, but not to subtract." A politician who challenges any existing lobby or program can expect all-out war—whereas a politician who simply adds to the existing pile of programs collects campaign contributions, support back home, and "Honorary Dairyman of the Year" awards.

President Clinton learned this lesson the hard way. During the Bush years, when some members of Congress suggested raising the heavily subsidized fees for grazing on federal land, ranchers' groups spent heavily to defeat them, laid siege to Capitol Hill, and denounced the reformers as "socialists" promoting "cultural genocide." Last year, the Clinton Administration's own proposal to raise land-use fees met with the same warm reception. Western land interests and their friends in the Senate made life so hot for the President that he beat a full retreat in the spring and then was mauled when he tried again in the fall. Eventually, if he tried hard enough, the President could get some of what he wants. But the cost in time, energy, and political capital would be enormous. And that is just for one little subsidy.

I'm not saying all subsidies are bad. Whether the Small Business Administration or rural electric subsidies or grazing subsidies or any other particular program is worthwhile is a matter of opinion. But that hardly matters, because it turns out that what a program actually does, or even how well it works, is irrelevant. Any politician, well-meaning or not, who tries to withdraw *any* group's program or subsidy, with justification or not, gets that group's fist in his face. It happens even when agencies try to rechannel money within an existing program. Even closing a local Agriculture Department office or an underused veterans' hospital is a nightmare.

The result is bizarre: *Government is stuck with almost everything it ever tries.* In 1993, Congress managed to get rid of four programs—most notably the super-conducting super collider—and four was rightly considered an exceptional haul (it took Ronald Reagan eight years to kill that many major programs). In the Agriculture Department, President Clinton sought to kill more than 200 small items, worth $160 million. (That may sound like a lot, but in fact it was a routine Presidential request.) Of those items, he bagged only three dozen, together worth $38 million—better than the Bush Administration had done, but still only 1/2000th of the department's budget. In the Education Department, Clinton tried to kill about a dozen programs, most of them, again, items that routinely show up on Presidential hit lists. All but one minuscule item sailed happily on.

In response to complaints that the Administration's "reinventing government" effort recommended only 15 program eliminations, the budget director, Leon Panetta, replied, "I would kiss the ground and thank God if we could eliminate 15."

So here is the fatal imbalance: As hard as it is for the government to adopt programs, adapting or getting rid of them, once the beneficiaries have dug in, is much harder still. As in the case of the unbalanced spaceship, at first this problem may seem minor. For a while, government can just add new things on top of old things. But only for a while.

Another thought experiment. Suppose you were chosen to rescue a dying company. But here's the catch: You can't drop a single product, close a single factory or scrap any equipment. You can develop new cars and computers, but you also have to keep all the

old cars and computers on the market—tail fins, vacuum tubes, and all. "Impossible!" you say. "No one could revitalize a company under such conditions!" And you're right.

But that's exactly the situation the federal government now faces. The government is like the old Soviet economy, in which old enterprises never shut down, preventing new ones from springing up. The Soviet economy was fairly modern in Stalin's day, but it failed to adapt. The same thing is happening to the U.S. government now.

Today, Washington spends five times more in constant dollars than it did in the late 1940s, when it could "afford" the Marshall Plan; it spends three times what it did in John F. Kennedy's day. Yet, for "lack of money," President Clinton's visionary national service plan was scaled down to a pea-sized $1.5 billion over three years, less than one year's cotton subsidy. Of course, this federal "poverty" isn't poverty at all. It's rigidity—alias demosclerosis. With every group fiercely defending every program, government can't reallocate resources. It gets stuck in its past, like a city buried in its own detritus.

An institution can't solve problems if it can't adapt. In a world where almost nothing works the first time, the key to solving problems is to experiment. President Clinton understands this; in his inaugural address, he pledged to "make our government a place for what Franklin Roosevelt called 'bold, persistent experimentation.'" The problem is that in a demosclerotic society, FDR's brand of experimental government cannot exist. When you're stuck with virtually everything you ever try, trial and error is impossible. You can't get rid of your mistakes, your failures, your anachronisms.

Instead, programs and policies and subsidies pile up and work to every end at once. Sometimes they make war on each other, as when turn-of-the-century antitrust law undercuts efforts to encourage strategic business partnerships. The government's farm disaster-relief program and its crop-insurance program work at cross-purposes, yet both are defended and both go on and on. Maladaptive programs create new problems, creating demand for still more programs, leading to still more interest groups and more seizing-up.

Bit by bit, program by program, the government turns dysfunctional. Eventually, it reaches the point of critical failure. That is, it begins to create at

least as many problems as it solves. The public believes that government has already reached that point. And the public is probably right.

"OK," say a lot of people, especially old-style Democrats, "let's pass new programs. That will fix it." But it won't. Remember, this is a *dynamic* problem, which is what makes it so insidious. Passing new programs is no solution because in a decade or two, after they're locked in, the new programs will be part of the old problem.

Take health-care reform. If major reforms are adopted, everyone will say, "That's the end of gridlock," and President Clinton will boast that Washington is back in action. But the glow will fade. Hard as it may be to adopt a health program, the much tougher problem will be to *adapt* it after enactment—or, tougher still, to get rid of it and replace it with something better. Lobbies will lock in every favorable provision, ensuring that re-allocating benefits—to say nothing of cutting them or rebuilding the whole program—is a political mare's nest. If lobbies calcify the health program, after a decade or two it will cause at least as many problems as it solves.

In its later stages, demosclerosis becomes weirdly convulsive. As government's flexibility dwindles, Washington scrambles ever more frantically, yet finds success ever more elusive. Enraged, the public turns against government and rails at politicians. But as politicians reply by piling new programs and subsidies on top of old ones, things get worse and the public becomes even angrier. Americans and their government become like the ill-tempered farmer and the arthritic nag. The farmer loads more and more on the nag, the nag becomes weaker and weaker, the angry farmer beats and whips the nag, the battered nag becomes weaker still. That's the chart.

It's important to understand that "change" is no escape if "change" just means piling programs, subsidies, and laws on top of other programs, subsidies, and laws. On the other hand, the answer also can't be simply to reduce the size of government. The issue isn't how to make government smaller (or larger) but how to make it more *flexible*.

In the fight against demosclerosis, standard pro-government liberal ideology ("More programs!") is counterproductive, and standard anti-government conservative ideology ("Less government!") is beside the point. We need to try something else. But what?

The forces of demosclerosis never just go away. They need to be fought unremittingly with a countervailing force, preferably one that attacks and weakens the lobbies themselves. That force is competition.

What lobbies want out of life is a comfy burrow to call home. They want a subsidy, tax break, or a favorable law or regulation that they can depend on year after year to shelter them from competition for resources. Such shelters take many forms and benefit every class of people. Farmers get cash subsidies; Medicare recipients get in-kind benefits; real estate agents get tax loopholes; textile makers get protective tariffs; taxi drivers get medallions that restrict competition.

I'm not saying that all benefits for everyone should be eliminated or that no programs are justified. I am saying that the true cost of such subsidies is much higher than the dollar figure in the federal budget: As subsidies become nesting places for lobbies and obstacles to adaptation, the ultimate victim is government itself. But if protection strengthens interest groups, competition can weaken them. And it can be harnessed in any number of ways.

- First, *force lobbies to compete with each other*. This turns out to be fairly hard to do. If the cattlemen propose to raise their subsidies by cutting the wheat farmers' benefit checks, they can expect to get the wheat farmers fist in their face. So lobbies seek a detente in which everybody goes along with everybody else's subsidies—and the bill is paid by taxpayers, consumers, or the unborn (that's the budget deficit).

How, then, to force confrontations? One way is to reduce the budget deficit, preferably over time to zero or even to surplus. Entirely apart from the economic benefits, when lobbies can't feed on the future, they must fight over a relatively smaller budget in the present. Meanwhile, when government reduces the deficit, it has to set priorities—a healthy exercise that stimulates adaptation.

Another way to force lobbies to compete is to decentralize. The economist Alice M. Rivlin—now of the Office of Management and Budget—has proposed a scheme in which Washington would cede to the states control of programs in education, job training, economic development, housing, transportation, social services, and others, in exchange for picking up broad social-insurance programs like health care and Social Security. True, states and localities are subject to the forces of demosclerosis, but they have an advantage over Washington: They compete with each other for people and jobs. That gives them less room to shelter lobbies than Washington's vast expanses provide.

- Second, and even more important: *clean out subsidies*, including tax breaks. Get rid of things to make room for things, and do it vigorously and on a broad scale. This weakens lobbies and strengthens government. The sugar lobby's mission is to defend the sugar subsidy. Get rid of the subsidy, and the lobby, while perhaps it won't vanish overnight, loses a lifeline. Moreover, resources pried from groups that captured them decades ago are freed for more pressing needs. Government gains space to adapt because funds can be used for new ventures.

For years, anti-government conservatives have talked about eliminating programs (though talk is about all they've done). Yet it is government's *friends* who should be scraping off barnacles, for the benefits ultimately flow to government itself. Liberals who never met a program they didn't like are loving government to death. They need to understand that without a determined and thorough housecleaning, government will rot.

Killing subsidies is, of course, exactly what interest groups exist to prevent. To beat them, it's critical to do the job wholesale, in a package big enough to show a real payoff. The model is the 1986 tax-reform bill, which swept away enough tax loopholes to allow major reductions in tax rates—pain rewarded with tangible gain. And the anti-model is the timid budget-plan President Clinton proposed last year. That plan failed to offer a visible payoff, either in the form of a dramatically lower deficit or a dramatically reformed government. Why support pain with nothing to show for it? No wonder no one wanted to vote for Clinton's plan.

- Finally, *expose entrenched interests to economic competition*. Domestically, government should hunt for and get rid of regulations and barriers that shelter specific industries and groups. The competition fostered by school choice, for example, is good for public schools in the long run, but it's bad for public-school employees' lobbies.

Perhaps most important of all, government should expose lobbies to *foreign* competition. Goods, money, and ideas from abroad fuel the innovation that makes ancient lobbies irrelevant and dissolves their political bases. That was one reason why so many groups hated the North American Free Trade Agreement.

NAFTA was good, but GATT, the General Agreement on Tariffs and Trade, is even better. Acting under its auspices, more than 100 countries recently agreed to reduce their trade barriers. Although multilateral trade negotiations are often slow and frustrating, they allow countries to attack *each other's* lobbies. Americans go after the European farm lobby and Europeans go after the U.S. maritime lobby. GATT is political reform in disguise.

Of all the counter-measures in the fight against demosclerosis, foreign competition may offer the best combination of effectiveness and accessibility. We know it helps, and we have the means to pursue it. Above all, foreign competition hammers entrenched lobbies every day. It's a sentinel that never sleeps.

To President Clinton's credit, 1993 brought progress on trade. On other fronts in 1993, however, he kicked away the opportunity for radical reform. Proposing only timid changes in government's structure, he tried to appease rather than confront the lobbies—which, whenever possible, returned the favor by humiliating him.

"He's a get-along, go-along kind of guy, fundamentally," says Rep. Timothy J. Penny, D-Minn., a prominent deficit hawk. "He's transitional in that he doesn't so much disagree with the old agenda but he's got a new approach. He's trying to layer the new on top of the old." Instead of trying to reorder the ramshackle, maladaptive mess that government has become, Clinton and Congress tried stacking more things on top of other things—the very strategy that created the mess to begin with. "Ross Perot was a wake-up call," says Penny, "and we hit the snooze button."

That isn't good enough. The forces of demosclerosis never just go away: The groups keep forming, the dynamic imbalance persists. True, hacking away at barnacles is no one's idea of fun. But for a glimpse of the future if Washington continues on its current course, look back at the chart. Then extend both lines. Though government is in bad enough shape already, make no mistake: It can get worse.

# Q: Are ethnic and gender-based special-interest groups good for America?

## Yes: These groups serve as useful way stations on the long road to political maturity.

**BY ANITA PEREZ FERGUSON**

*Ferguson is president of the National Women's Political Caucus in Washington and is a regular political analyst on To the Contrary, a syndicated television program.*

A current debate considers whether political activity by groups with similar characteristics or interests is good for our democracy. Without a doubt it is. Agencies that identify and advocate for specific groups—whether racial minorities, gender-based coalitions or the physically disabled—encourage the involvement of these groups in the electoral process and they deserve citizens' support. So-called "identity politics" provide a benefit as a preparation for mainstream political leadership, as a supportive network during life transformations and as an enhancement to our democratic process.

Some contend that such groups make their political decisions based only on a few criteria, such as race, gender or religious belief, and that politicians elected by so-called special-interest groups may ignore opposing concerns of their other constituents. However, such groups not only provide a necessary and appropriate orientation to the larger society, but those issues they select for special consideration indeed carry greater impact for the identified group and therefore deserve increased attention as political priorities.

The first engagement of an individual or group in identity politics can be compared to the process of maturation within a family setting. Early stages of either physical or political maturation are, by definition, stages of dependency and close-knit relationships. At this early stage we begin to develop fundamental skills for communication and learn to meet our basic needs for survival. At home, we learn to eat, speak, walk and dress. In the political arena, we learn to understand our rights

*(continued on page 181)*

## No: Contrary to the vision of America's Founders, identity politics balkanizes the electorate

**BY WARD CONNERLY**

*Connerly is chairman and founder of the American Civil Rights Institute in Sacramento and a member of the University of California Board of Regents.*

"One nation . . . indivisible."

Those three powerful words, contained in our Pledge of Allegiance, are the centerpiece of our democracy. They suggest a nation of people who share values and aspirations and who will pursue them within the context of some common, "indivisible" national purpose.

In reality, nothing could be further from the truth. America is not a nation without divisible parts; we have become a nation of a thousand tribes who view politics—public-policy issues—almost exclusively through the prism of our various identities.

"Identity" may be defined as some generic feature that serves as a distinguishing characteristic of an individual. These identities include ethnic background, gender, race, physical disability, age, religion and sexual orientation, to name a few. Our identity might be assigned to us by our society, or it might be voluntarily selected.

Although special-interest or "pressure" groups—public-employee unions, farmers, homebuilders, for example—also are a form of identity politics, groups that are formed around professional affiliations or occupations are not the kind of "identities" which have become so troubling to our political process.

Special-interest groups have existed and played a role in the American political process since the founding of the republic. Such groups are an inherent part of the governing process of a democracy. But, when the electorate divides into

*(continued on page 182)*

FERGUSON: *continued from page 180*

and responsibilities in our political system. Consider the tentative first steps a citizen takes to claim his or her rights in City Hall, or the stammering first sentence uttered to a member of Congress.

All political behavior is learned. However, not everyone is equally supportive of that learning process, especially when it comes to new citizens. In a 1993 article in the *Washington Post,* David S. Broder pointed out the cynical and cyclical relationship between election-reform proposals and immigrant waves in our American democracy. Broder astutely observes that many of our good government (even populist) reform movements actually may take power from special-interest or identity-politics groups and preserve it for socioeconomic elites. Campaign-reform movements have, Broder claims, suspiciously coincided with increases in Irish, German, Italian (and now Latin-American and Asian-Pacific) immigration patterns in the United States.

According to Michael J. Sandel in *The Politics of Community: Robert F. Kennedy vs. Ronald Reagan,* the contribution of identity politics to American political culture is a proven good: "The civic education and social solidarity cultivated in the black Baptist churches of the South were a crucial prerequisite for the civil-rights movement that ultimately unfolded on a national scale. What began as a bus boycott in Montgomery [Ala.] later became a general challenge to segregation in the South, which led in turn to a national campaign for equal citizenship and the right to vote. More than a means of winning a vote, the movement itself was a movement of self-government, an instance of empowerment. It offered an example of the civic engagement that can flow from local attachments and community ties." The work of the civil-rights movement is an example of identity politics which forever has changed our nation, and yet it is far from finished. Today, veterans of those early days who grew to political maturity within the movement serve as elected officials throughout the nation.

This is an example of an additional benefit of identity politics. While some individuals may choose to remain within the confines of their discrete political neighborhood with a specific racial, ethnic or gender group for their entire political lives, others will use the skills they have gained in a larger political context. Witness the example of eight-term Democratic Rep. Esteban Torres of California. His leadership skills were developed during the organizing days of a local labor union, and now he serves his varied constituents ably in the House of Representatives. As feminist author Betty Friedan has argued, business owners protecting their stores may develop into advocates for safer communities; PTA moms join the school board and then the legislature. In each case, the basic skills are honed through action taken in special-interest groups. And with the expansion of political skills comes an expanded understanding of the common needs and goals which many, if not all, groups share. "Different groups must come to see that the fates of their agendas are linked," according to Friedan.

Political-science Professor Amy Gutman writes that citizens should "educate for civic virtue." Writing in the spring 1996 issue of the journal *Responsive Community,* she urges: "Associate cooperatively. Speak responsively and respectfully. When we put these deliberative ideals into practice, they have conspicuously positive effects on our politics." Participation in

## Individuals are pulled into politics often through an identity group with whom they feel comfortable.

identity politics gives many people their first and best experiences in the education, association and speaking Gutman describes.

But let us not grow out of the old neighborhood of identity politics too quickly. Just as much civil-rights work remains unfinished, other identity groups (in particular the Hispanic/Latino community in the United States) still have much at stake in the political process. Hispanics—more than 25 million strong—will become the largest minority group in the country before 2010. The good news is that there already are more than 5,000 elected officials of Hispanic origin in the United States, according to the National Association of Latino Elected/Appointed Officials. The bad news is that more than 40 percent of Hispanic children in the United States live in poverty, according to the Committee for Hispanic Children and Families. Further, Hispanics are among the most fully employed Americans, but receive the lowest annual wages. Latino families are three times more likely than non-Latino families to have no health insurance. Latino women are four times more likely than non-Hispanic women to have received no prenatal care during pregnancy.

Given these challenging circumstances, it is little wonder that Hispanic political, policy and professional groups continue to exist and expand. Speaking at the 1996 convention of the Hispanic National Bar Association, Secretary of State Madeleine Albright pointed out: "This is precisely the kind of organization that makes our nation stronger. Your contributions to equal opportunity, education, civil rights and civil justice are helping to prepare us for the challenges ahead."

Identifying with the group means identifying with the group's challenges. More than three times as many Hispanic children drop out of school than their Anglo-American counterparts. They are exposed to violence at exceedingly high rates, and a large proportion lives in inadequate housing both in rural areas and in inner cities. Federal, state and—most of all—local action is needed, particularly at the local level.

As the late Tip O'Neill, former House speaker, rightly observed, all politics is local—and identity politics is nothing if not fiercely local. Perhaps this is the feature those who seek to move beyond these special interests find troublesome. Good identity politics stresses a broader sense of responsibility. The myopic interests described by Harvey J. Kaye, professor of social change at the University of Wisconsin, in *Tikkun* magazine is an example of bad identity politics. He writes: "In the past two years class talk has broken out all over.... So far, the most significant recent manifestation of class-based politics—Pat Buchanan's presidential campaign—has been far from progressive. While it revealed the anger of working people (especially white working men) and sent shivers up the spines of corporate and conservative elites . . . it espoused and tapped into strains of racism, anti-Semitism, sexism and homophobia that will have to be addressed by a new progressivism."

The all-important message of diversity has two essential parts: There are differences among Americans and those differences are good. Our differences are reflected in our family histories, which in turn influence our basic values, family configurations and measures of success in the modern world. The inherent goodness of these differences inspires creative approaches to national challenges and ensures a varied and pragmatic examination of our leaders and their proposed policies. The strategy of divide and conquer, which some of the 1996 political campaigns seemed to follow, neglected the second half of that message.

*American Demographics* magazine can shed light on the real story about identity politics. Their marketing studies closely have followed American trends among seniors, women and ethnic minorities. They also know how dynamic social positions in the United States can be. Just when you think you are ready for Main Street politics, your social identity changes and you are back in Politics 101—this time as a new parent, a recent retiree, a person with a disability or a crime victim.

You can be sure (and should be grateful) that there will be a special-interest group there to welcome you into your new phase of life.

Finally, little evidence exists to convince us that Americans automatically get involved in the political process because it is a natural or a good thing to do. In fact, the contrary is true. Fewer and fewer Americans are involving themselves in the political process at all. As with other social movements, participation is part of a push/pull experience. Individuals are pushed into political involvement because of a concern or problem, but they also are pulled into activity, often through an identity group with whom they feel comfortable. When we ignore or denigrate a particularized approach to the electorate, we actually are denying the possibility of participation to many people who never will respond to a homogenized political message.

Of course, Americans are affected by overriding economic concerns and trends toward downsizing in the 1990s. Social attitudes espoused in this state of scarcity create a backlash against racial, ethnic and gender-based politics. But those same socioeconomic factors affect these identity groups even more drastically than mainstream America. It neither is reasonable nor helpful to our democracy to discourage such political groupings. Rather, it remains our responsibility to encourage entrance into the democratic process through the nearest and most accessible doorway. In many instances this is the doorway of identity politics.

---

**CONNERLY:** *continued from page 180*

pressure groups along lines of group identities, the consequences are not what was envisioned by our Founders.

Identity politics not only is antithetical to the basic principle of one indivisible nation, it has the potential fatally to damage our democratic system of government. Consider the damage done by affirmative action, which has become a form of racial and gender patronage. It provokes and appeals to the most blatant form of identity politics imaginable.

To defeat Proposition 209—the California Civil Rights Initiative—its opponents tried to create a political equation of women and "people of color" against "angry white males." From a political standpoint, an identity campaign made sense for the opposition because white males constitute less than 35 percent of the California opposition.

The entire 209 opposition campaign was based on direct appeals to identity. Women were urged to oppose 209 because it allegedly would harm the specific interests of women. Latinos were exhorted to oppose 209 because it is "their turn" to benefit from affirmative action, and 209 would deprive them of that ability.

Asians were caught between a rock and a hard place. Supporting affirmative action would give them a preference in employment and contracting, but would give them a disadvantage in admission to more prestigious educational institutions, such as the University of California, Berkeley. The appeal to blacks

was blatant racism, even to the extent of injecting the Ku Klux Klan and David Duke into the campaign.

Although the pro-209 forces urged Californians not to vote on the basis of their identities, the final 209 vote reflected a classic experience in identity politics. Blacks opposed 209 by a 3-to-1 margin. The Latino vote almost was identical. Because of the conflicting interests of Asians, however, their vote was 45 percent in favor and 55 percent against 209.

As one examines the underlying features of identity politics, it becomes clear that the themes of "building diversity" by any means necessary and "celebrating our multicultural attributes" are the twin pillars of the identity-politics reality.

Diversity and multiculturalism promote and accentuate our "differences" and suggest that our identities are determined totally by those differences. Those themes argue against the goal of assimilation and the formulation of common identities.

Politicians are a major contributor to our practice of identity politics; it is much easier to pander to individual groups than it is to appeal to the overall best interest of the community at the national, state or local level.

One result of this game of identity politics is that we have bred a system with more political cowards per capita than at any time in our history. Republicans are afraid to take a position against race, gender and ethnic preferences because to do so might result in the loss of votes from blacks, Latinos and women.

Many Democrats support preferences—not because they believe it is the right thing to do but because they don't want to risk losing the support of the same groups to which the Republicans want to appeal. Of the two parties, however, Democrats are virtual captives of identity politics. Their convention likely has more identity caucuses than there are countries belonging to the United Nations.

During the 209 campaign in California, the proliferation of groups formed along identity lines was staggering. There even was a group that identified itself as "Black Gay and Lesbian Lawyers for Affirmative Action." This group combined professional status, sexual orientation and race.

The Congressional Black Caucus, the National Organization for Women, the American Association of Retired People—the list of organizations formed to protect and advocate for the interest of certain groups is endless. Some would argue that the public interest emerges from the battle taking place in the political arena between these warring identity groups. I don't believe that for a moment.

One of the worst examples of identity politics I have ever seen involved a congressional hearing conducted by the Congressional Black Caucus, or CBC, to address the plight of black farmers. Each member of the CBC empathized with the farmers who had been invited to the hearing, which was shown on C-Span, and promised that they would get to the bottom of the problem.

What was interesting about this hearing was the fact that not one nonblack member of Congress attended, although even black members without black farmers in their districts were present and promised to help solve the problems confronting black farmers. For Rep. Maxine Waters—the chair of the CBC, who presided over the hearing—the closest thing resembling a farm in her Los Angeles district are the ducks in the man-made lake at the Hollywood Race Track. Yet, she made it clear she regarded the black farmers as her constituents.

Unquestionably, it is appropriate for Congress to examine the question of whether black farmers have suffered discrimination. But why should this be the jurisdiction of the CBC? Why not the Agriculture committees? Certainly some white members of Congress have black farmers in their districts. Why, then, should those members not be invited to participate in such a hearing? When the problem is identified as a black problem to be solved by black politicians, that is identity politics in its most tasteless form.

President Clinton has been forced to practice identity politics more than any other president in our nation's history, and this trend is only likely to increase unless something happens to change our system. As one of the first acts following his election in 1992, the president announced that he wanted an administration that "looks like America." This was the ultimate expression and acknowledgment of identity politics in America.

Several days after Clinton's reelection, a representative of a women's group stated that she wanted the president to appoint women in direct proportion to the votes which women gave him toward reelection. Similar claims were made by "black leaders" who wanted to see more blacks in the Cabinet and by Latinos who wanted the president to make a Latino his next appointment to the Supreme Court.

Carried to its logical extreme, this approach to politics will result in campaigns based not on issues but on identities, or in policies formulated not on the overall public good, but on what a majority of the identity groups will accept, and in appointments based not on who is most qualified for the position but on electoral quotas.

---

# Practicing our politics on the basis of our identities forces us to choose sides on purely artificial grounds.

---

All of us contribute to identity politics by our preoccupation with race, gender, ethnicity and the concept of victimization. No institution in our society is more at fault, however, than the media, which always seem to find it necessary to call attention to the race or ethnic background of "minorities," even when it is totally irrelevant.

Jesse Jackson has run for president of the United States at least twice. In each instance he ran a relatively competitive campaign, gathering a significant number of Latino and white votes in addition to his strong showing among black people. This fact makes Jackson more than a "black civil-rights leader," which is the description I often see in the print media.

Although I am certainly no cheerleader for Jackson, it strikes me that such characterizations are unfair and unwittingly serve to devalue his legitimacy as a more universal political leader. When it comes to "minorities," there always seems to be that qualifier: the "African-American regent" or the successful "black businessman." Those are the qualifiers applied to me, almost without exception.

Imagine substituting "white" in either of those contexts. Clearly, it would be inappropriate. Why, then, is it acceptable to use such qualifiers in the case of Asians, blacks or Latinos?

Practicing our politics on the basis of our identities forces us to choose sides on purely artificial grounds, such as skin color, instead of thinking through our positions intellectually. When it comes to race, identity politics brings out the worst in us. It demands racial solidarity—loyalty to the race.

Our democracy cannot survive a system of politics based on our identities. Theodore Roosevelt seemed to understand this when he said, "The one absolutely certain way of bringing this nation to ruin, of preventing all possibility of its continuing as a nation at all, would be to permit it to become a tangle of squabbling nationalities—English-Americans, Scandinavian-Americans or Italian-Americans—each preserving its separate nationality."

If we allow identity politics to govern America, democracy is doomed.

# Trying Times

### BY LOUIS JACOBSON

THOUGH STILL A WASHINGTON POWERHOUSE, THE ASSOCIATION OF TRIAL LAWYERS OF AMERICA IS FACING THE STIFFEST CHALLENGES IN ITS HISTORY. NOT ONLY ARE ITS MEMBERS SCORNED BY THE PUBLIC, THEY'RE SPLIT OVER THE TOBACCO ISSUE AND UNDER FIRE FROM LAWMAKERS.

Two decades ago, Peter Kinzler was a Democratic congressional aide assigned to help pass a bill that would radically overhaul the nation's car insurance system. The legislation would have restricted traffic-accident lawsuits, which are the bread and butter of 80–90 per cent of all trial lawyers. One day, Kinzler recalls, Thomas Hale Boggs Jr. stopped in to see him. Boggs—then, as now, a superlobbyist for the Association of Trial Lawyers of America (ATLA)—told Kinzler that even if Congress added 75 amendments favorable to the trial lawyers, ATLA would fight the bill to its dying breath.

As it turned out, ATLA got its way on auto insurance through most of the 1970s. But now Kinzler is a lobbyist, and his Coalition for Auto-Insurance Reform is putting the issue back on Congress's agenda. An auto insurance reform bill—backed by House Majority Leader Richard K. Armey, R-Texas, and Sens. Joseph I. Lieberman, D-Conn., Mitch McConnell, R-Ky., and Daniel Patrick Moynihan, D-N.Y.—is garnering interest just in time to cause headaches for ATLA during a crucial moment in its history.

Virtually all of ATLA's foes agree that the 60,000-member trade association is still a powerhouse, but they suggest that it also faces some of the stiffest challenges of its two-decade tenure near the top of the Washington interest-group heap.

For starters, trial lawyers increasingly are finding themselves the object of public scorn. Attorneys involved in state and federal tobacco lawsuits are raking in huge fees that are unpopular with many Americans, providing an opportunity for ATLA opponents—such as a newly energized U.S. Chamber of Commerce—to score some public relations points.

And besides the auto insurance legislation, ATLA has other battles to fight on Capitol Hill. It is trying to stave off Congress's long-running attempts to curb lawsuits over defective consumer products, as well as lobbying to repeal the legal liability protections that managed care health insurance organizations currently enjoy. The trade group is also embroiled in the $368.5 billion national tobacco deal negotiated by state attorneys general and trial lawyers last summer. ATLA is fighting legislation based on the settlement that would end dozens of state and class action lawsuits and would restrict future lawsuits against the tobacco industry.

In the past, ATLA has faced—and won—several battles at once, and officials there downplay the degree of this challenge. But critics are hoping that the current panoply of issues could exacerbate tensions within the trade association. Already, a splinter group—high-powered trial lawyers who helped negotiate the tobacco settlement—has broken ranks with ATLA.

"No group I know of, other than ATLA, has gotten virtually everything on their dance card," said longtime business lobbyist Victor E. Schwartz, a partner at the Washington law firm of Crowell & Moring. "Now, for the first time, ATLA faces members of Congress [who are] saying, 'I can help you on auto insurance and medical malpractice, but not contingency fee reform.' And if ATLA demands absolute fealty, it will get a backlash. That's what can turn a lobbying superpower into an ordinary trade association."

## A FORMIDABLE FOE

Sherman (Tiger) Joyce, the president of the American Tort Reform Association, is just one of many ATLA adversaries who express great respect for the archenemy. "They are extremely formidable, and I say that in a very complimentary way," Joyce said.

ATLA's largesse certainly accounts for some of its success. It gave $3.5 million to candidates and parties during the 1995–96 election cycle, ranking third among all donors, according to the Center for Responsive Politics. ATLA also was the 12th-biggest provider of "soft money" to the parties. Its generosity was bolstered by six-figure donations from lawyers at several plaintiffs law firms, led by San Diego-based Milberg Weiss Bershad Specthrie & Lerach, which doled out $883,000.

For many years, ATLA has also benefited from the clout of the law and lobbying firm Patton Boggs. Tommy Boggs and a core group of seven or eight other lobbyists at the firm—Democrats and Republicans included—represent ATLA, which itself has four in-house federal lobbyists.

Such top-flight personnel have helped ATLA grasp the new political dynamics in Congress, where sentiment favoring changes to the legal system has grown. The 1994 elections not only ushered in a House Republican leadership committed to tort reform, but also ousted some lawmakers who were once ATLA's closest friends, including then-House Judiciary Committee chairman Jack Brooks, D-Texas. In addition, several Republicans with close ties to the trial lawyers have left the Senate since 1995.

Though the trade association still gives 85 percent of its money to Democrats, it has managed to win over enough Republicans that major tort reforms remain stalled. "Republican offices may not always agree with ATLA, but I have found that Republicans are more than happy to let you in the door and hear what you have to say," said Patton Boggs lobbyist Darryl Nirenberg, who once worked for Sen. Jesse A. Helms, R-N.C., and is the son of a trial lawyer. "On so many issues, ATLA is consistent with the conservative position—states' rights, a faith in juries, free markets and personal responsibility."

Top-drawer donations and connections alone, however, do not account for ATLA's influence. Both supporters and foes agree that the trade association has excelled at holding its membership to a single message, then dividing and wearying its opponents.

Business groups, for instance, have been petitioning Congress for almost two decades for stronger protections from lawsuits over faulty consumer products, but no comprehensive reform has been enacted. Over the past year, ATLA has exploited its opponents' differences so well on product liability that some say its critics spend as much time squabbling among themselves as they do opposing the trial lawyers.

ATLA did much the same thing to demolish proposals for no-fault auto insurance in the 1970s. "I think it was one of the most complete victories I've ever seen in the field of tort law," Schwartz said. "They just went into Baghdad and took out Saddam Hussein."

The trial lawyers also owe their success to their media savvy. The national organization and its state affiliates have avoided the public spotlight and left it up to their opponents to make the case for tort reform—a difficult task, considering that the issue traditionally has not been a sexy one. "Even in this period of heightened interest, the tort bar has grown ever more powerful," said Michael J. Horowitz, a Hudson Institute fellow and leading advocate of auto insurance reform.

When particular tort reforms have managed to grab media attention, ATLA and its consumer-group allies—most notably those affiliated with Ralph Nader—have often skillfully defended an individual's ability to sue as a fundamental right. "They are great at focusing away from what is in the bill to who is for it," Schwartz said. "Often, they will suggest that the groups for it are the drug companies, tobacco companies or chemical companies. Since ATLA believes the public perceives that those guys are up to no good, ATLA has been able to defrock their opponents and make them seem greedy, while casting themselves as saviors of the public."

> **NO CLARENCE DARROWS:** Trial lawyers used to be famous and well-liked. These days, they're targets of public criticism.

Even on the 1996 Bill Emerson Good Samaritan Food Donation Act, which shielded donors of food to the needy from liability, ATLA narrowed the bill's reach before passage. "You don't want a situation where a corporate entity like Kmart [Corp.] is dumping tainted meat on the homeless," said Linda A. Lipsen, the group's chief in-house lobbyist. "It was bad public policy. We did not take a pass just because of the sympathy surrounding it."

Faced with another bill in 1996 that banned lawyers from soliciting families who lost relatives in aviation disasters, ATLA persuaded lawmakers to keep it legal for families to contact attorneys on their own. Another time, ATLA successfully argued that the popular 1997 Volunteer Protection Act should offer limited immunity only to individual volunteers, not to large nonprofits, as the bill's sponsors had hoped. "Do you want a situation where an organization that monitors volunteers had no duty to make sure that whoever is watching your kids has no criminal record?" Lipsen said. "The entity has to be held accountable."

To the glee of ATLA's critics, a few narrowly tailored bills—ones that partially shield small businesses, makers of small airplanes, Amtrak and community homeless centers from liability—have sneaked through since 1994. Even ATLA's foes concede, however, that these small victories for tort reformers offer mostly psychological, rather than practical, advantage. "I think they are little chinks in ATLA's armor," Schwartz said. "But it does not in any way spell a partial or wholesale retreat by ATLA or a major change in its fortunes."

In fact, the trial lawyers' most skillful work, observers say, may be in shifting losing battles into arenas in which they are stronger. Most strikingly, ATLA rebounded from a string of tort reform losses with state legislatures and governors by petitioning state courts to overrule them. State judges have proven sympathetic: In the past two years, they have sided with the trial lawyers by a 2–1 margin. "They took broken eggs and made an omelette," said Lester Brickman, a law professor at the Benjamin N. Cardozo School of Law in New York City.

## LOOMING CHALLENGES

But as big as ATLA's recent triumphs are, its challenges are also substantial. The prospect of auto insurance reform, for instance, is worrying plenty of trial lawyers these days. Most of them don't try high-stakes tobacco, product liability or medical malpractice suits, but rather support themselves through smaller-scale car accident cases. "No-fault car insurance, if it passed, could be very, very damaging for ATLA," said John P. Coale, a prominent Washington-based trial lawyer.

If auto insurance reform is enacted, observers predict the impact could be serious because it could be used as a model for fixes to other areas of tort law. "The most dangerous thing for the trial lawyers would be if it passes and it works," Schwartz said. But ATLA and its allies feel confident about their prospects; Lipsen said that the auto insurance issue's reemergence has served to re-energize the organization's base.

Whether or not that confidence is justified, ATLA's opponents are ready to pounce on another issue: the trial lawyers' public image. Though ATLA's critics acknowledge that the freedom to sue remains popular, they suggest that accusations about ambulance-chasing lawyers, seemingly outrageous punitive-damage awards and the creeping litigiousness of American society are prompting a public backlash against trial attorneys.

Thomas J. Donahue, president and CEO of the U.S. Chamber of Commerce, said in an interview that "the single, universal thing I get a positive response on—from small companies and big companies, from individual proprietors and multinationals—is that something has gone seriously wrong with out legal system, that we've become a society where there always must be someone who's wrong and there always must be someone to sue."

The chamber has launched a multimillion-dollar assault—spearheaded by the new Institute for Legal Reform, headed by longtime chamber executive Lawrence B. Kraus—that will use advertising, lobbying and other tactics to highlight the cost of litigation to consumers, the size of attorney fees and the extent of trial lawyers' campaign donations to judges.

Supporters of reforming product liability laws say that one of their most successful advertisements—coopted from ATLA's playbook—is one about a child who cannot obtain a life-saving medical device because companies, fearing lawsuits, have stopped making them.

"I think we've been able to demonstrate that the American tort system is out of control," said Lawrence Smarr, chairman of the Health Care Liability Alliance, a tort reform group whose members include the American Medical Association, the American Hospital Association, insurance companies and pharmaceutical manufacturers. "Poll figures validate that the public is catching on to the fact that ordinary consumers pay dearly for the right to sue."

# ON THE DOCKET

The Association of Trial Lawyers of America (ATLA) is fighting on several fronts at once in Congress. This year's battles include:

**Auto insurance.** Congress is considering a proposal—opposed by ATLA, consumer advocacy groups and some insurers—that encourages states to adopt systems under which drivers insure themselves against only economic losses, primarily lost wages and medical expenses. Supporters say the bill would reduce insurance premiums, lawyers' fees and health care fraud. ATLA counters that gravely injured parties couldn't seek payments to cushion the blow of living with disabilities, that bad drivers would benefit at the expense of good drivers, and that the plan would impose a new federal bureaucracy on the states.

**Medical liability.** ATLA and many consumer advocacy groups support legislation sponsored by Rep. Charlie Norwood, R-Ga., that would, among other things, repeal the legal liability protections that managed care health insurance organizations currently enjoy.

**Product liability.** Lawmakers have been trying since the 1970s to restrict the type and nature of lawsuits that can be filed against manufacturers of defective consumer products, by, for example, capping punitive damages and limiting the targets of suits. ATLA and many consumer groups oppose the legislation, which many industry trade associations strongly support.

**Tobacco settlement.** ATLA, joined by many public health organizations, opposes all the congressional proposals for a national tobacco settlement that would provide legal protections to the tobacco industry. Ironically, in mid-April, the tobacco industry joined with ATLA in opposition to the settlement, for different reasons.

To be sure, as trial lawyers point out, Americans regard lawyers the way they do Congress—they tend to hate the trial bar but like their own lawyers. And some trial lawyers suggest that popular dissatisfaction with their Big Tobacco adversaries helps make them look good.

But one issue that may pack a punch is that the trial lawyers who have negotiated tobacco settlements in Texas, Florida and elsewhere are in line for windfalls worth billions of dollars. "We are unleashing a massive transfer of wealth to people about whom we have great questions of what the hell they're going to do with it," Donahue said.

Many trial lawyers—including Barry Nace, a Paulson & Nace partner who served as ATLA's president in 1993–94 and as its political action committee chairman from 1995–97—defend the payouts as legitimate. "The rest of us ought to sit back and say, 'They took a chance [on the tobacco cases] and have done a hell of a lot of good,'" Nace said. "How much is Shaquille O'Neal getting—and how much has he done to help people?"

Even some trial lawyers, however, acknowledge that the public fallout over fees could be damaging. "Certainly it's clear that as a PR and political matter, there are people in Congress and elsewhere who think there's a payoff in focusing attention on the attorneys' fees," said Arthur Bryant, executive director of Trial Lawyers for Public Justice, a group independent of ATLA that works on public-interest litigation and has attacked trial lawyers' fees in several instances. "To the extent that those fees are perceived to be unjustly large, it will hurt people's perceptions of trial lawyers."

Trial lawyer Coale, who helped craft the pending federal tobacco settlement, goes so far as to call billion-dollar fees "horrendous," adding, "It's terrible PR to come in and get a piece of the action like that." His national settlement would have an arbitrator decide the level of attorney compensation.

More serious than the disagreements over fees is the split over the pending tobacco legislation itself. ATLA's current leadership strenuously argues that Congress should not settle tobacco-related lawsuits that are not yet before it, while the negotiators of the settlement, including many ex-ATLA officials such as Coale, are pushing hard for its enactment. (Ironically, the tobacco industry's mid-April an-nouncement that it has changed course and is now going to fight the national settlement puts it on the same side as ATLA.)

For ATLA, which has had nary a schism in the past two decades, the internal split over the tobacco issue has been the subject of much discussion. Officials at the trade association downplay the significance of the discord, pointing out that its executive committee and board on three occasions have approved its stance on the issue. "There is no internal policy dispute," said Lipsen, who called the disagreements among its members "extremely respectful."

Nace is more sympathetic to ATLA's stance than to that of the federal settlement negotiators. "You're always in situations where you have to do what's best for your client," he said. He called the association's restiveness over tobacco understandable because the issue itself is unique, and agreed that his colleagues are handling the matter with maturity. "We've always come together on the critical issues," Nace said. "I saw at one point a potential for a real split, but I don't think that is materializing at all."

Others aren't so sure. "I think it's significant whenever you have four or five past presidents of ATLA on the other side of the issue," adds Michael A. Tongour, a Republican lobbyist who represented ATLA from 1995–97 and who now is lobbying in favor of a national tobacco settlement. "It would be worse if there were not a common front on other issues, but yes, it is a problem. I think the opponents of ATLA will try to utilize the schism."

Coale noted that ATLA has historically fought hard on issues that were favored by top-tier litigants, even when most trade association members didn't directly benefit. "They're being stupid by opposing the tobacco settlement," Coale said. "They need us for things like auto insurance, and they're wasting political capital by spreading themselves too thin."

As ATLA plots its strategy for coming battles, it can draw upon the strengths that long have made it a dominant Washington trade group. But its internal strife, combined with a bulging legislative agenda, gives its adversaries some optimism. "It doesn't tilt the playing field," said one anti-ATLA lobbyist, "but it does help level it."

# Did You Have a Good Week?

## *The new unit of political significance*

### James Fallows

When I read the newspaper at home, I always start with sports. But when I've been away for a while and am going through old papers, I find I can flip right past the sports pages. The close games and league races that are so absorbing when they are happening *right now* are boring once the suspense is gone.

More and more, it's the same with the real news. I'm not talking about covering political campaigns as if they were sporting events. This tendency has existed for decades and is well understood. Rather, I mean a development whereby most of the serious news we get is presented with the same artificial, short-lived intensity as sports. Precisely because we know that sports don't matter in a life-and-death sense, we can happily act for a while as if they did. In a few minutes it will all be over, and soon we'll have some other, equally interesting showdown to watch.

Through May and early June of this year, for example, the United States seemed headed toward a nuclear confrontation with North Korea. Numerous reports said that President Bill Clinton had come to his "testing time" and "moment of truth." Of course, the "day of reckoning," as *The Wall Street Journal's* political analyst Gerald Seib called it, did not come. I interviewed a South Korean diplomat, in Seoul, just after former President Jimmy Carter's visit, and he described the moment when he knew that the crisis had passed.

"It was when the O. J. Simpson car chase began," he said. "As soon as the American media had O. J. to deal with, you could *feel* the weight of CNN and the American pundits come off our shoulders."

North Korea's nuclear program returned to its natural dimensions, as a serious long-term problem but not one that required a response *right now.* By the time the American opinion machine was ready to deal with an issue other than O. J., the Whitewater hearings were at hand, along with the buildup for an invasion of Haiti. North Korea's nuclear rods, it goes without saying, were still there.

The Clinton years have come across as an endless stream of emergencies, each seeming to demand total attention while it is under way, but many forgettable as soon as they are done.

Zoë Baird. Kimba Wood. Travelgate. The haircut on the LAX tarmac. David Koresh and the Waco siege. Document-shredding at the Rose law firm. The death of Vincent Foster. Webster Hubbell. Barbra Streisand at the White House. The secrecy of the health-care task force. Casualties in Somalia. Criticism of Les Aspin and Warren Christopher. The Administration's fights for its political life over the first budget bill, over NAFTA, over the crime bill, over health reform. The showdown with China over human rights and with Singapore over caning. The latest skirmish in the trade war with Japan. Threats of action against Serbia, Haiti, North Korea, Cuba. Paula Jones. Whitewater recusals. Joshua Steiner and his diary. The disasters in Bosnia and Rwanda.

This list looks preposterously jumbled, and that is the point of it. Some of the events, in the Balkans and Rwanda, were world tragedies. Others, involving the Branch Davidians and Vincent Foster, were tragic on a smaller scale. Some—including the budget plan, health care, and NAFTA—will play a part in any account of the Clinton years. Others were temporary flaps, including quite a few whose plot lines are difficult to keep straight even now.

Yet every one of these issues, at least for a while, got right-now treatment by the press. We all recognize the signs that an issue has become an Issue: CNN specials, live C-SPAN or NPR hearings coverage, same-day discussion on *Nightline* and *Crossfire,* end-of-the-week wrap-ups on the Washington talk shows.

Journalists claim that they do their jobs by raising questions and looking on skeptically, and that the President and other politicians must do theirs by providing satisfactory answers. This sounds nice. Yet by moving constantly from one emergency to the next, our opinion system has changed the very nature of the political and governmental fight.

For politicians and the public, the struggle is not so much to make or hear convincing arguments. It is to concentrate on anything at all. By the time the Clinton health plan floundered, in August, the conventional wisdom was that the President had waited too long before turning his full attention to it. I wonder why! Hearing about the latest crisis on talk shows and op-ed pages is for the public like living with car alarms in New York: the constant warnings are enough to make you uneasy—but not quite enough to inspire action.

The right-now atmosphere has had at least two measurable effects, both bad, on the progress of Bill Clinton's Administration. First, it has played a part in the repeated premature obituaries for his presidency issued by the press. In May of last year, when Clinton had served eight percent of a four-year term, Elizabeth Drew was asked on the *McNeil/Lehrer NewsHour*

what was at stake in the upcoming House vote on his budget plan. "Nothing less than the Clinton presidency," she replied.

In fairness to her, it was not an overstatement by the standards of the time. Within the month *Time* had published its cover story on "The Incredible Shrinking President," and *Newsweek* had run a cover picture of Clinton with the caption "What's Wrong?" Then David Gergen came to the White House, Clinton was declared to have made a new start, and the obituaries were forgotten—until they were rolled out again later that year and throughout the current one.

Bill Clinton is known to feel that the press is biased against him. Every President since John Kennedy has felt the same way. Maybe, by now, some reporters and columnists do dislike Clinton and his associates. If so, it's a trivial point. The real problem is that so many members of the press are comfortable making overstatements they must know cannot be true.

The other effect has been to add a curious edginess to the public mood. The opinion industry has become a powerful but unacknowledged lobby in behalf of U.S. intervention, for intervention's sake, around the world. On talk shows and TV specials we see a nightmarish sequence of emergencies appearing out of nowhere. Their backgrounds are not explained, and each crowds the others for airtime. The bridge at Gorazde. The Rwandan refugee camps in Zaire. Flotillas from Guantanamo Bay.

The implied message of each of these scenes is "Do something *now!*" The message is conveyed not only by the suffering itself but also by commentators who say

that each case is a test of the President's "character" and "decisiveness." Some of the cases may demand immediate American action to relieve suffering. But the game-day mentality of the press has created a general enthusiasm for intervention almost as strong as the post-Vietnam fear of foreign entanglements. The enthusiasm sometimes wears off as an actual commitment nears, as with the intervention in Haiti. But while an Administration is deciding whether and how to get involved, the press chorus is saying, Act now!

I keep mentioning the political talk shows because they have been the most important force for turning real news into sports. Some of their effects are obvious. *The McLaughlin Group, The Capital Gang, Crossfire,* the Sunday-morning talk shows, and the countless local knockoffs of the Washington battling-journalists shows reward reporters for exhibiting all the wrong traits. These talk shows highlight personality rather than work product, opinion and attitude rather than reporting, and prediction—which is less accurate than the bookies' line on games and for which the journalists are less accountable than bookies—instead of analysis of what has actually occurred.

The Fox network and ESPN spend hours each Sunday on the buildup to the day's slate of NFL football games and, when the games are done, dispose of the results in a few minutes. The political talk shows follow the same plan. Since each of the Washington shows covers more topics than

any of the reporters can know about in detail, discussion naturally drifts to the one subject all the reporters do know: the pure mechanics of politics. ("How is Bob Dole likely to respond to this health-reform plan, Cokie?")

But the worst effect of the shows is so profound that it is barely noticed. This is to make the week the fundamental unit of political measurement. The central question on most of the shows is whether the President had a good week or a bad week. Getting a treaty ratified can mean a good week; a Travelgate-style staff shakeup can make a bad week. As in sports, the wins and losses are toted up as if they all had equal weight.

"It is rarely acknowledged, but asking 'Who won the week?' is a political act," Jay Rosen, of New York University, wrote last year in the magazine *Tikkun.* "The question . . . sets a rhythm to politics that permits the media to play timekeeper, umpire and, finally, judge. The question would not occur to an ordinary citizen."

Ordinary citizens, Rosen said, realize that politics concerns values and choices, not simply the up and down of each tactical fight. Will I pay more taxes? What will schools or health care be like? Will the Army have to stay and fight in Haiti or Bosnia? Most journalists recognize these issues, at least in theory. "But in . . . their day-to-day view of the scene," Rosen concluded, they "have accumulated a huge stake in the denial of meaning, the hollowing out of politics into a game of perceptions, to be played inside the media itself." They are, in other words, just playing the game.

# The 'New' Media and Politics: What Does the Future Hold?

**Doris A. Graber,** *University of Illinois at Chicago*

Beyond new technological advances, what makes the 'new' media new? I contend that the chief change brought about by the new media is the empowerment of media users. They now have greater control over incoming and outgoing messages, and their ability to contact literally millions of people has grown exponentially. These changes have sharply increased the need for new communications policies. I also argue that, despite an explosion of available information, the political information diet of average Americans will remain meager.

## The Changing Media Landscape

### The Growing Information Supply

During the closing decades of the twentieth century, over-the-air networks and cable television systems have multiplied, adding hundreds of broadcasting channels. Satellites carry vast numbers of radio and television programs beamed to customers' backyard satellite dishes. Senders of political messages now have available scores of inexpensive channels for sending customized political messages to diverse audiences. This is likely to improve the electoral chances of minority candidates and minority parties who can readily tailor their messages to the concerns of selected audiences. The needs and interests of specific audiences, such as groups differing in ethnicity, religious beliefs, or sexual orientation, or groups with special concerns related to their vocations and avocations are more likely to be addressed. Customizing also makes information transmission more effective than when depersonalized news is directed to heterogeneous mass audiences. Computers equipped with modems allow information seekers to gain access to the Internet system, which now carries a huge array of politically relevant messages. Other potentially rich sources for information that computer-literate individuals can tap are electronic mail networks and bulletin boards.

Unfortunately, while a great deal of effort has been devoted to creating new channels for carrying information, attention to the quality and diversity of the political content carried by these channels has lagged. When it comes to serious political information, choices offered by various channels, for the most part, amount to surface, rather than substance distinctions. Impartial, analytical information about public figures and public policy issues that would improve citizens' ability to appraise the political scene is all-too-scarce. Despite an explosion of politically oriented Home Pages on the World Wide Web, surprisingly little has been added that is genuinely new or that enriches the information supply beyond the offerings of the far smaller circle of 'old' media.

### Media User Empowerment

The new media have freed users from the tyranny of the time-clock. Twenty-four-hour news channels and computer news sources now make news available around the clock, rather than at times dictated by media delivery schedules. The rapid spread of home computers has increased the size of audiences who can reach computerized data at times of their choice. Video recorders allow average Americans to preserve particular information packages for use wherever, whenever, and as often as they wish. Eighty-five percent of America's households have at least one video recorder to selectively tape programs or play rented tapes. People can also buy political information stored on audio and video tapes and on CD-Rom.

The new media have also eased the control of professional journalists over the framing and interpretation of the news. Thanks to broadcasts of ongoing events, ready availability of full texts of messages, and interactive talk show broadcasts, people now can watch many happenings in real time, often in their entirety. While the initial choice of events to be broadcast is still reserved for journalists, the second step—editing and framing a story—can now be in news consumers' hands. CNN or C-Span viewers, for example, can make their own interpretations and draw their own conclusions while watching live broadcasts.

From *PS: Political Science and Politics*, March 1996, pp. 33–36. © 1996 by the American Political Science Association. Reprinted by permission.

Subscribers to on-line computer services can download full texts, including pictures, into their home computers. They can edit such information to suit their taste by adding, combining, or deleting data.

For those who like to ask newsmakers their own questions, numerous talk-show programs offer excellent opportunities. Politicians and media audiences like talk shows because most hosts, unlike peevish Washington reporters, allow their guests to present their arguments in their own words and from their own perspectives. Talk shows provide prized opportunities for direct interaction between ordinary folk and political leaders. The candidates' ample use of the talk show format during the 1992 campaign loosened the grip of traditional media over candidate messages. Audiences for talk shows were huge. Bill Clinton's one-hour appearance on *Donahue* was seen by nearly 8 million viewers. Television appearances on Larry King's show were seen by an estimated 2.5 million people. Candidates even appeared on rock-music-oriented MTV where a 1992 candidate forum attracted over 3 million—presumably elusive young American voters in the 18–34 age group. Campaigning on these programs also had a large echo effect. The standard mass media and individual pundits widely reported remarks made during talk shows, thus raising their profile and political significance.

## New Political Pressure Tools

Finally, thanks to the new electronic networks, individuals can now inform people worldwide and mobilize them for political action. Individuals and groups eager to spread their political messages no longer depend on media coverage to publicize their appeals. In cyberspace, a single private citizen can address hundreds of thousands of people via computer from the privacy of his or her home. Additionally, electronic publishing on home computers has vastly boosted the numbers of newsletters that vari-

ous social, professional, and trade communities can distribute.

By mid-1995, more than 25 million people in the United States—14% of the adult population—were connected to the Internet; worldwide audiences make the cyberspace community much larger. These numbers have been growing rapidly. However, there is likely to be a growth ceiling because the pool of computer-literate consumers is limited by educational, economic, and technical constraints.

---

**While available food for political thought has grown, despite much overlap and redundancy, the appetite for it and the capacity to consume it remain limited. The ceiling for the demand for political information has already been reached for most people.**

---

Projecting current user figures into the future, based on the demographic characteristics of the computer literate population, it seems unlikely that the majority of Americans will be cyberspace users in the foreseeable future.

## The Current Impact of New Media

What difference have the new media made thus far in the political lives of average Americans and what does the future portend? Unfortunately, information transmission capacity has vastly exceeded use. While available

food for political thought has grown, despite much overlap and redundancy, the appetite for it and the capacity to consume it remain limited. The ceiling for the demand for political information has already been reached for most people. The interest in talk shows recorded during the 1992 presidential campaign does not represent a major permanent spike in political interest and news consumption. Rather, it reflects a revived appetite for political fare when appealing formats compete with the current disliked offerings.

Unlike talk shows, political information available in cyberspace presents major challenges to the intellectual skills of information consumers. The fact that millions of American adults still are functionally illiterate when it comes to reading printed materials does not bode well for looking to a future when computer literacy will reach 90%. In practice, cyberspace riches are available only to individuals with superior education and financial resources. These are the publics who already participate far more in politics than their less privileged fellow citizens. As technology continues to evolve, the knowledge gap between the information privileged and the information underclass is likely to grow. Since knowledge means power, an information-deprived class is likely to suffer other power deprivations. It cannot readily avail itself of Internet resources that empower interest groups to use the information superhighway to organize and lobby for their causes. Hence the influence of educationally and economically privileged groups on politics, which has always been substantial, may be greatly enhanced. The end result may be a more fragmented polity, making political gridlock more likely.

## Reinventing Communications Policy

The multiplication of media, especially the growth of public computer networks, requires a complete rethinking of the scope and purposes of federal regulation of broadcast media. The Communications Act of 1934 was passed because transmission facilities were scarce. Congress wanted to make certain that the limited numbers of available broadcast channels were parceled out equitably and served broad public interests. Printed media were left largely outside the regulatory scheme. The first Amendment to the U.S. Constitution protects their independence from government intrusion. Fifty years later the basic regulatory framework remains intact although its ostensible raison d'être—the scarcity of transmission channels—has largely vanished. Government leaders and industry leaders, aware of the transformation of the communication delivery systems, agree that the 1934 Act must be revised. But there is no agreement on specific plans. Pressures for easing regulations are balanced by pressures to continue and even increase government controls.

### Regulatory Options

If the Communications Act of 1934 is put to well-deserved rest, the government has several basic policy options for dealing with the new media system. It can play a hands-off, laissez-faire role, allowing the system to grow according to the push and pull of market forces, with only minor controls to assure that the system operates effectively. Regulation would be limited to safeguards to protect national security, maintain social norms and privacy, and to guard intellectual property rights.

Media channels can also be treated as common carriers, like the telephone or rail and bus lines. Common carrier status makes transmission facilities available to everyone on a first-come, first-served basis. Congress, the FCC and various local governments like the common carrier concept that has been adopted for communications satellites. While court decisions make the power of Congress to impose common carrier features on the communication industry questionable, these decisions do not constrain state and local authorities.

As a third option, the government can confer public trustee status on communication enterprises. This status grants media owners full control over access to their channels, but requires them to meet certain public service obligations. Examples are equal time allotments to proponents and opponents of controversial public policies, or channel time for public and government broadcasts, including broadcasts serving public education, public safety, and medical and social services. The rationale for conferring trustee status on broadcasters lies in the potentially crucial impact that mass media have on American society. Trusteeship status has strong support in the United States and much of the world. Although it runs counter to the basic philosophy on which the American system was built, namely, that communication should be entirely free from government control, it appears to be the front-runner among the options available as a framework for future communications policy.

### Paying the Piper

Whether mass communication facilities are treated like any private enterprise, like a common carrier, or like a trustee, their costs have to be paid. There are several possibilities. The costs can be born by advertisers, by audience payments, by government subsidies, or by various combinations of these funding sources. Currently, advertisers pay the largest share of the nation's mass communication budget, although these costs are passed on to consumers in the form of higher prices. But advertisers' share is shrinking as multiplication of information channels splits audiences into smaller slices that are uneconomical targets for many advertisers.

What seems to be emerging in the new era is a system that is predominantly supported by audience payments. A major social drawback of such a system, which framers of new policies need to consider, is the plight of poor families who cannot afford many of the specialized programs that they need. Inequalities could be reduced through government subsidies but, given budgetary constraints, heavy government subsidies are unlikely. Shortage of public funds also means that the private sector will continue to finance the development of advanced communication networks. The likely consequence is continued emphasis on light entertainment fare that has mass appeal and attracts advertising dollars or user fees, rather than more serious programming.

### Hazards in the Information Marketplace

The new technologies have exacerbated a number of serious threats to major public and private interests. The protection of confidential information ranks high on that list. Safeguarding the secrecy of confidential public and private information as well as individual privacy presents major challenges in societies eager to preserve open access to data bases. Despite security codes, astute computer users can assemble scattered bits of information very quickly to gain insights into situations that should remain confidential. Current laws are inadequate to safeguard individual and collective privacy. If they are not revised, the information superhighway may become an Orwellian nightmare where individuals and organizations are exposed to every traveller's inquisitiveness.

The flurry of mergers and acquisitions approved by the government during the 1990s has raised concerns about excessive concentration of control over the public's information supply. Media entrepreneurs who dominate a large share of the information marketplace may become mouthpieces for special interests, and financial returns may become their programming lodestar. Many of the megamedia companies involved in these mergers are giant transnational corporations that exercise vast influence over the information tendered to the world's publics. This information shapes important economic and political issues throughout the world. Fortunately, excessive concentration, which leaves the field largely to the giants, has been partly balanced by the lush growth of specialized media, such as local cable television geared to serving particular community interests. Still, current merger policies raise worrisome issues.

Regulations to prevent inappropriate uses of the airways also need to be updated to cope with new problems. Currently, anarchy reigns in the fast-growing web of public and private computer networks that links millions of people around the globe. This state of affairs has allowed crooks to pursue get-rich-quick schemes to defraud the unwary among the hundreds of thousands of people exposed to these messages. Pornography flourishes in places where children can access it readily, while self-appointed censors hunt down messages that they consider offensive and destroy them. However, more effective government rules and regulations to guard against criminal and other antisocial behaviors in cyberspace are not enough. They must be supplemented by a new, more responsible user ethic.

## The Outlook for Progress

A look at communication technologies tells us what is possible, but it does not indicate what is likely to happen, particularly in the short run. A number of barriers block the full development of new mass communication technologies. They are political, economic, and social, along with typical patterns of resistance to major innovations and the tendency to adapt innovations to perpetuate rather than replace old procedures.

In the political arena, partisan and bureaucratic barriers must be surmounted. Many new developments never get off the ground because they are opposed for partisan reasons, or because bureaucracies impose too many regulations to guard against abuses. Frequently, unrealistically

high standards are prescribed, raising costs beyond economically feasible levels. The situation is complicated even further when state and local rules are piled on top of federal regulations. Setting requirements for public service and for open-access channels and for service for outlying areas requires controversial political decisions about matters apt to be very expensive. In sparsely populated areas, for example, costs of information services may exceed profits temporarily or permanently. Communication technologies involve large investments; their sudden obsolescence when regulatory agencies approve new technologies may become a crushing financial burden.

Early entrants into a technological field often develop a squatter's mentality about their rights such as access to certain broadcast frequencies or exclusive use of particular technologies. Latecomers to the mass communication field, on the other hand, are eager to reallocate facilities and to introduce even more advanced technologies. If their requests are granted, proven technologies may be sacrificed to new claimants whose prospects for success are uncertain. Meanwhile, technology continues its advance, raising fresh problems that further delay the green light for implementing new systems.

Whatever directions new communications policies take, they will have a profound impact on the directions of American politics generally. Unfortunately, the structure for making communications policy remains fragmented at all government levels and ill-suited to deal with existing problems, to say nothing of those that must be anticipated. Narrow, short-term issues are addressed, while far-reaching, long-term problems are ignored. Government leaders are unwilling to enter the thickets of communications policy making when so many other battles must be fought. Congress and the Federal Communications Commission (FCC), which over-

sees the information superhighway, thus far have done little beyond preliminary discussions and studies to cope with the flood of new problems that recent developments have raised. The FCC has not even tackled crucial issues of standardization of technologies so that investments in equipment and training can be kept moderate.

The ultimate prognosis remains clouded. There are bright dreams of high quality diverse information easily available to all travellers on the information superhighway. There are forebodings that the new highway will turn out to be a clone of older routes where the same dreary information cargo makes up most of the freight. And there are nightmares about gridlock, government and private spying on unsuspecting travellers, and propaganda barrages that obscure important facts. Which scenario will emerge? Much hinges on the willingness of industry and government leaders, as well as average citizens, to take control of communications issues to ensure the developments of a sound information system. A do-nothing policy that leaves developments to chance is irresponsible and dangerous.

## About the Author

**Doris A. Graber** is professor of political science at the University of Illinois at Chicago. She has written numerous articles and books on political communication topics including *Verbal Behavior and Politics* (1976), *Processing the News: How People Tame the Information Tide* (1993), *Public Sector Communication: How Organizations Manage Information* (1992), and *Mass Media and American Politics,* 5th ed. (1996). Her forthcoming book, *Virtual Political Reality: Learning About Politics in the Audio-Visual Age,* analyzes the political impact potential of audio-visuals in news broadcasts.

## Unit Selections

## Key Points to Consider

❖ What do you think is the single most important social welfare or economic policy issue facing the American political system today? The single most important national security or diplomatic issue? What do you think ought to be done about them?

❖ What factors increasingly blur the distinction between foreign and domestic policy issues?

❖ How would you compare President Clinton's performance in the areas of social welfare and economic policies with the way he has handled national security and diplomatic affairs? What changes has he tried to make in each of these areas?

❖ What policy issues currently viewed as minor matters seem likely to develop into crisis situations?

❖ What do you think is the most significant policy failure of American national government today? The most significant policy success?

❖ What do you think about the idea of devolution, which means giving state and local governments *more* responsibility for policy making and policy implementation and the national government *less*? What reasons are there to expect the state and local governments will do a better—or worse—job than the national government in such areas as welfare and health care benefits for the old and the poor?

 **Links**     **www.dushkin.com/online/**

These sites are annotated on pages 4 and 5.

"Products" refers to the government policies that the American political system produces. The first three units of this book have paved the way for this fourth unit, because the products of American politics are very much the consequences of the rest of the political system.

Dilemmas and difficulties in one policy area are often reflected in others. Indeed, tensions between fundamental values lie at the heart of much public policy making in all spheres: equality versus freedom, reliance on the public sector versus reliance on the private sector, collectivism versus individualism, internationalism versus isolationism, and so forth.

The health of the American economy is always a prominent policy issue in the American political system. One of the most remarkable consequences of 12 years under Presidents Reagan and Bush was enormous growth in budget deficits and in the national debt. Moreover, the nation's economy had entered a recession by the halfway mark of President Bush's term.

Since President Clinton took office in 1993, the United States has enjoyed steady economic growth and relatively low unemployment and inflation rates. Indeed, a healthy economy has been a foundation of President Clinton's popularity in public opinion polls and of his successful reelection campaign in 1996. In addition, continuing economic growth increased tax revenues to such an extent that the long-sought goal of a balanced budget was reached in 1998. It seems clear, however, that achieving and maintaining balanced budgets and even surpluses on an annual basis will depend on the health of the economy in the years to come.

Domestic public policy usually involves "trade-offs" among competing uses of scarce resources, and during his 1992 campaign Bill Clinton called attention to many such trade-offs in the area of health care. For example, are we as a nation content to spend a greater proportion of our national income on health care than any other industrialized country? If not, are we willing to limit medical spending when that may mean that some sophisticated and sometimes life-saving treatments become less available to middle-class Americans? Do we want to extend medical insurance to those millions of less affluent Americans currently uninsured, even though this might result in higher costs and/or less medical treatment for those who are already insured? As president, Clinton introduced a comprehensive health care reform proposal late in 1993. By the sixth year of the Clinton presidency, there has been no reform of the sort President Clinton had proposed.

Other domestic policy areas also involve trade-offs. To what extent should we make the unemployed who are receiving welfare payments work, and what responsibility should the government take for preparing such citizens for work and for ensuring that jobs are available? How much are cleaner air and other environmental goals worth in terms of economic productivity, unemployment, and so forth? Such trade-offs underlie debate about specific tax policies, social welfare programs, immigration policies, environmental problems, and the like.

For at least three decades, the United States and the Soviet Union each had the capacity to end human existence as we know it. Not surprisingly, the threat of nuclear war often dominated American diplomacy and national security policy making. Since World War II, however, the United States has used conventional forces in a number of military actions—in Korea, Vietnam, Grenada, Panama, and the Persian Gulf area. In 1991 the Soviet Union dissolved into 15 independent republics. This change left the United States as the world's sole remaining superpower and has greatly affected world politics and U.S. foreign policy ever since. Questions about the appropriateness of U.S. intervention in disparate places such as Bosnia-Herzegovina, Somalia, Haiti, Iraq, Kosovo, and even Russia have been at the forefront of foreign policy concerns since President Clinton assumed office. The threatened proliferation of nuclear weapons in North Korea also posed a difficult problem for the Clinton administration.

The foreign and defense policy process in the United States raises a host of related issues. One of these includes the struggle between legislative and executive branches for control of foreign and defense policy. Conflict between the branches sometimes takes place today in the context of the War Powers Resolution of 1973, which is itself a legacy of the Vietnam War. In 1991 Congress authorized war with Iraq, which was the first time since World War II that there has been explicit and formal congressional approval prior to commencement of military hostilities by the United States. In late 1995 President Clinton committed the United States to sending troops to Bosnia- Herzegovina as part of a multinational peace- keeping force. Despite some opposition in Congress, resolutions supporting the troops were passed. In late 1997, President Saddam Hussein of Iraq obstructed UN weapons inspection teams in his country. President Clinton responded by increasing the readiness of U.S. military forces in the Persian Gulf. In late 1998, in response to what the U.S. considered further provocation, there were several days of U.S. air strikes on Iraq. Another policy issue is the legitimacy of covert action. Finally, there is the recurring question of the relationship between foreign policy and democracy.

The traditional distinction between domestic and foreign policy is becoming more and more difficult to maintain, since so many contemporary policy decisions seem to have important implications for both the foreign and domestic scenes. President Clinton's emphasis on the connection between domestic and international economic issues in maintaining what he calls national economic security reinforces this point.

"Products" of American Politics

# The Entitlement Time Bomb

*John Attarian*

*John Attarian is a freelance writer in Ann Arbor, Michigan, who holds a doctorate in economics and has written on deposit insurance, pension insurance, the federal budget deficit, and Social Security.*

In recent years, Congress has periodically boiled with efforts to balance the federal budget—and with good reason. Federal spending has exploded out of control, due to spending for entitlement programs like Social Security, Medicare, and Medicaid.

This fiscal mismanagement has already exacted serious economic penalties, according to many analysts, including the General Accounting Office (GAO), the investigative arm of Congress. Moreover, if entitlement spending continues to go unaddressed, they say, America's economic future will be extremely grim.

Federal budget deficits mushroomed from fiscal 1981's $79 billion to sums exceeding $200 billion for most of the 1980s and '90s.

As of 1981, the national debt was $994.3 billion, or 33.5 percent of the gross domestic product (GDP). For the year 2000, it is projected to be $6.18 trillion, or 69.1 percent of GDP—a 522 percent increase in 20 years, while GDP rose only 202 percent. In other words, the federal government is spending and borrowing income far faster than America produces it.

And *entitlement spending*—transfer payments to people declared by law to be "entitled" by reason of income level, age, occupation, and so on to receive them—has been the cause. Major entitlements—such as Social Security, Medicare, Medicaid, government retirement benefits, unemployment compensation, food stamps, and the Earned Income Tax Credit (EITC), which the budget treats as an outlay—now consume over half the annual budget.

Moreover, the dynamics of the budget's components over the past 30 years prove that entitlements are the engine driving the growth in federal spending and deficits (see table).

## AN UNSTOPPABLE LOCOMOTIVE?

Entitlement spending has more than doubled as a share of the budget since 1965 and is the largest, fastest-growing sector today. Except for a temporary rise due to Ronald Reagan's defense buildup, the Pentagon's share has fallen since the Vietnam era. Likewise, the share for domestic discretionary spending—domestic spending that must be voted on by Congress, for items like government operations, education, infrastructure repair, and so on—has dropped substantially.

But thanks to chronic large deficits stoked primarily by soaring entitlements, spending for net interest on the national debt has risen steadily.

How did America come to this pass? Briefly, according to political observers, thanks to an ideology of activist government and a prosperity that gave the impression that such activism was easily affordable, many new entitlements—such as Medicare and Medicaid (both enacted in 1965), Supplemental Security Income (1972), and the EITC (1975)—were created in the 1960s and '70s, and existing ones such as Social Security were expanded, with little thought or provision for future costs.

The overwhelming bulk of entitlement spending is for such non-means-tested programs (i.e., those that distribute benefits to all who qualify for them, regardless of income or assets) as federal retirement benefits, Social Security, and Medicare. As of fiscal 1995, non-means-tested programs cost $609.3 billion and were 40.1 percent of total outlays and 77.1 percent of major entitlement spending.

Two programs—Social Security and Medicare—now dominate entitlement spending and the budget as a whole. At $333.3 billion in fiscal 1995, Social Security is the largest single item in the budget. Medicare, costing $156.9 billion, is the fourth-largest, after defense and interest on the debt. Combined, Social Security and Medicare now consume $490.2 billion—almost a third of all federal spending.

■ *A nation barreling toward bankruptcy:* As more people swell the ranks of America's senior citizens, the fiscal burden of entitlement programs like Social Security and Medicare mounts.

By contrast, major means-tested entitlement programs (i.e., programs benefiting only people with lower incomes and assets) cost $181.1 billion and accounted for just 11.9 percent of federal spending in fiscal 1995. Social Security outlays alone are almost twice those for all federal poverty programs.

It follows that focusing on cutting poverty programs will not solve the problem. Whatever welfare's flaws, budget busting is not one of them. The conclusion is inescapable: America's fiscal crisis cannot be resolved without radical reform of Social Security and Medicare.

As is widely known, entitlement outlays are not subject to annual appropriations votes by Congress. Adding entitlements and net interest payments on the national debt (a legal obligation of the government), about two-thirds of federal spending is essentially beyond congressional control.

The data (see next page) also show that entitlement spending is insensitive to the economy's position in the business cycle. It was far higher in 1985, a good year, than in 1975, a re-

. cession year. And entitlement outlays for 1995, a good year, far exceed those for 1990, a recession year. This is mostly true even of the one major entitlement responsive to economic fluctuations: unemployment compensation.

In good and bad times alike, the spending valve is now stuck open. In short, thanks to entitlements, America has lost control of federal spending. Hence the plunge into debt.

## THE ECONOMIC CONSEQUENCES

Growing far faster than both total outlays and GDP, more than doubling as a share of both in 30 years, entitlements are outstripping the U.S. economy's capacity to finance them. They are also creating a serious drag on American economic performance.

The chronic massive deficits, economists say, are devouring America's seed corn: the savings that finance investment. Over the past 30 years, government deficits have consumed an increasing share of the country's declining national savings. Net national saving—private-sector

saving after public-sector deficits are subtracted—averaged 8.1 percent of GDP in the 1960s and 7.2 percent in the 1970s, but only 3.7 percent in the 1980s and a mere 1.7 percent in 1990–93.

Just a tiny sliver of national output, then, is now available for investment to sustain American productivity and living standards in future years.

Another indicator of the growing diversion of moneys from productive investment to deficit finance is the federal government's share of total net borrowing in the credit market. In 1965, the government did only 5.8 percent of total borrowing. By 1980, its share of borrowing had hit 21.4 percent. It reached a staggering 55.3 percent in 1991 and 57.5 percent in 1992. This was the real, if unadmitted, cause of the "credit crunch" and recession of the early 1990s: Government borrowing to finance budget deficits was diverting credit from business, the phenomenon known to economists as *crowding out.*

Financing the budget deficit devoured a still-massive 49.3 percent in 1993. As of 1995, the government did 23.9 percent of total net borrow-

## MAJOR ENTITLEMENTS AND THE BUDGET, 1965-1995
(dollar amounts in billions; fiscal years)

| ITEM | 1965 | 1970 | 1975 | 1980 | 1985 | 1990 | 1995 | % Growth |
|---|---|---|---|---|---|---|---|---|
| Social Security | 17 | 30 | 64 | 117 | 186 | 247 | 333 | 1,859 |
| Medicare | — | 6 | 12 | 31 | 64 | 96 | 157 | 2,517 |
| Medicaid | — | 3 | 3 | 14 | 23 | 41 | 89 | 28,667 |
| Federal retirement | 3 | 6 | 13 | 27 | 39 | 53 | 66 | 2,100 |
| Veterans benefits | 4 | 7 | 13 | 14 | 16 | 16 | 20 | 400 |
| Unemployment comp. | 2 | 3 | 13 | 17 | 16 | 17 | 21 | 950 |
| Food and nutrition | — | 1 | 7 | 13 | 17 | 21 | 34 | 3,300 |
| Supplemental Security | — | — | 4 | 6 | 9 | 12 | 25 | 525 |
| EITC | — | — | — | 1 | 1 | 4 | 15 | 1,400 |
| Family support | 3 | 4 | 5 | 7 | 9 | 12 | 17 | 467 |
| **Tot. Major Entitlements** | **29** | **60** | **134** | **247** | **380** | **519** | **777** | **2,579** |
| Total as % of outlays | 25 | 31 | 40 | 42 | 40 | 41 | 51 | 104 |
| Total as % of GDP | 4 | 6 | 9 | 9 | 10 | 10 | 11 | 175 |
| Total outlays | 118 | 196 | 332 | 591 | 946 | 1,253 | 1,519 | 1,187 |
| GDP | 671 | 986 | 1,511 | 2,645 | 3,971 | 5,460 | 7,005 | 944 |
| Deficit | 1 | 3 | 53 | 74 | 212 | 221 | 164 | 16,300 |
| National debt | 332 | 381 | 542 | 909 | 1,817 | 3,206 | 4,921 | 1,382 |
| Net interest | 9 | 14 | 23 | 53 | 130 | 184 | 232 | 2,478 |
| ... as % of outlays | 8 | 7 | 7 | 9 | 14 | 15 | 15 | 88 |
| DDS* | 26 | 39 | 67 | 129 | 146 | 183 | 252 | 869 |
| ... as % of outlays | 22 | 20 | 20 | 22 | 15 | 15 | 17 | -23 |
| Defense | 51 | 82 | 88 | 135 | 253 | 300 | 274 | 437 |
| ... as % of outlays | 43 | 42 | 27 | 23 | 27 | 24 | 18 | -58 |

SOURCE: OFFICE OF MANAGEMENT AND BUDGET

ing—a considerably smaller share, to be sure, than earlier in the decade, but still over *four times* as much as the government took in 1965, just before the entitlement explosion began.

In short, public-sector elephantiasis, driven by mushrooming entitlement spending, contributed mightily to the stagnation of productivity and real wages since the early 1970s, and to the recession of the early '90s.

Such has been the performance and economic impact of entitlement spending in the recent past. What of the future?

### THE TICKING BOMB

The economic feebleness of the deficit-dominated early 1990s warns that the United States is running the risk of getting caught in a vicious circle of entitlement-fueled spend-

> **Entitlement spending has more than doubled as a share of the budget since 1965 and is the largest, fastest-growing sector today.**

ing, deficits, and stagnation. The trap can be described as follows:

• The deficits that finance the spending devour the savings that should be invested to create jobs and productivity growth.

• The resulting stagnation curtails revenue growth and helps drive up entitlement spending, borrowing to cover the entitlement spending, and spending on interest on the borrowing.

• The deficits thus grow from both sides of the ledger, feeding another round of spending, borrowing, and stagnation.

Ominously, according to many economists, the United States is sitting on a huge, ticking time bomb.

They say that the ongoing healthcare cost inflation and the aging of the American population will, if current policies remain unchanged, drive entitlement spending to unsustainably high levels.

The Congressional Budget Office projects that, under current law, entitlement spending, thanks mostly to Medicare and Medicaid spending growth, will be about $1.62 trillion in 2005, or 60.1 percent of total outlays and 14 percent of GDP, and that the budget deficit will be $472 billion.

After 2010—as the baby boomers born between 1945 and 1965 begin to retire and draw Social Security, Medicare, and civil service and military retirement benefits—the outlook gets worse yet. Again assuming no change in current law, the President's Bipartisan Commission on Entitlement Reform projected that, by 2012, entitlement spending plus interest on the national debt will require all federal tax revenue.

And by 2030, the commission said, Medicare, Medicaid, Social Security, and federal retirement programs *alone* will devour all federal revenues. That is, revenues will not suffice to cover all entitlement spending, let alone the rest of the budget.

When the huge baby boom generation retires, the population of Social Security beneficiaries will grow much faster than the population of workers paying taxes to finance their benefits. Tax revenue will no longer suffice to cover benefit costs, and Social Security will have to cash in the government bonds in its "trust funds."

According to the Board of Trustees' actuarial analysis, using pessimistic demographic and economic assumptions, which former Chief Actuary A. Haeworth Robertson has argued are the most realistic, the Social Security payroll tax will no longer generate a surplus over benefit outlays after 1999. Social Security's Old Age Survivors and Disability Insurance trust funds will be bankrupt in 2016 under the pessimistic assumptions, in 2029 under intermediate ones.

## MEDICARE, MEDICAID TEETERING

The crisis will arrive even sooner for Medicare. In 1995, its expenditures exceeded income, and it began draining its Hospital Insurance trust fund. Under both the "low-cost" and intermediate assumptions of Medicare's Board of Trustees, the trust fund will be exhausted in 2001. Un-

der pessimistic ("high-cost") assumptions, exhaustion will occur in 2000.

To obtain money to pay off the Treasury debt from the trust funds, the federal government will have to cut spending elsewhere in the budget, raise taxes, or, most likely, increase borrowing from the public, which will drive budget deficits higher. Assuming that all redemption of the trust funds' government debt is financed by new borrowing, under the Social Security trustees' pessimistic assumptions, the deficit from Social Security and Medicare *alone* will be $66 billion in fiscal 2000, $175 billion in 2005, $341 billion in 2010, and $686 billion in 2015.

When the funds are totally exhausted, unless Social Security and Medicare benefits are radically cut or their payroll taxes drastically increased, deficits will soar higher yet.

While the demise of Social Security and Medicare certainly constitutes the lion's share of the lurking menace of runaway entitlements, other entitlement programs also have vast potential for trouble:

• The Congressional Budget Office projects that Medicaid outlays will be almost triple their 1995 level in just 10 years, hitting $148 billion in 2000 and $232 billion in 2005.

• The present value of future civil service retirement benefits promised under current law—that is, the amount of money that would have to be invested today to pay for them—is now over $1.1 trillion. Unfortunately, no money has been reserved to cover these future obligations.

• Similarly, unfunded military retirement benefits promised under current law have a present value exceeding $713 billion, and the estimated present value of unfunded veterans' benefits is over $190 billion.

Simply to provide retirement benefits to its own people, then—never mind Social Security and Medicare beneficiaries—the government has committed itself to spending over $2 trillion, but without providing the means to make these commitments good. Even while confronting Social Security and Medicare bankruptcy, the government will have to find money to honor these obligations, too.

All in all, entitlement spending mandated under current law is a recipe for ruinous deficits. Indeed, in 1995, the GAO, using a long-term growth model to simulate the economic impact of future deficits, projected that under current tax and spending policies, by 2025 federal

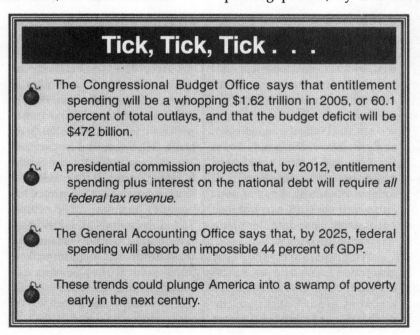

## Tick, Tick, Tick . . .

The Congressional Budget Office says that entitlement spending will be a whopping $1.62 trillion in 2005, or 60.1 percent of total outlays, and that the budget deficit will be $472 billion.

A presidential commission projects that, by 2012, entitlement spending plus interest on the national debt will require *all federal tax revenue.*

The General Accounting Office says that, by 2025, federal spending will absorb an impossible 44 percent of GDP.

These trends could plunge America into a swamp of poverty early in the next century.

spending will absorb 44 percent of GDP and the budget deficit will exceed 23 percent of GDP. Net interest on the debt would be roughly 30 percent of total federal spending in 2025.

## THE NATION'S SLIDE INTO POVERTY

To finance chronic huge deficits, government borrowing would devour virtually all available credit. The resulting crowding out would make the credit crunch of the early 1990s recession trivial. Businesses would be unable to maintain existing plants and equipment, let alone expand or upgrade them.

America's capital stock would shrink accordingly, as would productivity, output, and employment. The GAO projected that by 2025 investment would disappear, our capital stock would be less than half its

> **The entitlement state has the potential to make America an economic backwater choked with poverty.**

1994 level, and real per-capita GDP would have barely grown since 1994.

With deficits consuming most domestic savings and foreign lenders unlikely to prop up a bankrupt government, there would be little choice but for the Federal Reserve Bank to purchase U.S. government bonds, a practice known as *monetizing* the

deficits. When what is essentially one branch of the government finances the rest of the bureaucracy, the country starts to print money at a furious pace, expanding the money supply and risking hyperinflation.

The entitlement state, then, has the potential to make America an economic backwater choked with poverty.

Perhaps even worse than the size of the entitlement time bomb and its potential for devastation, observers say, is the deafness of America's politicians to its ticking. So far, little effort has been made, by either President Clinton or the Republicans in Congress, to confront the entitlements issue, to educate the American people about the need for making deep sacrifices, and to actually undertake those sacrifices.

The country still has some time left, but it is running out fast.

# THE SHAM OF SAVING SOCIAL SECURITY FIRST

*From an essay by **Robert B. Reich** in the May/June issue of* The American Prospect. *Reich, the former secretary of labor in the Clinton Administration, is currently University Professor of Economics and Social Policy at Brandeis University.*

America is richer now than it has ever been—almost a third wealthier than it was just fifteen years ago. It is, in fact, the richest nation in the history of the world. Yet despite all this affluence there remain basic things—things that other less wealthy nations accomplish, like giving all children a decent education and providing all citizens with adequate health care—that America still can't seem to afford to do. It's not that these basic goals are anathema to us; it's just that every time we approach the point where they seem attainable, we decide that we can't afford them quite yet.

When the Cold War officially ended in 1989, there was a brief debate over how to spend the so-called peace dividend. But then our leaders decided that the more prudent course was to keep most of our military intact, at an average cost of nearly $300 billion per year, just in case it might still be needed. "We have more will than wallet," George Bush ruefully intoned at the time.

There was rekindled hope when the Democrats took over the White House in 1993, but the President and the Democratic Congress concluded that, before we could attend to any other reforms, the budget deficit must be reduced. We resolved to cut it by half (at the start of the Administration, it amounted to approximately 4.7 percent of our GDP) before embarking on the social agenda that was the foundation of Bill Clinton's presidential campaign.

The deficit waned, but the bar was lifted again in 1995 when a Republican Congress, backed by several noted Democrats, threatened a constitutional amendment to balance the budget. In order to block such an attempt, the Administration pushed aside the agenda until the budget was in fact balanced. Now it is 1998. The budget is balanced. There are even surpluses. But it appears that the bar has been lifted once again.

In his most recent State of the Union Address, President Clinton laid out for us in broad terms his plan for the Administration's remaining years. He spoke about education and about Medicare, and offered some proposals that would take the nation a few steps toward fulfilling the unfinished agenda. True, the steps are small when compared with the size of the problems they seek to address (Medicare expansion, for example, is expected to reach no more than 300,000 early retirees and laid-off workers over the age of fifty-five, out of the 3 million in this group, which itself is a small portion of the 41 million Americans lacking health care). And true, most of the new initiatives are focused more on people earning middle-class wages than on the working class and the poor. But the President has at least signaled something of a return to the themes with which he began his presidency.

Yet to focus on the benignity of the proposals themselves misses a deeply troubling aspect of what the President has said, or, more accurately, has failed to say. Rather than offering a larger vision for how the nation might afford to achieve the larger goals, both now and in the future, by capitalizing on our thriving economy, the President took pains to reassure the nation that his modest proposals would not dip into the budget surplus.

From *Harper's,* June 1998, pp. 26-29. Excerpted from the article "My Dinner with Bill" by Robert Reich, Professor of Economic and Social Policy at Brandeis University, appearing in *The American Prospect,* May/June 1998. © 1998 by *The American Prospect,* P.O. Box 383080, Cambridge, MA 02138. All rights reserved.

For their financing they will depend instead on proceeds from a hoped-for tax on tobacco, and from various "loophole closers" in the tax code, all of which will be fought over in Congress. The budget surplus, he emphasized repeatedly, calling attention to his and by extension the nation's fiscal responsibility, will go expressly to "save Social Security first."

Therein lies the problem. By failing to consider any use for the budget surpluses other than saving Social Security, the President has finally raised the bar so high as to render any larger social agenda virtually unattainable. "Social Security First" implies that Social Security is in grave danger and that only the fiscally reckless would focus on anything other than stanching this gaping wound. According to projections from the actuary of the Social Security trust fund, Social Security revenues (plus interest) will exceed Social Security expenditures through the year 2018. By 2019, when the great wave of postwar baby boomers begins to hit the retirement shore, expenditures will begin to exceed income. Without "corrective actions," by 2029 the fund will be unable to pay all its obligations—unless, of course, the Treasury simply issues more debt to cover them.

This crisis-mongering is simply wrong. As a former trustee of the Social Security trust fund, I can tell you that the actuary's projections (made, by the way, before anyone expected the budget to be balanced by 1998) are based on the pessimistic assumption that the economy will grow only 1.8 percent annually over the next three decades. Crank the economy up just a bit, to a more realistic 2.2 percent a year (which is below the projection the White House uses in its new budget), and the fund is nearly flush for the next seventy-five years. Its solvency could be assured by any number of fairly small changes, such as eliminating the ceiling on income subject to the payroll tax, or raising the retirement age by two years, or reducing Social Security payments to wealthy retirees. And if lower-wage earners were ever to get a larger share of the economic pie, Social Security revenues would, of course, be much higher.

The President's Social Security First campaign is also an open invitation to those who argue that we must use any budget surpluses in future years to eliminate the federal debt. Since Social Security is a pay-as-you-go system, any effort to "shore up" the Social Security trust fund now is, in effect, an effort to pay down the debt. Once you concede that paying down the debt is a good thing to do, there's no obvious stopping place. Why not apply every penny of surplus in future years to this noble objective? Conservative think tanks, editorial writers, followers of Ross Perot, Concord Coalitioners, and all other advocates of public austerity and private profligacy will happily slide down this hill.

Saner voices should be clear: public debt is not necessarily bad. Not only may debt occasionally be useful for stabilizing the economy (in the long run, John Maynard Keynes is not dead), but its proceeds might be used to hasten economic growth. As the President argued early in his Administration, public investment in education, infrastructure, and basic research are as important to future growth as is private investment. Families and businesses borrow all the time in order to invest. As long as the economy grows faster than the national debt, the exact size of the debt isn't worrisome. And that is precisely what has been occurring. In 1997, the federal debt totaled about 50 percent of the nation's GDP. This year, it will be below that even if we were to spend every penny of the surplus, and it will continue to drop if the budget stays balanced. Economic growth is the key, and the way to grow faster is to invest—privately and publicly.

It is worth noting, by the way, that federal investments in education, infrastructure, and research have continued to fall over the last three administrations. They represented 2.5 percent of GDP in 1981, fell to 1.8 percent by the time Ronald Reagan left office in 1988, and ten years later remain at 1.7 percent—lower than at any time since 1962. The trend is well documented in a table in the back of the annual budget books distributed by the Government Printing Office. Even if enacted, the budget initiatives of

which the President spoke in his State of the Union Address would notch public investment up only incrementally.

Without a larger vision, Social Security First is, at best, a momentary stay. The other crowd champing at the bit is the tax cutters, whose members include most Republicans now holding office or harboring political ambition. Tax cuts are wildly popular, of course, although they have been trumped, temporarily, by the Social Security scare. When the choice is between cutting taxes and "saving" Social Security, the latter wins. But since no meaningful alternative for how the nation might invest its resources for the public good has been proffered, Republicans have found their platform for 2000 and beyond. Now that the budget is balanced, they will continue to clamor to cut taxes, pushing various "flat" variants that are likely to favor the wealthy. As soon as Social Security is deemed to be out of danger, the tax cutters will compete for floor space with the debt cutters. The conversation over the public good thus has been reduced to this cramped debate.

But because we have grown so breathlessly wealthy, America can afford to do much more than what this debate implies. Social Security can easily be saved, we don't need to pay down the debt, we can cut taxes on the middle and working class, and we can *still* afford to do what a rich nation must do for all its people. That would require, though, a consideration of several options that lie outside the bounds of current political debate—including a progressive tax on the accumulated wealth of Americans whose assets have swelled in recent years.

There is no longer any talk of universal health care. Our schools, especially those in poor and working-class neighborhoods, continue to deteriorate. Despite the fact that the nation, as a whole, is richer than any nation in the history of the world, the current conversation has been framed so narrowly that it excludes the possibility of using this wealth to address our citizens' most pressing needs. As our coffers overflow, we have been led to believe, yet again, that something even more pressing must come first.

# Do It Yourself

*Washington—and Americans—are at a crossroads between the collective approach to social security and medicare and the corporate trend toward self-reliance. Workers may become more prudent consumers as they assume responsibility for retirement and health care costs, but the disadvantaged may find it difficult to provide for their own needs.*

## JULIE KOSTERLITZ

Once upon a time, not so very long ago, we were all in it together. With the creation of social security in the wake of the Great Depression, continuing with the spread of company pension and health plans after World War II and climaxing with the passage of medicare in 1965, Americans constructed a public and private social welfare system to provide themselves with greater economic security.

Mostly these were collective arrangements through which working Americans of great and modest means alike pooled their resources for financial protection against often random, but universal, hazards. Chief among these were the risk of illness or injury and the risk of outliving one's savings. Industrial Age substitutes for the extended family, these arrangements have run on cross-subsidies—the healthy supporting the sick, the young shoring up the old and, often, high-wage earners helping those with low wages.

Now, however, that system of social welfare is up for grabs. Pools are breaking apart, and the guarantees are disappearing. In their place are new programs that require individuals to take on the responsibility and risk of providing for their own financial security. "We're coming to a series of turning points, whether we realize it or not," departing Labor Secretary Robert B. Reich said in an interview.

These changes bring the likelihood of more unequal outcomes: Some will undoubtedly improve their lot, while others, just as surely, will face greater hardship.

---

*The old guarantees are vanishing as employers make workers responsible for retirement and health care. Medicare and social security may follow suit.*

---

The transformation is already well under way in the private sector. Employers' traditional pension plans with their guaranteed fixed payments are being supplanted by voluntary, individually owned and controlled, tax-subsidized retirement savings accounts. Earlier this year, Congress approved—as a limited experiment—tax subsidies to medical savings accounts (MSAs), an individualized alternative to traditional employer-sponsored group health insurance. MSAs essentially allow workers to leave the health insurance risk pool, taking their premium contributions with them to help finance their own care.

It may not be long before social security and medicare, traditionally politically insulated from fundamental change, undergo a similar transformation. With the medicare trust fund's costs already outstripping its income, and social security's expected to follow suit in the not-too-distant future, calls are mounting in some quarters for fundamental change: converting social security to a system of private individual savings accounts, and medicare to a system of vouchers to be put toward the cost of private health plans or MSAs.

What's driving these changes? Clearly some economic forces are at work: Slower growth makes it tougher to finance the ever more sophisticated health care and the longer retirements we have come to expect. An increasingly competitive business environment makes employers more cost-conscious about benefits. A growing disparity between incomes makes these programs' egalitarian features an increasing drag on the prospects of the well-to-do. And the changing nature of the labor market makes rewards for long service less enticing to workers and bosses alike. Most workers nowadays don't intend to spend their careers at one job, and employers are reluctant to encourage all of their workers to stay.

Demography hasn't helped either. Longer life expectancies and a rapidly aging population will greatly accelerate the nation's cost of supporting retirement. Rising health care costs compound the problem.

Political attitudes have also changed with time. Increasing public disillusion with government may have its corollary in the rising emphasis on individual responsibility and self-reliance. These attitudes are also encouraged by the powerful business interests that stand to make money on the new "do-it-yourself" arrangements: mutual funds and insurance companies to name two.

Some see a broader cultural shift. "It's part of the fragmentation of America, the breakdown in the idea of community, the ethic that we share some responsibility for each other," said John C. Rother, the director of legislation and public policy for the American Association of Retired Persons, who is on sabbatical from that post to research policy options for the graying of America.

Others of a more libertarian or conservative bent believe that the collective arrangements are bringing about their own demise because they mask the true cost of benefits and fuel overconsumption. "The ability to rely on politics, to plan a life based on political redistribution of income is going away. It's not sustainable," author and former Bush Administration aide James P. Pinkerton said in an interview.

To those critics, a move toward self-provision beats the alternative: more redistribution of wealth and rationing of benefits. David Frum, a Toronto-based senior fellow at the conservative Manhattan Institute, writes in his recent book, *What's Right:* "The right sort of entitlement reform must not only liberate Washington from impossible spending commitments; it must liberate people from the Washington social-welfare system, by moving them toward individual control of their own pension and health plans."

But to others, this trend signals danger. "The potential problem has to do with what I call 'the secession of the successful,' " Reich said. "You've got to be very careful that we don't simply create back doors through which the wealthier, the healthier and the better-off can simply remove themselves from risk pools, thereby leaving the sicker and the less-well-off facing even higher premiums and fewer ways of making it."

Over the next decade, Congress and the President will be asked to make a basic choice: whether to try to shore up the traditional public and private collective arrangements and their egalitarian ideals or to embrace self-reliance. "The issue here is how much risk we're going to bear societally and how much we're going to put on individuals," Robert D. Reischauer, a Brookings Institution senior fellow and former Congressional Budget Office director, said.

It's the same debate Americans have had with themselves periodically, since at least the days of the New Deal. But such sweeping questions are never answered once and for all: Societies change their institutions to reflect changing circumstances and public preferences.

---

*In the boom days after World War II, with employers eager to attract workers and still-ascendant labor unions flexing their muscles, employee benefit plans spread throughout corporate America.*

---

The public, however, has shown massive ambivalence. In the early 1990s, Americans clamored for guaranteed health care coverage but blanched at the elaborate government orchestration President Clinton proposed. Voters reacted harshly to reports of Republicans' meddling with medicare yet returned them to control both chambers of Congress.

This debate's outcome could depend heavily on how it is framed. "Once you define [the debate as] taking care of

themselves as opposed to having government take care of them, you're on a very different slope, in my judgment," Theodore R. Marmor, a professor of public policy and management at Yale University, said.

And they may break down along class lines. "Those who do well in life tend to view the world as a fair place. Their success is indication of hard work and prudent decisions," Reischauer said. "For those on the other end, the world is a slightly unfair place, where external forces relegate them to the bottom."

Americans' ambivalence, memorialized by their recent vote to keep a divided government, guarantees a continuing struggle in Congress on these critical issues.

## BENEFIT PLANS STALL

In the boom days after World War II, with employers eager to attract workers and still-ascendant labor unions flexing their muscles, employee benefit plans spread throughout corporate America.

But for at least the past decade, the trend has stalled. The share of the population covered by employer pension plans leveled off around 49 per cent in 1987; the share of the nonelderly with job-related health coverage fell from 69.5 per cent in 1988 to 63.8 per cent in 1995, according to the Employee Benefit Research Institute (EBRI). The institute says this means that in 1995 roughly eight million more nonelderly Americans lacked health insurance than in 1988.

Just as important, however, the character of the benefit arrangements is changing. The traditional pension plan of the postwar era, specially structured to reward long tenure with a company, guaranteed all workers a "defined benefit" for the duration of their retirement—however long that might be. The onus was on employers to come up with the money and to insulate workers from the downside risks of investments.

Starting in the late 1970s, an increasing share of employers began promising to make only a "defined contribution" toward a worker's retirement fund. The onus was still on employers to come up with the contributions, and workers benefited from the investment savvy of the collective pension fund. They were, however, no longer guaranteed a predetermined benefit.

But after 1981, encouraged by a change in Internal Revenue Service regulations, an increasing number of employers moved another step away from the world of guarantees, setting up retirement plans that merely offered workers the opportunity to contribute their own money to tax-deferred retirement savings plans. Known to the public by their tax code nomenclature, 401(k)s, these savings accounts have also acquired another name: "do-it-yourself" plans. With these plans, what workers draw in retirement depends on how much they save (many employers match part of workers' contributions), on their investment savvy and on the vagaries of the stock markets.

The change was, in part, a response to a more competitive business climate. Plans rewarding seniority no longer made sense, Dallas L. Salisbury, president of the EBRI, said. "In an environment where you're reengineering [for efficiency], the last thing you want is a tool that encourages everyone to stay, because the ones it proves most effective in keeping are those with the lowest marketability."

But the change has also both reflected and magnified a growing disparity in wages between the top and bottom earners. The old-style plans typically required everyone to participate, provided some subsidies (both from those who died before collecting benefits and sometimes from shareholders) and set contribution levels that were proportional to salaries. The new plans, with their emphasis on voluntarism, have different sets of incentives and subsidies, which tend to favor those with higher incomes. "The wage gap is being mirrored in a benefits gap," Reich said. "Companies are providing fairly generous compensation packages to top-level executives, not only wage packages and stock-option packages, but also benefit packages of all sorts. The further you go down in the company ranks, the more you see these wages dropping, but also the cost of benefits being shifted to employees or dropped altogether."

Efforts to preserve the egalitarian ideal in retirement plans have stumbled and arguably have even backfired. In 1986 and again in 1993—concerned at the growing drain on the Treasury and anxious to ensure that retirement plans didn't merely become tax shelters for the wealthy—Congress imposed an array of rules designed to curb benefits at the top of the income scale and to assure some measure of parity between high and low-income earners.

But employers argued that the rules were cumbersome and counterproductive and that they discouraged employers from setting up such plans. Congress responded earlier this year by relaxing some of the rules governing the retirement savings plans. *(See NJ, 9/21/96, p. 2003.)*

Before that, however, top corporate executives had already begun circumventing the restrictions by opting out of or supplementing their companies' retirement plans with separate, corporate-subsidized—although somewhat riskier—arrangements for themselves. A recent *New York Times* series documented the rapid rise in the use of these "deferred-compensation" arrangements. Under these arrangements, executives opt to let their companies retain and invest some of their pay—effectively deferring taxes on that money until the executives receive it years later. Unlike 401(k) plans, there are no limits on how much can be put away. Some companies guarantee high interest rates and offer matching contributions on the deferred pay.

These developments don't merely ratify a greater disparity of benefits, they also sever the link between upper-income and lower-income workers. Before the equity-oriented 401(k) rules were liberalized, top executives had a self-interest in seeing that their low-wage counterparts contributed to 401(k) plans. The new rules permit indifference. Similarly, as *The Times* notes, separate deferred-compensation plans for top officials remove the executives' personal stake in the viability or the generosity of the corporate retirement plans for the rank and file.

## COSTS SHIFT TO WORKERS

The nature of corporate health care plans is also changing. Already corporate plans are shifting more costs to workers: According to Labor Department data, the share of employers who pay the full freight for workers' health coverage dropped from 74 per cent in 1980 to just 37 per cent in 1993.

Moreover, some employers appear to be moving—as many in the pension arena already have—away from the guarantee of broad health care benefits over to the lesser guarantee of a fixed-dollar contribution toward the cost of a health plan. Jack A. Meyer, president of the Economic and Social Research Institute in Washington, reports that two private coalitions he works with that bring together small businesses to purchase health care services are on the verge of introducing such a system; several large businesses have also suggested they may move in this direction.

Meyer said the goals, to introduce competition by health plans and cost consciousness by consumers, are appealing. But over time, this could split up the broader risk pool, with the wealthier and those in ill health opting to pay more for privileges such as wider selection of physicians.

The limited introduction of tax-subsidized MSAs could also fundamentally alter the nature of health insurance—doing away with most risk sharing and fragmenting risk pools.

*The limited introduction of tax-subsidized medical savings accounts could also fundamentally alter the nature of health insurance—doing away with most risk sharing and fragmenting risk pools.*

Here's why: MSAs substitute low-deductible plans that have high premiums with high-deductible, or catastrophic illness insurance plans that charge lower premiums. Employers or employees can stash away pre-tax dollars in the savings accounts to help defray costs below the deductible, as well as any uncovered expenses. What they don't use builds up with tax-free interest. Cash can be taken out and spent for other things, but the withdrawn amount is slapped with taxes and a penalty.

Many analysts, including those at the American Academy of Actuaries, believe these plans would be attractive to the healthy (who are unlikely to use up all the cash on medical care) and the wealthy (because they can afford possible out-of-pocket expenses and because their higher tax brackets make tax-free savings more attractive).

MSAs are likely to be unattractive to that small share of the population with chronic illnesses, people who know that they'll require more care and who will spend their own money each year to meet the deductible. They may also scare off low-income people, who are loath to take the risk of having to pay out of pocket for health care. Those people will be left in an increasingly costly risk pool. "You have relatively few people who account for most of [the health insurance] claims," said Anna M. Rappaport, a principal at the Chicago office of William M. Mercer Inc., a New York City-based employee benefits consulting firm. "It's a social question who will pay for them, if not everyone contributes" to the cost of their care.

MSA advocates dispute this analysis, arguing that the plan will have universal appeal and benefit. More important, they argue, it's the best means for controlling costs without having government or health maintenance organizations impose rationing. "Risk pooling distorts incentives for any kind of consumption. When the item consumed is health care, the distortions are the worst," according to John C. Goodman, president of the Dallas-based National Center for Policy Analysis, who came up with the MSA concept in the mid-1980s. "There's going to be draconian rationing unless people set aside funds" for their own care, he said.

It was after a protracted and bitter battle over just such issues that Congress approved the limited version of tax-subsidized MSAs. Among the limitations: Only 750,000 taxpayers working for small businesses or for themselves can set them up. After evaluating the results of the experiment at the turn of the century, Congress will have to vote on whether to expand the MSAs' availability.

Goodman, of course, is betting the plans will prove so popular that Congress will have no choice. "There will be pressure to let more people in," he said.

Ironically, the controversial MSA measure was attached to a broader bill that was intended to shore up the traditional system of pooling risk. The Health Coverage Availability and Affordability Act restricts insurers' ability to deny people coverage because of preexisting conditions and guarantees most workers the right to keep their health insurance when they leave their jobs.

That Congress passed both measures at the same time, despite their conflicting philosophies, is perhaps a reflection of both public ambivalence on the deeper issues and the challenges facing divided government in tackling the issues.

"This society has to make a choice—we'll make it implicitly or explicitly," Reich said. "The choice is whether we try to somehow prop up the private system of social [welfare] or whether we embark upon a new system of [public] social insurance for the middle class or below." A critical problem with the second option, he conceded, is that "we don't have the money."

Still, Reich maintains that it is possible to use the resources of government selectively to plug holes in the private-sector safety net. Case in point: The Clinton Administration's proposal to create a narrow, publicly financed health insurance program for the short-term unemployed—a proposal for which, Reich insists, financing has already been identified.

There is, Reich concedes on reflection, a third alternative: "Sink or swim . . . that is, everyone is on his or her own. That's the direction we're moving in right now."

## THE EGALITARIAN IDEAL

It may prove difficult enough, however, just to maintain the public social insurance programs we already have. The question is not whether to cut social security and medicare: Some retrenchment in both programs is a given.

The more nettlesome question is about whether it's possible, or indeed desirable, to preserve the programs' universal and collective nature and their egalitarian ideals.

Last year's dustup between Clinton and the Republican Congress over medicare may have been a preview of the battles to come. The '96 campaign trail rhetoric notwithstanding, the fight was not exclusively, or even principally, about how much to "cut" (or, in Republican parlance, how much to "slow the growth of") medicare spending. Indeed, Congress's final spending proposal wasn't radically different from the President's.

The deeper differences were over the government's promise of providing equal treatment for the elderly. Republicans billed their plan as an opportunity for medicare beneficiaries to take advantage of health plans that were more diverse and efficient.

Congressional Democrats and the Clinton Administration, however, argued that the GOP plan would have fragmented medicare's broad risk pool, because it provided inadequate safeguards against health plans that use subtle methods to skim off the good health risks, leaving everyone else in an anorexic public program. Democrats argued that it also would have made access to certain types of plans dependent on the ability to pay. "You easily could have gotten risk segmentation and a class-based system," Brookings's Reischauer said.

The political coup de grâce from the Democrats' standpoint is that the GOP measure, which was part of a broader budget reconciliation bill that Clinton vetoed, included a proposal to give medicare patients access to MSAs—a further threat to the medicare risk pool.

But don't think some of the same issues won't be back, and soon. Congress and the President may partially dodge the medicare bullet with smaller fixes to next year's budget that would also push back the date of medicare's rendezvous with bankruptcy, now projected for 2001. But as the baby boomers start retiring, medicare's costs will become so large that most analysts doubt the feasibility of raising taxes to cover them.

"As an abstract philosophical issue, it's hard for people to say, 'We choose not to do social insurance,' " said Gail R. Wilensky, a senior fellow at the nonprofit health foundation Project Hope who ran medicare for two years during the Bush Administration. But faced with vastly higher taxes, she said, "people may be willing to take a second look."

The government may well be forced to choose between two unpalatable alternatives: continuing to offer all beneficiaries an equal, but deteriorating level of care or, following the private employers' lead, limiting its own financial liability and offering beneficiaries a defined contribution toward the cost of care. Patients who could afford to pay extra for better-quality plans would be free to do so, and the rest would have to take what they could get.

---

*The problem isn't merely that there are no painless solutions. It is also that one consequence seems inevitable: the program becomes an increasingly unattractive financial proposition for the well-to-do.*

---

Reischauer concedes that sooner or later, fiscal constraints may force the government to abandon medicare's classless character. "It would be impossible not to sacrifice that somewhat under any of the alternatives," he said.

Although social security's fiscal problems aren't nearly as severe, reform quickly raises some similarly thorny questions.

The problem isn't merely that there are no painless solutions. It is also that,

no matter how the pain is distributed—whether taxes are raised, the retirement age extended, or cost-of-living increases reduced—one consequence seems inevitable: The program becomes an increasingly unattractive financial proposition for the well-to-do.

Until recently, despite the program's built-in redistribution to the less-well-off, all recipients got more in benefits than they put in—thanks to rising payroll taxes and to favorable economic and demographic trends.

Already, however, high-income single men who retired in the past decade are projected to receive less in lifetime benefits than they contributed to social security, and other high-income groups will eventually face the same prospect. Cuts in the program only exacerbate the problem. "It becomes a very bad deal for younger workers, and that's especially true at upper-income levels," William J. Beeman, director of economic studies at the corporate-sponsored think tank Committee for Economic Development, said. Low-income workers still get a positive rate of return on their contributions when they retire, he said, but "of course, political pressures are more heavy from middle and upper-income people."

Converting social security to a system of private individual savings accounts might eventually obviate that problem—it would lessen redistribution of income. Fans of this approach contend that because the money can be invested in stocks and bonds, everyone—including low-income elderly people—would get a better return on their money than they do from social security. The rich might benefit disproportionately from the change, they admit, but what does that matter if everyone's better-off?

Social security's defenders don't buy this economic scenario, for a host of reasons. Instead, they argue, many low-income and middle-income retirees would

face greater risk of ending up worse-off. *(For more about privatization of social security, see NJ, 12/23/95, p. 3136.)*

But one level below the dizzying technical arguments about how to overhaul social security—and indeed the entire social welfare system—are profound philosophical disagreements about the value of collective action, the pooling of risk and trying to ensure everyone an equitable financial outcome.

"Besides the fiscal problem, there's a growing realization that insuring all the actions anyone takes, takes responsibility away from the individual and causes more irresponsible behavior," David D. Boaz, executive vice president of the libertarian Cato Institute in Washington, said.

Libertarians, Yale professor Marmor countered, imagine that all people have equal capacity to fend for themselves, "to distribute their income over the life cycle and to protect themselves from [financial] risks . . . even when the sources of these risks are largely outside the individuals' control.

"It's the lake Wobegon problem: All the children are above average and all the women are good-looking," he paraphrased.

Boaz agreed that many events in a lifetime are beyond an individual's control. But he argued, "We would be a healthier, stronger, more prosperous people if we act as though we can control all the consequences. Some people will suffer" in such a system, "but over-all suffering will be less than where everyone is guaranteed against the consequences of their actions."

Marmor, however, believes that such a world would reward privilege rather than virtue. "If the world were as genial a place as it is for those who have a good education and scarce skills, rich families or trust funds," he said, U.S. society would not need a cushion. But, he noted, well-off people "are a trivial proportion of the population."

# Ten Essential Observations on Guns in America

## James D. Wright

*James D. Wright is the Charles and Leo Favrot Professor of Human Relations in the department of Sociology at Tulane University. He has written widely on problems of firearms and gun control, including two books. His current researches are on the effect of poverty on the urban underclass, alcohol and drug treatment programs for the homeless, and health problems of street children in Latin America.*

Talk of "gun control" is very much in the air these days. Emboldened by their successes in getting the Brady Act enacted, the pro-control forces are now striking on a number of fronts: bans on various so-called assault weapons, mandatory gun registration, strict new laws against juvenile acquisition and possession of guns, and on through the list. Much current gun-control activity springs from a recent and generally successful effort to redefine gun violence mainly as a public health issue rather than a criminal justice issue.

Increasingly, the ammunition of the gun control war is data. Pro-control advocates gleefully cite studies that seem to favor their position, of which there is no shortage, and anti-control advocates do likewise. Many of the "facts" of the case are, of course, hotly disputed; so too are their implications and interpretations. Here I should like to discuss ten essential facts about guns in America that are not in dispute—ten fundamental truths that all contestants either do or should agree to—and briefly ponder the implications of each for how the problem of guns and gun violence perhaps should be approached. These facts and their implications derive from some twenty years of research and reflection on the issues.

1. *Half the households in the country own at least one gun.* So far as I have been able to determine, the first question about gun ownership asked of a national probability sample of U.S. adults was posed in 1959; a similar question asking whether anyone in the household owns a

gun has since been repeated dozens of times. Over the ensuing thirty-five years, every survey has reported more or less the same result: Just about half of all U.S. households own one or more guns. This is probably not the highest gun ownership percentage among the advanced industrial societies (that honor probably goes to the Swiss), but it qualifies as a very respectable showing. We are, truly, a "gun culture."

Five important implications follow more or less unambiguously from this first essential observation.

The percentage of households owning guns has been effectively constant for nearly four decades; at the same time, the total number of guns in circulation has increased substantially, especially in the last two decades. The evident implication is that the increasing supply of guns has been absorbed by population growth, with newly formed households continuing to arm themselves at the average rate, and by the purchase of additional guns by households already owning one or more of them. In fact there is fairly solid evidence that the average number of guns owned by households owning any has increased from about three in the late 1970s to about four today.

The second implication is thus that many (and conceivably nearly all) of the new guns coming into circulation are being purchased by people who already own guns, as opposed to first-time purchases by households or individuals who previously owned no guns. I think it is also obvious that from the viewpoint of public safety, the transition from N to N + 1 guns is considerably less ominous than the transition from no guns to one gun. If this second implication is correct, it means that *most of the people in the gun shops today buying new guns already own at least one gun*, a useful point to keep in mind when pondering, for example, the alleged "cooling off" function to be served by waiting periods imposed at the point of retail sale.

Furthermore, it is frequently argued by pro-control advocates that the mere presence of guns causes people to do nutty and violent things that they would otherwise never even consider. In the academic literature on "guns as aggression-eliciting stimuli," this is called the "trigger pulls the finger" hypothesis. If there were much substance to this viewpoint, the fact that half of all U.S. households possess a gun would seem to imply that there ought to be a lot more nuttiness "out there" than we actually observe. In the face of widespread alarm about the skyrocketing homicide rate, it is important to remember that the rate is still a relatively small number of homicides (ten to fifteen or so) per hundred thousand people. If half the households own guns and the mere presence of guns incites acts of violence, then one would expect the bodies to be piled three deep, and yet they are not.

Fourth, gun ownership is normative, not deviant, behavior across vast swaths of the social landscape. In certain states and localities, it would be an odd duck indeed who did not own a gun. Surveys in some smaller southern cities, for example, have reported local gun ownership rates in excess of 90 percent.

And finally, to attempt to control crime or violence by controlling the general ownership or use of guns among the public at large is to attempt to control the behaviors of a very small fraction of the population (the criminally or violently inclined fraction) by controlling the behaviors and activities of roughly half the U.S. population. Whatever else might be said about such an approach, it is certainly not very efficient.

2. *There are 200 million guns already in circulation in the United States*, give or take a few tens of millions. It has been said, I think correctly, that firearms are the most commonly owned piece of sporting equipment in the United States, with the exception of pairs of sneakers. In any case, contestants on all sides of the gun debate generally agree that the total number of guns in circulation is on the order of 200 million—nearly one gun for every man, woman, and child in the country.

It is not entirely clear how many acts of gun violence occur in any typical year. There are 30–35,000 deaths due to guns each year, perhaps a few hundred thousand nonfatal but injurious firearms accidents, maybe 500,000 or 600,000 chargeable gun crimes (not including crimes of illegal gun possession and carrying), and God knows how many instances in which guns are used to intimidate or prey upon one's fellow human beings. Making generous allowances all around, however, the total number of acts of accidental and intentional gun violence, whether fatal, injurious, or not, cannot be more than a couple of million, at the outside. This implies that the 200 million guns now in circulation would be sufficient to sustain roughly another century of gun violence at the current rates, even assuming that each gun was used once and only once for some nefarious purpose and that all additions to the gun supply were halted permanently

and at once. Because of the large number of guns already in circulation, the violence-reductive effects of even fairly Draconian gun-control measures enacted today might well not be felt for decades.

# Most of the people in the gun shops today buying new guns already own at least one gun.

Many recent gun-control initiatives, such as the Brady Act, are aimed at the point of retail sale of firearms and are therefore intended to reduce or in some way disrupt the flow of new guns into the domestic market. At the outside, the number of new guns coming onto the market yearly is a few million, which adds but a few percent to the existing supply. If we intend to control gun violence by reducing the availability of firearms to the general public, as many argue we should, then we have to find some workable means to confront or control the vast arsenal of guns already circulating through private hands.

Various "amnesty," "buyback," and "please turn in your guns" measures have been attempted in various jurisdictions all over the country; in one well-publicized effort, teenagers could swap guns for Toys R Us gift certificates. The success of these programs has been measured in units of several dozen or at most a few hundred relinquished firearms; the net effect on the overall supply of guns is far too trivial to even bother calculating.

3. *Most of those 200 million guns are owned for socially innocuous sport and recreational purposes.* Only about a third of the guns presently in circulation are handguns; the remainder are rifles and shotguns. When one asks gun owners why they own guns, various sport and recreational activities dominate the responses—hunting, target shooting, collecting, and the like. Even when the question is restricted to handgun owners, about 40 percent say they own the gun for sport and recreational applications, another 40 percent say they own it for self-protection, and the remaining 20 percent cite their job or occupation as the principal reason for owning a gun.

Thus for the most part, gun ownership is apparently a topic more appropriate to the sociology of leisure than to the criminology or epidemiology of violence. Many pro-control advocates look on the sporting uses of guns as atavistic, barbaric, or just plain silly. But an equally compelling case could be made against golf, which causes men to wear funny clothes, takes them away from their families, and gobbles up a lot of pretty, green, open space that would be better used as public parks. It is, of course, true that golf does not kill 35,000 people a year (although middle-aged men drop dead on the golf course quite regularly), but it is also true that the sport and recreational use of guns does not kill 35,000 people a year. There are fewer than a thousand fatal hunting accidents annually; death from skeet shooting, target practice, and such is uncounted but presumably very small. It is the violent or criminal *abuse* of guns that should concern us, and the vast majority of guns now in circulation will never be used for anything more violent or abusive than killing the furry creatures of the woods and fields.

# The sport and recreational use of guns does not kill 35,000 people a year.

Unfortunately, when we seek to control violence by controlling the general ownership and use of firearms among the public at large, it at least *looks* as though we think we have intuited some direct causal connection between drive-by shootings in the inner city and squirrel hunting or skeet shooting in the hinterland. In any case, this is the implication that the nation's squirrel hunters and skeet shooters often draw; frankly, is it any wonder they sometimes come to question the motives, not to mention the sanity, of anyone who would suggest such a thing?

4. *Many guns are also owned for self-defense against crime, and some are indeed used for that purpose; whether they are actually any safer or not, many people certainly seem to feel safer when they have a gun.* There is a fierce debate raging in gun advocacy circles these days over recent findings by Gary Kleck that Americans use guns to protect themselves against crime as often as one or two million times a year, which, if true, is hard to square with the common assumption of pro-control advocates that guns are not an efficacious defense against crime. Whatever the true number of self-defensive uses, about a quarter of all guns owners and about 40 percent of handgun owners cite defense against crime as the main reason they own a gun, and large percentages of those who give some other main reason will cite self-defense as a secondary reason. Gun owners and gun advocates insist that guns provide real protection, as Kleck's findings suggest; anti-gun advocates insist that the sense of security is more illusory than real.

But practically everything people do to protect themselves against crime provides only the illusion of security in that any such measure can be defeated by a sufficiently clever and motivated criminal. Dogs can be diverted or poisoned, burglar bars can be breached, home alarm systems can be subverted, chains and deadbolt locks can be cut and picked. That sales of all these items have skyrocketed in recent years is further proof—as if further proof were needed—that the fear of crime is real. Most people have also realized, correctly, that the police cannot protect them from crime. So people face the need

to protect themselves and many choose to own a gun, along with taking many other measures, for this purpose. Does a society that is manifestly incapable of protecting its citizens from crime and predation really have the right or moral authority to tell people what they may and may not do to protect themselves?

Since a "sense of security" is inherently a psychological trait, it does no good to argue that the sense of security afforded by owning a gun is "just an illusion." Psychological therapy provides an *illusion* of mental wellness even as we remain our former neurotic selves, and it is nonetheless useful. The only sensible response to the argument that guns provide only an illusion of security is, So what?

5. *The bad guys do not get their guns through customary retail channels.* Research on both adult and juvenile felons and offenders has made it obvious that the illicit firearms market is dominated, overwhelmingly, by informal swaps, trades, and purchases among family members, friends, acquaintances, and street and black-market sources. It is a rare criminal indeed who attempts to acquire a gun through a conventional over-the-counter transaction with a normal retail outlet. It is also obvious that many or most of the guns circulating through criminal hands enter the illicit market through theft from legitimate gun owners. (An aside of some possible significance: Large numbers of legitimate gun owners also obtain guns through informal "street" sources.)

As I have already noted, many efforts at gun control pertain to the initial retail sale of weapons, for example, the prohibition against gun purchases by people with felony records or alcohol or drug histories contained in the Gun Control Act of 1968, the national five-day waiting period, or various state and local permit and registration laws. Since felons rarely obtain guns through retail channels, controls imposed at the point of retail sale necessarily miss the vast majority of criminal firearms transactions. It is thus an easy prediction that the national five-day waiting period will have no effect on the acquisition of guns by criminals because that is not how the bad guys get their guns in the first place.

Having learned (now more than a decade ago) that the criminal acquisition of guns involves informal and intrinsically difficult-to-regulate transfers that are entirely independent of laws concerning registration and permits, average gun owners often conclude (whether rightly or wrongly) that such measures must therefore be intended primarily to keep tabs on them, that registration or permit requirements are "just the first step" toward outright confiscation of all privately held firearms, and that mandated registration of new gun purchases is thus an unwarranted "police state" intrusion on law-abiding citizens' constitutional rights. Reasoning in this vein often seems bizarre or even psychotic to proponents of registration or permit laws, but it is exactly this reasoning that accounts for the white-hot ferocity of the debate over guns in America today.

And similar reasoning applies to the national waiting period: Since it is well known that the bad guys do not generally obtain guns through normal retail channels, waiting periods enforced at the point of retail sale can only be aimed at thwarting the legitimate intentions of the "good guys." What conceivable crime-reductive benefit will a national five-day waiting period give us? If the answer is "probably very little," then the minds of average gun owners are free to speculate on the nefarious and conspiratorial intentions that may be harbored, consciously or not, by those who favor such a thing. The distinction between ill-considered and evil is quickly lost, and the debate over guns in America gets hotter still.

---

## The national five-day waiting period will have no effect on the acquisition of guns by criminals because that is not how the bad guys get their guns in the first place.

---

That the illicit gun market is supplied largely through theft from legitimate owners erodes any useful distinction between legitimate and illegitimate guns. Any gun that can be owned legitimately can be stolen from its legal owner and can end up in criminal hands. The effort to find some way to interdict or interfere with the criminal gun market while leaving legitimate owners pretty much alone is therefore bootless. So long as anybody can have a gun, criminals will have them too, and it is useful to remember that there are 200 million guns out there—an average of four of them in every second household.

6. *The bad guys inhabit a violent world; a gun often makes a life-or-death difference to them.* When one asks felons—either adult or juvenile—why they own and carry guns, themes of self-defense, protection, and survival dominate the responses. Very few of the bad guys say they acquire or carry guns for offensive or criminal purposes, although that is obviously how many of them get used. These men live in a very hostile and violent environment, and many of them have come to believe, no doubt correctly, that their ability to survive in that environment depends critically on being adequately armed. Thus the bad guys are highly motivated gun consumers who will not be easily dissuaded from possessing, carrying, and using guns. If sheer survival is the issue, then a gun is a bargain at practically any price. As James Q. Wilson has argued, most of the gun violence problem results from the wrong kinds of people carrying guns at the wrong time and place. The survival motive among the bad guys means exactly that the "wrong kinds of people" will be carrying guns pretty much all the time. The

evident implication is that the bad guys have to be disarmed on the street if the rates of gun violence are to decline, and that implies a range of intervention strategies far removed from what gun control advocates have recently urged on the American population.

7. *Everything the bad guys do with their guns is already against the law.* That criminals will generally be indifferent to our laws would seem to follow from the definitions of the terms, but it is a lesson that we have had to relearn time and time again throughout our history. So let me stress an obvious point: Murder is already against the law, yet murderers still murder; armed robbery is against the law, yet robbers still rob. And as a matter of fact, gun acquisition by felons, whether from retail or private sources, is also already illegal, yet felons still acquire guns. Since practically everything the bad guys do with their guns is already against the law, we are entitled to wonder whether there is any new law we can pass that would persuade them to stop doing it. It is more than a little bizarre to assume that people who routinely violate laws against murder, robbery, or assault would somehow find themselves compelled to obey gun laws, whatever provisions they might contain.

8. *Demand creates it own supply.* That "demand creates its own supply" is sometimes called the First Law of Economics, and it clearly holds whether the commodity in demand is legal or illegal. So long as a demand exists, there will be profit to be made in satisfying it, and therefore it will be satisfied. In a capitalist economy, it could scarcely be otherwise. So long as people, be they criminals or average citizens, want to own guns, guns will be available for them to own. The vast arsenal of guns already out there exists in the first instance because people who own guns like guns, the activities that guns make possible, and the sense of security that guns provide. "Supply side" approaches to the gun problem are never going to be any more effective than "supply side" approaches to the drug problem, which is to say, not at all. What alcohol and drug prohibition should have taught us (but apparently has not) is that if a demand exists and there is no legal way to satisfy it, then an illegal commerce in the commodity is spawned, and we often end up creating many more problems than we have solved.

Brazil and several European nations manufacture small arms; the Brazilian lines are relatively inexpensive but decent guns. In fundamental respects, the question whether we can disarm the American criminal population amounts to asking whether an organized criminal enterprise that successfully illegally imports hundreds of tons of Colombian cocaine into the U.S. market each year would not find the means to illegally import hundreds of tons of handguns from Brazil. And if this is the case, then it seems more or less self-evident that the supply of firearms to the criminal population will never be reduced by enough to make an appreciable difference.

9. *Guns are neither inherently good nor inherently evil; guns, that is, do not possess teleology.* Benevolence and malevolence inhere in the motives and behaviors of people, not in the technology they possess. Any firearm is neither more nor less than a chunk of machined metal that can be put to a variety of purposes, all involving a small projectile hurtling at high velocity downrange to lodge itself in a target. We can only call this "good" when the target is appropriate and "evil" when it is not; the gun itself is immaterial to this judgment.

Gun-control advocates have a long history of singling out "bad" guns for policy attention. At one time, the emphasis was on small, cheap handguns—"Saturday Night Specials"—which were thought to be inherently "bad" because no legitimate use was thought to exist for them and because they were thought to be the preferred firearm among criminals. Both these thoughts turned out to be incorrect. Somewhat later, all handguns, regardless of their characteristics, were singled out (as by the National Coalition to Ban Handguns); most recently, the so-called military-style assault weapons are the "bad guns of the month."

Singling out certain types of guns for policy attention is almost always justified on the grounds that the type of gun in question "has no legitimate use" or "is designed only to kill." By definition, however, all guns are "designed to kill" (that is, to throw a projectile downrange to lodge in a target), and if one grants the proposition that self-defense against predation and plunder is a legitimate reason to own a gun, then all guns, regardless of their type or characteristics, have at least some potentially "legitimate" application. It seems to me, therefore, that the focus in gun-control circles on certain "bad" guns is fundamentally misplaced. When all is said and done, it is the behavior of people that we should seek to control. Any gun can be used legitimately by law-abiding people to hunt, shoot at targets, or defend themselves against crime; and likewise, any gun can be used by a criminal to prey upon and intimidate other people. Trying to sort firearms into "inherently bad" and "inherently good" categories seems fundamentally silly.

10. *Guns are important elements of our history and culture.* Attempts to control crime by regulating the ownership or use of firearms are attempts to regulate the artifacts and activities of a culture that, in its own way, is as unique as any of the myriad other cultures that comprise the American ethnic mosaic. This is the American gun culture, which remains among the least understood of any of the various subcultural strands that make up modern American society.

There is no question that a gun culture exists, one that amply fulfills any definition of a culture. The best evidence we have on its status as a culture is that the single most important predictor of whether a person owns a gun is whether his or her father owned one, which means that gun owning is a tradition transmitted across generations. Most gun owners report that there were firearms in their homes when they were growing up; this is true even of criminal gun users.

The existence and characteristics of the American gun culture have implications that rarely are appreciated. For one, gun control deals with matters that people feel strongly about, that are integral to their upbringing and their worldview. Gun-control advocates are frequently taken aback by the stridency with which their seemingly modest and sensible proposals are attacked, but from the gun culture's viewpoint, restrictions on the right to "keep and bear arms" amount to the systematic destruction of a valued way of life and are thus a form of cultural genocide.

Guns evoke powerful, emotive imagery that often stands in the way of intelligent debate. To the pro-control point of view, the gun is symbolic of much that is wrong in American culture. It symbolizes violence, aggression, and male dominance, and its use is seen as an acting out of our most regressive and infantile fantasies. To the gun culture's way of thinking, the same gun symbolizes much that is right in the culture. It symbolizes manliness, self-sufficiency, and independence, and its use is an affirmation of man's relationship to nature and to history. The "Great American Gun War," as Bruce-Briggs has described it, is far more than a contentious debate over crime and the equipment with which it is committed. It is a battle over fundamental and equally legitimate sets of values.

Scholars and criminologists who speculate on the problem of guns, crime, and violence would thus do well to look at things, at least occasionally, from the gun culture's point of view. Hardly any of the 50 million or so American families that own guns have ever harmed anyone with their guns, and virtually none ever intend to. Nearly everything these families will ever do with their firearms is both legal and largely innocuous. When, in the interests of fighting crime, we advocate restrictions on their rights to own guns, we are casting aspersions on their decency, as though we somehow hold them responsible for the crime and violence that plague this nation. It is any wonder they object, often vociferously, to such slander?

# Clinton's Foreign Policy: A Victim of Globalization?

*by Moisés Naím*

**B**ill Clinton presides over the most militarily and economically powerful nation on Earth. He does not need to worry about getting reelected, and he is recognized, even by his most implacable critics, as intelligent and knowledgeable about the central challenges facing today's world. Yet, in the United States and abroad, the view is widely held that, unless a drastic change occurs within the next year or so, President Clinton is unlikely to be remembered for his foreign policy record. Why? Why is a man known for his huge appetites not showing much appetite for changing the world? Is it a desire to please everyone? An obstructionist Congress? An indifferent public? Or is it that new conditions, many of them global, constrain the autonomy of presidents, be they from the United States or any other country?

We asked our contributing editors to share their sense of how Clinton and his foreign policy are perceived in their corners of the world. We did not anticipate much of a convergence of views: We were wrong.

Each of their assessments has a regional focus and highlights different issues and events. Nonetheless, a common theme emerges: Clinton's lack of a coherent, long-term strategy or vision. From Tokyo, Yoichi Funabashi points to a "notable lack of the 'vision thing' "; France's Jacques Attali notes, "lacking a long-term vision, his administration seeks to impose its fancied solutions on an ad hoc basis." Commenting on U.S. policy toward Latin

America, Jorge Domínguez exclaims, "I long for Bush's 'vision'!"; while in Moscow, Yegor Gaidar concludes that "one of the chief distinguishing characteristics of President Clinton's foreign policy has been his unwillingness to make clear choices or to provide a coherent vision." From London, Rupert Pennant-Rea observes that "it is surely fair to be disappointed by Clinton's foreign policy record: relentlessly tactical and never in the cause of strategy"; and, with regard to the Middle East, Fawaz Gerges laments that "more than any other recent president, Clinton appears to conduct foreign policy on an ad hoc basis, often gearing it toward satisfying domestic constituencies." From Hamburg, Christoph Bertram writes that "while Kohl's agenda is clear, Clinton's, if it exists at all, is difficult to decipher"; a point echoed in Hong Kong by Nayan Chanda, who regretfully observes that in Asia "the indirection that has marked Clinton's policy toward the region has only confirmed the initial apprehension of 1992."

FOREIGN POLICY's contributing editors are not alone in these dim assessments. According to the results of a study by the Pew Research Center for the People & the Press, most opinion leaders identify a lack of direction as the president's greatest failing in handling U.S. relations abroad.

The reasons for the administration's strategic void are many, but one that seems to dominate is the primacy Clinton gives to political calculations. The *New York Times* reports that even "senior [administration] officials concede that political considerations often eclipse policy commitments"—a perception shared by some

---

MOISÉS NAÍM *is the editor of* FOREIGN POLICY.

Reprinted with permission from *Foreign Policy*, Winter 1997/1998, pp. 34-37. © 1997 by the Carnegie Endowment for International Peace.

of the president's peers. Witness the comments last July by Canada's Jean Chretien. As reported by CNN, he told two fellow prime ministers that Clinton's commitment to NATO expansion had less to do with reasons of state than "short-term political reasons, to win elections." (see box, "With Friends Like These . . .").

Accusing any president of being too political is like criticizing a ballerina for being too skinny. It comes with the job, the training, and, perhaps, the genes. But just as ballerinas can become dangerously thin, presidents can take the political nature of their jobs too far. Clinton's political reluctance to tackle tough issues—another theme of our contributors—until the last minute (whether Bosnia or the Chemical Weapons Convention) usually followed by a heroic *Sturm und Drang* that is then spun by the White House into an epic triumph, has allowed problems with allies and friends to fester, fueled public cynicism, and wasted time and energy on needless come-from-behind victories. And as the President's disastrous legislative defeat in November on fast-track authority shows, sometimes there is no substitute for sustained leadership in the face of political opposition.

On the other hand, perhaps the president deserves a break. Although countless words have been written about Clinton's shortcomings as a policymaker, not enough attention has been given to the flip side of the coin: the environment in which policy is made. Leading a nation today may or may not be more difficult than it used to be, but it is definitely very different. In addition to reckoning with a radically changed strategic landscape, Clinton must contend with constraints that hinder presidential action across a broad range of fronts.

## THE NEW CONSTRAINTS

The demise of the Soviet Union—and the concomitant spread of the ideology of free markets and open societies—has opened many new opportunities for the United States, paving the way for America's current global pre-eminence. But as the rosy afterglow of freedom's victory in the "long, twilight struggle" begins to fade, new limits—or old limits given new force—on the president's ability to conduct foreign policy are beginning to emerge. Take the limits on the financial resources available to support government policies abroad or the influence of nonstate actors

### With Friends Like These . . .

At the NATO summit in Madrid, Spain, on July 9, 1997, an open microphone inadvertently caught Canadian prime minister Jean Chretien joking about Bill Clinton's priorities, especially his political reasons for expanding NATO. As CNN's Wolf Blitzer reported at the time, Chretien held the following exchange in French with the prime ministers of Belgium and Luxembourg, Jean-Luc Dehaene and Jean-Claude Juncker, as they waited for Clinton to arrive, unaware that they were on the air:

"It's not reasons of state. It's all done for short-term political reasons, to win elections. Take the quarrel over whether to admit the Baltic states. That has nothing to do with world security. It's because in Chicago, Mayor [Richard M.] Daley controls lots of votes for the nomination."

The three leaders laughed. Still waiting for Clinton, Juncker asked, "And if we started without them?"

"To prove that we know what to do without them," Dehaene added.

"To prove we're independent. He [Chretien], he's used to not doing what they want," said Juncker.

"I make it my policy," Chretien responded. "But it's popular. The Cuba affair. I was the first to stand up [against U.S. efforts to tighten the embargo against Cuba]." The three men chuckled.

on the formulation and execution of these policies. Both have always shaped policy preferences and outcomes. Now, with the integration of financial markets and the plummeting costs of international communication and transportation, their impact has become even more pronounced.

Although the full shape and force of these changes are just becoming apparent, four factors are worthy of integration into any appraisal of the president's performance: first, the repercussions of more rigid fiscal constraints; second, the increase in the number and the influence of nonstate actors who can shape different aspects of U.S. foreign policy; third, the growing role of the media and its impact on public opinion and, therefore, on politics; and fourth, the internationalization of

*Ronald Reagan, Leonid Brezhnev, and François Mitterand all enjoyed greater financial flexibility than Bill Clinton, Boris Yeltsin, and Jacques Chirac.*

public-sector actors at all levels of government, from the federal to the municipal.

*Less Money*

Around the world, deficit spending is out and balanced budgets are in. Heads of state everywhere complain that they have much less money to do their jobs than their predecessors: Ronald Reagan, Leonid Brezhnev, and François Mitterand all enjoyed greater financial flexibility than Bill Clinton, Boris Yeltsin, and Jacques Chirac, for example.

Recently, Secretary of State Madeleine Albright pleaded: "We cannot lead without tools. It costs money to detect cheating at a nuclear facility in North Korea or Iraq.... It takes money to help our partners build peace and democracy and to defeat transnational crime.... The amount we seek for everything from aid to Ukraine to promoting Kentucky's exports to assisting students abroad equals about one percent of our total budget. But that one percent may determine fifty percent of the history that is written about our era."

It has become common to attribute this new fiscal austerity to the domestic preoccupations and short attention spans of American tax-payers recently delivered from the communist threat. Several commentators have seized on the fact that one-third of the members of Congress do not have a passport to illustrate just how provincial the world's only superpower has become.

Although there is more than a grain of truth to these observations, it is also true that governments today face sterner fiscal limitations. Taxpayers and the private money managers that buy government bonds have lost most of their past tolerance for governments that spend much more than their normal reve-

nues. The Cold War used to provide a fiscal fig leaf for what would now be immediately denounced as profligacy. Today, not only are the Cold War's spending justifications gone, but the financial consequences of running large budget deficits are more immediate and severe. As international financial markets have become more integrated, new technologies permit—indeed, encourage—the instant and massive transfer of funds from countries with shaky economic fundamentals. Large deficits have become a sharp warning signal for international investors.

Moreover, new economic policies in a multitude of countries now offer investors, large and small, new opportunities. Countries have to compete more intensely to attract the money to fund their operations or to stop foreign investors from fleeing their stock markets. They can compete either by offering low risk in the form of sound economic and political fundamentals or by offering higher returns to the buyers of government bonds. Paying more to bond holders means that less money will be available for government programs, thus creating even more problems for governments that are already under fiscal pressure.

European heads of state who are striving to meet the fiscal and monetary targets of the Maastricht Treaty, or their counterparts in Africa, Central Europe, East Asia, and Latin America who are operating under the tight conditions of the International Monetary Fund (IMF), are familiar with the political consequences of rigid external constraints on their public expenditures. In the United States, the power of the bond market became painfully evident to Clinton as soon as he was first elected. Lloyd Bentsen, then secretary of the treasury, Federal Reserve Chairman Alan Greenspan, and Robert Rubin, then chairman of the National Economic Council, told the rookie president and his political advisers that many of the social programs they were so enthusiastic about could not be funded. Implementing them would increase the government deficit, scaring the bond markets and leading to higher interest rates, lower tax revenues, and higher costs of servicing the federal debt. These effects would in turn further reduce the money available to fund social programs.

The message was not lost on the Clinton team. One of the president's political strategists, James Carville, who helped him run an election campaign based on the slogan, "It's the economy, stupid," noted: "I used to think if there was reincarnation I wanted to come back as the President, the Pope or a .400 baseball hitter. But now I want to come back as the bond market. You can intimidate everyone."

The need to reduce the federal deficit and the inward-looking political mood prevalent in the U.S. Congress have had dramatic results. The amount of funding allocated by Congress for international affairs has plummeted and is now less than half of what it was in 1984. Today, the United States has the lowest number of consulates abroad since 1820. Its foreign aid budget has decreased from the $12 billion spent on economic and humanitarian assistance during the Cold War to $9 billion in 1997, and it now lags behind countries such as Japan, Germany, and France as a contributor to international development. Since Clinton first took office, America's unpaid debts to international institutions such as the United Nations and the World Bank have become a constant source of embarrassment abroad.

*More Players*
The funds deployed by billionaire philanthropist George Soros to support a smooth transition to democracy and free markets in Eastern Europe and the former Soviet Union now rival those invested by the United States. Ted Turner's $1 billion donation to the United Nations stands in vivid counterpoint to the United States' chronic, large-scale arrears. Whether from Boeing or Fidelity Investments, the heads of multinational corporations and large investment funds have as much access to governments around the world as most top U.S. officials.

But these days you do not have to be a billionaire or the CEO of a global corporation to make a significant difference in international affairs. Jody Williams won the 1997 Nobel Peace Prize for her contribution to the International Campaign to Ban Land Mines. Her efforts helped bring together more than 1,000 human rights, children's, medical, arms-control, religious, women's, and environmental voluntary organizations in nearly 55 countries to ban antipersonnel land mines. In just one year, the NGO coalition, together with Canada and a handful of other countries, succeeded in pushing through a new treaty to ban these weapons despite the initial opposition of all five of the major powers. Bowing to public pressure, three of them—Britain, France, and Russia—have since switched and now support the campaign. When asked to name the main instrument she used to wield such global power, Jody Williams answered, "e-mail."

Presidents have always had to take into account the interests of pressure groups in their policymaking. In recent years, however, nongovernmental organizations have boomed in number, resources, and influence. Many, such as Greenpeace or the land mine coalition, can project their views worldwide. Again, at the core of their new strength are the revolutionary changes that have lowered the costs of telecommunications and transportation. Coupled with a freer political environment, these technological innovations have not only spurred international trade and investment but have formed the sinews of an emerging civil society where nongovernmental organizations increasingly limit the autonomy of governments.

*Closer Public Scrutiny*
"Great mountains grow more impressive as you get closer to them. Great men don't." As this saying suggests, proximity and power are a corrosive mix. A president's main asset is his credibility. But today's new journalistic ethos and media technologies have made presidential credibility even more difficult to preserve. Global coverage, the demand for instant reactions to complex policy dilemmas, the opening to public scrutiny of previously private arenas, and the growing population and popularity of policy pundits have turned the once lofty realm of presidential foreign policy pronouncements into a free-for-all, with presidents and their cabinet members struggling to put their "message" out before a cynical press and distracted public.

As the post-Watergate media has become more aggressive in its coverage of public figures, the aura of power and majesty that once made phrases like "leader of the free world" believable has all but evaporated. A half century ago, the press refrained from showing photos of President Franklin D. Roosevelt in his wheelchair; when Clinton tore a tendon in his right knee, they did not hesitate to splash photos of the free world's leader smiling as he was forklifted into *Air Force One*. Never mind the obvious contrast between the media establishment that allowed President Kennedy's philandering to go unnoticed and the one now scrutinizing the deepest recesses of Clinton's private life. One can debate the merits of these respective approaches. But beyond the self-serving rationalizations advanced by both schools of thought, it is clear that the rules of the game have changed. As journalist Adam Gopnik noted, "The reporter used to gain status by dining with his subjects; now he gains status by dining on them."

Commentators (usually joined by policymakers behind closed doors) regularly decry the influence of global coverage on policymaking. Writing in this magazine in 1994, Johns Hopkins professor Michael Mandelbaum noted that "televised pictures of starving people in . . . Somalia . . . created a political clamor to feed them, which propelled the U.S. military. . . . [into the Horn of Africa in 1992]." Fittingly, when heavily camouflaged American troops staged a supposedly secret night landing on their Somalian beachhead, shots of their painted faces blinking into the spotlights of waiting television crews were beamed around the world. A year later, television had the opposite effect. Footage showing a cheering mob of Somalian warlord General Mohammed Farah Aidid's followers dragging a dead American soldier through the streets of Mogadishu sparked public outrage in the United States and prompted an abrupt troop withdrawal.

Often overlooked amid all the handwringing about the impact of the media is the enthusiasm that policymakers bring to orchestrating media coverage of foreign policy issues when it serves their interests. And in this area, the Clinton administration has shown exceptional zest and zeal. Secretary Albright's success at raising the profile of American diplomacy both at home and abroad is one positive side of the equation. But every hour that the president, the secretary of state, the secretary of defense, and the national security advisor and their respective staffs devote to delivering speeches, arranging press conferences, staging events, and generally schmoozing with reporters and columnists is an hour that cannot be spent solving problems, thinking about the future, or forging better relations with foreign counterparts.

*More Diffuse Government*

New actors with the ability to constrain presidential power are also proliferating inside the state. Devolution has gone global. From England to India and from Japan to Argentina, Russia, and the United States, power is shifting from federal to state and local governments. In this decade, the proportion of national budgets administered by state and local governments has steadily increased. Vot-

*Leaders must be willing to be not just chief executives but chief coordinators.*

ers are also playing a larger role in defining, through elections and referenda, important decisions that used to be Washington's prerogative, including foreign policy.

Decisions by state and local governments that directly impinge on U.S. foreign policy are nothing new. Just think of the protests over the Vietnam War, nuclear-free zones, and apartheid. Recently, however, this trend seems to be accelerating. More than 15 state and local governments currently impose—or at least threaten to impose—sanctions against companies that do business in countries with poor human rights records. The Massachusetts legislature, for example, outraged by the conduct of the military junta ruling Burma, passed a bill in June 1996 barring official purchases from companies that conduct business there. And in October 1997, Stuart Eizenstat, Clinton's undersecretary of state for economic affairs, attacked Alan Hevesi, New York City's comptroller, for undermining U.S. foreign policy toward Switzerland. Even as the State Department worked to persuade Swiss banks to contribute funds for Holocaust survivors and their families, Hevesi took a different approach, barring the Union Bank of Switzerland from participating in a $1 billion bond offering as punishment for its alleged dealings with Nazi Germany. Eizenstat noted: "Confrontation with the banks will achieve far less than cooperation. . . . I don't question the motives of New York City, but I am concerned that its approach will be counterproductive."

Power is not only shifting from the nation's capital to states and cities. It is also increasingly slipping away from the White House to other federal agencies. This erosion goes beyond the perennial presidential complaint about the tendency and ability of civil servants to distort or even derail a president's initiatives. Increasingly, regulatory agencies, from consumer safety to telecommunications to banking supervision or antitrust, find that they cannot do their jobs adequately within domestic limits. Coordination with similar agencies abroad is often indispensable.

Just as private businesses, nongovernmental organizations, terrorist groups, and scientists are exploiting the new opportunities created by globalization to join forces with like-minded institutions around the world, many government agencies are developing strong alliances with their peers abroad. Sometimes these alliances bear fruit in formal international treaties. Agencies of different governments that share a similar agenda may also develop agreements and common initiatives that enmesh them in a global web of commitments, which in turn effectively constrain the flexibility of the executive.

In 1989, for example, the industrialized nations of the world established the Financial Action Task Force, an ad hoc organization of 26 states trying to coordinate their efforts to combat money laundering. Since its low-key creation eight years ago, the task force has endorsed 40 recommended countermeasures and implemented a system for monitoring the individual efforts of member states. The agreements reached by the group often frame the policy options available to the president and other agencies.

The State Department's declining role is one consequence of the internationalization of the public sector. In the past, most U.S. government officials deployed abroad were from the State Department, the armed forces, or intelligence agencies. In the last 10 years, the number of Department of Health and Human Services employees serving abroad has more than doubled and the Justice Department has expanded its international postings by more than 70 percent.

## From Chief Executive to Chief Coordinator

Sympathizers claim that given the severe political constraints under which Clinton's administration has had to operate, his foreign policy achievements are nothing short of miraculous. Just witness the Asia-Pacific Economic Cooperation (APEC) forum, North American Free Trade Agreement (NAFTA), the World Trade Organization (WTO), the Bosnian peacekeeping operation, improved relationships with China and Japan, the Chemical Weapons Convention, the successful Mexican bailout, dramatic reductions in the nuclear threat from North Korea, Russia, and Ukraine,

a relatively smooth political and economic transition in Russia and, last but not least, NATO expansion. These, Clinton's friends say, all mark important goals for the United States and even for the world at large, and they fit within a coherent strategic vision.

Yet there is also a consensus that these accomplishments fall short of what is needed or, even, what is to be expected of an American president free to focus more on the history books than on the opinion polls. In Clinton's second term, in particular, the scope of his ambitions seems more modest than his personal history, his rhetoric, and his country's world dominance would lead one to expect.

In the eyes of the president's critics these shortcomings are not surprising. What else could be expected from a president who is not a statesman, but just a lucky politician whose stint as governor of a small, relatively backward state has shaped his instincts? To them, Clinton is a compromiser. In his White House, achieving narrow, short-term, political goals will always take precedence over attaining broad strategic objectives.

Clinton's backers counter that his travails have less to do with personal foibles than the dire political circumstances that have haunted him since he took office. As a result of having lost control of Congress in 1994, the president's political difficulties have become even more acute. For his supporters, Congress bears as much, if not more, responsibility than the administration for any shortcomings in recent U.S. foreign policy.

This controversy is just another small chapter in the long-standing debate about what role the personality of leaders plays in changing the course of history. To some scholars, history is shaped by forces largely immune to the personality of leaders, who are only the temporary custodians of fleeting power whose nature is tightly constrained by circumstances beyond their control. Others point to Gengis Khan, Napoleon, Churchill, Mao, and many more, as incontrovertible evidence that dominant individuals can mold history.

The Clinton administration will not decide this debate. But from a short-term perspective it is hard to argue that the president's personality is irrelevant for American actions abroad. It is equally difficult to discount the effect of the current American mood. Its manifestation in congressional initiatives reveals an American public that is inward-looking and distrustful of government, ideologically victorious while feeling economically insecure and uninterested in foreign affairs.

Even so, politics and personality alone cannot explain the administration's performance overseas. Changed global realities are clearly at work. What their lasting repercussions will be cannot yet be foretold. Yet it seems increasingly apparent that in order to succeed presidents will need more than just a vision and the obsessive will to execute it. These traits may be indispensable. But in today's world, even a strong willed, visionary president will not achieve much unless he or she has the capacity to create and coordinate coalitions formed by numerous disparate actors, some of which may not even be formal organizations but "virtual communities." Leaders must be willing to be not just chief executives but chief coordinators. Without an organizational structure designed to work effectively within some of today's constraints, any head of state will have a rough time making the new conditions and trends work for, and not against, his or her initiatives.

The New American Consensus

## Our Hollow Hegemony

### Why Foreign Policy Can't Be Left to the Market

**By Fareed Zakaria**

Sometime this summer the post-cold-war world ended. It was a brief, giddy age. We were thrust into it headlong barely 10 years ago, when the Berlin wall cracked, Eastern Europe freed itself and the Soviet Union disintegrated. Suddenly the United States became not just the sole surviving superpower but the repository of the sole surviving ideology. Countries around the globe fell over themselves to embrace capitalism, democracy and the American way—from mutual funds to Madonna. As if conscious of the need to play its part, the American economy surged to historic highs.

The new forces of globalization swept the world. Economics and technology reigned supreme and ancient civilizations struggled to become emerging markets. Western nations moved furiously into a postindustrial, information age with explosions of new industries and wealth. As economies intertwined, cyberspace took off and capital (and capitalists) sloshed around the world at a heady pace, the old world of international politics and national security seemed utterly obsolete. Even thinking in terms of national boundaries was considered old-fashioned. "We treat the world as a single nation," declared Alfred Zeien, C.E.O. of Gillette.

The new world order found a new world stage. Where international attention was once focused on the General Assembly of the United Nations or U.S.-Soviet summits, for the last decade it has been lavished on Davos, an

---

*Fareed Zakaria is the managing editor of Foreign Affairs.*

Alpine ski resort in Switzerland. There, each year in late January, the international business and media elite gathered at the World Economic Forum, and developing countries strove mightily to impress the conferees by dispatching their presidents and prime ministers or, better still, their economists. Once the most dazzling figures on the international scene were diplomats—Acheson, Eden, Kissinger; now they were economists—Chubais, Cavallo, Summers. Every country worth its salt had a brilliant young economist charting its new course. (He was always young and always brilliant.) Every year a new reformist regime bubbled with promise. Ukraine, Tunisia and Portugal all had their 15 minutes of fame—and their country funds a resulting 15 percent uptick.

It is difficult to mark the end of an era with precision, but just as Russia's embrace of the Western model ushered in the beginning of a new age in world affairs, so the collapse of Russian reform this past July heralded its end. There were other signs. The Asian financial crisis, Japan's deepening depression, nuclear explosions in South Asia, and emboldening of Saddam Hussein and the return of terrorism all wore at the easy assumptions of peace and prosperity that have characterized the 1990's. It remains difficult to see on the horizon a worldwide depression or a large-scale war, but gone is the expectation that the post-cold-war world was inexorably evolving into something new and better.

Three times this century the United States waged and won a world war against an evil empire. Each time—in 1919, 1945 and 1989—it hoped that, with this struggle over, with this evil vanquished, with this empire defeated, international affairs would be quite different from the past. The dismal cycle of war and destruction would be replaced by an ever-expanding realm of peace, prosperity and liberty. And for the third time this century, that hope has faded as politics returns to the world of nations.

What is different this time is that, when finally the entire world seemed to admit that the American dream was their dream too, America lost interest.

After World War I, and again after World War II, the United States worked hard to bring about changes in the world that made it, more than ever before, hospitable to free markets, liberal democracy and international cooperation. Today, however, it is not the world that has given

From *The New York Times Magazine,* November 1, 1998, pp. 44-47, 74, 80. © 1998 by The New York Times Company. Reprinted by permission.

up on America but America that has given up on the world. Historians will surely look back on this decade and be struck that at America's moment of greatest global triumph—when all the world looked to Washington for leadership—and in the midst of an almost-unprecedented economic boom, Americans became uncharacteristically small-minded in their ambitions.

THE OPEN WORLD ECONOMY—WHATEVER THE RHETORIC OF BUSINESSmen and economists—is a *political* construct, neither natural nor self-sustaining. In its current incarnation, it is the product of concerted American policies since 1945. By sheltering Western Europe from the Soviet threat, Washington made it unnecessary for those nations to have their own (possibly competing) national policies and thus helped promote an unprecedented era of cooperation in Europe. Washington pumped public money around the world. It constructed a regime of fixed exchange rates anchored by the dollar, creating for a generation a stable environment in which the world economy could flourish without panics and crashes.

Perhaps most important, like Britain in the 19th century, Washington practiced unilateral free trade, opening the American market to foreign goods even when others would not reciprocate—thus fueling the growth of Europe, East Asia and Latin America. Globalization—which entails not simply the opening of markets but also societies—has been a product of American foreign policy over 50 years. But as the global economic system confronts its first, deep crisis, America has lost interest in its own handiwork.

This is not a problem that can simply be laid at the door of Bill Clinton or Newt Gingrich or politicians generally. Apathy about the world pervades every aspect of American society today. Coverage of foreign news by networks and newsmagazines has plummeted. The number of foreign news reports broadcast by NBC dropped from 1,013 in 1988 to 327 in 1996. For decades, White House news conferences were dominated by questions about foreign policy. Today, even at a joint meeting with Clinton and Yeltsin, reporters ask a few obligatory questions about foreign policy and quickly move to the domestic crisis of the moment. Book publishers are uninterested in publishing anything about world affairs.

These trends reflect an increasingly competitive business environment and an increasingly frivolous public culture, but at the heart of things lies the simple fact that the average American is simply not interested in the world.

The United States, we are often told, is isolationist at its core. The settlers came to the New World to escape the court intrigues and internecine power struggles of the Old. And, indeed, America's lack of interest in the world beyond is real and deep-rooted. But American isolationism is a curious thing. The relentless march of 13 colonies north, south and west across a continent can hardly be called isolationism. This territorial expansion required a complex series of negotiations with France, Spain, Britain and Mexico—and wars with three of the four—in addition to a stream of bloody battles with the Native Americans. More curious still is American behavior in this century. While sometimes disengaging from the international scene altogether (during the 1930's, for example), America also conceived of and sponsored the most ambitious international projects in this century, or any other for that matter. The League of Nations, the United Nations, the Marshall Plan, the Helsinki Final Act—all are products of American power and principle. How to explain this national split personality?

America's most basic attitude toward the world abroad mirrors that of its cultural homeland—Great Britain. Like the United States, Britain for centuries saw itself as an island nation separate from, and superior to, the scheming continent it abutted. In one of the first authentic expressions of English nationalism, Shakespeare's John of Gaunt defines his country as

*This fortress built by Nature for herself*
*Against infection and the hand of war. . . .*
*This precious stone set in the silver sea,*
*Which serves it in the office of a wall,*
*Or as a moat defensive to a house,*
*Against the envy of less happier lands.*

About 35 years after Shakespeare wrote "Richard II," John Winthrop, the Governor of Massachusetts, declared the new American colonies "a city upon a hill." And while he did not go on to describe the envious and infected lowlands around the hill, the implication is obvious. If the world as it exists is evil, what follows is that it can either be ignored or transformed but never accepted. International politics is to be transcended, not engaged in.

Thus dealing with European great powers for the purpose of westward expansion was proper, since the goal was the Americanization of these lands. But any kind of alliances or involvement at Europe's congresses and conferences was dangerous, for their evil ways would corrupt the young republic. President John Quincy Adams's July 4 speech from 1821 famously asserts that "America does not go abroad in search of monsters to destroy." But Adams goes on to explain why America should not take up even a good cause abroad: "She well knows that by once enlisting under other banners than her own . . . she would involve herself . . . in all the wars of interest and intrigue, of individual avarice, envy, and ambition. . . . She might become the dictatress of the world. She would be no longer the ruler of her own spirit."

This suspicion of the world goes well beyond Presidents and secretaries of state. Randy Newman's satirical song "Political Science" captures most Americans' irritation with the world.

*We give them money, but are they grateful?*
*No, they're spiteful and they're hateful.*
*They don't respect us, so let's surprise 'em!*

*We'll drop the Big One and pulverize 'em.*
*Boom goes London! Boom Paree!*

The historian Walter McDougall points out insightfully that the lyrics, written during the cold war, do not read: "Boom goes Moscow! Boom Beijing!" It is dealing with friends and allies—in other words conducting routine diplomacy—that frustrates Americans. Woodrow Wilson best exemplified this attitude in his ambivalence about American participation in World War I. He wanted to enter the war to change the world, but he could not bring himself to engage in traditional balance-of-power politics, i.e. to take sides. He tried in vain in January 1917 to get all countries in battle to simply renounce their war aims and accept a "peace without victory." (Georges Clemenceau, future French Premier, called that speech "so fine a sermon on what human beings might be capable of accomplishing if only they weren't human.") Finally Wilson was forced to take America into the war, but he did so with his nose high in the air. Washington fought not as an "ally" of the British and French but as an "associated power," implying that it had other, purer goals than they. And indeed it did. "We shall fight," Wilson declared in his war message to Congress, "for a universal dominion of right . . . as shall bring peace and safety to all nations and make the world itself at last free."

It is easy to mock this hope for a new and better world as European "sophisticates" have done for decades. The world is intractable, they say; human beings are fallible; problems are endemic; foreign policy is an ongoing process. There is wisdom in these Burkean cautions. But, in fact, the dream is worth dreaming. Free markets, free trade, an open world economy and political cooperation are an alluring alternative to war, pestilence and disease. Washington sponsored and nurtured an open world economy, which is at the heart of the hope to transform a poor and envious world into a prosperous and secure one. For developing countries, hitching their wagons to the global economy has proved to be the only way out of thousands of years of poverty. Over the last 30 years, East Asian nations brought literally hundreds of millions of people out of medieval conditions of malnutrition, sickness and despair—easily the fastest rate of poverty alleviation in human history. And in the 1990's so many countries around the world seemed poised to follow that example.

So why did these promising developments go awry? Who lost the post-cold-war world? Well, transforming the world is a tall order. The realities of international politics always intrude on dreams. But they have done so in these last few years more quickly and thoroughly than they might have because Americans—leaders and public alike—lost faith in their own ideals. Exhausted by its long struggle with the Soviet Union, without fears of war or depression, America in the 1990's has still wanted to transform the world, but it has not wanted to work the transformation itself—or to pay for it.

CENTRAL TO ANY TRANSFORMATION OF THE POST-COLD-WAR WORLD WAS the transformation of Russia. As with Germany and Japan in 1945, an enduring peace required that Moscow be integrated into the Western world. Otherwise a politically and economically troubled great power—which strides continents and has the world's second-largest storehouse of nuclear weapons—would remain bitter and resentful about the post-cold-war order. In the early 1990's, the most important Russian leaders wanted Russia to go down this path and be partners with the West—Yeltsin himself, but also others like Boris Federov, Anatoly Chubais, Yegor Gaidar and Andrei Kozyrev.

What is striking, however, is that throughout the 1990's few American statesmen—with the notable exception of Richard Nixon—ever wanted to make the transformation of Russia an American goal.

"Russians will define Russia's future," Bill Clinton has said many times, as if to absolve America (and himself) of "losing" that country. The United States has certainly tried to help liberalize Russia's economics and politics, but considering the size of that country and the history of

**Problems that might be solved by bombing, we readily undertake. Problems that cannot be addressed by this method, we ignore.**

its problems—and when compared to the initiatives of the 1940's and 50's in Europe and Japan—these efforts have been weak and half-hearted. Much of the time, we have accommodated to Russian realities—its autocratic democracy, weak state institutions, enduring Communist elite—rather than trying to change them. "De-Communization" was never even a goal as de-Nazification was, even if the latter was incompletely carried out.

While George Bush was generous in his treatment of the defeated Soviet Union, he recounts in his recent memoir how miserly he felt he had to be in helping out the new democratic Russia. A senior Bush official recalls: "We never challenged domestic and budgetary constraints and said to the American people: 'This is a world historic moment. We have a chance to make an enormous difference.' By 1992, Bush was under attack for being a foreign-policy President and Russia got lost in these fears." The Clinton Administration was even less ambitious. To date, all American aid to Russia over the decade—including our share of the International Monetary Fund and every other international organization's grants and loans—stands around $15 billion. The Marshall Plan alone was six times its size.

We would have wasted the money, we are now told. Russia, after all, is a corrupt, feudal country with a legacy of Communism and no Enlightenment, Renaissance or Reformation. (And, of course, at this point, with Russian reform in tatters, its reformers unemployed and the country on the verge of chaos, any large-scale aid effort would be futile.) But you did not hear such cultural determinism in the late 1940's. After all, Japan had no Enlightenment, Renaissance or Reformation either, and its feudal history was deeper and more sustained than Russia's. Germany's past had its own problems. And both countries had been at war with America, killing, torturing and maiming Americans with savage brutality. And yet a few years later, Americans committed themselves to rebuild these countries and thus transformed ever-warring Europe into a benign trading bloc. Who knows how hopeless a defeated Japan or Germany would have looked 10 years after World War II without major American involvement? Who knows what Russia could have looked like today if the United States had been truly ambitious?

AND THEN THERE IS ASIA. WHEN THE TURMOIL IN EAST ASIA FIRST BROKE, Americans looked on as if it were a freak show. Many commentators took it as an opportunity to gloat about the virtues of the American way of life and the poverty of Asian values. Policy makers seemed to believe that matters could be left to the I.M.F. and that no political response was necessary. Globalization would do the work for them. The market would force countries to become genuinely free economies. The discrediting of Communism would make nations naturally accept liberal democracy and the rule of law. Goldman, Sachs, Morgan Stanley and other banks and mutual funds would do the work of transformation. Washington would watch and cheer.

"We can't want reform in any country more than its government and its people do," Lawrence Summers, the Deputy Secretary of Treasury, often intones, perfectly expressing this view of America, and of the average American, as concerned spectator. But until yesterday the United States wanted certain kinds of reform more than the government and the people themselves. We have cajoled, urged, bribed and threatened regimes to liberalize their economies along Anglo-American lines. To take just one example, during the last decade Washington has pressured East Asia's emerging economies to make their currencies fully convertible. American financial firms pushed hard for this change because they wanted easy access to these growing markets. Any thought of a phased transition, in which countries moved gradually to expose themselves to the fury of global capital markets, was ruled out even though that is how convertibility came to Western Europe (which had stable financial institutions and centuries of experience with capitalism). This "reform" was a crucial factor in the East Asian boom and bust—as billions of dollars moved in and out free and fast.

THE MODESTY OF AMERICAN AMBITION HAS NOT BEEN MATCHED BY A modesty of rhetoric. In 1992, it is worth recalling, Bill Clinton accused his predecessor of spending too much time on foreign policy, but his criticisms of Bush's policy at least implied an even more ambitious and expensive one. Clinton accepted all Bush's concerns, but added to them the need to restore Bosnia to its unified multi-ethnic status, pressure China to democratize, help Haitians in despair, rebuild the Somali nation and assist further in Russia's reforms. All this from an Administration promising to pay less attention to foreign policy! Of course, most of this proved to be merely rhetoric.

Over the last year and a half, Washington has insisted on keeping tight control of the international response to the global economic crises—while offering very little by way of policy ideas, initiatives, organization or money. Last year, the Japanese Government, which has provided far more in aid to Southeast Asia than the United States, offered to set up a $100 billion "Asian Monetary Fund" to prevent a further loss of confidence in that region. Washington instinctively vetoed it.

Ever since the collapse of the Soviet Union, Washington has enjoyed playing the part of sole superpower—being visited by all, making glorious speeches, strutting around the globe. But it has not wanted to pay the bills in political capital, energy, attention or dollars. We are eager to lead on any problem that can be solved quickly and on the cheap. We trumpeted NATO expansion as the most ambitious new project for the security of Europe, and then quickly explained that it would cost virtually nothing. We declared that the restoration of Bosnia as a single, multi-ethnic nation was vital, but made it clear that we had no intention of paying the high price that this would entail. We have sought to bring order to the periphery—Haiti, Somalia—because it was easier than stabilizing the core: Russia.

The way foreign policy is made nowadays has exaggerated this fitful leadership. (Now you see us, now you don't.) Crises that flash vividly onto television take on an urgency that may have little to do with their intrinsic importance, which explains America's continued indifference to the (untelevised) horrors in Sudan, which outstrip as a humanitarian catastrophe anything happening in the Balkans. While public support for serious international initiatives has always been fragile, politicians used to be able to build support for them steadily, over months and years. The public was, after all, initially against American involvement in World War II, the Marshall Plan, the gulf war and almost all free-trade agreements.

But politicians have increasingly become unwilling, and unable, to educate and guide public opinion. Last year, President Clinton could not convince his own party to give him authority to negotiate trade agreements, the first time such authority has been denied in a generation. (And at a time when the American economy was at a 35-year peak and unemployment was 4.7 percent!) Since politicians do not want to lead and the public does not want to be led, foreign policy is increasingly being made by narrow interest groups (business lobbies, ethnic organizations) often with a single agenda, who pressure Congress and the Administration to enact their favorite policy. Thus American manufacturers lobbied for Japan-bashing in the early days of the Clinton Administration, Polish- and Hungarian-Americans fought for NATO expansion, African-American lobbyists pushed for the invasion of Haiti, Cuban-Americans have sought harsh sanctions on Cuba and so on.

It is a new Wilsonianism, full of unilateral declarations, righteous rhetoric and spasmodic inventions. Economic sanctions and air power have become the indispensable handmaidens of today's foreign policy because they offer, in Eliot Cohen's phrase, the allure of modern courtship: gratification without commitment. With a few exceptions, sanctions provide the opportunity for cheap moralizing—taking a stand that pleases some domestic group, while in fact doing little to change the reality on the ground. (According to the Institute of International Economics, a Washington think tank, a third of all American sanctions this century have been instituted in the 1990's.) Bombing makes it possible to reap the glory and rewards of military action with none of its usual costs. Problems that might be solved by bombing, we readily undertake. Problems—often more serious and long-term—that cannot be addressed by this method we ignore. We have become a nation of cheap hawks.

Our current path is an alluring alternative to real international leadership, with its hard choices, gray areas and persistent struggle. The Truman Administration, for example, rebuilt and secured Western Europe and Japan but ignored the Communist takeover of China. It put into place containment policies that would have to be pursued steadily for decades before they bore fruit. It dealt with dictators

and guerrillas and financed political parties and intellectual groups—whatever was necessary to promote American interests and ideals. Despite an extraordinary position of power, it yielded to its allies in negotiations time and time again. In other words, it engaged in international politics, and in so doing, transformed it.

Just as important, the Truman Administration educated the American people about the world they lived in. This was a time—and it was no coincidence—when the lives of ordinary Americans intersected with great world events. Timothy Naftali, a historian at the University of Virginia, explains: "During World War II and the early cold war, personal lives and public life became connected. Hundreds of thousands of Americans took part in the war effort, the Marshall Plan, the Korean War and other such projects. It is this generation of Americans that cares about foreign policy, buys books on international affairs, politics and history, watches news shows and documentaries. Generations since have seen no connection between their own lives and the world beyond."

Perhaps this isn't so bad. Perhaps the ambition to change the world was absurd to begin with, and it is for the best that America renounces it. Perhaps America must become a "sophisticated" country, willing to accept the world as it is. This would represent a tremendous loss of faith, but could bring a different kind of stability to the world and a sense of limits to American politics. It would mean a scaling back of lofty aims along with a willingness to share the benefits and burdens of global leadership with its allies.

But this is not what has happened. There are no signs that the Clinton Administration—or the American people—are ready for realism. What we have now is the rhetoric of transformation but the reality of accommodation; a hollow hegemony.

# Index

# AE Article Review Form

We encourage you to photocopy and use this page as a tool to assess how the articles in **Annual Editions** expand on the information in your textbook. By reflecting on the articles you will gain enhanced text information. You can also access this useful form on a product's book support Web site at **http://www.dushkin.com/ online/.**

NAME: _____ DATE: _____

TITLE AND NUMBER OF ARTICLE: _____

BRIEFLY STATE THE MAIN IDEA OF THIS ARTICLE: _____

LIST THREE IMPORTANT FACTS THAT THE AUTHOR USES TO SUPPORT THE MAIN IDEA:




WHAT INFORMATION OR IDEAS DISCUSSED IN THIS ARTICLE ARE ALSO DISCUSSED IN YOUR TEXTBOOK OR OTHER READINGS THAT YOU HAVE DONE? LIST THE TEXTBOOK CHAPTERS AND PAGE NUMBERS:




LIST ANY EXAMPLES OF BIAS OR FAULTY REASONING THAT YOU FOUND IN THE ARTICLE:




LIST ANY NEW TERMS/CONCEPTS THAT WERE DISCUSSED IN THE ARTICLE, AND WRITE A SHORT DEFINITION:

ANNUAL EDITIONS revisions depend on two major opinion sources: one is our Advisory Board, listed in the front of this volume, which works with us in scanning the thousands of articles published in the public press each year; the other is you—the person actually using the book. Please help us and the users of the next edition by completing the prepaid article rating form on this page and returning it to us. Thank you for your help!

## ANNUAL EDITIONS: American Government 99/00

### ARTICLE RATING FORM

Here is an opportunity for you to have direct input into the next revision of this volume. We would like you to rate each of the 47 articles listed below, using the following scale:

**1. Excellent: should definitely be retained**
**2. Above average: should probably be retained**
**3. Below average: should probably be deleted**
**4. Poor: should definitely be deleted**

Your ratings will play a vital part in the next revision. So please mail this prepaid form to us just as soon as you complete it. Thanks for your help!

**We Want Your Advice**

### RATING

#### ARTICLE

1. The Declaration of Independence, 1776
2. The Constitution of the United States, 1787
3. The Size and Variety of the Union as a Check on Faction
4. Checks and Balances
5. The Judiciary
6. What Good Is Government?
7. Chomp!
8. What's Wrong with America: Open Season on Uncle Sam
9. When Naptime Is Over
10. Race and the Constitution
11. Vigilante Justices
12. Breaking Thurgood Marshall's Promise
13. More than Sex: Why the Courts Are Missing the Point
14. The Case for Impeachment
15. The Case against Impeachment
16. The Separated System
17. Hooked on Polls
18. The Governor-President, Bill Clinton
19. There He Goes Again: The Alternating Political Style of Bill Clinton
20. Beyond Monica: The Future of Clinton's Past
21. Imperial Congress
22. The Town That Ate Itself
23. In the Money: A Congressman's Story
24. Few in Congress Grieve as Justices Give Line-Item Veto the Ax

### RATING

#### ARTICLE

25. The Rehnquist Reins
26. Indicting the Courts: Congress' Feud with Judges
27. A Judge Speaks Out
28. Gaveling Back the Imperial Presidency
29. Census: A Political Calculation
30. Why I Do What I Do: Howard Smith, I.R.S. Agent
31. Running Scared
32. Lost Opportunity Society
33. Democracy v. Dollar
34. Campaign Financing: Four Views
35. Alice Doesn't Vote Here Any More
36. March Madness: How the Primary Schedule Favors the Rich
37. Demosclerosis
38. Q: Are Ethnic and Gender-Based Special-Interest Groups Good for America?
39. Trying Times
40. Did You Have a Good Week?
41. The 'New' Media and Politics: What Does the Future Hold?
42. The Entitlement Time Bomb
43. The Sham of Saving Social Security First
44. Do It Yourself
45. Ten Essential Observations on Guns in America
46. Clinton's Foreign Policy: A Victim of Globalization?
47. The New American Consensus: Our Hollow Hegemony

(Continued on next page)

NO POSTAGE
NECESSARY
IF MAILED
IN THE
UNITED STATES

## BUSINESS REPLY MAIL
FIRST-CLASS MAIL PERMIT NO. 84 GUILFORD CT

POSTAGE WILL BE PAID BY ADDRESSEE

**Dushkin/McGraw-Hill**
**Sluice Dock**
**Guilford, CT 06437-9989**

---

## ABOUT YOU

Name                                                    Date
_____    _____

Are you a teacher? ☐   A student? ☐
Your school's name
_____

Department
_____

Address                          City              State      Zip
_____

School telephone #
_____

## YOUR COMMENTS ARE IMPORTANT TO US !

Please fill in the following information:
For which course did you use this book?
_____

Did you use a text with this *ANNUAL EDITION*?  ☐ yes  ☐ no
What was the title of the text?
_____

What are your general reactions to the *Annual Editions* concept?
_____

Have you read any particular articles recently that you think should be included in the next edition?
_____

Are there any articles you feel should be replaced in the next edition? Why?
_____

Are there any World Wide Web sites you feel should be included in the next edition? Please annotate.
_____

May we contact you for editorial input?  ☐ yes  ☐ no
May we quote your comments?  ☐ yes  ☐ no
_____